Animal Rights/Human Rights

Animal Rights/ Human Rights

Entanglements of Oppression and Liberation

David Nibert

ROWMAN & LITTLEFIELD PUBLISHERS, INC.
Lanham • Boulder • New York • Toronto • Plymouth, UK

ROWMAN & LITTLEFIELD PUBLISHERS, INC.

Published in the United States of America
by Rowman & Littlefield Publishers, Inc.
A wholly owned subsidary of The Rowman & Littlefield Publishing Group, Inc.
4501 Forbes Boulevard, Suite 200, Lanham, Maryland 20706
www.rowmanlittlefield.com

Estover Road
Plymouth PL6 7PY
United Kingdom

British Library Cataloguing in Publication Information Available

Library of Congress Cataloging-in-Publication Data

Nibert, David Alan, 1953–
    Animal rights/human rights : entanglements of oppression and liberation / David Nibert.
        p.   cm.
    Includes bibliographical references and index.
    ISBN 0-7425-1775-6 (cloth)—ISBN 0-7425-1776-4 (paper)
    1. Animal welfare.   2. Human rights.   3. Exploitation.   4. Marginality, Social.   5. Violence.   6. Social status.   7. Animals and civilization.   I. Title.
    HV4708 .N59   2002
    179'.3—dc21   2002001779

Printed in the United States of America

♾ ™ The paper used in this publication meets the minimum requirements of American National Standard for Information Sciences—Permanence of Paper for Printed Library Materials, ANSI/NISO Z39.48-1992.

To Julie and Taylor

Contents

Foreword

This brilliant and well-referenced book, long overdue, is an incisive critique of the *global problematique* of Western civilization and the American Way. It shows the connections between the oppression and exploitation of people and of other animals, and affirms the socioeconomic, environmental, cultural, political, bioethical, and spiritual relevance of the "Liberation of Life" movement. This book provides considerable wisdom and momentum to this survival imperative and evolutionary choice. Freedom and dignity for all beings are the hallmarks of a humane society and a sustainable global community and economy.

The increasing collaboration of animal and environmental protection and human rights organizations with multinational corporations, motivated by the need for money and the allure of power, is a matter of growing concern to me. So is the linkage, as David Nibert shows, between corporate capitalism and the World Trade Organization, the World Bank, the International Monetary Fund, and other leading institutions in the promotion of aid and development programs in developing countries in ways that facilitate the globalization of capitalism—a type of capitalism that in its present form is neither socially just, environmentally friendly, nor ecologically sustainable. In the long term, then, it is not economically viable. In the short term, as this book shows, it is responsible for the demise of America's once-thriving rural farming communities, thanks in large measure to the corruption of farm subsidies into corporate profits, and for an increasingly toxic environment and food chain.

The unbridled capitalism of the petrochemical–pharmaceutical, medical, and agricultural and energy industrial complex, combined with the military and other government and nongovernmental establishments and organizations, has created a huge market and much wealth out of the exploitation and degradation of human and other life, harming the soil, our food, our health, and our quality of life. Linked with the politics of either secular democracy or totalitarian socialism, or of some fascist regime or feudal theocracy, capitalism—the concentration of wealth and power—as history informs, harms more than it benefits. Professor Nibert asks if capitalist systems—which treat humans and other animals and the land as industrial fodder, as so many production units—can be reformed. Is reform possible when costly government regulations—such as pesticide and antibiotic uses, food irradiation, and genetic engineering—prove ineffectual in real-world risk management and containment scenarios? Such scenarios are quite distinct from scientific risk determinations by the virtual realists of the scientific and biomedical, industrial, and research establishments that exert considerable control over Congress.

Is reform possible when antitrust and antimonopoly laws are rarely enforced? When academia and public educational institutions, from the curriculum content of most state schools to the defilement of public museums, promote corporate interests and revise history? Take, for example, this scenario at America's most hallowed Smithsonian Natural History Museum—what I call the "Orkin Syndrome." In a letter to the *Washington Post* (January 27, 2002), the former director of this museum, Porter M. Kier, wrote:

> During my term as director of the Smithsonian's Museum of Natural History, we built an insect zoo. The purpose of the exhibit was to convince museum visitors that insects were "fun" and a vital part of our lives and our environment. Now this exhibit has been refurbished and renamed the Orkin Hall in honor of a corporation dedicated to convincing the public that insects are dangerous pests that must be eliminated [*Style*, January 18]. Surely this is too high a price to pay for financial support for an exhibit. In the past Congress and the American people supported their museum. Why not now?

We are seeing the corporate takeover of museums, public education, academia, as well as the entertainment, sports and information media, the Church, the heart and mind of America—and the globe. As this book shows, this process includes the incorporation of values and beliefs that are antithetical to the bioethics of equalitarianism, biodemocracy, the conservation of biodiversity and cultural diversity, and respect for human and nonhuman interests, and democratic entitlements.

This book should be essential reading for all undergraduate students in the sciences and the humanities. David Nibert helps show us the way to a more humane and viable future.

Michael W. Fox, DSc, PhD, Bvet Med, MRCVS
Washington, D.C.

Acknowledgments

As I traveled on this sociological journey through the relationship between humans and other animals, I was assisted along the way by Katie Gantz, Melinda Kanner, Amy Achor Mickunas, Randy Shields, Stephen Kaufman, Jerry Pankhurst, Rob Russell, Rebecca Plante, and Christine McIntyre, all of whom gave me useful documents, articles, or books. Thanks also are due to Leah Lind and Brian Luke, who took the time to read the entire manuscript and provide useful comments; Holli Kendall, who reviewed chapter 4; and Bill Winders and Philip McMichael, who read a section from chapter 4.

Several people deserve special thanks. I am indebted to Bonnie Berry, both for her invaluable review and critique of the manuscript and for her support and enthusiasm for this project. Randy Shields devoted hours to his thorough reading of the manuscript—including multiple reviews of sections I was finding difficult—and provided insightful comments and penetrating questions. Conni Narcho provided invaluable assistance in preparing the manuscript in its early stages of production. Special thanks also go to Dean Birkenkamp at Rowman & Littlefield for his support and encouragement and to the Rowman & Littlefield production staff for their expertise.

Like many others who have had their minds opened to the oppression of other animals, I owe a debt of gratitude to Henry Salt, Peter Singer, Tom Regan, Carol Adams, ecofeminists, and others, too numerous to name, who have had the courage to challenge the oppression of other animals.

I am thankful for my longtime friendship with Sally Cooper, who has contributed greatly to my ongoing recovery from socialization in a profoundly patriarchal society.

A number of personal friends also have been invaluable in opening my eyes and my heart to the worth and personhood of other animals. Some of these friends no longer walk the Earth but still hold a place in my heart; they include Athena, Hoot, Tomás, Naro, and Friedreich. My longtime friend and companion, Iris, continues to keep company with me as I work to complete this project.

Finally, this book would have been nearly impossible without the support and assistance of my spouse, Julie Ford. She not only superbly edited each new chapter and successive draft of the manuscript but also offered valuable comments and feed-back. She helped me make the time and afforded me the space I needed for such an undertaking—as my files, notes, and stacks of papers and documents overflowed my office, invaded our dining room, and finally threatened to overrun virtually every open space capable of accommodating a stack of books or a box of documents. I am also indebted to my son, Taylor, for the inspiration he supplies. His deep concern and respect for both humans and other animals sustains my hope for the possibility of social transformation and a better world for all.

Introduction

A 1972 anthropocentric book titled *Animals in the American Economy* opened in the customary fashion of many such books, past and present: "In myriad ways animals of land, air and sea have contributed to the cultural, spiritual, and economic well-being of mankind."[1] The truth is just the opposite: In myriad ways the oppression of other animals has been devastating for the cultural, spiritual, and economic well-being of the vast majority of humans. What is more, the oppression of devalued groups of humans has been, and remains, disastrous for other animals. This book shows how the oppression of humans and other animals is deeply entangled.

Ecofeminist writers like Carol Adams, Josephine Donovan, and Marti Kheel have illuminated the ideological entanglements to a considerable degree, and their work has been invaluable in increasing my own awareness of the close relationship between the oppression of humans and other animals. The ideological entanglements between exploitation of humans and other animals are fueled by, and intertwined with, economic-based oppression—particularly under corporate capitalism. The liberation of devalued groups of humans or of other animals is unlikely in a world that increasingly uses both as fodder for the continual growth and expansion of transnational corporations, particularly agribusiness. The bodies of other animals increasingly are used to provide luxury, privilege, and desirable cuts of "meat" for the affluent around the world. The same practices that cause enormous suffering for other animals also take a terrible toll on workers, the Third World, the global environment, and consumers. These terrible consequences are rendered largely invisible to the majority in affluent nations.

Increased awareness of the entanglement of many critical problems confronting humans in the twenty-first century with the oppression of other animals is important for the overall struggle for social justice. However, many who are active in movements for the liberation of devalued humans are generally unreceptive to this reality, due in part to a lack of awareness of both the atrocious treatment of other animals under capitalism and the integral part that other animals have played in human oppression, past and present. Correspondingly, many in the animal rights movement are unaware of the entanglement of the oppression of humans and other animals and how oppression of other animals is fueled by the structure of political-

economic arrangements. This book draws on sociological theory to increase awareness of such factors and also to urge more unity among advocates for other animals
and other progressive forces in society. Unity and cooperation are necessary to forestall the undemocratic, exploitative—and ultimately unsustainable—advance of
global capitalism and to foster increased tolerance, acceptance, and respect for all.

Toward that end, this book features a new look at the history of western "civilization," one that takes into account the interrelated suffering of oppressed humans
and of other animals. It accentuates the economic and elite-driven character of prejudice, discrimination, and institutionalized oppression of humans and other animals
alike. This examination of the economic entanglements of the oppression of humans
and other animals is combined with an analysis of some of the ideological forces that
legitimate them and a review of the uses of state power that protect them.

Chapter 1 opens with a description of the little-known massacres of devalued others in Hinckley, Ohio, and Panzos, Guatemala. It introduces the perspective and
theory that guide this exploration of the causes and entanglement of the oppression
of humans and other animals. Chapter 2 provides a brief examination of the roots
of Western oppression, coupled with an exploration of how exploitation of humans
and other animals is entangled—and how oppression has intensified with the emergence of capitalism, particularly in the United States. Chapter 3 looks at the economic underpinnings of the expansion and intensification of oppression in the
twentieth century, its basis in the capitalist system, and the consequences for the vast
majority of the inhabitants of the Earth. The pharmaceutical industry is featured as
an example of the abominable practices of contemporary multinational corporations. Chapter 4 looks specifically at the effects of the Green Revolution, the growth
of corporate-dominated agribusiness, and their consequences for other animals, the
Third World, the environment, agricultural workers, communities with factory
farms and slaughterhouses, and consumers. Chapter 5 brings into focus the nature
of the state, with a historical look at how elites have used the various powers of the
state and law as tools to maintain control of their societies. This review is followed
by an examination of how the U.S. state has been used to blunt efforts for progressive change, with a particular emphasis on legislation and court decisions pertaining
to other animals. Chapter 6 is an examination of the role of ideology in the oppression of devalued humans and other animals, with examples of pervasive, insidious,
and day-to-day social, political, and economic indoctrination. Chapter 7 provides a
summary of the main points and suggests that both the Left and advocates for other
animals must reevaluate their philosophical and strategic approaches to social
change. Fundamentally altered economic, political, ideological, and social arrangements are necessary to stop the oppression of both humans and other animals; such
elemental changes require an understanding of the causes of oppression and more
unity among all working to relieve and eliminate suffering.

One of the ways in which oppression masquerades as somehow right and natural,
particularly in more affluent nations, is through the use of language. The very words
we use exert considerable control over our consciousness and our views of the world.
I have struggled with the English language in my attempt to use words and phrases

that do not automatically reflect hierarchical rankings of living beings. For example, I largely refrain from using the terms *people, nonhuman,* and *animals,* choosing instead to use *humans and other animals.* This wording emphasizes human commonality with other inhabitants of the planet, rather than fostering a perception of separateness and "otherness" that helps rationalize disregard and mistreatment of other animals. The frequent use in this book of the broad and oversimplified category title of "other animals" for the many and varied groups on the Earth is troubling for me, but I have not yet found a more respectful way to proceed. The term *the Left* is used in a broad, ecumenical sense, especially in chapter 7, and generally refers to all those working for progressive causes: workers, public interest groups, civil rights activists, consumer groups, environmentalists, and liberation activists of all stripes. Similarly, the term *animal rights* is also used loosely here and is intended to be largely synonymous with the term *animal liberation.* This sidesteps debates about the pros and cons of efforts to improve the lives of other animals primarily by promoting legal rights for them—a question not addressed at length in this work.

Words and expressions that are disparaging to other animals and euphemisms that tend to disguise the reality of oppression (such as the term *meat,* which disguises the reality that other animals' dead bodies are used for food) are placed in quotation marks. While this may make the text somewhat awkward at times, it is much preferable to using smoother language that implicitly supports oppressive arrangements. The distracting effect of highlighting commonly accepted, euphemistic terms actually may serve to make horrid practices and conventions more visible and real to some readers. The use of the term *murder* for the killing of other animals in many settings, for example, is more likely to promote reflective thought than such terms as *culling, taking,* or even *hunting.* When other writers are quoted, however, their use of words will be presented unaltered.

While I speak frequently of the liberation of oppressed humans and other animals, I am not attempting to lay out what an oppression-free existence should look like or map in detail how it should be achieved. Suffice it to say that a world in which other animals can live largely free from violence and from use as mere objects at the hands of humans would in itself represent a profound global transformation.

The point of view presented here sometimes takes issue with some of the views of prominent advocates for other animals and some writers from the Left. The fact that I might take issue with certain of their ideas should be seen not as a general critique of their work but as an attempt to expand on their ideas, foster dialogue, and further the struggle against oppression. I have learned a great deal from all the progressive writers discussed on the following pages, and I have great respect for their integrity and commitment to creating a world free of oppression and suffering.

NOTE

1. John A. Sims and Leslie E. Johnson, *Animals in the American Economy* (Ames: Iowa State University Press, 1972), vii.

1

~~❧~~

Toward a Sociological Analysis of Animal Oppression

The first thing you've got to do, in any kind of change, is to recognize the forms of oppression that exist.

—Noam Chomsky[1]

In the cold, early-morning hours of Christmas Eve, 1818, six hundred humans surrounded a snow-covered landscape in rural northeastern Ohio called Hinckley Township, named after the "owner," a prosperous Massachusetts judge. The group, directed by those with experience in warfare, assembled in four lines that boxed in an area of about five square miles. Some carried guns, while others brandished hayforks, hatchets, knives, and bayonets attached to poles. With the sounding of horns and conch shells, the armed assembly began its advance toward the center, taking care to create a great deal of noise and commotion to announce their approach. The aim was to kill every being trapped inside the box they formed. As the march proceeded, frantic deer were seen running in every direction. Some darted desperately at the terrible line, hoping to break away from the peril descending on them—only to be shot and killed as they approached the advancing throng. The humans who had guns advanced ahead of the others, taking aim at everyone they spotted, especially bears and wolves. As the box of death tightened, hundreds of beings were massacred. Some deer who avoided being shot with guns were lanced in midair as they desperately sought to leap over the horrible line. As the box continued to close in, some humans climbed trees and fired down on the panicked and terrified inhabitants of the forest.

The human box became inescapable as the density of the lines doubled and trebled from the increasing concentration. In a last act of desperation, terrified bears, deer, wolves, turkeys, and others sought refuge under the edge of the bank of a frozen stream. Eventually discovered, and pinned with nowhere to flee, they were massacred as lead balls rained down on them. By late afternoon the sounds of musket

1

blasts and the shrieks and cries of those ruthlessly stalked and trapped eventually ceased. An estimated seventeen wolves, twenty-one bears, and three hundred deer were dead.[2] The number of other smaller beings who were slain was not recorded. Judge Hinckley's land was thus "cleared" of troublesome others.

On 29 May 1978, hundreds of Guatemalan subsistence farmers, most of whom were Quiche "Indians" from several different villages, converged on the town of Panzos. The inhabitants of one village had been ordered there by a group of Guatemalan soldiers. Residents from another community were told to go to Panzos, where they would be given an official response to their appeal for government recognition of their rights to the land they lived on. Residents from another village joined the others in order to protest recent murders in their community by military death squads. An estimated eight hundred to one thousand subsistence farm families— campesinos—arrived on the 29th and made their way to the town plaza. The day before their coming an army detachment had arrived.[3]

After the Quiche gathered in the plaza, soldiers blocked the streets to box them in. Then the villagers were angrily addressed and insulted by a delegation of large landowners, one of whom said that the landowners "had the authorization of the President and Minister of Government to kill you."[4] A scuffle broke out between two soldiers and a campesino, and suddenly both soldiers and landowners began firing on the unarmed crowd, many shooting from balconies and rooftops. Bullets rained down on the Quiche, and many fell in their tracks. Panicked and terrified, the crowd rushed the soldiers blocking the streets—only to face blasts of gunfire. In an act of desperation, terrified villagers, including women holding screaming babies, drowned trying to escape by crossing the Polochic River. After the initial deadly volley of bullets, assaults against the fleeing campesinos were directed by a local plantation owner, riding in a jeep with a military officer.

After the blasts of gunfire ended and the shrieks and cries of those ruthlessly stalked and trapped eventually ceased, an estimated 140 Quiche, including many women and children, were dead, with some 300 wounded. Soldiers prevented anyone from giving medical assistance to the injured and to those who lay bleeding to death. Army reinforcements and helicopters were called in to comb the mountainsides to kill those who had escaped.

By afternoon, the Panzos mayor claimed the corpses were already in a state of putrefaction, and by 4:00 P.M. the dead were buried in a common grave—dug two days before the massacre. The military immediately cordoned off the Quiche land. From the 1960s through the 1980s, numerous such incidents were used to rid Guatemala of "troublesome others"; tens of thousands were murdered by police and military forces.

In the summer of 1998, Willow Grear was out for a walk with her companion Cassidy, a dog, in their Dayton, Ohio, neighborhood. Grear, who has been blind since birth and is a member of the "working poor," heard the sound of approaching bicycles just before one crashed into Cassidy. Cassidy's cries of fear and pain produced laughter from a group of boys as they sped away. A bystander approached Grear and told her she saw one of the boys deliberately run into the dog. The trauma Grear suffered from the attack was also so profound for Cassidy that her personality and perspective on the world were dramatically affected, prompting Grear to state, "She'll never be the same dog she was."[5]

These episodes of violence and horror may appear to be isolated anomalies, but such incidents are all too prevalent over the course of recorded history. As this book will attempt to show, such events are connected, not by time or place but, rather, by the similar nature of the economic, political, and ideological systems that led to them—systems that rely on oppressive and violent practices to protect and expand privilege. These causes of oppression, rooted in history, remain a profound, indeed determinative, part of the twenty-first century and continue to restrain the development of enlightened thought and ethical social and economic practices.

I will maintain that horrendous episodes such as those that occurred in Hinckley, Ohio, and Panzos, Guatemala, are linked to the more everyday, small-scale—but pervasive—incidents of abuse and violence such as the casual yet devastating attack on Willow Grear and Cassidy. As a human with a disability, a person who is economically marginal despite the fact that she works, Willow Grear was, and remains, at risk in a society that has a long history of disrespect for and devaluation of such individuals. Vulnerability accompanies devaluation. Those whose worth is minimized, or totally unacknowledged, are susceptible to abuse, exploitation, and violence.

Just as groups of humans are devalued, other animals, like Cassidy, are highly vulnerable in our society. The exploitation of other animals and the justification of their mistreatment not only closely resemble human oppression but are inextricably tied to it. While the primary focus of this book is human oppression of other animals, the thesis is that such oppression is motivated primarily by economic interests and, what is more, that it is profoundly and permanently entwined with human oppression of other humans.

This book will explore these fused forms of oppression by way of reflections on Western history and on developing economic practices, political processes, and belief systems. It will avoid the treatment of other animals as mere resources or tools for the "inevitable ascent of human progress and civilization," as most human members of society—particularly in the West—have been taught. Such a view has served to legitimate ruthless oppression and to blunt awareness of and sensitivity to such oppression. Rather, this book will document how the historical oppression of humans and other animals has provided a benefit primarily for a relatively *small* number of humans, particularly those with substantial privilege and power.

The mistreatment of devalued humans and other animals has been, and continues to be, driven largely (although not exclusively) by individual material interests and the broader economic systems that condition them—not by biology or innate prejudice. This observation comes from a sociological approach to the experiences of devalued humans and other animals, an approach grounded in a tradition of examining the structural and institutional underpinnings of human ideas and behavior. Because this examination of oppression draws from the sociological perspective, a brief look at several important sociological ideas and assumptions will help provide a context for the analysis of oppression that is to follow.

A SOCIOLOGICAL APPROACH TO OPPRESSION

Sociologists primarily search out and study broad social patterns. One of the most important and pervasive patterns is the devaluation of certain groups in society. Many sociologists question why some among us, such as women, humans of color, children, humans with disabilities, humans who are older or poor, and those with different sexual orientations, seem particularly vulnerable to violence and abuse and are disproportionately afflicted with adversity and privation. Sociologists have come to believe that racism, sexism, classism, and the like have historical and social structural causes that are rooted largely in unjust social arrangements—arrangements that significantly shape human consciousness and that are reflected in individual behaviors.[6] It is from this perspective that some have chosen to look more closely at massacres, such as those in Guatemala, as well as individual experiences of assault, such as the attack on Willow Grear and her companion Cassidy. It is in such a context, I will argue, that we must view the massacres like the one at Hinckley and humans' overall horrendous treatment of other animals, past and present.

This general idea that various forms of oppression have structural causes has received substantial support in academic literature over the past two decades. Social scientists and liberation activists alike promote the idea that the oppression of various groups is deeply grounded in the institutional arrangements and belief systems of society. For instance, sociologist Daniel Rossides reflects the findings and perspectives of many scholars when he writes that discrimination against devalued groups is "socially induced and maintained."[7] This is to say that oppressive treatment of groups of humans is not natural or inevitable; rather, it is part of a tightly woven set of cultural practices that are deeply established in social arrangements. *Moreover, the oppression of various devalued groups in human societies is not independent and unrelated; rather, the arrangements that lead to various forms of oppression are integrated in such a way that the exploitation of one group frequently augments and compounds the mistreatment of others.*

Margaret Anderson and Patricia Hill Collins are among a rapidly growing number of sociologists who maintain that categories such as race, class, and gender are "interlocking" and "interactive systems" that should be analyzed in the context of "social institutions and belief systems."[8] Changing these social arrangements is key in expanding justice and freedom for all. Social activist and writer Suzanne Pharr puts it this way:

> It is virtually impossible to view one oppression . . . in isolation because they are all connected. . . . They are linked by a common origin—economic power and control—

and by common methods of limiting, controlling and destroying lives. There is no hierarchy of oppressions. Each is terrible and destructive. To eliminate one oppression successfully, a movement has to include work to eliminate them all or else success will always be limited and incomplete.[9]

I will argue that, to reduce the potential for future massacres like those in Guatemala, episodes like the one at Hinckley must become deplorable, inexcusable, and unacceptable—and vice versa. Oppression of humans causes much of the mistreatment of other animals, and the awful treatment of other animals fuels human exploitation. As we shall see, one of the most important entanglements, and one of the most tragic, has been the practice of considering other animals as *food* for humans. For instance, in chapter 2 we will see that the initial organized killing of other animals for food and the use of their body parts as resources contributed significantly to the devaluation of women. Correspondingly, the devaluation and oppression of women facilitated and compounded the oppression of other animals. Similar entanglements between devalued groups of humans and other animals are commonplace throughout history and in contemporary social arrangements.

The oppressive treatment of different devalued groups—including exploiting a being's labor, raising others for food and resources, and physically displacing or exterminating other groups—is entwined not only materially but also with the systems of beliefs and values that guide human society. Oppression has to be rationalized and justified. It relies heavily on hierarchical views in which certain groups are believed to be undeserving of consideration and fair treatment, promoting a ranking based on purported virtue or worth. The ideological entanglement of hierarchical views of both humans and other animals has been the topic of several scholarly works, particularly by ecofeminists.[10] This book will attempt to contribute to existing ideas about the related ideological foundations and entanglements of these related oppressions with additional sociological reflections.

This analysis of oppression will also bring into focus the role of the state and the development and use of law. Both privilege and its corollary, oppression, are embedded in and largely protected by the state and by the laws and practices it produces. This point is important because challenges to oppression are frequently political ones. Those working for justice and liberation of devalued groups should understand that, with the state as it exists today, they face a formidable obstacle to the achievement of their objectives. It is very much in the interests of liberation movement activists to become more united across causes in the face of such power. By understanding the nature of the state, past and present, social change strategies can be undertaken with realism and clarity.

This book will maintain that those involved in any one liberation movement should realize their entanglement with all other oppressed groups and their common purpose. We will see that Suzanne Pharr's insight—"to eliminate one oppression successfully, a movement has to include work to eliminate them all or else success will always be limited and incomplete"—*must be expanded to include the liberation of other animals*. At the same time, advocates for other animals should expand their awareness of the relationship between oppressive treatment of other animals and human stratification and suffering. Such understanding and political solidarity are vital if real advances are to be achieved in the liberation and quality of life for countless humans *and* other animals.

THE OPPRESSION OF "MINORITIES"

Over the past three decades, a number of important scholars and activists have denounced "speciesism," comparing it explicitly to racism and sexism. The application of the sociological perspective in general, and selected minority group theory in particular, to animal oppression holds a great deal of promise for expanding our understanding of the causes of speciesism and its relationship to, and entanglement with, the oppression of devalued groups of humans.

Although a theoretical position arising from sociological minority group theory will guide this review of the treatment of devalued humans and other animals, it is necessary to make a brief digression to challenge the customary definition of two important terms to begin to bridge a theory of human oppression with the oppression of other animals. First, we will reconsider the meaning of the term *minority group* and suggest a more accurate and inclusive term in its place. Then, we will review uses of the term *speciesism* and interpret it from a sociological vantage point.

The term *minority group* was created early in the twentieth century to refer to groups that differed from the one that controlled society. Initially used to refer to *ethnic* minorities, sociologists now commonly use the term to refer to any group in human society whose members differ from the controlling group.[11] Unfortunately, for many years most sociologists portrayed controlling group members as normative or typical members of society, while minority group members have been viewed as "alien" or "special."[12] What is more, traditional academic definitions of minority group have largely soft-pedaled the causes, consequences, and realities of the frequently oppressive social arrangements imposed on minority groups, often making them appear to be both natural and inevitable. Ethnic conflict, for instance, is widely viewed as a universal, normal, and cyclical phenomenon. As a result, the term *minority group* has been used extensively in our culture because it does not imply a critique of the status quo.

Not surprisingly, due in part to the widespread usage of the euphemistic term *minority group,* most who benefit from the privilege that stems from the exploitation of such groups are seldom motivated or encouraged to become aware of and reflect on their material and psychological stake in oppressive social arrangements. Consequently, I believe it is time to replace the ostensibly objective term *minority groups* with one that is more accurate and straightforward—*oppressed groups.*

The following definition of *oppressed group* is derived in large part from an analysis of oppression developed by Iris Young.[13] *An oppressed group shares physical, cultural, or economic characteristics and is subjected, for the economic, political, and social gain of a privileged group, to a social system that institutionalizes its exploitation, marginali-*

zation, powerlessness, deprivation, or vulnerability to violence. This term is more forth-right than *minority group,* its euphemistic counterpart, and is inclusive of humans of color, humans living in poverty, women, humans who are older, humans with disabilities, humans with different sexual orientations, and *other animals.*[14] The term *oppressed group* is not only more appropriate and honest but also avoids the human-centered concept of minority groups and helps challenge the prevailing view that human use and mistreatment of other animals lies in the realm of "natural affairs."

Some writers promoting social justice and liberation of devalued human groups eschew the term *oppression* because they believe that such terminology treats deval-ued others primarily as passive victims of discrimination and exploitation.[15] While I am sympathetic to their concerns, I am reluctant to downplay the term *oppression.* Rather, in this book I will make widespread use of the terms *oppression* and *oppressed groups,* as they help punctuate the nature of social structural arrangements and their consequences. I believe it is possible to use these powerful terms while still recogniz-ing the subjective experiences of those who are oppressed and their frequently bold and courageous resistance to such arrangements. Such resistance has ranged from, for example, efforts to resist displacement and extermination to revolts by the enslaved, from attempts to escape captivity to struggles for political change. These efforts by countless individuals and groups, in the United States alone, have been responsible for real improvements in the general quality of life.

The second theoretical adjustment needed for the inclusion of other animals into the theoretical realm of oppressed groups is reconsideration of the term *speciesism.* The view that speciesism is prejudice, a view promoted by many advocates and defenders of other animals, hampers somewhat the analysis of the social structural causes of oppression of other animals. An example of such use goes back to the important and ground-breaking work of Richard D. Ryder, credited with coining the term *speciesism* in 1970. He wrote:

> Speciesism and racism are both forms of prejudice that are based upon appearances—if the other individual looks different he is rated as being beyond the moral pale. . . . Speciesism and racism (and indeed sexism) overlook or underestimate the similarities between the discriminator and those discriminated against and both forms of prejudice show a selfish disregard for the interests of others, and for their sufferings.[16]

In his classic book, *Animal Liberation,* Peter Singer also compared the oppressive treatment of animals to racism and defined speciesism as prejudice. "Speciesism . . . is a prejudice or attitude of bias in favor of the interests of members of one's own species and against those of members of other species."[17]

Philosopher and activist Tom Regan, author of *The Case for Animal Rights*—an important philosophical treatise first published in 1983—followed Ryder and Sing-er's lead in regarding speciesism as prejudice.[18] Then, in 1985, the *Oxford English Dictionary* defined *speciesism* as "discrimination against or exploitation of certain animal species by human beings, based on an assumption of mankind's superiority."[19] Reflecting on the various uses of the term, in 1985 Ryder observes, "Speciesism is, I suppose, a compromise word. . . . It describes the doer's negative attitudes and actions. . . . It denotes not merely discrimination but prejudice, and, far more importantly, the exploitation, oppression and cruel injustice which flow from this prejudice."[20]

These exceptional writers are correct when they assert that speciesism and other forms of oppression are comparable. However, sociologists tend to use the suffix *-ism* in a more specific way than what is generally meant by those talking about speciesism. Most sociologists consider racism, as well as sexism, classism, and other "isms" to be ideologies. That is, they are neither prejudice nor mistreatment. Rather, an *ideology* is *a set of socially shared beliefs that legitimates an existing or desired social order*. Prejudice, on the other hand, is an individual predisposition to devalue a group of others. As sociological theorist Donald Noel notes, "As an attitude prejudice is a characteristic of an individual—not of a cultural structure. It may be a very widespread, common attitude but its locus, nonetheless, remains the individual and it is not analyzed in terms of institutional processes but in terms of psychological processes."[21]

It is relevant to note at this point that the contemporary sociological emphasis on institutionally based oppression is something of a recent development. For example, until the late 1960s most sociologists, like the public, largely viewed racism as the consequence of individual prejudice, and many prejudiced individuals were believed to suffer from some form of personality disorder.[22] This perspective hindered a thorough sociological examination of the role of existing social arrangements in the formation and maintenance of racism. The relative silence about the social structural and economic causes of racism essentially portrayed these forces as benign[23]—much like the contemporary analysis of the oppression of other animals. Such a conservative view among early sociologists is not surprising when one considers that during the first half of the twentieth century the emerging discipline of sociology was striving for legitimacy and general acceptance. Eventually, however, most sociologists came to challenge the psychological reductionistic, system-supporting, "scientific" explanation of racism that paraded as "objective science."

For example, in his 1972 book *Racial Oppression in America,* Robert Blauner helped spearhead the emerging consensus as outlined in the following passage:

> Social science experts assumed that . . . movement toward equality depended primarily on the reduction of prejudice in the white majority, rather than on the collective actions of the oppressed groups themselves or upon basic transformations in the society. Here sociologists were reflecting the general ethos of American culture, which minimizes a consciousness of, and concern with, group power—with the structure of institutions and their constraints—emphasizing in their stead the ideas and attitudes of individuals. . . . I would not deny that ideas of white superiority are powerful in their impact, and that stereotypes of racial minorities have a tenacious hold on the conscious and unconscious mind. But prejudiced attitudes are not the essence of racism. . . . racism is institutionalized. The processes that maintain domination—control of whites over nonwhites—are built into the major social institutions. These institutions either

exclude or restrict the participation of racial groups by procedures that have become conventional, part of the system of rules and regulations.[24]

Slowly, sociologists came to subscribe to the idea that, rather than causing racism, prejudice emerged primarily to support and sustain racial exploitation and oppression. Noted sociologist Herbert Blumer maintained that, when a group acquires certain privileges at the expense of another group, prejudice arises as a mechanism to protect those privileges. James Vander Zanden summarizes Blumer's position as follows:

> Prejudice arises . . . through a collective process in which spokesmen for a racial or ethnic group—prominent public figures, leaders of powerful organizations, and intellectual and social elites—operating chiefly through the mass media publicly characterize another group. Such spokesmen foster feelings of racial superiority, racial distance, and a claim to certain rights and privileges. Other members of the dominant group, although having different views and feelings, fall into line fearing ingroup ostracism. The sense of group position serves as a special kind of social norm, especially for individuals who strongly identify with the ingroup. In this fashion a sense of group position—with its encompassing matrix of prejudice—becomes a general kind of orientation. It is a hypothesis, then, that views the dominant group as having a vested interest in another group's subordination; the dominant group has a stake in preserving an order characterized by privilege and advantage. Prejudice becomes an instrument for defending this privilege and advantage.[25]

Hence, the view of prejudice as a primary *cause* of ethnic oppression was seriously challenged in the 1960s, and an institutional analysis of oppression came to the fore. Institutional analysis reveals that racism is not prejudice; prejudice is an individual attitude. Nor is racism discrimination; discrimination is action—differential and unequal *treatment* of the members of a specific group solely because they are members of that group. Racism, as well as sexism, classism, and the like, are ideologies. Various types of prejudice and discrimination are outgrowths of these *invidious* ideologies that are created to protect privilege.

This level of specificity is important if we are to gain a better understanding of the structural causes of oppression of humans and other animals. Don Noel made the argument for such specificity in a 1972 essay on racism; his reasoning easily and necessarily transfers to speciesism.

> To identify racism with discriminatory acts . . . may be adequate to the worthy task of educating the public to the horrors and gross injustice of racism and discrimination, but such conceptual imprecision destroys the possibility of unraveling the causal relationship between a racist ideology and a discriminatory social structure. . . . Racism must be rigorously distinguished from concepts which refer to actual behavior if the relationship between the ideology and a given structure of race relations is to be meaningfully explored.[26]

So, it follows that speciesism is also an ideology—that is, a set of widely held, socially shared beliefs. As we will see, speciesism, like racism, sexism, and classism, results from and supports oppressive social arrangements.

Creating more precise definitions is far easier than changing cultural perceptions that prejudice, and related amoral attitudes, are the *primary* causes of oppression. When the psychological and moral (or immoral) bases of oppression are accentuated, social structural forces are downplayed or overlooked entirely. That approach generally has characterized much of the modern movement for rights and justice for both humans and other animals, prompting many simply to wring their hands, shake their heads, and assume a "when will we ever learn" or "why can't we all just get along" attitude. Such sentiments may well prompt educational efforts, challenges to specific businesses practices, and even modest political reforms, but they tend to stifle any realization of the need for social structural change.

Many important works on the liberation of other animals tend to follow this individualistic and psychologically oriented explanation of oppression. In *Animal Liberation,* for instance, Peter Singer does not offer an explanation for the cause of racism, sexism, or speciesism but primarily suggests that the attitudes underlying them are ethically flawed and should be challenged through education. He does not call into question the social system that promulgates speciesism, although throughout *Animal Liberation* he repeatedly acknowledges the institutional underpinnings of speciesism. For example, he writes:

> Nor is the task of reform made any easier by the large companies involved in the profitable businesses of breeding or trapping animals and selling them, or manufacturing and marketing the cages for them to live in, the food used to feed them, and the equipment used to experiment on them. These companies are prepared to spend huge amounts of money to oppose legislation that will deprive them of their profitable markets. . . . The people who profit by exploiting large numbers of animals do not need our approval. They need our money.[27]

Singer not only questions the dynamics of the economic and political systems but also criticizes a culture and mass media that devalue and depersonalize other animals.

> [M]ost of the "information" about farm animals to be gained from watching television is in the form of paid advertising, which ranges from ridiculous cartoons of pigs who want to be made into sausages and tuna trying to get themselves canned, to straightforward lies about the conditions in which broiler chickens are reared. The newspapers do little better. Their coverage of nonhuman animals is dominated by "human interest" events like the birth of a baby gorilla at the zoo, or by threats to endangered species; but developments in farming techniques that deprive millions of animals of freedom of movement go unreported.[28]

Despite these insightful and powerful criticisms of social institutions, in the last analysis Singer largely sees individual attitudes and moral deficiencies as underlying the problem of animal oppression.

One book that has compared speciesism and racism, and has explored the roots of both forms of oppression, is Marjorie Spiegel's important work *The Dreaded Comparison.*[29] Spiegel's work expresses strong criticism of the economic system.

> To a large extent, the heightened *institutionalization* of oppression of blacks (in the form of legalized slavery), and animals (in factory farming and vivisection), can be attributed to the profit motive. Indeed, eighteenth- and nineteenth-century anti-abolitionists contended that the end of slavery would bring with it the collapse of the economic structure of the United States, while in our own century C. W. Hume wrote that "the major cruelties practiced on animals in civilized countries today arise out of commercial exploitation, and the fear of losing profits is the chief obstacle to reform."[30]

Exploring the causes of the oppression of both human and other animals, Spiegel considers important issues of ideology and power. However, while recognizing the complexity of causation, she deemphasizes the role of economic factors in oppression, past and present. "For while the profit motive serves to explain some aspects of vivisection," she writes, "factory farming and the black slave trade, it fails miserably at explaining, for example, lynching or segregation, or the calculated cruelty involved in many 'scientific' experiments, or the joy people derive from killing. Oppression is carried far beyond the point of profitability and mere economic exploitation."[31]

Like Singer, Spiegel emphasizes *individual transformation* as the best course for ending oppression of humans and other animals. She states:

> If we are to succeed in stemming our destructiveness and learning to once again live sustainably and harmoniously with the earth and all its inhabitants, it is the urge to commit violence that must be addressed—both on a societal level, and, perhaps most importantly, in ourselves as individuals.
>
> Ultimately, the true battle against oppression will be waged within each of us, because that is where all violence begins. And that is also the only place where violence—with enough work—can finally, everlastingly, be brought to an end.[32]

In *The Case for Animal Rights*, Regan suggests that the cruel treatment of other animals is linked to specific economic practices but not to the essential structure of contemporary economic arrangements. As he sees it, "[t]he rights view is not antagonistic to business, free enterprise, the market mechanisms, and the like."[33]

Leading animal rights activist Kim Stallwood further separates the oppression of other animals from consideration of economic arrangements, stating, "[I]n every human society, whether communist, capitalist, or developing world, the labor of nonhuman animals is used without any moral consideration to provide services and to produce commodities for human consumption."[34] This viewpoint presents a problem from a sociological vantage point because moral considerations are largely conditioned by economic circumstances; the level and intensity of oppression and the *possibilities* for improving the treatment of other animals are very different in "communist" and "capitalist" societies and the "developing world"—as we will see.

One common aspect, then, of these praiseworthy writers and advocates for other animals is their tendency to overlook or minimize the social structural basis of oppression of other animals. Their writings emphasize the primary importance of overcoming prejudice and immoral reasoning in order to secure liberation for other animals. While individual business owners, or even entire industries, occasionally may be criticized, the overall system is largely viewed as benign.

As noted earlier, many sociologists use a structural analysis to provide insight into other forms of oppression. They have long grappled with the *causes* of class, racial, and gender-based oppression and the accompanying roles played by both prejudice and institutional arrangements, with the latter coming to be viewed as producing the former. As we look at the causes of animal oppression and the role of individual and structural forces, then, it seems both useful and appropriate to look for insights from sociological theory of oppressed groups.

OPPRESSION: THE THREE BASIC FACTORS

In 1968, Donald Noel developed a system-based theoretical framework to explain the origin of ethnic stratification.[35] He maintained that ethnic stratification was the product of three interactive forces: (1) competition for resources, or some form of exploitation of one group by another; (2) unequal power; and (3) ethnocentrism— "the view of things in which one's own group is the center of everything, and all others are scaled and rated with reference to it."[36] While his theory made room for psychological considerations, they were placed in the context of structural forces. The value of Noel's theory is not just its close linking of material motivation with issues of power and belief systems but also its distillation of complex and interdependent social forces into a compact and readily understood model.

Noel's model will be revised somewhat in this analysis of the oppression of humans and other animals into a three-pronged theoretical device that accentuates what many sociologists and liberation activists have come to regard as the economic context of most episodes of competition and exploitation.[37] Moreover, in this analysis the consideration of unequal power will be focused largely on the use of the various powers that are vested in those who control the state. Finally, the concept of ethnocentrism will be expanded to include a larger system of ideological control.

As we shall see in the chapters to follow, this modified version of Noel's theory of ethnic stratification—which will be referred to from here on as the *theory of oppression*—has substantial application to the oppression of other animals. The motivating factor—the pursuit of economic self-interest—is easily applied to human displacement, exploitation, and extermination of other animals as human society expands. First, humans compete with other animals for economic resources, including the use of land. Second, exploitation of other animals serves numerous economic ends for human animals, providing sources of food, power, clothing, furniture, entertainment, and research tools. However, we will see in the chapters that follow that such exploitation primarily has served to enhance the lives and fortunes of a few at a considerable cost to the many.

This theory also points to the importance of power. One important aspect of power is the ability of one group to exert its will against another, regardless of resistance. Abuses of power are seen throughout history as various human groups devised weapons and techniques to dominate other animals and to displace, control, capture, exploit, or exterminate them. The most concentrated form of power for most of the past ten thousand years has been the *state*.

Finally, ideological conditioning is the third essential requirement for oppressive social arrangements. Oppression requires rationalization and legitimation; that is, it must appear as the right thing to do, both to the oppressing group and in the eyes of others. A set of ideas that devalues an entire group—an ideology, such as racism, sexism, or speciesism—thus is socially constructed. That ideology provides explanation and support for the development and perpetuation of social institutions that are deeply rooted in the elimination or exploitation of the oppressed group. Moreover, the ideology justifying that action is promulgated throughout the social system in order to garner public acceptance and reduce dissent. Over time, these socially constructed ideas will come to be accepted as real and true, and the "lower" or "special" position of the oppressed group will be viewed as the natural order of things, promoting ethnocentrism and anthropocentrism.

These three factors are necessary for the development and perpetuation of oppression of humans and other animals:

- Factor 1—Economic exploitation/competition
- Factor 2—Unequal power, largely vested in control of the state
- Factor 3—Ideological control

Generally speaking, then, humans tend to disperse, eliminate, or exploit a group they perceive to be unlike themselves (an outgroup or the "other") when it is in their economic interests to do so. Next, the oppressing group must have the power to subordinate members of the at-risk group. While physical force is the key to this subordination, such force is usually vested in part in political control. Those who exercise political control wield the power of the state, with the ability to make and enforce law. Finally, ideological manipulation fuels prejudiced attitudes and discriminatory acts that help protect and maintain oppressive economic and social arrangements. Such arrangements are made to appear natural, thus making the oppression invisible to those who enjoy privilege and who gain some benefit from such oppression. The theory of oppression is presented graphically in figure 1.1.

This model is based on the supposition that oppressive treatment of entire groups is a systemic phenomenon, not reducible to individualistic explanations such as prejudice or innate tendencies toward violence. This perspective is grounded in a synthesis of several macro- and microsociological ideas, which will be expanded in some detail as we proceed. Significantly, while this model depicts systemic oppression as occurring in a linear fashion, in reality the various aspects of the system are largely

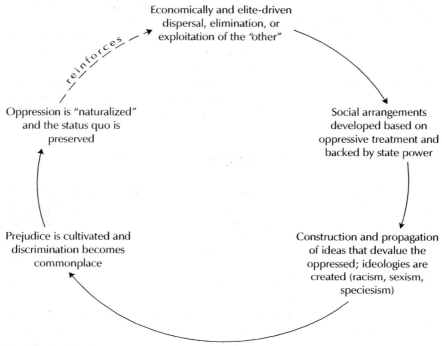

Figure 1.1   Theory of Oppression

interdependent and operate more or less simultaneously. The reciprocal influences, however, are not entirely symmetrical, due to the primary influence of material and economic considerations.[38] The theory of oppression will serve as a sort of "causal compass" to guide our examination of the systemic and entangled oppression of humans and other animals.

One last note on this theoretical model is in order before we move on. While theoretical models serve to illuminate understanding of complex social phenomena, they can also mask complex linkages. In the case of the theory of oppression, for example, since ideological devaluation and uses of unequal power are prompted largely by material circumstances, they can be reduced—creating possibilities for increased tolerance—when oppression of a devalued group no longer serves the interest of the oppressors. Such is the case, for example, of the gray wolf in the United States. Humans waged upon the wolves "a relentless war" with "rifles, traps, and poisons for more than three hundred years."[39] Today, human friends of the wolves, and their many supporters among the general public who no longer perceive the wolf as an economic threat, are nurturing their return in several western states.

Conversely, increased ideological disparagement of an already devalued group can occur, and expansion of tyrannical use of power will result, when new opportunities for exploitative pursuit of self-interest arise. This was seen, for example, in Germany in the early twentieth century after European Jews had attained a degree of social acceptance and integration. The economic and social disorganization after World War I led to scapegoating, a form of exploitation, and European Jews faced increased and ruthless oppression, with catastrophic consequences.

Human social systems are not fixed in stone, and specific economic motivations for oppression—and resulting societal arrangements and ideas—are subject to change. This is where we find hope and the prospect for societal transformation.

OPPRESSION AND CAPITALISM

The social structural basis and the deep entanglement of the oppression of humans and other animals alluded to thus far may well have provoked deep skepticism in some readers already. Most human members of society have been deeply immersed, all their lives, in a culture that largely devalues other animals and legitimates humans' self-interested use of other animals' lives and bodies. Challenges to such deeply ingrained ideas and practices are understandably difficult for many to accept. Similarly, many friends and advocates of other animals, although embracing a viewpoint that ties efforts to liberate other animals to other liberation movements, may balk when such an analysis is grounded in a critique of capitalism. They—like most members of society—have been taught and conditioned to believe that capitalism, if not the ideal system, is at least the best economic and social system humans can develop.

As stated earlier, the thesis of this book is that oppression of humans and other animals is entangled and that such exploitation is motivated primarily by economic interests. Furthermore, there is compelling evidence that the economic forces fueling oppression have intensified with the development of capitalism. Indeed, as we shall see, contemporary capitalism and the new global economy it has produced—while benefiting the most powerful and privileged members of the most affluent nations—are increasing the disparities in the global distribution of wealth. Millions of humans are subjected to serious material privations. For instance, the gap in income between the richest one-fifth of the human global population and the poorest one-fifth "was 74 to 1 in 1997, up from 60 to 1 in 1990 and 30 to 1 in 1960."[40] Today "350 billionaires have as much wealth as one-half the world's population."[41] A 1999 United Nations report declared that "global inequalities in income and living standards have reached grotesque proportions."[42]

At the same time, *billions* of other animals with whom we share the planet now endure unspeakable acts and unimaginable suffering. The scale and intensity of misery inflicted on other animals have also increased with modern capitalism. Anthropologist Barbara Noske notes:

> In the earlier stages of domestication humans invaded and became part of animal social systems. . . . But under industrial capitalism these systems are no longer intact so that

animals have become reduced to mere appendages of computers and machines. . . .
[P]resent-day capitalism tends to eliminate anything in the animal which cannot be
made productive. The animal is modified to suit the production system, and its offend-
ing parts are simply cut off.[43]

Due to the vigorous promotion and support of the capitalist system that takes
place in the United States, most of those who work in defense of other animals do
not challenge capitalism—although many working in other liberation movements
are more inclined to do so. The profound role that capitalism plays in the oppression
of other animals, however, prompted philosopher and activist Susan Finsen to
finally ask, *"Is corporate capitalism compatible with animal rights?"* (emphasis
added).[44]

While sociological theory of oppressed groups conveniently emphasized the individual causes of oppression until the 1960s, as noted earlier, not all theorists downplayed institutional and economic forces. For example, W. E. B. DuBois believed
capitalism and racial oppression were inextricably tied together and that racism and
colonialism were the twin pillars of capitalist society. The quest for private profit
resulted in the "miserable modern subjugation" of humans of color around the
world, he argued. The following passage from a 1944 analysis of neocolonialist relations between the United States and the Third World provides an example of
DuBois's critique of the capitalist system.

> [I]n the most beautiful part of the New World, the overwhelming mass of the inhabi-
> tants [suffer from] poverty, ignorance, disease and disfranchisement from taking any
> part in modern civilization. White citizens of the United States and most Englishmen
> find nothing unusual or alarming in this situation. They have argued from the days of
> the slave trade that not more than a tenth of the Caribbean peoples are capable of mod-
> ern civilization or conceivable participants in political and cultural democracy. . . . [I]n
> most modern instances, the wealthy country is thinking in terms of profit, and is
> obsessed with the long-ingrained conviction that the needs of the weaker country are
> few and its capacity for development are narrow or nonexistent. In that case, this eco-
> nomic partnership works to the distinct disadvantage of the weaker country. The terms
> of sale for raw materials, the prices of goods and rent of capital; even the wages of labor
> are dictated by the stronger partner, backed by economic pressure and military power.[45]

DuBois believed that one could not effectively challenge racism while remaining a
supporter of capitalism.[46]

Another prominent scholar of the early twentieth century, whose insightful work
generally was not widely embraced, was Oliver Cromwell Cox. Cox's work also promoted the idea that racism served the interests of elites by justifying the oppression
of another group. Cox maintained that modern racism essentially began in the 15th
century to legitimate the European quest for profits.

> Western civilization began to take on its characteristic attributes when Columbus
> turned the eyes and interests of the world away from the Mediterranean toward the

Atlantic. . . . The socioeconomic matrix of racial antagonism involved the commercialization of human labor in the West Indies, the East Indies, and in America, the intense competition among businessmen of different western European cities for the capitalist exploitation of the resources of this area, the development of nationalism and the consolidation of European nations, and the decline of the Roman Catholic Church with its mystical inhibitions to the free exploitation of economic resources. Racial antagonism attained full maturity during the latter half of the nineteenth century, when the sun no longer set on British soil and the great nationalistic powers of Europe began to justify their economic designs . . . work had to be done, and if not voluntarily, then some ideology had to be found to justify involuntary servitude. "The Indians were represented as lazy, filthy pagans, of bestial morals, no better than dogs, and fit only for slavery, in which state alone there might be some hope of converting them to Christianity."[47]

The capitalist exploiter of the colored workers, it should be observed, consigns them to employments and treatments that [are] humanly degrading. In order to justify this treatment the exploiters must argue that the workers are innately degraded and degenerate, consequently they naturally merit their condition. . . . This, then, is the beginning of modern race relations. It was not an abstract, immemorial feeling of mutual antipathy between groups, but rather a practical exploitative relationship with its socio-attitudinal facilitation. . . . The capitalist exploiter, being opportunistic and practical, will utilize any convenience to keep his labor and other resources freely exploitable. He will devise and employ race prejudice when that becomes convenient.[48]

The perspective cultivated by DuBois, Cox, and numerous other writers, and now shared by many sociologists and activists working in human liberation movements, is important here for two reasons. First, it epitomizes and supports the general sociological assumption that prejudice is a *tool* of oppression and not its cause—an insight that is important to the contemporary struggle for the liberation of humans and other animals. Second, it indicts capitalism as a primary factor in perpetuating and expanding oppression into the twenty-first century. As we shall see in more detail in the chapters that follow, capitalism's growth and development depended on the terrible oppression of both humans and other animals—and this remains true today.

CONCLUSION

In sum, in this chapter I have attempted to construct a sort of theoretical scaffolding around which to build an analysis and understanding of oppression. The term *minority groups* has been replaced with the more appropriate, powerful, and inclusive term *oppressed groups*. Use of the term *speciesism* has been examined, and we see that it is actually an ideology, a belief system that legitimates and inspires prejudice and discrimination.

Noel's theory of ethnic stratification was introduced, revised, and recast as a general theory of oppression for our use in exploring the basis for the oppression of humans and other animals. This theoretical scaffolding will help to explain the massacres at Hinckley and in Guatemala, how the structure of human society put

Cassidy and Willow Grear at high risk for mistreatment, and why adolescent boys reveled in their assault. It will help explain why the analyses of the entanglement of oppression observed by many writers is incomplete until they include speciesism.

While I have suggested that capitalism is profoundly related to oppression, there is no question that the oppression of humans and other animals preceded capitalist society. In the next chapter, we will briefly reflect on the roots of western oppression and then examine how exploitation of humans and other animals continued, and in many ways intensified, with the emergence of capitalism.

NOTES

1. Noam Chomsky, *Robbing People Blind: The U.S. Economic System,* audio interview with David Barsamian at MIT, Part 2, 31 October and 3 November 1995 (Boulder, Colo.: Alternative Radio, P.O. Box 551, 80306).

2. Milton P. Peirce, "The Great Hinckley Hunt," *The American Field,* 4 January 1890, 4.

3. Robert G. Williams, *Export Agriculture and the Crisis in Central America* (Chapel Hill: University of North Carolina Press, 1986), 148–49.

4. *Green Revolution* 37, no. 5 (1981): 19.

5. Mary McCarthy, " 'Fun' May Have Ruined Woman's Guide Dog," *Dayton Daily News,* 5 July 1998, 1B and 3B.

6. See, for example, Richard C. Edwards, Michael Reich, and Thomas E. Weisskopf, *The Capitalist System,* 3d ed. (Englewood Cliffs, N.J.: Prentice Hall, 1986); Scott G. McNall, *Political Economy: A Critique of American Society* (Glenview, Ill.: Scott Foresman, 1981).

7. Daniel W. Rossides, *Social Stratification: The Interplay of Class, Race, and Gender,* 3d ed. (Upper Saddle River, N.J.: Prentice Hall, 1997), 19.

8. Margaret L. Anderson and Patricia Hill Collins, *Race, Class, and Gender: An Anthology* (Belmont, Calif.: Wadsworth, 1992), xii and xiii.

9. Suzanne Pharr, *Homophobia: A Weapon of Sexism* (Little Rock, Ark.: Chardon, 1988), 53.

10. See, for example, Carol J. Adams, *The Sexual Politics of Meat: A Feminist-Vegetarian Critical Theory* (New York: Continuum, 1992); Joan Dunayer, "Sexist Words, Speciesist Roots," in *Animals and Women: Feminist Theoretical Explorations,* ed. Carol J. Adams and Josephine Donovan (Durham, N.C.: Duke University Press, 1995), 11–31; for a sociological treatise, see Arnold Arluke and Clinton Sanders, *Regarding Animals* (Philadelphia: Temple University Press, 1996).

11. For an expanded discussion of this application, see Edward Sagarin, *The Other Minorities* (Toronto: Ginn, 1971).

12. For a more developed version of this position, see David Nibert, "Minority Group as Sociological Euphemism," *Race, Gender & Class* 3, no. 3 (1996): 129–36.

13. Iris Young, *Justice and the Politics of Difference* (Princeton, N.J.: Princeton University Press, 1990).

14. Nibert, "Minority Group as Sociological Euphemism," 135.

15. See, for example, Gerda Lerner, *The Creation of Patriarchy* (New York: Oxford University Press, 1986), 234.

16. Richard D. Ryder, *Victims of Science: The Use of Animals in Research,* rev. ed. (London: National Anti-Vivisection Society Limited, 1983 [1975]), 5.

17. Peter Singer, *Animal Liberation,* rev. ed. (New York: Avon, 1990), 6.

18. See, for example, Tom Regan, *All That Dwell There: Animal Rights and Environmental Ethics* (Berkeley: University of California Press, 1982), 184–85.

19. Marc Bekoff and Carron A. Meanney, *Encyclopedia of Animal Rights and Animal Welfare* (Westport, Conn.: Greenwood, 1998), 320.

20. Richard D. Ryder, *Animal Revolution: Changing Attitudes toward Speciesism* (Cambridge, Mass.: Blackwell, 1989), 328.

21. Donald L. Noel, *The Origins of American Slavery and Racism* (Columbus, Ohio: Merrill, 1972), 159.

22. See, for example, Joe Feagin and Clarice Feagin, "Theoretical Perspectives in Race and Ethnic Relations," in *Race and Ethnic Relations: Contending Views on Prejudice, Discrimination, and Ethnoviolence,* ed. Fred L. Pincus and Howard Ehrlich (Boulder, Colo.: Westview, 1994).

23. See, for example, Robert W. Friedrichs, *A Sociology of Sociology* (New York: Free Press, 1970).

24. Robert Blauner, *Racial Oppression in America* (New York: Harper & Row, 1972), 8–10.

25. James W. Vander Zanden, *American Minority Relations,* 4th ed. (New York: McGraw-Hill, 1983), 81; Vander Zanden summarizes a chapter written by Herbert Blumer titled "Race Prejudice as a Sense of Group Position," in *Race Relations,* ed. Jitsuichi Masuoka and Preston Valien (Chapel Hill: University of North Carolina Press, 1961).

26. In Vander Zanden, *American Minority Relations,* 158.

27. Singer, *Animal Liberation,* 93 and 161.

28. Singer, *Animal Liberation,* 216.

29. Marjorie Spiegel, *The Dreaded Comparison: Human and Animal Slavery* (New York: Mirror Books, 1996).

30. Spiegel, *The Dreaded Comparison,* 83.

31. Spiegel, *The Dreaded Comparison,* 90.

32. Spiegel, *The Dreaded Comparison,* 106.

33. Tom Regan, *The Case for Animal Rights* (Berkeley: University of California Press, 1983), 341.

34. Kim Stallwood, "Utopian Visions and Pragmatic Politics: Challenging the Foundations of Speciesism and Misothery," in *Animal Rights: The Changing Debate,* ed. Robert Garner (New York: New York University Press, 1996), 195.

35. Don Noel, "Theory of Ethnic Stratification," *Social Problems* 16 (1968): 157–72.

36. William G. Sumner, *Folkways* (Boston: Ginn, 1906), 13.

37. See, for example, Scott G. McNall, *Political Economy: A Critique of American Society* (Glenview, Ill.: Scott, Foresman, 1981).

38. While the primacy of economic factors will be accentuated, this analysis should not be characterized as an exercise in "vulgar Marxism" or "reductionistic economic determinism" so eschewed by the defenders of twenty-first-century capitalism. Rather, a dialectical approach to the causes and maintenance of speciesism will be developed, and the role of powerful political and social forces, as well as prejudice and other social psychological factors, will be discussed. Nonetheless, the primacy of economic forces—particularly under capitalist society—will be asserted.

39. Douglas H. Chadwick, "Return of the Gray Wolf," *National Geographic* 193, no. 5 (May 1998): 78.

40. David McGowan, *Derailing Democracy: The America the Media Don't Want You to See* (Monroe, Maine: Common Courage, 2000), 38.

41. Robert W. McChesney, *Rich Media, Poor Democracy: Communication Politics in Dubious Times* (New York: New Press, 2000), 299.

42. McGowan, *Derailing Democracy,* 33.

43. Barbara Noske, *Beyond Boundaries: Humans and Animals* (New York: Black Rose, 1997), 20.

44. Susan Finsen, "Obstacles to Legal Rights for Animals: Can We Get There from Here?" *Animal Law* 3 (1997): ii.

45. W. E. B. DuBois, *Against Racism: Unpublished Essays, Papers, Addresses, 1887–1961,* ed. Herbert Aptheker (Amherst: University of Massachusetts Press, 1985), 230 and 234.

46. Manning Marable, *How Capitalism Underdeveloped Black America* (Boston: South End, 1983), 11–18.

47. At this point in the text, Cox quotes Francis Augustus MacNutt, *Bartholomew De Las Casas* (Cleveland: Clark, 1909), 25.

48. Oliver Cromwell Cox, *Caste, Class, & Race: A Study in Social Dynamics* (New York: Doubleday, 1948), 330–34.

2

Economic Basis of
Animal Oppression

[P]ractical ethics does not so much determine practical economics as it adjusts
to it.

—Robert S. Lopez[1]

E very year thousands of schoolchildren take highly anticipated field trips to science and natural history museums, including one known as the Center of Science and Industry (COSI) in Columbus, Ohio, pouring out of a virtually endless
stream of yellow school buses. The children's "scientific" outing is one of many such
experiences that will shape their views, their values, and their dreams. Inside, child-
friendly mechanical gadgets demonstrating various principles of physics are inter-
spersed with exhibits that glorify the "progress of mankind" and make existing social
arrangements appear as natural and inevitable as the movement of the planets
around the sun.

One particularly large and theatrical exhibit that occupied COSI for years, until
the museum relocated in 1999, was the "Tunnel of Time." By way of elaborately
crafted life-size scenes that depicted various periods in human history, the exhibit
was a sort of historical scrapbook. In the very first scene, ostensibly representing the
dawn of human history, a group of humans were in the act of killing another animal
in what appeared to be an organized hunt. The action was violent and grisly, and
many children stared, wide-eyed and silent, at the spectacle, the silence punctuated
by "cool" and "awesome." This powerful ideological lesson about the "natural"
relationship between humans and other animals presented as science, in this exhibit
and countless others like it still in existence, is actually quite misleading. Notwithstanding such exhibits and popular myths, the truth is that planned hunting of other
animals is a relatively recent cultural and social structural practice, one that is no
more natural to humans than smoking cigarettes or polluting rivers.

The human species has existed for at least five million years, but many scientists

21

believe that the hunting of other animals is a fairly recent development in human history. For example, anthropologist Steven Mithen maintains that australopithecines, who lived between 4.2 and 1 million years ago—and who many believe to be ancestors of today's humans—were largely vegetarians. "Did the australopithecines hunt at all? Probably not, or at least no more than chimpanzees today. Indeed, the robust australopithecines evolved into specialized vegetarians, with massive jaws and chewing muscles fixed onto a crest of bone."[2]

Some scholars believe that widespread organized hunting of other animals started only about twenty thousand years ago.[3] Author Jim Mason, for example, writes:

> Neither is it true that we have been mighty hunters throughout . . . evolution. Some anthropologists now believe that humans probably first took to meat-eating as scavengers, occasionally grabbing a bit of meat and bone left among the remains of animals killed by true predators. That and the occasional killing of rodents, lizards, and other small animals surprised in the course of foraging kept animal flesh in the diet for millions of years. Evidence now suggests that true, planned, coordinated hunting of large animals began only about 20,000 years ago.[4]

According to leading biological anthropologist Matt Cartmill, "There is no reason to think that hunting is natural in the sense of being instinctive for human beings. (Probably most of the people who ever have lived have never hunted.)"[5]

Cartmill writes that early humans, "(like most people today) had eaten a 'preponderantly vegetable diet.' "[6] This is because the primary method by which we human animals acquired food and resources for most of our existence has been not hunting but foraging. In general, food and other material resources were obtained by searching for edible plants, seeds, fruits, nuts, and other forms of vegetation, perhaps supplemented by the sporadic consumption of the remains of recently deceased other animals scavenged along the way. In all probability, the human relationship with other animals was mainly one of relatively peaceful cohabitation. As Sherwood Washburn and C. S. Lancaster put it, "Prior to hunting, the relations of our ancestors to other animals must have been very much like those of other noncarnivores. They could have moved close among the other species, fed beside them, and shared the same waterholes."[7]

One explanation for why organized hunting of other animals began only relatively recently in our history is that, for most of our existence, hunting was an ineffective and inefficient way of obtaining resources. Foraging was a much more practical and productive means of economic production.

Over tens of thousands of years humans became adept foragers. Human experience determined where to search, what to look for, and how to use and distribute foraged resources. This experience-based knowledge was formulated into custom and was handed down from one generation to the next as *learned* behavior. It was, and still is, important for humans to teach succeeding generations how to survive in any given time because humans have little of what is called ancestral memory or instinct—that is, memory or knowledge about how to behave, possessed at birth.

What is more, human animals not only create survival skills but also construct entire ways of thinking and behaving, as well as systems of social organization. This information is transmitted to each new generation in the form of *culture* and *social structure*. Culture is composed of common beliefs, values, language, customs, and norms; social structure refers to the ways humans are organized to coordinate actions and work toward established goals. Since human animals, interacting with one another, invent culture and social structure, we say these things are *socially created*. Throughout eons of human prehistory, the foraging life, with its rules, customs, and structure, was regarded as "natural" and right. Our prehistoric ancestors were unaware of any other way of relating to one other and to other animals.

Many believe that a change in this socially constructed reality, a modification that began to place more emphasis on organized hunts, became feasible after the Ice Age glacier movements expanded prairies and grasslands, creating conditions that accommodated the movement of large groups of other animals.[8] Since such massive migrations facilitated successful and efficient capturing and killing of other animals in order for humans to ingest them as food, humans began to devote time to this pursuit. Humans desiring to stay in or migrate into very cold or arid regions became particularly adept at using the bodies of other animals for food and fashioning their skin, hair, bones, horns, and sinews into clothing, shelters, tools, and other necessities.

So, the change from a socially created culture that relied on foraging to one that included occasional to frequent hunting of other animals was economically motivated behavior, cultivated as the potential for effective hunts grew. It was not necessary for human survival, as hominids had existed for the better part of five million years, but simply furthered nonessential interests. Still, even though the hunting of other animals became an established way to acquire food and resources, in many societies plant-based foraging typically still provided at least 60 to 70 percent of the food for many groups.[9]

This change in the relationship between humans and other animals, from cohabitors to hunter and quarry, eventually affected relations between humans, most notably women's relationships to men.[10] Women and men most likely functioned as equals through most of prehistory, when humans foraged close to campsites and even when early forms of organized hunting began. However, when the tracking and killing of other animals began, particularly with the use of spears and other projectiles, a division of labor developed that changed that relationship. According to anthropologist Leith Mullings:

> The division of labor was associated with the development of hunting with projectile weapons—pursuing and killing large mobile animals—as opposed to earlier forms of hunting, such as drives, individual hunting of small animals or "surround" hunting. It was in the specific conditions where meat became a regular part of the diet and resources were scarce, thus making dispersal into small groups a necessity, that projectile hunting was associated with a sexual division of labor. As the ability to remain inconspicuous and to surprise the animal was key in this type of hunting, small groups became more

efficient, as opposed to drive hunting or surround hunting where large groups were required to surround or drive the animal.

It was with the development of these socioecological circumstances, characterized by small groups and projectile hunting, that a woman with children found herself encumbered as a hunter.[11]

Hunting shaped relations between female and male humans largely because the bodies of other animals became a valued economic resource, and killing them enhanced male prestige and privilege. Men accrued elevated prestige through the acquisition and distribution of resources derived from the bodies of other animals. While women generally provided more routine, and more reliable, forms of nourishment from plants, their foraging work produced less skin, hair, bones, and other such "resources" that were converted to clothing, tools, and related materials. What is more, the decrease caused by hunting in men's participation in foraging and in caring for children and others needing assistance no doubt created a need for women to devote a greater amount of their time to these tasks—resulting in decreased time for rest and leisure. Concomitantly, the increased labor and caretaking tasks exacted from women freed males to increase the time they could devote to hunting. This developing mistreatment of women and other animals was based on, and compounded by, each other's exploitation.

Evidence to support this position on the historical relationship between hunting and the devaluation of women—and the idea that hunting facilitated the hierarchical placement of males in such communities—also comes from the work of twentieth-century anthropologist Valerio Valeri. Valeri studied a community of forest-dwelling humans in the Moluccas, the Huaula—a community relatively untouched by the cultures and practices of wealthy nations. He observed that, for the Huaula people, "hunting being a noble activity . . . is one basis of two acts of hierarchical discrimination: of men from women, and of 'great men' . . . from lesser or 'ordinary men.' "[12] Thus, inequalities between human females and males (and the beginnings of significant social distinctions between males) are rooted to a substantial degree in organized hunts of other animals—an early entanglement of the oppression of devalued humans and other animals.

So, then, human pursuit and killing of other animals during the later prehistoric period occurred because the activity provided economic benefits. That is, the practice was driven by material interests, not innate animosity and prejudice. Such predatory behavior on the part of the human species was socially created and cultivated, not instinctive. Prehistoric humans came to accept the altered relationship with other animals, and between females and males, as "natural" and right, not realizing that their culture and the structure of their small community were socially manufactured. Although this new predation toward other animals was no doubt terrifying and horrific for those who were stalked or killed during prehistory, the vast majority of other animals continued to live largely free of human interference.

About ten thousand years ago, a dramatic technological development—the planting and harvesting of edible vegetation, early agriculture—put many human societies on a path toward profound transformation. This change in the method of economic production eventually led to increased provisions and population growth in human societies. As human settlements slowly changed from transient to relatively permanent, larger numbers of other animals, such as sheep, goats, cows, and pigs, were held and bred in captivity and their bodies used for food and resources. As agricultural techniques developed, the labor power of such animals as elephants, oxen, yaks, horses, and donkeys also was exploited to till soil, pull sledges and wagons, power millstones and pestles, and perform other tasks in relation to human economic production.

Oppression of nonhuman animals for their flesh and labor power was soon to be joined by another economic-related reason for their oppression: direct competition. The clearing of land that accompanied the advent and growth of agricultural society cost countless nonhuman animals dearly as the land they lived on was cleared for grazing or prepared for cultivation. Innumerable other animals were displaced, orphaned, or killed as their homelands were burned or razed. Adapting to the expansion of human society and humans' ever-increasing control of the Earth, some other animals sought food from human-cultivated or harvested vegetation. These other animals came to be viewed as "pests" because their existence and needs conflicted with human economic goals. Wolves, coyotes, large cats, and other carnivorous species also were seen as direct competitors both for the other animals who were now held captive and domesticated and for free-living species that humans viewed as desirable "quarry." Consequently, these competitors also came to be regarded as troublesome and were eradicated because of their perceived harm to human material interests.

At the same time, nascent agricultural society brought with it mass exploitation of humans. One sociological account of early agricultural society holds that priests came to claim many of the resources produced through early agriculture for the appeasement of the gods—resources the priests themselves began to consume. Thus, while the majority cultivated the soil, the early agrarian priests cultivated a distinct, nonlaboring, privileged position within the community.[13]

The existence of agriculture-based products also created the need for a new class of societal members—warriors. This group protected planted-based harvests and the highly coveted domesticated other animals from marauding human groups, while also keeping the increasingly exploited and disgruntled laboring masses under control. High-ranking warriors eventually used the coercive power of their position to exert a strong influence over the management of the society, exacting considerable privilege for themselves.

Just as the early devaluation of women was tied to the oppression of other animals, so, too, were the deep divisions within the ranks of males. The devaluation of humans who labored in the fields, and who produced the food and goods of the society, legitimated not only the intensive and exploitative use of their labor but also the privations they were forced to endure. This intraspecies oppression occurred because the surplus food and resources produced by the masses of humans in early agricultural society—particularly "meat"—were not plentiful. Such "food" products were distributed unequally, a practice justified by evolving ideas about the greater value and importance of the elite and the lowly status of those who labored—self-serving ideas created and promulgated by the powerful themselves.

The shortage of "meat" arose largely because it was difficult, if not impossible, to raise the large number of other animals needed to provide it for everyone; such a population of captive other animals would have required enormous areas of lush rangeland. However, while many humans merely did not get much "meat," others frequently went hungry, as land suitable for cultivation was often set aside for grazing other animals rather than raising plant foods to feed the growing human population.

Moreover, in many areas other animals forced into domestication for the production of "meat" or "milk" who grazed during warm weather required reserves of feed during the winter. Consequently, a large portion of the harvest of edible plants was held for "livestock" consumption. The privileged could thus enjoy "meat" during the winter, and the "herd" of captive other animals could survive into the next year. Holding food derived from plants for the consumption of captive other animals must have contributed to hunger for many devalued humans, particularly during periods of meager harvests. Indeed, anthropological studies of skeletal remains have found that chronic malnutrition was much more prevalent in agricultural societies than in earlier groups of foragers.[14] Devaluation of the masses of humanity and the elites' practice of eating cows in ancient India, for instance, generated suffering for humans and cows alike. Writing of the human consequences, Jeremy Rifkin remarks, "While the poor teetered between survival and famine, the victims of periodic floods and droughts, the Brahmin caste and the Vedic chieftains continued to slaughter the cattle of India, consuming enormous amounts of beef. . . . Angry, the peasants lashed out, demanding equity and admonishing their rulers for their callous disregard. The rulers of India turned a deaf ear."[15]

Other animals were so valued as a scarce resource and coveted by the elite that they were used as, and became interchangeable with, currency, helping buttress highly stratified social and economic systems. Indeed, early coins often bore the images of such animals as oxen and goats. Author Hermann Dembeck writes:

Words still very much in use reflect the lasting influence of trade in animals over the ages. The Latin word for wealth in cattle and in cash has found its way into our language. In Rome, cattle were called *pecus,* and the word for a herd of cattle was *pecunia.* Since the Romans usually had to pay for cattle in cash, pecunia ultimately became the term for money in general. *Pecuniary* is derived from it, and our word *fee,* which in Old English meant cattle, is cognate with *pecus.*[16]

The oppression of other animals, and the closely associated oppression of humans, was motivated by material interest—the creation and hoarding of privilege. Just as with other animals, over time the oppression of humans assigned to devalued social positions also came to be viewed as a natural and normal aspect of worldly existence. The vast majority of human animals on the Earth would be relegated to the socially created position of peasant, serf, or slave, and other animals generally would be relegated to positions of livestock, quarry, or pests. Their lowly positions and ill treatment were woven into the fabric of the economic, political, religious, and social systems and thus *institutionalized*.

OTHER ANIMALS IN WAR AND ENTERTAINMENT

Agriculture-based human societies grew in size through widespread oppression of humans and other animals, as well as through the imperative for warfare and repression inherent in systems that oppress other animals. During the hundreds of thousands of years of foraging society, prestige was obtained through the ability to find resources that were shared by the entire group. In the more "civilized" agrarian society, prestige was achieved largely through military prowess and conquest. Countless humans and other animals suffered miserably or were killed as elites or would-be elites undertook endless military expeditions and conflicts.

Of course, constant warfare was not the result just of power-hungry, egotistical rulers. More important, war served significant economic development purposes in societies based on oppression of humans and other animals. First, the agrarian-based economies gradually exhausted the land. The crude agricultural techniques of the time devitalized the soil, and the grazing of large numbers of captive other animals depleted pastures. The relationship among enslaving and restraining the movements of cows and the depletion of grazing lands and warfare (as well as the health implications of a "meat"-eating diet) are noted by Socrates in the following dialogue with Glaucon, as represented in Plato's *Republic*:

> [A]nd there will be animals of many other kinds, if people eat them?
> Certainly.
> And living this way we shall have much greater need of physicians than before?
> Much greater.
> And the country which was enough to support the original inhabitants will be too small now and not enough?
> Quite true.
> Then a slice of our neighbor's land will be wanted by us for pasture and tillage, and they will want a slice of ours, if, like ourselves, they exceed the limit of necessity, and give themselves up to the unlimited accumulation of wealth?
> That, Socrates, will be inevitable.
> And so we shall go to war, Glaucon. Shall we not?
> Most certainly, he replied.[17]

Territorial expansion and invasion of areas claimed by other rulers were vital to obtain new areas of arable land and grazing areas.

Second, possession of other animals represented wealth. Warfare was a way to increase the elite's possession of other animals held captive by other societies. For example, Hermann Dembeck notes:

> The Egyptians, too, carried off vast herds of cattle from the lands they conquered in the Near East. After the repulsion of the Egyptians from Mesopotamia, the Assyrians . . . treated their defeated neighbors in exactly the same way. They appropriated the herds of the subject peoples, destroyed their cities, and killed a considerable portion of the population. The animals had to be driven to Assyria by the victims, and then guarded for the new owners.[18]

A great deal of wealth, power, and personal prestige came through the plundering that accompanied war-related expansionism. Historian Gordon Childe observes, "[T]he military conqueror has become the ideal for the ruling classes. To such, wealth is booty to be taken, not produced, or rather the product of the 'oldest labour saving device'—robbery."[19]

And, there was a third economic function of warfare in agrarian society. As populations grew, so did the need for basic infrastructure such as roads and aqueducts. The ruling class demanded elaborate temples, palaces, and monuments, both to assuage their egos and to inspire awe and fear—and, thus, compliance—in the masses of oppressed humans. War, then, was also a source of human labor power, as many prisoners of war were relegated to the position of slave. It was not uncommon for entire societies to be enslaved by conquering armies. Humans who became the spoils of war suffered horrendous exploitation and misery.

Women were particularly affected by warfare. The devaluation of women that began with the ascent of organized hunting increased in tandem with the expanded oppression of other animals in agricultural society. Just as many other animals came to be viewed as personal property, so, too, did women come to be viewed as the property of men. Women could be given in marriage, with no say in the matter, and many families sold their daughters into slavery. Great numbers of female infants were killed or left to die from exposure so as not to put a strain on family resources, particularly when necessitated by dowries. Noting one of the consequences of war for women under such circumstances, Susan Brownmiller describes a tactic of the ancient Greeks that both preceded them and continues even in warfare today: "Among the ancient Greeks, rape was also socially acceptable behavior well within the rules of warfare, an act without stigma for warriors who viewed the women they conquered as legitimate booty, useful as wives, concubines, slave labor or battle-camp trophy."[20] The widespread and frequent warfare characteristic of agricultural society also brought hardship, terror, and death to incalculable numbers of individuals who were used as combatants or weapons.

Other animals were also harmed by large, hierarchical human societies' penchant for warfare. The relationship between hunting and warfare is noted by scholars Andree Collard and Joyce Contrucci in their reflection on the thoughts of Aristotle. "Over 2,000 years ago," they write, "Aristotle had rationalized the justice of war with . . . [this] reasoning. Wars were necessary to secure slaves (people *born* inferior) and good soldiers acquired their skills by practicing on animals (hunting)."[21]

Other animals were further exploited as instruments of warfare. The exploitation of dogs for military purposes, for example, dates back to at least four thousand years ago, the eighteenth century B.C., when Hammurabi, ruler of Babylon, supplemented his army with large dogs. Ancient writers and artists noted the use of dogs in military campaigns and frequently portrayed them in suits of armor.[22] Horses as tools of warfare also go far back in recorded history. At least a thousand years B.C., the Hittites are believed to have used horse-drawn chariots as weapons of war. The Scythians of northern Asia are thought to have invented reins and saddles to facilitate the use of horses in battle; they hung the scalps of those they killed from the bridle reins.[23] From ancient times to well into the twentieth century, mounted cavalries have been integral components of military organization. Elephants were also used as transportation and weapons for centuries. Asian elephants are reported to have been used in warfare from at least the seventeenth century B.C., and African elephants were used by the ancient Carthaginians in wars with the Romans. Thus, countless humans and other animals were instruments or victims of war—costly "fodder" for socially created systems built on the desire of elites for animal flesh and luxury.

The exploitation of oppressed humans and other animals for entertainment purposes was also common in ancient agricultural society. One of the most infamous examples of such cruelty is the horrific exploitation that occurred in ancient Rome. Human contestants were forced to battle to the death for the entertainment of the powerful and a citizenry debauched by an existence characterized by varying degrees of deprivation, ruthlessness, and tyranny. Other animals also were frequently pitted against each other or against humans, or simply slaughtered as entertainment. For example, in 80 A.D., the huge Roman amphitheater known as the Colosseum was inaugurated by the Emperor Titus, who advertised fights to the death between more than ten thousand human prisoners and five thousand other captive animals in the first one hundred days. During recorded history, few humans have undertaken to chronicle the experiences of other animals, and their experiences of ruthless oppression can only be imagined. However, author F. R. Cowell has envisioned the scene in Rome as the forced battles between humans concluded:

> The few survivors retired to get their laurel crowns, their bags of gold and to anticipate the adulation of Rome. Squads of little men ran into the arena with ropes and metal hooks to drag the bodies of the dead and wounded to a mortuary cell where valuable weapons and armor were retrieved and sorted out. The gasping, bleeding, groaning wounded were finished off, for nobody had any use for a maimed gladiator who, if nursed back to health, might never fight again. The bodies were then piled into carts to be taken and flung into a nameless common grave. . . .
>   A great novelty followed. Ostriches and giraffes, which few Romans had seen before, were released after a long captivity. Scenting fresh air and enjoying a new-found freedom, they sought to get back the use of their legs and to run joyously round the arena, to the vast amusement of the crowd. It was a short-lived respite. Bands of archers ran into the arena and the slaughter began. Wounded and startled animals fled in all directions as the arrows hissed and struck, vainly seeking an escape from which the pitiless high walls of the arena barred them. It was soon strewn with the dead and dying.[24]

During some periods, elephants were a particular favorite for such cruel sport, due no doubt not only to their size and the dramatic spectacle of their death but also likely because of the large amount of "meat" they produced. After such "contests," the flesh of the other animals was frequently given to members of the plebeian class, as some small recompense for the extreme privations they suffered due to the excesses of the patricians. The debasement of the citizenry and the exploitation of the unfortunate "contestants" were further fueled by a gambling industry that capitalized on these exhibitions. The taking of bets brought in income that perpetuated the contests and heightened their popular interest.

The exploitation of devalued humans and other animals for entertainment throughout the agricultural era can also be seen in the development of zoos and menageries. The ancient Egyptians maintained large temple menageries, and the Empress Hatshepsut organized the first animal-collecting expedition when she sent a special fleet to Punt to bring back species of dogs, monkeys, leopards, and giraffes. The soldiers of Alexander the Great brought back "strange creatures" for the populace to gape at, and the famous elephants of Carthage were put on show in a public park when they were not needed for military use. There were also well-stocked menageries in Rome, though these were usually devoted to supplying the arena.[25]

At the same time, humans with various types of disabilities also were exhibited for entertainment. In Rome in the fourth century B.C., for example, wealthy families kept humans with disabilities to amuse their guests; in the second century, the viewing of those with disabilities became a source of public entertainment.[26] Likewise, the male elite in some societies enslaved women in order to have them perform for the amusement and gratification of guests, and numerous societies held women in brothels for paying customers.

Social systems that regarded other animals, women, humans with disabilities, and the enslaved as property and objects of entertainment did not bode well for children. Children were valued in small, socially integrated foraging societies, but their status plummeted in the oppressive atmosphere of agrarian society. Because of the exploitation and privations the elite imposed on the masses of humans, many children did not survive infancy—particularly during periods of meager harvests and food shortages. Those perceived as weak or defective were often killed, and infants with disabilities frequently were believed to be possessed by evil spirits. Children who survived infancy could be used by their family in a variety of ways that furthered the family's aims. Children were regularly sacrificed to the gods to atone for parental misdeeds, or they could be sold into slavery or used as security or payment for debts. Most surviving children, however, were sent to the fields when they were old enough to be productive. Adults expected children to be obedient and, as with similar groups of "others"—those defined as lesser, inferior beings—beating became a common method of controlling them.

From this brief look of Western history thus far, we can see that humans' economic arrangements have exerted a profound influence over their relationships with other animals. For most of human history, other animals and humans were largely cohabitors—a reality conditioned by the foraging way of life. Changing climatic

conditions facilitated the emergence of hunting. This change in the method of material accumulation was necessarily accompanied by ideas that assuaged human guilt,
ideas that were embedded in social and religious practices and beliefs. The ascent of
agricultural society gradually transformed human oppression of other animals into
a mundane practice.

Interhuman relationships also changed profoundly during these periods, and not
for the better. The mistreatment of humans and other animals was not stimulated
by prejudice; rather, prejudice resulted from the socially constructed ideological systems that legitimated oppression. Significantly, the ruthless treatment of humans
and other animals was entangled. Hunting and devaluation of women went hand in
hand, "meat" production and hoarding brought hunger to many, the ever-growing
need for grazing lands prompted expansion and warfare, mounted soldiers and the
use of elephants in battle led to the assembly of larger armies, and thus even more
mounted soldiers and elephants. Tremendous levels of violence banalized ruthless
killing, and a debauched humanity was encouraged to revel in public displays of the
slaughter of humans and other animals—and on and on. The horrid treatment of
other animals and devalued humans over the ages was conditioned by economic
arrangements and validated by political and ideological systems that supported the
oppression.

OPPRESSION IN THE MIDDLE AGES

In the Western world the Roman Empire, weakened by excess, greed, and corruption, eventually collapsed in the fifth century. No longer bound together by the force
of Roman legions, much of Europe succumbed to parochial battles for control of
land, with widespread pillaging ensuing. Many devalued and exploited humans
agreed to serve new masters, the manorial lords, in return for protection from
marauding bands in the early Middle Ages. Often, however, the lords' terrible conduct inside their fiefdoms was not much better than that of the pillagers from whom
they ostensibly guarded their communities. Cruelty and oppression continued
largely unabated as the manorial system merely replaced centralized tyranny with a
more decentralized form of despotism, exploitation, and cruelty; this situation was
intensified by constant warfare. Writer Sibylle Harksen notes:

> In the early Middle Ages the exploitation of the peasants by the feudal lords was . . .
> severe. . . . [The peasants] more than anyone else had to bear the burden of the great
> wars as well as any lesser strife, since the aggressor always endeavored to weaken his
> adversary by damaging his property, by destroying his villages by fire and laying waste
> the fields of his peasants. Poverty and unremitting hard work characterized the life of
> the peasantry—both men and women.[27]

The social position of women in the agrarian-based, war-afflicted world of the
early Middle Ages was little improved over their position in the ancient world. The

patriarchy and misogyny that characterized the earlier period continued. Women in the Middle Ages spent their lives under the guardianship of men: fathers, husbands, or overlords. In some areas during the Middle Ages, the custom emerged called the *jus primae noctis,* or "right of the first night." Under this custom the manorial lord had the right to "take the virginity" of the bride of any of his vassals or serfs unless the bride and bridegroom made a prescribed payment. Women of the privileged feudal class were given the right to inherit property if no male heirs existed; however, they were never actually permitted to control the estate. Under feudalism, an overlord took the income generated from the estate until the heiress married, and she either married a man of the overlord's choice or forfeited the estate.

The tyrannical life of the manor took its toll on children as well. Infant mortality was high due to poor nutrition, disease, polluted water, and houses that did not provide adequate shelter. Fewer than half of the children born survived to maturity. Until children reached seven years of age, a sign that they would probably survive to adulthood, many were often treated with indifference and neglect, particularly during the demanding harvest seasons. At about the age of seven, children were ushered into the adult world and the prescribed social positions assigned to them.

Cruelty and indifference, compounded by superstitions relating to demonic possession, continued to plague humans with disabilities, although some were desired for their entertainment value. "Fools" and "jesters" were both common sources of amusement and status symbols for manorial lords and monarchs. Some humans with disabilities also were prized by early entrepreneurs who displayed them profitably during the Middle Ages in "side shows" or "ships of fools" that sailed from port to port displaying their "cargo."

Other animals remained costly to raise and maintain and thus were "owned" mainly by the affluent as a symbol of their wealth and status. The flesh of other animals was expensive and destined "essentially for the rulers' tables."[28] Nick Fiddes notes that the elites' consumption of other animals as food was high during the Middle Ages, writing, "Throughout the Middles Ages the greatest differences in eating patterns were not so much between geographical areas as between the mass of the population and a numerically small but outstandingly wealthy elite whose diet was marked by conspicuous consumption in terms of quality, quantity and variety."[29]

A historical example of such a medieval "feast" comes courtesy of Henry VIII, unmerciful in his dealing with humans and other animals alike:

> In a single day of feasting, Henry VIII and his courtiers consumed 11 beef carcasses, 6 sheep, 17 hogs and pigs, 45 dozen chickens, 15 swans, 6 cranes, 384 pigeons, 648 larks, 72 geese and 4 peacocks; the meat is flavored by 3,000 pears and 1,300 apples. Three thousand loaves of bread and 400 dishes of butter are also consumed. . . . By 1541, Henry's waist will expand from 37 inches to 57 inches.[30]

Noting the social symbolism of practices in medieval England, Jeremy Rifkin observes:

[T]he nobility spent personal fortunes and countless time and energy preparing elaborate meat-eating feasts in an effort to outdo one another. Among the wealthy, food and its preparation became the primary means of expressing rank and privilege. . . . Meat was used as a political and social tool at each lord's table to clearly delineate the appropriate rank and status of the invited guests. The high table was always served first, followed by the next table of rank, and so on. The best cuts of meat were alloted [*sic*] to those first served. The less desirable cuts were distributed down the line. When venison was served, the entrails or "umbles" of the deer were always distributed last to the guests of least distinction, thus giving rise to the popular expression "to eat humble pie."[31]

As in the preceding ages, the most "humble" paid for the "meat"-eating excesses of the elite with their own hunger and starvation and through warfare-related deaths, as the powerful few fought to expand pastures and to acquire "booty."

Before experiencing horrid death in order to grace the dining halls of the elite, other animals also no doubt were terrorized by, and were frequently victims of, the constant fighting and warfare that characterized the Middle Ages. Historian Jean Gimpel writes, "A medieval chronicler tells us that even the livestock were conditioned to war. As soon as the animals—horses, oxen, pigs, and sheep—heard the signal of the watchman of approaching men-of-arms, they would rush back to the safety of the city walls."[32]

Like those with disabilities, the oppression of other animals also took the form of entertainment, and the amusements were frequently latent with symbolic value. Henry VIII, for instance, considered bear-baiting "a splendid diversion, and many herds of bears were maintained for that purpose. Henry had his own bear-pit and his own Master of the King's Bears."[33] Elephants, scarce in northern Europe, were displayed and paraded before the masses to demonstrate the greatness and majesty of the elite who "owned" them. Among many "high personages with a passion for possessing strange and wild animals"[34] was Henry III of France, who in the mid–sixteenth century cultivated a large collection of other animals, only to order them killed after he dreamed they were going to eat him.[35] Among humans with less socially bestowed distinction or privilege, some enterprising individuals exhibited "trained goats, ponies, horses, and bears who were forced to dance on their hind legs in the squares of the market towns. On holy days in England, bulls and bears were frequently baited for the delight of villagers."[36] A stark indication of the web of oppression that served the interests of the elite of this period is seen in this example recorded by Gerald Carson: "When dwarfs were objects of fashionable amusement, a French duchess had a locksmith make a pair of iron collars, one for the neck of her dwarf girl, Belon, the other for Her Grace's monkey."[37]

In the fourteenth century, the plague's decimation of the European population and the disruption of feudal and manorial systems had even more unfortunate consequences for European women ascribed to positions of peasants. Because of high rates of male mortality, from both disease and war, and the cloistering of eligible males in guild organizations that accompanied the early stages of capitalism, many women were not marrying. They were forced to seek wages in nascent towns and cities, and many found no opportunities except prostitution.

While this social instability and changed behavior of women were the result of war, pestilence, and poverty, efforts of women to adapt to the changing conditions alarmed the leadership of the Christian church. Women were scapegoated for the disorganization of the time, and the witch hunts emerged. In the early fourteenth century, the Catholic Church began persecuting women, mostly peasant women, as witches. Handbooks were even created to aid the inquisitors in identifying and exacting confessions from those accused of consort with the devil. The practice continued for several hundred years and became intricately related to religious and political struggles of the time. Mary Nelson observes:

> Eventually, the trials came to be used by other organizations to persecute their own demons. The Protestants killed Catholics as witches, the Catholics burned Protestants, and certain judges burned whole villages, male and female, in order to confiscate their victims' wealth. In the end, the witch trials became a secular political tool. . . . Throughout both the Protestant and Catholic witch crazes, a large number of peasant women who were not particularly involved in political conflicts at the root of the accusations found themselves accused nonetheless, for it was common practice to first accuse a few women and then, through the use of torture, elicit the names of suspected (male) political enemies or rivals from them. The enemies were thus indicted and brought to trial not as Catholics or Protestants but as witches, making it impossible for them to defend themselves. The continued execution of women along with political enemies served to reaffirm the validity of the fundamental witch beliefs. If all witchcraft accusations had been brought against political rivals, the political motivations would have become too transparent for the populace to tolerate.[38]

The ability of the powerful few in Western Europe to oppress "others" for accumulation of wealth eventually spread to other areas of the globe. The expansion of their control was prompted in the fourteenth century after the Ottoman Empire of Turkey took control of Constantinople and limited access to overland trade routes from Europe to the far East. Western aristocrats lost access to many luxury goods, particularly spices that were used to enhance the taste of "meat" (and to mask the fact that it was often rancid). Seeking alternative routes to the eastern producers, they turned to the sea.

Around 1415, a Portuguese monarch, Prince Henry, sent out explorers to seek direct contact with the gold-producing areas of Africa and an alternate route to the Far East. The early explorations along the western coast of Africa proved beneficial to the Portuguese monarchy, as the explorers bartered for or simply stole precious metals and other resources for the realm. As the Portuguese monarchy's search for an alternate route to the Far East continued, the oppressive consequences compounded. Historian R. R. Palmer notes:

> In 1498 the Portuguese Vasco da Gama, having rounded Africa in the wake of other intrepid explorers, found himself in the midst of this unknown world of Arab commerce. He landed on the Malabar coast (the southwest coast of India), where he found a busy commercial population—Arabic, Hindu, Parsee, Jewish, Nestorian Christian.

These people knew at least as much about Europe as Europeans knew about India . . .
and they realized that the coming of the Portuguese would disturb their established
channels of commerce, through which they had long moved from the interior of India,
or from the East Indian islands where the spices originated, through the Red Sea or
Persian Gulf to the markets of the eastern Mediterranean. Da Gama, playing upon local
rivalries, was able to load his ships with the coveted wares, but on his second voyage, in
1502, he came better prepared, bringing a fleet of no less than twenty-one vessels. A
ferocious war broke out between the Portuguese and Arab merchants, the latter supported in one way or another by the Egyptians, the Turks, and even the distant Vene-
tians, all of whom had an interest in maintaining the old routes of trade. For the
Portuguese . . . no atrocities were too horrible to commit against the infidel competitors
whom they found at the end of their heroic quest. Cities were devastated, ships burned
at their docks, prisoners butchered and their dismembered hands, noses, and ears sent
back as derisive trophies; one Brahmin, mutilated in this way, was left alive to bear them
to his people. Such, unfortunately, was India's introduction to the West.[39]

Thus was the state of the preindustrial world in which, according to Alexander
Cockburn, "90 per cent of the world was peasant and 10 per cent 'other,' with the
latter living off the surplus of the former. From this world came most of our values
and sentiments about the animals we have domesticated for work, companionship
and food."[40]

ENSLAVEMENT AND RAVAGING
OF THE NEW WORLD

Similar tragedies resulted from Spanish and Portuguese forays into the Western
Hemisphere. By the early fifteenth century, Bartolome de las Casas, a Catholic priest
living in the West Indies, was inspired to denounce the European enslavement of
indigenous humans that had become rampant in the Western Hemisphere. He
began preaching against the evils of the *encomiendas,* huge plantation-like systems
worked by enslaved humans, and eventually gained an audience with the Spanish
monarch. The king responded with a law that called for better treatment of the
enslaved. However, when the wealthy beneficiaries of the encomiendas protested,
the law was rescinded. Paradoxically, in his later attempts to ameliorate the brutal
conditions experienced by the indigenous enslaved, Las Casas suggested that Africans could be imported to do the work instead. As the population of indigenous
humans drastically declined as a result of genocide and imported disease like small-
pox, the elite turned to Africa.

The Portuguese had begun enslaving humans from Africa and selling them in
Mediterranean slave markets soon after the Europeans' initial incursions along the
western coast of Africa in the early fifteenth century. The demand for labor by Spanish and Portuguese planters and miners in the Western Hemisphere significantly
increased the volume of the trade in humans. Enslaving and selling humans from
Africa proved to be even more profitable for the Portuguese than expropriating Afri-

can gold. Wealthy Spanish, English, and Dutch merchants soon challenged the Portuguese monopoly and sought part of the lucrative market in human beings for themselves.

By all accounts, traders of enslaved humans were ruthless and greedy. Africans captured for slavery were so tightly packed into cargo ships, and so poorly treated, that as many as half died in the horrible passage across the Atlantic. Such loss of life was regarded by traders and merchants as merely an acceptable business loss. In this era of plunder, colonialism, and enslavement, countless humans had their lives destroyed and were forced to endure unimaginable suffering as wealthy Europeans conquered and colonized much of the world for the sake of economic expansion, greater wealth, and endless supplies of "meat." All the while, innumerable other animals faced their own version of the Middle Passage as they were transported to the New World as both supplies of food and laborers. In the Western Hemisphere, colonizers appropriated vast areas of land, much of it used to graze cows to satisfy the European elite's taste for "meat," especially "beef." The entanglement of the elite's oppression of cows and those humans who controlled them on a daily basis can be seen in the following passage by Jeremy Rifkin:

> Cattle, chattel, and capital went hand in hand during the colonization of the Americas. Conquistadores, missionaries, and later landed aristocrats colonized the new lands with cattle. Indian and African slaves, and later poor European immigrants, were put to work tending herds on both continents. The Americas, from the southwestern region of what is now the United States to the boot of Chile, were awash in cows and New World serfs. The new herdsmen went by different names in different countries: in Chile, the *hauso;* in Argentina, the *gaucho;* in Venezuela, the *llanero;* in Mexico, the *vaquero*—all were part of a new indentured class of migratory labor, poorly paid, mercilessly exploited, whose only distinction lay in their mounted steeds. . . . They helped secure the fortunes of both the Spanish crown and the new landed gentry in the Americas.[41]

Those who found wealth in the flesh and skin of cows "established a hierarchical herding culture, steeped in violence and subjugation and maintained by ruthless exploitation of native peoples and lands."[42]

In the colonized areas of the Americas, indigenous other animals were being displaced and killed as land speculators and human settlers wreaked havoc on their lives and homelands. Most colonizers viewed other animals much as they viewed indigenous humans—as troublesome pests and competitors, obstacles to maximum economic control of the area. Early officials offered bounties for the scalps of such other animals as wolves, bears, panthers, and squirrels.[43] Invading humans frequently cleared land of other beings by forming a large circle around a piece of land and making their way to the center, killing everyone they could trap inside.

Such were the circumstances underlying the Hinckley massacre described in chapter 1. In 1818, the Ohio country was in the final stages of invasion and of preparation for economic production. The Hinckley massacre was preceded by a protracted period of interhuman warfare as European powers fought for control of the economic opportunities in North America. By 1760, armies under British control had wrested control from the French of Canada and of areas east of the Mississippi River. Then, wealthy colonists shrewdly enlisted the masses to take arms against the British and, with the help of the French, took economic and political control of the North American territory. These "new Americans" then set their sights on the next obstacle to control of the land and its economic promise—Native Americans. Indigenous humans were systematically displaced and exterminated. While most courageously fought to save their homelands, others, such as the Delawares of Ohio, offered no resistance and remained peaceful, even accepting the religion of the invaders. How-ever, pacifism and religious conversion simply reduced the Native Americans' capac-ity to resist the power of those who wanted their land. For example, on 7 March 1782, a Pittsburgh-based militia scapegoated the Delaware pacifists for resistance offered by other Native American societies. The militia captured sixty-two adults and thirty-four children who were attempting to harvest the corn fields they had been forced to abandon the previous autumn. The following day all ninety-six cap-tives were methodically slaughtered. According to historians Eugene Roseboom and Francis Weisenburger, "[T]he murder by a band of frontiersmen, supposedly Chris-tians, of a group of noncombative neutrals who had been taught to regard nonresis-tance as a Christian virtue is almost without parallel."[44]

The British were finally forced out of the area after the War of 1812—a war fought in part over control of the lucrative trade in the skin and hair of other ani-mals—and the Native American resistance in Ohio effectively was silenced when U.S. military forces killed Tecumseh in 1813. Ohio was almost prepared for its full profit-making potential. However, non-"domesticated" other animals were regarded as a threat to profitable crop production and to the raising of sheep whose hair would be used as fodder for the growing New England textile mills. Paramilitary massacres, such as that conducted in Hinckley in 1818, were repeated again and again in the "New World" and other rapidly colonizing areas of the globe to exter-minate or displace any other animals that were perceived as an obstacle to maximum economic efficiency.

The slaughter of hundreds of other animals in Hinckley (like the War of 1812, the killing and displacement of Native Americans, the enslavement of humans from Africa, etc.) was a product of the developing system of economic organization of the time. The old *command economies* of medieval agrarian systems, in which lords and potentates issued commands on matters of economic production and distribution, were being eclipsed by a system promoted by Adam Smith in the *Wealth of Nations*. Smith believed that the collective good was best served by a system of economic organization that operated as an autonomous, self-regulating system, one outside of the hand of the government. Unfortunately, wealth, luxury, and "meat" continued to be prized under the capitalist system and oppression served the interests of the new capitalist class as much as it served other elites over the ages. Like the agricul-tural "meat"-hoarding elites of the past whose oppressive practices were driven by the need for new agricultural and grazing lands and more labor power, the emerging capitalist elite's quest for similar possessions—as well as sources of investment capital and expanded markets for their products—stepped up the tradition of exploitation and plunder. Such developing arrangements caused increased numbers of other animals to have their labor exploited to power equipment and provide transportation, while others were raised and slaughtered for the economic utility of their hair, skin, and flesh in rapidly increasing numbers. Other animals that were not yet subjected to captivity, or that were defined as pests or competitors, increasingly were sought for the profits that could be obtained from their skin and hair. While small, subsistence farmers, struggling to survive, turned to trapping for income, more humans relied exclusively on trapping for their livelihoods. Professional trappers were successful in capturing such other animals as beaver, mink, and fox, killing them and selling their skin and hair for profit. For many, the trade in the skin and hair of other animals was quite lucrative. For instance, beginning in 1670 the Hudson Bay Company flourished on the killing of countless other animals whose hair was used in fashionable garments worn by the privileged in Europe. The wearing of fur became so strong a symbol of high social status in England that for years "commoners were prohibited by law from wearing clothing fashioned from gold or silver cloth, velvet, furs, and other 'luxury' materials."[45]

While the suffering and death of innumerable humans and other animals on the face of the Earth fueled the growth and development of nascent capitalism, the other animals beneath the ocean surface fared little better. For example, in the seventeenth century, the hunting and killing of whales became big business for Great Britain, Holland, and Germany. Whale hunting had long been gainful due to the demand for baleen, which was used in the construction of such items as military wear and corsets. Oil and other extracts from the bodies of whales came to be used in the manufacture of a number of products, including soap, margarine, cosmetics, lubricants, textiles, paints, and varnishes. Spermaceti, a substance found behind the sperm whale's frontal bone, was used for the manufacture of ointments, candles, and other products. From 1835 to 1872, whalers from the United States alone killed an estimated 300,000 whales in order to sell 6.5 million tons of oil and 3.6 million barrels of spermaceti, valued at $272 million.[46]

While some capitalist investors and business owners grew rich, most of those actually killing the whales merely hoped for subsistence. Whaling crews were paid only if their voyages were profitable for those who financially controlled the "industry," and crews were subjected to dangerous and arduous toils. Whaling business operators frequently sought out African Americans in order to obtain sufficient crew members. (Moreover, on more than one occasion, after a shipwreck forced surviving crew members to resort to cannibalism, African Americans were the first to be eaten.)[47]

One of the North American communities that relied most heavily on the hunting and killing of whales in the eighteenth and nineteenth centuries was Nantucket Island. Early Nantucket whaling boats were staffed primarily by Native Americans, members of the Wampanoag Nation, who were compelled to contribute their labor to "whaling" by a system of debt servitude that was nurtured by the island inhabitants of European ancestry.

Just like many humans who have been cruelly oppressed throughout the ages, some whales resisted the pervasive and ruthless slaughter of members of their communities, and by the mid–nineteenth century accounts of whales attacking "whaling" ships were not uncommon.[48] After the destruction of tens of thousands of whales, historian Nathaniel Philbrick observes, an increasing number of whales were "fighting back."[49]

All the while, "resources" expropriated from the Americas, stained with the blood of the enslaved and massacred, flowed to Europe and stimulated capitalist economic activity in growing towns and cities as an archaic system of oppression was slowly being eclipsed by a new one.

In the seventeenth and eighteenth centuries, powerful European landowners—forced to abandon old manorial systems and to join the market economy—sought more efficient, and more profitable, forms of agricultural production. In early eighteenth-century England, for example, Vincent Townshend boosted agricultural production by promoting crop rotation, and Jethro Tull is credited with first planting seeds in organized rows rather than scattering them throughout the field. These and other innovations dramatically increased agricultural production. Such changes increased agricultural production with the use of fewer farmers and farm laborers. The motivation behind the development and implementation of these changes is commonly touted as benevolent in nature. However, historian E. P. Thompson notes, "[W]e should remember that the spirit of agricultural improvement in the 18th century was impelled less by altruistic desires to banish ugly wastes or—as the tedious phrase goes—to 'feed a growing population' than by the desire for fatter rent-rolls and larger profits."[50]

The rise of industrial capitalism was greatly enhanced by these less than benevolent changes in agricultural production. As historian E. J. Hobsbawm observes, increased agricultural output carried out three fundamental functions in the era of capitalist-driven industrialization.[51] First, it supplemented the accumulation of revenues for the developing capitalist sectors of the economy to use for manufacturing equipment and resources. Second, it provided developing urban industries with a large pool of cheap and exploitable labor, in the persons of former serfs and peasants whose labor was no longer required on farms. The newer agricultural practices, compounded with the increased exploitation of sheep and other animals, reduced the need for agricultural workers, with whom at least some minimal yields had to be shared, and landowners could realize higher profits. (It is true that many humans who were once confined to the social position of serf or peasant were eventually permitted to buy their freedom, but for most that freedom was limited to migrating to developing urban areas to compete with others like them for wage work.) Third, increased agricultural production helped meet the demand for food by a rapidly growing, nonagricultural population—the urban proletariat—whose exploited labor was bringing industrial capitalism to life.

Another development that forced countless humans into the ranks of the growing urban proletariat was known as "enclosure." The growth of the textile industry in Europe in the late Middle Ages prompted the aristocrat-controlled governments to pass Enclosure Acts, granting powerful individuals possession of what by custom had been communal land. These acts forced "peasants" off land that traditionally had been available for humans of limited means and status to cultivate gardens, to pasture small groups of other animals and as a source of wood. According to historian William Stearns Davis, the beneficiaries of the enclosures were the "great landlords." He writes:

> It was discovered that there was excellent money in sheep grazing, with Flanders providing an insatiable market for English wool. "The foot of the sheep has turned the land to gold," became the saying. But to develop great sheep runs the landlords used every unscrupulous means to force the "customary tenants," the peasants, to abandon their rights to the common village farms. . . . By 1560 an enormous number of small farmers, cotters, and rural handicraftsmen lost their hold on the land by this ruthless process of "enclosures"—conversion to strictly private ownership. . . . Furthermore, the demand for sheep runs implied the deliberate turning back of plowland into grazing land. One shepherd can tend the flocks where once the arable lands gave honest work for twenty men.[52]

In Britain, the acts of Parliament that gave large tracts of land to privileged humans to graze sheep also reserved for the new property owners the exclusive right to hunt other animals. This policy stood in stark contrast to the long-standing tradition that other animals such as deer, rabbits, squirrels, and various type of birds were "fair game" for anyone who could kill them. Under the Enclosure Acts, only the landholding aristocrats were permitted to hunt other animals. Since the population of other animals had been decimated by hundreds of years of hunting and human expansion, the powerful sought to keep the "pleasure" of hunting, killing, and eating the remaining other animals for themselves. For many deprived humans, the enclosures not only exacerbated hunger but also reinforced the idea that eating "meat" was a symbol of elevated status and power.

While the European elite engaged in oppression and the appropriation of resources domestically and globally, British rulers also expanded the exploitation of their near neighbor, Ireland. This piece of history is remarkable for its stark demonstration of the entanglement of the oppression of humans and other animals.

Many today believe that the long-running conflict between the Irish of Northern Ireland and the English has been motivated exclusively by religious and ethnic differences. While these differences have been a factor, the early conflicts and many of the still-contentious issues are profoundly economic in nature. In the twelfth century, British rulers invaded Ireland and seized the land, and by 1700, British landowners "owned" 86 percent of Ireland.[53] Historian Ronald Takaki notes:

> The landlords sought to bring Ireland into the British market. Between 1750 and 1810, Irish exports increased from two million to six million pounds. During a visit to Ireland in 1771, Benjamin Franklin reported that British colonialism and its emphasis on exports had reduced the Irish people to "extremely poor" tenants, living in the most sordid wretchedness, in dirty Hovels of Mud and Straw, and cloatheed only in Rags." The Irish had been forced to survive on "Potatoes and Buttermilk, without Shirts," so

that the "Merchants" could export "Beef, Butter, and Linen" to England. . . . "Progress" for the landlords meant pauperization for the peasants.[54]

Subsistence farming was replaced by cash crop production as English colonizers of Ireland exported the bodies of other animals, "dairy" products, and grain to England to feed an ever-growing proletariat—a population that faced rampant abuse at the hands of the industrialists and that might have been more inclined to rebel if food prices increased substantially beyond their paltry wages. Rifkin writes:

> Shortages of foodstuffs and rising prices were fueling discontent among the new working class and middle class of the cities, threatening open rebellion. British officials and entrepreneurs quieted the masses with Scottish and Irish beef. Historians of the period point out that, were it not for the Celtic pasture lands of Scotland and Ireland, it might well have proved impossible to quell the growing unrest of the British working class during the critical decades of British industrial expansion.[55]

The large amount of land in Ireland given over to "livestock" production left little for subsistence, and Irish farmers turned to potatoes as an acre-economizing crop. The ill-fated potato crop of 1846 brought famine on the Irish and induced widespread emigration. This British-produced calamity provided the opportunity for an even more thorough invasion of Ireland and increased exploitation of other animals. Eric B. Ross observes:

> What was most interesting was that, in the midst of this crisis, the export of Irish grain and livestock not only continued but intensified. Indeed, far from inducing any modifications in English colonial rule, the Great Famine of the 1840s actually provided England with an incredible opportunity, while the peasantry was virtually prostrate, to intensify pre-famine trends in land clearance and cattle rearing. . . . Just from the period 1846–49 to 1870–74, the number of Irish cattle exported to England climbed from almost 202,000 to about 558,000.[56]

The increased scale of exploitation of other animals, particularly cows and sheep, required the eradication and removal of humans in Ireland, and many of the Irish who survived the famine moved on to expand the ranks of the exploited working class in Britain and the United States.

PRE–TWENTIETH-CENTURY CAPITALISM AND ENTANGLED OPPRESSION

In the sixteenth through the nineteenth centuries, most of the humans in Europe who were forced into towns and cities in hopes of finding wage labor suffered terribly. While some found new freedoms and opportunities with the rise of capitalism, many fared poorly in the economic marketplace, forced to sell their labor at subsistence wages and to compete in the economic free-for-all that emerged.[57] Reflecting on this experience, Robert Heilbroner and Lester Thurow write:

[T]he economic freedom of capitalism came as a two-edged sword. On the one hand, its new freedoms were precious achievements for those individuals who had formerly been deprived of the right to enter into legal contracts. For the up-and-coming bourgeois merchants, it was the passport to a new status in life. Even for some of the poorest classes, the freedom of economic contract was a chance to rise from a station in life from which, in earlier times, there had almost been no exit. But economic freedom also had a harsher side. This was the necessity to stay afloat by one's own efforts in rough waters where all were struggling to survive. Many a merchant and many, many a jobless worker simply disappeared from view.[58]

Seeking to minimize production costs and maximize profits, early capitalists automated whenever possible to reduce labor costs. When human workers were required, business owners sought cheap and compliant labor; children, much abused in the past, now became fodder for the growing capitalist machine. By 1835, approximately one-third of the factory workers in the textile industry in England—much of it focused on production of "wool" products—were children, half of them under the age of fourteen. Writer Davis Wasgatt Clark notes:

Physical strength was no longer needed when artificial power could be applied. A man was not needed when the weaver's heavy beam was discarded. The skill of an adult also was not required when automatic machinery took the place of the primitive spindle and shuttle. The possibility of utilizing children at low wages, in the place of skilled spinners and weavers, thus presented itself. Greed took advantage of opportunity, and soon, to the little slaves of the mines and brickyards of England, were added those of the mills. The barbarism practiced under this system is incredible, and defies exaggeration.[59]

Typically children worked from five-thirty in the morning until eight in the evening, and the cramped positions required for many of the tasks caused various physical deformities in the younger children. The extreme hours the children were required to work resulted in constant fatigue and lack of sleep. Nonetheless, girls and boys who were late for work, fell asleep on the job, or moved too slowly were beaten with straps and sticks by overseers.

Other animals were also subjected to this awful exploitation. For instance, the nineteenth-century novelist Emile Zola realistically depicted the abuse of both humans and other animals who worked in French coal mines in *Germinal.* In one particularly poignant passage, he gives us a glimpse into the terrible and cruel confinement of horses underground:

The signal hammer had beat out four blows; they were bringing down the horse. This was always exciting, because sometimes the horse would become so terrified that it would be dead when it was unloaded. At the top of the shaft, bound in a net, it would paw wildly; then, as soon as it felt the solid ground give way, it would become petrified and sink from sight without so much as a tremble of its hide, its eyes wide and staring. The one being brought down now was too big to pass between the guides and had to be suspended from the bottom of the cage, its head pulled down and tied to its flank. The descent lasted about three minutes. . . . At last it appeared, as motionless as stone, its staring eyes dilated with terror. It was a bay, scarcely three years old, called Trompette. . . .

Soon Trompette was set down in a heap on the iron flooring. He still had not moved; he seemed to be caught in the nightmare of this bottomless, dark hole, this huge room ringing with noise. They were just beginning to untie him when Bataille, just unharnessed, came up and stretched out his neck to sniff at this new arrival fallen from the earth above. . . . Bataille grew animated. Perhaps he recognized the smell of fresh air, the almost forgotten scent of the sun on the grass. And suddenly he broke into a loud whinny, a song of happiness in which there was also a wistful sob. It was his welcome— joy at this whiff of things long past, and grief over this new prisoner who would never return to the surface alive.[60]

The physical conditions of the early industrial towns reflected the oppressive environment of the workplace. Company owners constructed housing for the workers very close to the factory. These quarters were usually small, one-roomed, and windowless. Poor sanitary conditions were conducive to disease, and epidemics of tuberculosis and typhoid fever contributed to high mortality rates. Devoid of pure water supplies, public lighting, sewage systems, parks, or other amenities, the early industrial towns were miserable places.[61] As these towns grew into cities, such conditions seldom improved—and frequently intensified.

Hardship and suffering associated with the dreadful working and living conditions in Europe were compounded by low wages, and conditions and pay were no better in the United States. In the industrial sectors there, the paltry wages paid to most workers, particularly women, were not enough to support them. Desperate, many women turned to prostitution to sustain themselves and their families. In 1858, Dr. William Sanger surveyed two thousand prostitutes in New York City's jails. Of his findings, Barbara Mayer Wertheimer writes:

One quarter of the women Sanger surveyed were sewers: tailoresses, milliners, seamstresses, vestmakers, dressmakers, hat trimmers, or flower makers. Although almost half of the total, some 933, worked as servants, earning $5 a month or less for being on call twenty-four hours a day, Sanger found no single group as badly off as the sewers. "Working from early dawn until late at night," he wrote, "with trembling fingers, aching head, and often empty stomach, the poor seamstress ruins her health to obtain a spare and insufficient living." He did not see that she had any way out. Milliners and women working in paper-box factories seemed just as badly off. So did tobacco packers and book folders. Over half of those he interviewed had averaged only $1 a week before turning to prostitution. Another 336 women had earned no more than $2 weekly. Three out of every four were under twenty-five years of age; almost half were between fifteen and twenty. . . . Sanger castigated employers for buying labor at the lowest possible price, and consumers for saving pennies at the expense of the workers, whose wages and working conditions they never thought to ask about before they bought. . . . But Sanger's words fell on deaf ears.[62]

This web of oppressive practices created a social system that fueled and energized the developing capitalist order. An emerging capitalist elite obtained fortunes from the bodies and labor of other animals, benefited from the displacement and extermination of indigenous humans, and squeezed profit from the enslavement of Africans and the wretched lives of exploited workers.

An example of the new elite was John Jacob Astor, the son of a butcher, who in the late eighteenth century turned the pursuit of the skin and hair of other animals into a personal fortune. His ruthless treatment of other animals went hand in hand with his debasement of indigenous humans and the devaluation of his employees.[63] Ben B. Seligman writes:

> Tight-fisted and penny-pinching, he sent scores of trappers across the wilderness of America to gather pelts, making the business profitable enough for him to enter the shipping business as well. The West was his province, and intruders were expelled, often under threat of arms. The Indians were plied with liquor, the easier to cheat them, and whatever laws existed were simply ignored with impunity. Profit was gathered from two sources: by overcharging for the items sold at the trading post and by cheating on purchases. . . . [A]stor was not always willing to part with a man's share, and on occasion a trapper returning home to collect his back pay was assassinated. . . . [Astor] died in 1848, aged eighty, feared by many and thoroughly disliked by most. . . . He left nine-tenths of his fortune to his son William, little to charities, and nothing to his servants and employees.[64]

Astor had become one of the wealthiest men in the United States with a fortune estimated at $25 million, wealth derived in large part from selling the skin and hair of other animals.

The economically motivated and entangled nature of oppression of humans and other animals can be seen again in the process popularly referred to as the "opening of the West." In the seventeenth and eighteenth centuries, Native American societies in the eastern part of North America were obliterated, and most survivors were forcibly settled on reservations west of the Mississippi. However, in the nineteenth century, societies of humans indigenous to the west continued to resist expropriation of their homelands, vast areas that capitalists wanted as grazing lands for cows and sheep. Moreover, the vastness of the western lands provided a safety valve for the potentially rebellious effects of exploitation and poverty experienced by the masses of humans in the east. Many were exhorted by the elite to "go west," an entreaty backed up by exaggerated reports of gold in western lands.

The unrelenting encroachment into the homelands of Native Americans was accompanied by massacres perpetrated by the U.S. Army, such as the notorious episodes at Sand Creek and Wounded Knee.[65] At the same time, "[m]ilitary commanders encouraged the slaughter of bison . . . as [w]ithout the buffalo, Plains Indians could not effectively resist American expansion."[66] An estimated four million buffalo suffered the same fate as many Native Americans who stood in the way of profitable use of western lands. Buffalo skin and hair were turned into revenue by both established and nascent entrepreneurs, and mass killings provided a thrill for the elite and privileged. Rifkin writes:

[In just a few years] the buffalo were eliminated entirely from the western range after thousands of years of habitation. . . .

The mass extinction of the American buffalo remains, to this day, one of the most gruesome tales in the ecological history of the country. . . .

Buffalo hunters usually received between $1 and $3 per hide. The hides were often tanned with the fur on and made into coats, robes, and overshoes. Many of the hides were purchased by the British Army, which regarded buffalo leather more highly than calf leather because of its elasticity and flexibility. Buffalo leather was even used to make belts for industrial machinery and could be seen in the finest homes as padding and covering for furniture. . . .

For wealthy easterners and European royalty, special buffalo game shoots became the rage in the 1870s. Buffalo Bill Cody, the best-known of the buffalo hunters, recounted a shooting match that had been arranged between himself and another famed buffalo hunter, named Comstock, for the entertainment of a group of wealthy sports enthusiasts from St. Louis. Cody remembers that he had killed thirty-eight to Comstock's twenty-three on the first run. He attributed his victory to his finesse in corralling the creatures, allowing him to increase his count "I had 'nursed' my buffaloes, as a billiard player does the balls when he makes a run." After "the run" the visitors from St. Louis celebrated by setting out "a lot of champagne, which they had brought with them and which proved a good drink on a Kansas prairie."[67]

With the near extermination of Native Americans and the buffalo, as well as of prairie dogs and other "pests," cultivation of large numbers of cows in the western plains became increasingly profitable. Many cows, however, resisted being enslaved and being driven long distances. J. Frank Dobie reflected on the experience of such cows in his 1941 book, *The Longhorns*. He notes that the humans whose job it was to control and drive the cows referred to the difficult ones as "outlaws." Dobie, however, takes issue with the term.

The word "outlaw," however legitimized by common usage, is a betrayal. The cattle I am thinking of made their reputation in fierce, hardy, persistent, resourceful, daring efforts to maintain freedom. They refused to be "dumb driven cattle." . . . Instead of being outside the law, they followed the law of the wild, the stark give-me-liberty-or-give-me-death law against tyranny. They were not outlaw anymore than a deer or a wild cat in evading man is an outlaw.[68]

Dobie recounts one story by a "cattle driver" about an elusive and determined cow whose individuality, personhood, and persistent quest for freedom were sadly eclipsed by the cultivated taste for his flesh:

As we approached this range, a big snow-white steer with the widest set of horns I had ever seen outside of a house kept lifting his head and looking away towards the Diablo Mountains. . . . As soon as we turned him loose, he pulled out for the Diablos. He got in the roughest part of them. Those roughs were his natural home. . . .

I wintered the steers and the next fall began shipping. We got the white steer in a roundup, but failed to hold him. So he went back to the Diablos for another year. He was as wild as any blacktail deer I ever saw but more cunning in keeping out of sight.

Lack of timber prevented his staying permanently hidden. We rounded in Old Whitey once more, took extra precautions, and this time held him. . . .

One evening we shut him up, along with several hundred other steers, in the shipping pens at Sierra Blanca. We had to hold over until next morning before loading out. . . . I stayed in the little Sierra Blanca hotel that night, and the next morning before going to the pens met a man . . . [who] had seen our white steer going in a long lope towards the Diablo Mountains.

One day after cold weather came, I took a long-range rifle, a couple of pack mules and a *cowpuncher* [emphasis added] and went to the Diablo roughs. I shot the steer. He must have weighed fifteen hundred pounds. That night the beef froze where it was hanging outside. It was tender as calf when cooked. . . . I believe it was the best [beef] I have ever eaten.[69]

Such "problem" cows, like their human counterparts who resisted their oppression, were subjected to particularly ruthless treatment. Dobie writes:

Sometimes the eyelids of the outlaws were sewed up so that they would blindly follow other cattle, trying to avoid all limbs. Again, to prevent running, the head was tied down to the front foot; a hind foot was tied to the end of a tail; a hamstring or a knee tendon was cut; a thong was bound tightly around the leg just above the hock. To take the fight out of the worst scalawags and to make them more drivable, horns were chopped off with axes or knocked off with heavy sticks, were shot into with bullets from six-shooters. Another way to make a bad critter come a-walking was to slit the cartilage of the nose, tie one end of a rope through the hole, and pull the other with a saddle horn. The hole could pull through, however.[70]

While military posts and western towns and cities provided a growing number of buyers for the flesh of such other animals, a transcontinental railroad system was needed to help connect western rangelands with the huge eastern and European markets. Countless horses and mules, pulling skids and wagons, were driven relentlessly to transport enormous amounts of timber to railroad construction sites, and immigrant labor was exploited mercilessly by greedy railroad magnates working to achieve a "manifest destiny"—one that would accommodate huge "livestock" shipments. The abuse of Chinese workers in this undertaking was particularly severe. Paid considerably less than other laborers, Chinese workers also were concentrated in some of the most dangerous areas. For example, Takaki notes:

Determined to accelerate construction, the Central Pacific managers forced the Chinese laborers to work through the winter of 1866. The snowdrifts, over sixty feet in height, covered construction operations. The Chinese workers lived and worked in tunnels under the snow, with shafts to give them air and lanterns to light the way. Snowslides occasionally buried camps and crews; in the spring, workers found the thawing corpses, still upright, their cold hands gripping shovels and picks and their mouths twisted in frozen terror. "The snow slides carried away our camps and we lost a good many men in those slides," a company official reported matter-of-factly; "many of them we did not find until the next season when the snow melted."[71]

Seeking to expand financial gains by saturating the now more available eastern and European markets, ranchers raised increasing numbers of cows. By the mid-1880s, an estimated 7.5 million cows lived on the Great Plains north of Texas and New Mexico alone, numbers too large to be sustained by the overgrazed and depleted rangeland.[72] Dry, hot summers left millions of cows underfed, dehydrated, and in poor condition to face the winter. "The natural tendency of cows to move en masse towards the south in bad weather"[73] was controlled by the creation of barbed wire. The terrible, flesh-tearing barbs "provided a cheap, flexible and effective means of controlling the movement of cattle without human intervention."[74] Barbed wire also has severely injured and killed countless other animals who have tried to get over, under, or through it—and continues to do so. Richard White describes the winter of 1886 and the inability of cows to escape its deadly grasp:

> Beginning with a blizzard in November, winter gripped the northern plains and pummeled them unmercifully. Howling winds and bitter cold that dropped temperatures as low as −46 degrees Fahrenheit kept ranchers and their cowboys confined to their houses and bunkhouses. On the range, the cattle died. In the spring the cowboys found the rotting corpses of cattle piled in coulees and lying in rows against the fencelines. . . . Even those animals that survived were weak, emaciated, and often maimed, with their tails, ears and feet frostbitten.[75]

The spectacle of so much suffering and death was so horrifying that one hardened rancher found the whole business "distasteful," prompting him to later write, "I never again wanted to own an animal that I could not feed and shelter."[76] The many millions of cows who survived the deprivation, harsh environment, and cruel treatment of the late nineteenth century eventually were driven mercilessly for miles to railroad yards where, crammed into railways cars, they would then suffer intense crowding, discomfort, fear, and pain. They finally reached Kansas City, Chicago, or some other slaughterhouse destination where they would be fattened in feedlots and then subjected to a cruel and agonizing slaughter.

All the while, ranchers of Mexican descent, with legal title to western lands, were driven out by squatters and miners of European heritage. One common tactic was to kill the "foreigners' " cows. Large "cattle" companies, with government assistance, also appropriated the land of small Chicano villages. White writes:

> The small landholders and communal villagers of northern New Mexico suffered crippling losses, first through the frauds that deprived many villages of their lands and then, more seriously, by the refusal of Congress and the Court of Private Land Claims, established in 1891, to grant them title to traditional communal holdings. . . . As these lands fell into the hands of large cattle companies, the villagers could no longer maintain their own herds. To replace herding in the economy, men began to migrate out of the villages to seek seasonal work in the mines, railroads, ranches, and farms of Colorado and New Mexico. By the early twentieth century whole families were becoming migrant workers.[77]

The ruthless treatment of Mexican Americans, buffalo, Native Americans, cows and "steers," Chinese immigrants, and the multitudes of other animals killed because they posed some perceived threat to maximum economic production, did not benefit all other humans equally. For instance, reflecting on privilege and poverty in Britain, Rifkin writes:

> In the period between 1884 and 1886, 43,136 tons of fresh beef were shipped to the British Isles. It should be noted that not everyone shared equally in the new beef glut. The middle and upper classes in England consumed the lion's share of the American . . . beef. The military consumed much of the rest—each soldier was guaranteed 12 ounces of meat per day. Working-class Britons were still largely excluded from the beef culture, being able to afford only small amounts and inferior cuts. Within working-class families, the little beef that was consumed was distributed unevenly, the adult males receiving most of the available supply, while women and children received little or no meat.[78]

An example of one who profited enormously from the killing of "steers," cows, and other animals was Philip Armour. Driven by a desire for personal wealth—the definition of success in the capitalist system—Armour turned from unsuccessful prospecting in California goldfields to slaughtering other animals as a wholesale supplier of "meat." Avoiding the military draft during the Civil War by paying $300 for a substitute, Armour began supplying the Union army with provisions derived from the bodies of pigs. It is estimated that Armour was killing nine hundred thousand pigs a year by 1865, when he expanded into cow production and "processing." Armour not only made his fortune at the expense of millions of other animals but, like Astor and others of the new elite, also had no compunction against profiting from the cultivated misfortunes of humans as well. Predicting the end of the Civil War, and thus the end of lucrative federal contracts, Armour astutely maneuvered to increase his personal wealth before the markets faltered. Matthew Josephson writes:

> It was Armour who consummated one of the most famous business "coups" of the period. In 1865, watching the progress of Grant's armies toward Richmond with a clairvoyant eye, and being completely persuaded of the early approach of victory and peace, he had suddenly rushed to New York and sold quantities of pork short at the prevailing high prices of around $40 a barrel. After Appomattox, the crash of commodity markets, involving especially pork, ruined hundreds of traders, made thousands of farmers the poorer, but permitted Armour to "cover" his short contracts in pork at about $18 a barrel, so that he gained overnight $2,000,000 in quick profits and his praises were sung in high financial circles. With this capital he swiftly increased his meat business, buying out weaker competitors and improving his plant until it became one of the most . . . prosperous industries in all the land.[79]

Reflecting on the concentration of the "meat" industry, and its quest to exact even greater profits from the bodies of others, Ben B. Seligman notes:

The industry began to use by-products, making a variety of goods out of the parts of the carcasses once dumped into the river. Fertilizer, glue, buttons, combs, bristles, felt, glycerine, and oleomargarine were some of the items that chemists rescued from bones and hair. Armour was particularly fond of German chemists, who were quite clever in devising new by-products. He once told a supervisor to receive cordially an expected visiting German, as he "may have something more in his head besides dandruff."

Inevitably, all the major packers began to "cooperate" with one another. Small firms were bought up by the larger ones, and distributing agencies were established in Omaha, Kansas City, and St. Louis. The Big Four—Armour, Swift, Hammond (later merged with Armour), and Morris—fixed prices and divided sales territories.[80]

Like cow herders in other countries, the romanticized American icons—the cowboys—made a sparse living by containing the movements of cows and then relentlessly driving them to their slaughter. If cows (like Whitey) were able to escape to wooded areas and forests it often was difficult for paid hands to find and control them. The techniques that were developed to identify, intimidate, and control large numbers of cows and prevent their escape before slaughter came to be celebrated in rodeos. Started as a form of entertainment for those who worked controlling and driving the cows, rodeos expanded as their profit-making potential became clear. Rodeo events, such as cow roping and wrestling, were a spectacle many would pay to watch. The spectacles of the rodeo are reminiscent of the Roman Colosseum. R. A. Marchant writes:

> Another of the rodeo events, the bull-dogging, is almost exactly the same as a spectacle that used to thrill the crowds at the Roman Colosseum. In this, a cowboy has to fling himself from his horse, seize the horns of a steer and attempt to force it to the ground. The Roman equivalent was introduced into the arena by Julius Caesar when he imported Thessalonian horsemen to chase bulls and wrestle them to the ground by gripping their horns and twisting their necks.
>
> The ways in which many other animals are used in entertainments such as films and circuses are also often almost identical in form and spirit to the Colosseum spectacles.[81]

Use of other animals and humans with disabilities for entertainment purposes also intensified under early U.S. capitalism. Some, like P. T. Barnum, made millions from their exhibitions. Before Barnum's era, acts involving horses were the mainstay of circuses in the eighteenth century, but "wild animal" acts were common by century's end. In the United States, various species of other animals were held captive aboard circus ships, which displayed other animals who were forced to perform "acts" for paying customers at seaports and major river towns.

Barnum first profited from exhibitionism in 1835 when he purchased and displayed Joice Heth, a woman of color whom he claimed was 160 years old and had been George Washington's nurse. In the 1840s, he expanded his exhibition by including human "freaks" and seldom-seen species of other animals. Such displays eventually earned him boasting rights of delivering "the greatest show on earth." Barnum published several books, including *How I Made Millions* and *The Art of*

Money Getting. While there are several notable exceptions, contemporary circuses follow Barnum's formula, still resembling the ancient Roman circus. Again, Marchant writes, "The Romans were not content with teaching their performing elephants remarkable feats of balance and other acts, but had to dress them up in tawdry finery and costumes to get laughs as well, and this lamentable custom still has many imitations today."[82]

Virtually unrestricted and vastly expanded use of other animals under capitalism also resulted in their use by vivisectionists. Ostensibly for public benefit, widespread use of other animals as research subjects, with its often extreme callousness, seems to have begun in the nineteenth century. Reviewing some of this history, Richard Ryder notes the practices of one early nineteenth-century vivisector, François Magendie:

> There is no doubt that Magendie's callousness was outstanding even for the age he lived in, and shocked some of his contemporary physiologists. John Elliotson wrote: "In one of his barbarous experiments, which I am ashamed to say I witnessed, he began by coolly cutting out a large round piece from the back of a beautiful little puppy as he would from an apple-dumpling."
>
> All of Magendie's experiments and nearly all of those carried out by his successors . . . were of course entirely without any form of anaesthesia. Moreover, each of these experiments and demonstrations continued for some time and the agonies of the subjects must have been not only intense but also prolonged. We know . . . that dogs were cut open in preparation "an hour or more" before the actual demonstrations took place. We also know that they were not destroyed immediately afterwards, but if still alive were available for further operations by students.[83]

This brief glimpse of oppression throughout Western history suggests that human mistreatment of other animals does not spring from some instinctive or universal force of nature—any more than does human exploitation of other humans. The changing human view of other animals, from relatively peaceful cohabitants to "inferiors," "pests," "quarry," and "property," relatively recent in origin, was the result of humans, particularly the elite, pursuing their material interests and domination of the earth. These socially created, oppressive practices are largely destructive, produce great suffering, and generate conflict.

The oppression of humans and other animals developed in tandem, each fueling the other. From human male domination over females, to hunger generated by the elite's feeding and consumption of "domestic" animals, to warfare necessitated by the need for new grazing areas (with the added "bonus" of claiming women and other animals as the spoils), to the use of other animals as instruments of warfare, to the sacrificing of devalued humans and other animals in the Colosseum to entertain and placate the impoverished masses, to the debasement and extermination of the Irish by the British (in large part for the appropriation of land to raise sheep and cows), to the exploitation and extermination of indigenous Americans (in part for the skins and hair of other animals and for acquisition of grazing land), to the violence and discrimination against humans of Mexican descent (for land acquisition for increased populations of cows raised for slaughter)—the oppression of devalued groups of humans has been intimately and thoroughly tied to the oppression of other animals. Indeed, for the past ten thousand years those who were vulnerable to some form of materially motivated exploitation have become the stepping stones for what is euphemistically referred to as "the development of civilized society."

The 1818 incident in Hinckley, then, was not an anomaly—nor, as we will see in the chapters that follow, were the massacres in Guatemala or the attack on Cassidy and Willow Grear. Nor was it necessitated by an urgent need for food. Rather, it was the result of socially created practices set in motion centuries earlier, in a system that primarily served the interests of the elite. In the Hinckley case, Judge Hinckley of Massachusetts benefited materially from land speculation made profitable by the killing of Native Americans, the killing of other animals, and the captivity and breeding of sheep whose hair was turned into cloth by exploited women and children in New England textile mills.

The theory of oppression, with its emphasis on the underlying economic/competitive motivation for oppression, easily applies to the treatment of devalued humans and other animals from the start of hunting through the development of capitalism. Such oppressive treatment over the ages stemmed largely from the material and related competitive advantages accrued by elites and were reflected in prejudices and in induced tendencies of humans to subjugate and exploit those whom they defined as lesser beings.

Not surprisingly, the economic/competitive motivation for oppression was not alleviated under conditions of pre-twentieth-century capitalism. The emerging capitalism, with its emphasis on self-interested and egotistical pursuits, was quite compatible with oppressive practices. Indeed, capitalism intensified and expanded oppressive conditions throughout the world through domestic exploitation and colonialist predation—practices that, while creating a new class of powerful elites, also facilitated the development of a nascent middle class, particularly in industrial capitalist countries. While paying tribute to the technical capabilities ushered in by the capitalism system, Karl Marx and Friedrich Engels note the continuance of tyranny and repression in the capitalist system in the following passages from the *Communist Manifesto:*

> Modern industry has established the world market, for which the discovery of America paved the way. This market has given an immense development to commerce, to navigation, to communication by land. This development has, in its turn, reacted to the extension of industry, commerce, navigation, railways extended, in the same proportion the bourgeoisie developed, increased its capital, and pushed into the back ground every class handed down from the Middle Ages.
>
> The modern bourgeois society that has sprouted from the ruins of feudal society has not done away with class antagonisms. It has only established new classes, new conditions of oppression, new forms of struggle in place of old ones.[84]

Oppression continued because, while capitalism did eventually break down the monarchically controlled economic and political systems of previous centuries, the new elite coveted privilege at least as much as the monarchs and continued to obtain it through the subjugation of others. Capitalism defined the pursuit of one's individual economic self-interests as both natural and morally desirable. Accumulation of wealth came to be a driving force in social affairs, and the acquisition of personal wealth generally became the sine qua non of human existence. Social relationships with both humans and other animals increasingly came to revolve around pecuniary considerations, as evidenced by the practices of Astor, Armour, Barnum, and countless other celebrated "entrepreneurs." Reflecting on the effect of capitalism on human social organization, Robert Heilbroner observes, "[T]he pattern of economic maximization was generalized throughout society and given an inherent urgency that made it a powerful force for shaping human behavior. In a word, the drive to maximize income became a new mode of *social coordination and control*."[85] A socially constructed reality characterized by great emphasis on personal gain and egocentrism yields a world in which "others" largely are categorized as tools for, or obstacles to, one's aspirations for pecuniary gain and self-gratification.

Through the nineteenth century, then, capitalism with its development of efficient methods for the production of economic goods created new possibilities for liberation and justice. For industrial capitalists, employing a free but exploited workforce was more profitable than maintaining slave labor, and manufacturers needed a market for their goods. These realities resulted in expanded freedom and opportunities for some. However, such developments were fueled by terrible oppression of others; as it expanded, capitalism promoted the expansion of oppression of countless humans and other animals as its possibilities for progressive change were substantially eclipsed by its self-serving ethos that justifies the procurement of growing levels of private profit.

CONCLUSION

This historical review provides evidence in support of the assertions made in chapter 1. First, the motivation for the development and institutionalization of oppressive practices is primarily material, not attitudinal. Such arrangements are not genetic or innate, and prejudice is the product of these arrangements—not the principal cause. Second, oppressive practices generally serve the interests of a powerful elite and, to a lesser degree, other privileged humans. The vast majority of humans and almost all other animals are ill served. Third, the oppression of devalued humans and the oppression of other animals have common origins and are usually entangled in such a way that increased exploitation of one group compounds the mistreatment of the other.

The economic underpinnings of the expansion and intensification of oppression in the twentieth century, its basis in the capitalist system, and the consequences for the vast majority of the inhabitants of the earth will be explored in the next chapter.

NOTES

1. Robert S. Lopez, *The Commercial Revolution of the Middle Ages, 950–1350* (Englewood Cliffs, N.J.: Prentice Hall, 1971), 18.

2. Steven Mithen, "The Hunter-Gatherer Prehistory of Human-Animal Interactions," *Anthrozoos* 12, no. 4 (1999): 195–204.

3. Mithen, "The Hunter-Gatherer Prehistory of Human-Animal Interactions," 195–204.

4. Jim Mason, *An Unnatural Order: Uncovering the Roots of Our Dominion of Nature and Each Other* (New York: Simon & Schuster, 1993), 72.

5. Matt Cartmill, *A View to a Death in the Morning: Hunting and Nature through History* (Cambridge, Mass.: Harvard University Press, 1993), 242.

6. Cartmill, *A View to a Death in the Morning,* 6. This assertion is also made by the American Dietetic Association; see Jane Brody, *Jane Brody's Nutrition Book* (New York: Bantam, 1987), 437, cited in Nick Fiddes, ed., *Meat: A Natural Symbol* (New York: Routledge, 1991), 181.

7. Sherwood Washburn and C. S. Lancaster, "The Evolution of Hunting," in *Man the Hunter,* ed. Richard B. Lee and Irven DeVore (Chicago: Aldine, 1968), 293–303, cited in Cartmill's *A View to a Death in the Morning,* 13.

8. Mason, *An Unnatural Order,* 84.

9. Richley H. Crapo, *Cultural Anthropology: Understanding Ourselves and Others,* 2d ed. (Guilford, Conn.: Dushkin, 1990), 56.

10. See, for example, Janet Saltzman Chafetz, *Sex and Advantage: A Comparative, Macro-Structural Theory of Sex Stratification* (Totowa, N.J.: Rowman & Allanheld, 1984).

11. Leith Mullings, "Notes on Women, Work, and Society," in *Anthropology for the Nineties: Introductory Readings,* ed. Johnnetta B. Cole (New York: Free Press, 1988), 314.

12. Valerio Valeri, *The Forest of Taboos: Morality, Hunting and Identity Among the Huaulu of the Moluccas* (Madison: University of Wisconsin Press, 2000), 173.

13. Kurt B. Mayer, *Class and Society* (New York: Doubleday, 1955).

14. Stephen K. Sanderson, *Macrosociology: An Introduction to Human Societies* (New York: Harper & Row, 1988), 74–76.

15. Jeremy Rifkin, *Beyond Beef: The Rise and Fall of the Cattle Culture* (New York: Plume, 1992), 35.

16. Hermann Dembeck, *Animals and Men: An Informal History of the Animal as Prey, as Servant, as Companion* (New York: Doubleday, 1965), 166.

17. This dialogue appeared in Dudley Giehl. *Vegetarianism: A Way of Life* (New York: Barnes & Noble, 1979), 98.

18. Dembeck, *Animals and Men,* 168.

19. Gordon Childe, *What Happened in History* (Baltimore: Penguin, 1971 [1941]), 184.

20. Susan Brownmiller, *Against Our Will: Men, Women and Rape* (New York: Bantam, 1975), 25.

21. Andree Collard and Joyce Contrucci, *Rape of the Wild: Man's Violence Against Animals and the Earth* (Bloomington: Indiana University Press, 1989), 38.

22. Ronald A. Marchant, *Man and Beast* (New York: Macmillan, 1968), 48.

23. Dembeck, *Animals and Men,* 217.

24. Frank Richard Cowell, *Life in Ancient Rome* (New York: Wideview/Perigee, 1961), 175–76.

25. Marchant, *Man and Beast,* 78–79.

26. David Nibert, "The Political Economy of Disability," *Critical Sociology* 21, no. 1 (1995): 59–80.

27. Sibylle Harksen, *Women in the Middle Ages* (New York: Schram, 1975), 12.

28. Norbert Elias, *The Civilising Process* (New York: Urizon, 1978 [1939]), 118, cited in Nick Fiddes, *Meat: A Natural Symbol* (New York: Routledge, 1991), 22.

29. Fiddes, *Meat: A Natural Symbol,* 22.

30. William Grimes, "The 800-Year-Old Dessert, and More," *New York Times,* 29 December 1999, B1.

31. Rifkin, *Beyond Beef,* 53 and 54.

32. Jean Gimpel, *The Medieval Machine: The Industrial Revolution of the Middle Ages* (New York: Penguin, 1976), 226.

33. Beatrice Saunders, *Henry the Eighth* (London: Redman, 1963), 24.

34. Gerald Carson, *Men, Beasts, and Gods: A History of Cruelty and Kindness to Animals* (New York: Scribner's, 1972), 22.

35. Carson, *Men, Beasts, and Gods,* 22.

36. Carson, *Men, Beasts, and Gods,* 23.

37. Carson, *Men, Beasts, and Gods,* 23.

38. Mary Nelson, "Why Women Were Witches," in *Women: A Feminist Perspective,* 2d ed., ed. Jo Freeman (Palo Alto, Calif.: Mayfield, 1979), 458 and 465.

39. Robert Roswell Palmer, *A History of the Modern World* (New York: Knopf, 1950), 92.

40. Alexander Cockburn, "A Short, Meat-Oriented History of the World from Eden to the Mattole," in *Dead Meat,* ed. Sue Coe (New York: Four Walls Eight Windows, 1995), 28.

41. Rifkin, *Beyond Beef,* 50.

42. Rifkin, *Beyond Beef,* 51.

43. Michael B. Lafferty, *Ohio's Natural Heritage* (Columbus: Ohio Academy of Science, 1979), 10–11.

44. Eugene H. Roseboom and Francis P. Weisenburger, *A History of Ohio* (Columbus: Ohio State Archaeological and Historical Society, 1953), 41.

45. Gideon Sjoberg, *The Preindustrial City: Past and Present* (Glencoe, Ill.: Free Press, 1960), 127.

46. Dembeck. *Animals and Men,* 117.

47. Nathaniel Philbrick, *In the Heart of the Sea: The Tragedy of the Whaleship Essex* (New York: Viking, 2000).

48. Philbrick, *In the Heart of the Sea.*

49. Philbrick, *In the Heart of the Sea,* 224.

50. Edward Palmer Thompson, *The Making of the English Working Class* (New York: Pantheon–Random House, 1964), 217.

51. Eric J. Hobsbawm, *The Age of Revolution: 1879–1848* (New York: Mentor, 1962).

52. William Stearns Davis, *Life in Elizabethan Days: A Picture of a Typical English Community at the End of the Sixteenth Century* (New York: Harper, 1930), 175–76.

53. Ronald Takaki, *A Different Mirror: A History of Multicultural America* (Boston: Back Bay, 1993), 141.

54. Takaki, *A Different Mirror,* 141 and 142.

55. Rifkin, *Beyond Beef,* 57.

56. Eric B. Ross, "An Overview of Trends in Dietary Variation from Hunter-Gatherer to Modern Capitalist Societies," in *Food and Evolution: Toward a Theory of Human Food Habits,* ed. Marvin Harris and Eric B. Ross (Philadelphia: Temple University Press, 1987), 31.

57. Robert L. Heilbroner, *The Making of Economic Society: Revised for the 1990s,* 8th ed. (Englewood Cliffs, N.J.: Prentice Hall, 1989), 37.

58. Robert Heilbroner and Lester Thurow, *Economics Explained* (Englewood Cliffs, N.J.: Prentice Hall, 1982), 9.

59. Davis Wasgatt Clark, *Child Labor and the Social Conscience* (New York: Abington, 1924), 87.

60. Emile Zola, *Germinal* (New York: Signet, 1970 [1885]), 49–50.

61. Friedrich Engels, *The Condition of the Working Class in England* (Stanford, Calif.: Stanford University Press, 1968 [1844]).

62. Barbara Mayer Wertheimer, *We Were There: The Story of Working Women in America* (New York: Pantheon, 1977), 102–3.

63. See Matthew Josephson, *The Robber Barons: The Great American Capitalists 1861–1901* (New York: Harcourt, Brace, 1934), 12.

64. Ben B. Seligman, *The Potentates: Business and Businessmen in American History* (New York: Dial, 1971), 53–54, 72, and 74.

65. See Dee Brown, *Bury My Heart at Wounded Knee: An Indian History of the American West* (New York: Holt, Rinehart & Winston, 1970).

66. Richard White, *It's Your Misfortune and None of My Own: A New History of the American West* (Norman: University of Oklahoma Press, 1991), 219.

67. Rifkin, *Beyond Beef,* 74, 75, and 76.

68. J. Frank Dobie, *The Longhorns* (New York: Grosset & Dunlap, 1941), 283.

69. Dobie, *The Longhorns,* 284–85.

70. Dobie, *The Longhorns,* 310.

71. Ronald Takaki, *Strangers From a Different Shore: A History of Asian Americans* (New York: Penguin, 1989), 85–86.

72. White, *It's Your Misfortune and None of My Own,* 223.

73. Reviel Netz, "Barbed Wire," *London Review of Books* 22, no. 14 (20 July 2000): 31.

74. Netz, "Barbed Wire," 30.

75. White, *It's Your Misfortune and None of My Own,* 224.

76. White, *It's Your Misfortune and None of My Own,* 224–25.

77. White, *It's Your Misfortune and None of My Own,* 240.

78. Rifkin, *Beyond Beef,* 95.

79. Josephson, *The Robber Barons,* 102.

80. Seligman, *The Potentates,* 174–75.

81. Marchant, *Man and Beast,* 70.

82. Marchant, *Man and Beast,* 71.

83. Richard D. Ryder, *Victims of Science: The Use of Animals in Research,* rev. ed. (London: National Anti-Vivisection Society, 1983), 123.

84. Karl Marx and Friedrich Engels, *The Communist Manifesto* (New York: Washington Square Press, 1964 [1848]): 57 and 58.

85. Robert Heilbroner, *The Making of Economic Society,* 9th ed. (Englewood Cliffs, N.J.: Prentice Hall, 1993), 60.

3

Capitalist Expansion
and Oppression

Every large mammalian species in the eastern part of America has been destroyed by modern man—except those he has chosen to protect for his own selfish purposes. . . . Large or small, all suffered crushing devastation if any profit was to be gained thereby; or if they seemed to pose even the threat of competition with our rapacious appetites.

—Farley Mowat[1]

In the early 1980s, an African American neighborhood in Columbus, Ohio, was threatened by the proposed construction of a freeway. The freeway was necessary, said the business elite, to provide a more direct link between downtown Columbus and the local airport. Neighborhood opponents challenged the project and suggested that the new route would shave only a few minutes off the commute. Rush-hour bottlenecks could be eased, they suggested, by more development of mass transit between downtown businesses and hotels and the airport.

The downtown interests bristled at the neighborhood resistance. The suggestion to improve mass transit service was brushed off by one member of the Columbus City Council who declared that "people have always loved their automobiles and will not ride on buses and shuttles."[2] In the end, the downtown elite launched a well-financed media campaign and convinced voters to approve the project. Like countless others throughout the country since the mid–twentieth century, the neighborhood was ravaged by freeway construction.

The assertion by the Columbus politician that people have always loved their cars, however, is another popular yet inaccurate historical reconstruction. The "American love affair with the automobile" might be described more accurately as an aggressive suitor forcing its intentions on a reluctant public. Over time, the manufactured demand for automobiles has contributed to environmental degradation, resource depletion, urban sprawl, social and economic segregation, and other ills. The brief account of the rise of the automobile in the U.S. culture and economy that follows illustrates how economic elites can effectively promote terrible social practices in their pursuit of private profit—policies that are harmful to the public and devastating for other animals.

For many decades, horses carried human animals and their goods in town and country alike. However, in the nineteenth century, the growing cities required the ability to transport masses of humans. Some met this need by use of the omnibus, a horse-drawn vehicle that accommodated about twelve passengers. The omnibus was supplemented in some areas with the "horsecar," a larger vehicle attached to rails and designed to carry forty to seventy passengers. In the latter part of the nineteenth century, there were more than fifteen hundred horsecars in New York City alone, and the labor of roughly twelve thousand horses powered them.[3] The lives of those assigned to the position of "car horse" were deplorable. Gerald Carson writes:

> It was a matter of common observation to one who cared to look that New York was hell for car horses. On the evening of February 11, 1868, for instance, a Third Avenue car was seen carrying sixty persons inside the car, with forty on the platforms and others both on the roof and hanging out the windows. The weight of the load was estimated at 21,000 pounds, with two feeble horses struggling to move the car up the steep grade that then existed between Twenty-second and Thirty-sixth streets. Sometimes a pedestrian with an ear attuned to that kind of thing could hear the labored breathing of the horses as far as a block away. . . . And so it was that the animals arrived, handsome and healthy, only to leave broken and crippled, usually passing to new owners for a nominal sum, often farmers who bought up town horses for whatever strength they had left and literally worked them to death on the farm.[4]

In the first two decades of the twentieth century, electric-powered streetcars began to replace omnibuses and horsecars in many U.S. cities. This particular development of early twentieth-century capitalism eventually helped to alleviate much of the suffering of horses bound to omnibuses. However, such relatively efficient and sensible forms of public transportation were soon eclipsed by a self-centered quest for private profit.

Those who controlled the growing steel, oil, and rubber industries foresaw the enormous profit potential of the automobile. The production of the first automobiles was received rather coolly by the public, particularly by those in large cities who were users and supporters of mass transit and who had developed a "love affair" with electric streetcars. In the face of poor market demand, corporate strategists promoted—indeed, forced—public acceptance of and reliance upon the automobile by undermining streetcar systems in many large cities and by using their political clout to redirect government transportation funds into the construction of roads and highways.[5] Advertising as well as films and other popular media turned the car into a cultural icon, symbolizing freedom, mobility, and status. The tactics and strategies used by the automakers and other industrial powers resulted in enormous corporate growth and expansion and huge profit. For most of the twentieth century, a substantial portion of individual and family income has been spent on the purchase, fueling, maintenance, and insuring of automobiles.

The forced reliance on automobiles developed in the mid– to late twentieth century created fortunes for a few and jobs for many. However, it has also rapidly depleted valuable global energy resources and severely damaged the environment. The cost to taxpayers of creating and maintaining the system of highways in the United States is enormous. Writing in 1985, policy analysts J. Allen Whitt and Glenn Yago observed, "[I]nfrastructure investment in highways is a costly and rapidly expanding burden. It is becoming evident that the commitment to highway transportation exacts great fiscal and social costs. Direct federal expenditures since 1956 for the national highway program total between $200 and $300 billion; . . . it will take even more than that amount to repair and maintain those same roads."[6]

The cultivated reliance on automobiles not only has led to depletion of natural resources, spoiled the environment, saturated many areas with toxic fumes, and taken huge shares of both family and public resources, but also has cost more than two million human lives in the United States alone—and led to countless debilitating injuries—from automobile accidents over the decades. Auto accidents are the third leading cause of death in the United States, and the leading cause for humans between the ages of fifteen and thirty-four.[7]

The web of greed and tragedy that has been generated by the automobile industry takes in other animals as well, at staggering levels. An estimated 365 million other animals are killed on U.S. roads and highways alone *every year,*[8] many enticed into the road by fast-food scraps and packages from the likes of McDonald's, Burger King, and Wendy's thoughtlessly thrown from car windows. Their writhing, mangled and smashed bodies are regarded as mere refuse by hurried motorists. Meanwhile, countless others have been, and continue to be, displaced or killed by highway construction projects, parking lots, and urban sprawl—a contemporary form of the practice of "kill and clear" reminiscent of incidents like the one in Hinckley, Ohio, that characterized earlier periods of American "settlement."

The urban sprawl facilitated by the automobile not only continues to destroy the homes and environments of millions of other animals every year but also has contributed to the decline and abandonment of downtowns, neighborhoods, and entire communities. This occurs due to the tendency for those who control capital to disinvest in and desert areas with limited purchasing power and to continually relocate to areas with greater profit potential. Older shopping centers and malls that once drew business activity away from formerly flourishing downtown business districts are in turn abandoned as profit-induced sprawl leads to incessant razing of the landscape for the new malls and "superstores" that take their place. In a society singularly focused on profit accumulation, the potential for reinvestment, revitalization, and recommitment to neighborhoods and communities is eclipsed by more profitable "cut-and-run" tactics.[9] This practice is evidenced by the countless forsaken and impoverished areas that blight both urban and rural landscapes.

The destructiveness associated with the growth of the automobile industry, and the consequent waste, havoc, and death, exemplifies the character of corporate capitalism, particularly as it developed in the twentieth century.

CORPORATE CAPITALISM AND
INTENSIFIED OPPRESSION

The growth in technology under late nineteenth- and early twentieth-century capitalism was not without its benefits. The late U.S. socialist and scholar Michael Harrington noted that "real wages were up between 1850 and 1914 in all industrialized countries; in France and Great Britain they almost doubled during that period."[10] A generally rising standard of living accompanied the "enormous growth in the consumption of the masses within the advanced nations."[11] The improved standard of living was due in part to the pressure workers and nascent labor organizations put on business owners to improve working conditions—as well as to the capitalists' realization that workers needed incomes high enough to be able to afford to consume the goods they produced.

During this period of rapid industrialization and urban growth, many humans living in the United States struggled as small-business owners, family farmers, and sharecroppers—each with various degrees of economic self-determination under the conditions of nineteenth-century capitalism. For most, however, their relative self-determination was being rapidly eclipsed by economic concentration. Why did this occur?

During this period powerful economic elites such as plantation owners, large mill operators, factory and slaughterhouse owners, bankers, and financial speculators dominated the U.S. economy. Most of these large business enterprises were still owned by a single person or family or by a small partnership. Mammoth business corporations began to emerge, however, because the capitalist system is characterized by an inherent tendency for continued growth and expansion. Douglas Dowd explains this imperative:

> A competitive capitalist economy is one where the only protection a given firm has is its own strength. That strength finally depends upon its profitability. In the modern world, this means that each firm must adopt the latest in technology, for both defensive and offensive reasons. With all or most firms in a given industry doing so, both production and productivity increase. The market must expand to absorb the increased production. In the normal course of such processes, some firms continue to expand, in themselves and by gobbling up others. The result is large-scale production, large-scale ownership, and large-scale control; a tendency towards monopoly. Along with economic expansion, both facilitating it and required by it, is geographic expansion—expansion of foreign markets, access to increasingly-needed foodstuffs and raw materials, and profitable foreign investments.[12]

This characteristic of capitalism, a predacious type of growth that is grounded in, and fueled by, so much oppression and death, was intensified by the emergence of giant business enterprises in the late nineteenth century. The personal fortunes of individuals like John D. Rockefeller, Andrew Carnegie, J. P. Morgan, Philip Armour, Gustavus Swift, and other owners of business empires of the period were acquired in such a way that they frequently were referred to as "robber barons." For instance, the same large "meat" packers that sold the United States spoiled and tainted "meat" during the Civil War sold hundreds of thousands of pounds of "beef" to the army during the Spanish American War. Noting that 5,462 U.S. soldiers died in various theaters of operations and in camps while only 379 died in battle, Howard Zinn ponders how many war-related deaths of U.S. soldiers were the result of food poisoning.[13] He writes:

> In May of 1898, Armour and Company, the big meatpacking company of Chicago, sold the army 500,000 pounds of beef which had been sent to Liverpool a year earlier and had been returned. Two months later, an army inspector tested the Armour meat, which had been stamped and approved by an inspector of the Bureau of Animal Industry, and found 751 cases containing rotten meat. In the first sixty cases he opened, he found fourteen tins already burst, "the effervescent putrid contents of which were distributed all over the cases." . . . Thousands of soldiers got food poisoning. There are no figures on how many of the five thousand noncombat deaths were caused by that.[14]

While such unscrupulous practices brought profit and business growth, expansion was made possible by the emergence and proliferation of the corporate form of business ownership. Unlike the proprietorships and partnerships that previously had been the norm, corporations had the advantage of providing limited liability for shareholders, who are not legally responsible for corporate crimes and debts. Investors can lose their personal investment, but they cannot be sued by the corporation's victims or creditors. Consequently, business corporations initially were viewed warily as monopolistic and corruptible. An early nineteenth-century economist, Daniel Raymond, wrote, "The very object . . . of the act of incorporation is to produce inequality, either in rights or in division of property. . . . [Corporations] are always created for the benefit of the rich."[15]

For most of the nineteenth century, corporations were seldom used in businesses, and organizing a corporation required a special act of a state legislature. As the century advanced, however, the expenses of industrial machinery and other expansion costs grew. Capitalists sought alternative ways of raising the required venture capital—ways that would protect their personal fortunes, and those of their financiers, from the risks of investment. So, despite public mistrust, in the latter half of the nineteenth century government chartering of business corporations became commonplace.

The corporate structure facilitated the growth of private enterprises that sought to reduce competition, which many business moguls viewed as a wasteful and unnecessary aspect of commerce. (This view was held notwithstanding capitalist rhetoric that extols robust competition as one of the essential features of a "consumer-driven" market economy.) A great deal of business competition was eliminated in the early twentieth century as enormous corporations either bought others out or drove them out of business through pools, trusts, predatory price fixing, and other even more disreputable tactics.[16] While such practices were personally benefi- cial for the few, they were very damaging for the many. The profit-driven trend toward increased business size, with enormous enterprises that acquire or ruin smaller ones (economic concentration) and the placement of economic power in fewer and fewer hands (centralized control), is frequently referred to as monopoly capitalism.[17] Monopoly capitalism also perpetuated and increased social injustice and privation. However, even before the drive toward centralization and monopoli- zation began in earnest, by the mid–nineteenth century U.S. capitalism had pro- duced extreme economic disparity. Historian Mary Beth Norton and her associates write:

> Wealth throughout the United States was becoming concentrated in the hands of a relatively small number of people. In New York City between 1828 and 1845, the wealthiest 4 percent of the city's population increased their holdings from an estimated 63 percent to 80 percent of all individual wealth. By 1860, the top 5 percent of Ameri- can families owned more than half the nation's wealth.
>
> A cloud of uncertainty hung over working men and women. Many were afraid that during hard times they would become unemployed. They feared the competition of immigrant and slave labor. They feared the insecurities and indignities of poverty, chronic illness, disability, old age, widowhood, and desertion. And they had good rea- son. Poverty and squalor stalked the urban working class as cities grew.[18]

Commenting on the state of the society in the late nineteenth century, economist Ben B. Seligman writes:

> Life was no longer measured by the seasons, but by the clock, and the whirl of the machine. The city, with its belching smokestacks, began to dominate the landscape as the economy moved from extractive industries to manufacturing. The change was a haphazard one, and its ugliness was to generate problems that have persisted down to the present.
>
> The city became an instrument of industrial development to be manipulated freely by those who controlled its resources and who could gather personal gain in the process. Everything that was engaged in was directed toward material ends only. . . . Everything seemed to reflect an overwhelming pressure to measure success by the only standard that counted—money.[19]

While wages generally increased and consumption grew, workers were considered to be just another expense for giant business enterprises, and many employers con- tinued to keep wages as low as possible—particularly for those groups who were traditionally devalued and oppressed. Children and young women were preferred workers because they were viewed as more easily exploited and controlled. Not only were wages kept at meager or below-subsistence levels, but also the costs of improved working conditions and safety precautions were considered an unnecessary expense. Children, women, and men alike (particularly men of color, immigrants, and the unskilled) were killed or disabled by appalling working conditions and frequent accidents. One famous tragedy, for instance, occurred in 1911 at the Triangle Shirtwaist Factory in New York City. A fire broke out in the crowded garment factory, and 146 young women, many recent Jewish and Italian immigrants, were killed—trapped and unable to escape the fire due to faulty fire escapes and exits that had been blocked to keep them in and union organizers out.

Throughout the nineteenth and early twentieth centuries, many exploited human laborers attempted to organize themselves into unions in order to resist abuses by their employers, and some were successful.[20] In response to labor organizing efforts, large business owners and corporate directors solicited workers from around the globe, especially from Ireland, Southern Europe, Asia, and Latin America. Immigrants in the United States were easily exploited due to their willingness to work for meager payment, and Machiavellian employers also capitalized on the newcomers' presence to factionalize workers. The following reflection by Douglas Dowd highlights the relationship between ethnic oppression and capitalism:

> Although immigration had been increasing since the 1850s . . . it was during the 1880s that the great wave of immigration from the poorer parts of Europe and Asia began. . . . These people came at a time when industrialization had taken strong hold and when conditions of factory and city were becoming increasingly ugly. From the viewpoint of settled Americans . . . these newcomers were also "increasingly ugly."
>
> America had been well-prepared for a translation of all this into divisions and hostility that were many-faceted. It had been prepared by our own habituation to oppressing and even exterminating red, black, and brown peoples. . . . From the mid-1890s on, Jim Crow laws spread and deepened, and lynching became so common that it went unnoticed in the press (there were as many as one thousand a year officially recorded). The prior and continuing oppression of Native Americans joined with stepped-up oppression of black people. . . . Savage developments in the eastern half of the country combined with savage developments in the western half, as Spanish-speaking and Asian immigrants were mistreated and killed . . . while being exploited in the fields, mines, factories, and railroads.
>
> Racial oppression and ethnic and religious hatreds did not begin in the United States, it should go without saying. But the combative atmosphere of the United States, taken together with the long-standing and well-entrenched acceptance of the Puritan work ethic and its corollary of economic individualism, made it easy for bigots and unscrupulous businessmen to exploit these pervasive inclinations.[21]

Powerful industrialists and growing corporations not only factionalized the working class but also used violence and repression when necessary to suppress organizing efforts or break strikes. For example, in the late nineteenth and early twentieth centuries: ten miners leading resistance against the coal mining industry were denounced as members of a radical Irish fraternal organization, the Molly McGuires, and executed; at least fifty workers were killed during the great railroad strike that swept the nation in 1877; ten workers died in the Homestead steel strike in 1892; six working-class leaders were scapegoated and hung as a result of the Haymarket incident of 1886; scores of mine workers in West Virginia and the Rocky Mountains perished in strikes during the 1890s; entire families were massacred by Rockefeller company gunmen during a 1914 strike in Ludlow, Colorado—the list goes on and on.[22] The level of violence directed at the U.S. working class during this period was viewed as unprecedented and extreme, even by politically conservative Europeans. Noam Chomsky observes, "[U.S.] labor history is extremely violent. Incomparably more so than Europe. . . . [H]undreds of workers were getting murdered by the security forces. This went on until the late 1930s. [There was] nothing like it in Europe. In fact, the right wing European press was appalled by the treatment of American workers, right through the turn of the early part of the [twentieth] century."[23]

Pursuit of profit at any cost also motivated expansion and oppression outside the country's borders. By now the United States was a well-established capitalist power, and the elite followed the colonialist and imperialist lead of their militaristic European counterparts. For instance, even before the push toward the corporate business structure, powerful interests—including land speculators and white slaveholders who resented Mexican antislavery laws—encouraged the government to provoke a war with Mexico. The conflict resulted in the expropriation of a significant portion of Mexican territory, including what is now California, Texas, New Mexico, Arizona, and Colorado. Racist ideologies and concomitant prejudice were manufactured or encouraged to legitimate the appropriation of Mexican land and resources. As seen in chapter 2, this racism also justified the later appropriation of land legally held by U.S. citizens of Mexican heritage—much of it used to graze cows who would be sent to giant packing houses to be killed and dismembered—and the exploitation of the labor of these dispossessed citizens, as well as later generations of immigrants from Mexico and other Central American countries.

Similarly, the United States' war with Spain in 1898—also prompted by industrial and corporate interests—resulted in the "liberation" of Cuba, Puerto Rico, and the Philippines, a liberation that actually subjected their populations and land to domination and control by U.S. corporations. The economic benefits that were sure to accrue to importers, sugar producers, bankers, steamship owners, and the like gave them vested interests in preventing the territories' economic or political independence.[24] Regarding U.S. interests in Cuba, for example, Howard Zinn observes:

> Americans began taking over railroad, mine, and sugar properties when the war ended. In a few years, $30 million of American capital was invested. United Fruit moved into the Cuban sugar industry. It bought 1,900,000 acres of land for about twenty cents an acre. The American Tobacco Company arrived. By the end of the occupation in 1901 . . . at least 80 percent of the export of Cuba's minerals were in American hands, mostly Bethlehem Steel.[25]

Filipinos had long resisted Spanish colonization and similarly resisted U.S. control when it became clear that the U.S. Army was an occupying—not a liberating—presence. The force with which the United States crushed the Philippine independence movement was particularly ruthless. Historian Kenneth C. Davis notes, "[T]he Philippine incursion . . . carried with it all the earmarks of a modern imperial war: massive strikes against civilians, war atrocities, and a brutality that had been missing from American wars with Europeans. Fighting against the 'brown' Filipinos removed all excuses for civility."[26]

The U.S. government also used military power to stifle the will and interests of the indigenous people of Hawaii as the islands were expropriated and claimed as U.S. territory—an action that mainly served the interests of the sugar cane industry. Meanwhile, humans from China, Japan, Korea, the Philippines, and India in the nineteenth and early twentieth centuries were induced to migrate to Hawaii and the U.S. mainland, where their labor was exploited by agriculturalists and mining and railroad companies. Again, racist ideologies were created and propagated to justify their exploitation. Eventually, many immigrants sought to improve their lives by starting their own farms and businesses. However, their pursuit of security and self-determination increased the level of economic competition in the areas they settled—escalating the level of racism and violence against them.[27]

The denigration and exploitation of workers, ruthless economic competition, imperialist practices, and the drive toward economic concentration and centralization—all compelled by the capitalist system—fanned the flames of prejudice and ethnocentrism against all potentially exploitable and devalued groups. Humans with disabilities, for example, faced continued oppression under such arrangements. Many were still exhibited as "freaks," more "animal than human," and used to turn profits for shadowy entrepreneurs, while increasing numbers were confined to atrocious state institutions and forcibly sterilized. Humans with disabilities were scapegoated as the powerful and privileged promulgated the belief that their "kind" had caused widespread poverty and social disorganization in the United States. Some capitalist-friendly scientists recommended that the labor power of people with developmental disabilities be tapped for profitable ventures, as illustrated by the following passage from a 1918 book by Paul Popenoe and Roswell Hill Johnson, the latter a professor at the University of Pittsburgh:

> Feeble-minded men are capable of much rough labor. Most of the cost of segregating the mentally defective can be met by properly organizing their labor, so as to make them as nearly self-supporting as possible. It has been found that they perform excellently such work as clearing forest land . . . and great gangs of them might profitably be put to work, . . . waste humanity taking waste land and . . . making over land that would otherwise be useless. . . . No manufacturer of today has let the product of his plant go to waste as society has wasted the energies of this by-product of humanity.[28]

Meanwhile, despite the abolition of slavery, humans of color were still terrorized and lynched, particularly if they were perceived as challenging the U.S. form of apartheid and the economic benefits it provided for the privileged, their minions, and any others who derived some benefit, real or imagined, from their oppression. In the classic 1937 sociological work *Caste and Class in a Southern Town,* John Dollard discusses some of the material advantages of oppression that accrued to many white middle-class southerners under the Jim Crow system:

> For one thing, they [the white-middle class] avoid the manual work and the more monotonous types of work. . . . Middle-class people seem generally to make use of Negro house servants, cooks, chambermaids, nurses for children, and houseboys. . . . In the main, middle-class people do not mow their own lawns, cook their own meals, clean up their own houses, not to speak of farming their own land. . . . The middle group has a larger share of the goods and services which flow from the common operation of the socio-industrial machine in Southtown and county. They have better houses and lawns, more fans, electric iceboxes, radios, screens, better food, newer cars and clothes, more movies, books and travel, and more efficient schools and colleges accessible to their children.[29]

In contrast to many other writers of the period, Dollard does not isolate innate personality or psychological causes for these oppressive conditions, but, rather, also plants them firmly in institutional and economic arrangements.

> We must note that whites are as automatically caught in this socio-economic situation as are the colored. The middle-class whites are playing their social roles with no more, but no less, greed and acquisitiveness than any other man in our society exhibits. They are acting as they have to act in the position within the social labor structure which they hold, that is, competing as hard as they can for maximum returns.[30]

As can be predicted by the theory of oppression, an economic system that exploits workers and pits them against one another for jobs also fuels animosity against perceived competitors. The following passage from the autobiography of novelist Richard Wright, also written in 1937, embodies the theory:

> There is but one place where a black boy who knows no trade can get a job, and that's where the houses and faces are white, where the trees, lawns, and hedges are green. My first job was with an optical company in Jackson, Mississippi. . . .
>   I worked hard, trying to please. For the first month I got along O.K. Both Pease and Morrie seemed to like me. But one thing was missing. And I kept thinking about it. I was not learning anything and nobody was volunteering to help me. . . . I asked Morrie one day to tell me about the work. He grew red.
>   "Whut yuh tryin' t' do, nigger, get smart?" he asked.
>   "Naw; I ain't tryin' t' git smart," I said.
>   "Well, don't, if yuh know whut's good for yuh!"
>   I was puzzled. Maybe he just doesn't want to help me, I thought. I went to Pease.
>   "Say, are yuh crazy, you black bastard?" Pease asked me, his gray eyes growing hard.
>   I spoke out, reminding him that the boss had said I was to be given a chance to learn something.
>   "Nigger, you think you're *white*, don't you?"
>   "Naw, sir!" . . .
>   Pease shook his fist in my face.
>   "This is *white* man's work around here, and you better watch yourself!"
>   From then on they changed toward me. They said good-morning no more.[31]

Similarly, some observers see economic factors as the primary reason for the anti-Semitism that grew so strong in the United States during the first half of the twentieth century and that has persisted, in varying degrees, to this day. According to some scholars, powerful U.S. Gentiles actually cultivated anti-Jewish ideology to justify the exclusion of Jewish-Americans from profitable industries and to create another scapegoat for the deplorable economic conditions that accompanied industrial capitalism and its corollary, concentrated economic power.[32] Gay liberation activist Bob McCubbin suggests that homophobia also serves as an "instrument of bourgeois class rule" to "divide the international working class."[33] Moreover, some sociologists maintain that the status of older humans declined with the advent of western capitalist society, and continued with the development of monopoly capitalism. According to sociologist James J. Dowd:

> By most accounts, the "great transformation" in the status of the aged occurred with industrialization, because legal land ownership in an industrial economy brought the landowner less status than in the previous agricultural economy. Factory work became the major occupational pursuit, creating two large classes of capitalists and workers. . . . In general, the changes that accompanied industrialization were . . . "disastrous for the old."
>
> One of the consequences of the shift from an agricultural to an industrial economy . . . has been a decline in the power of old people relative to the power of other age groups. . . . The status of the aged (as measured by relative income, health, weeks worked, and education) was higher in the United States, for example, in 1940 than in 1969. . . .
>
> When discussing the problems and status of the aged in the twentieth century, one realizes that the main factor that determines the nature of intergenerational relations in Western societies is the society's political economy.[34]

The hardship, deprivation, and humiliation experienced by humans of color and other devalued groups motivated W. E. B. DuBois, Oliver Cox, and others to study the problems' capitalist underpinnings, as we saw in chapter 1. These writers, however, were ignored or denigrated by both the corporate establishment and many social scientists who submitted to the forces and demands of corporate-dominated society.[35]

TWENTIETH-CENTURY CAPITALISM AND ENTANGLED OPPRESSION

As could be expected, the harsh and cruel treatment of humans remained mirrored in and inextricably entangled with the oppression of other animals. For example, the use of assembly-line production methods to reduce the need for highly skilled workers, a tactic that made workers easily replaceable and more exploitable, was pioneered and refined in slaughterhouses—and the consequences for other animals were horrific. Other animals, such as cows and pigs, were prodded, jabbed, and driven up ramps to the top floor of slaughterhouses where they were shackled, suspended by belts and propelled downward by gravity to suffer agonizing death on a "disassembly line." The gruesome treatment of other animals in the early twentieth-century Chicago slaughterhouses was described in Upton Sinclair's classic novel *The Jungle*. In a stark and poignant passage, Sinclair introduces the public to the reality of the experience of other animals in a rapidly mechanizing society.

[T]here was a great iron wheel, about twenty feet in circumference, with rings here and there along its edge. Upon both sides of this wheel there was a narrow space, into which came the hogs at the end of their journey; . . . chains . . . [were] fastened about the leg of the nearest hog, and the other end of the chain they hooked into one of the rings upon the wheel. So, as the wheel turned, a hog was suddenly jerked off his feet and borne aloft.

At the same instant the ear was assailed by a most terrifying shriek. . . . The shriek was followed by another, louder and yet more agonizing—for once started upon that journey, the hog never came back; at the top of the wheel he was shunted off upon a trolley, and went sailing down the room. And meantime, another was swung, and then another, and another, until there was a double line of them, each dangling by a foot and kicking in frenzy—and squealing. . . .

It was all so very businesslike. . . . It was pork-making by machinery, pork-making by applied mathematics. And yet somehow the most matter-of-fact person could not help thinking of the hogs; they were so innocent, they came so very trustingly; and they were so very human in their protests. . . . And each of them had an individuality of his own, a will of his own.[36]

At the same time, workers on this notorious "kill-line" were forced to work at a rapid, relentless pace, and serious injury was commonplace. The callous treatment of workers was inextricably linked with, and driven by, the same insatiable thirst for personal wealth that caused the monstrous, and increasingly mechanized, treatment of other animals. Jeremy Rifkin writes:

Production increased dramatically following the introduction of the disassembly line. In 1884, five splitters handled 800 head of cattle in a ten-hour day. By 1894, four splitters were handling 1,200 head a day. . . .

[F]orced to work in an environment that was as hazardous as it was hellish, packing-house laborers fought back, demanding better working conditions and better pay. Some of the bloodiest labor battles of the waning years of the nineteenth century were fought between the fledgling beef-packing unions and the Beef Trust.[37]

During many strikes, the slaughterhouse operators "kept the plants operating with waves of new immigrant laborers and poor blacks."[38] In another powerful passage, Sinclair describes the plight of Marija, who loses her job because of union activity but finds another as a "beef trimmer":

She had about made up her mind that she was a lost soul, when somebody told her of an opening, and she went and got a place as a "beef trimmer." She got this because the boss saw that she had the muscles of a man, and so he discharged a man and put Marija to do his work, paying her a little more than half what he had been paying before. . . . She was shut up in one of the rooms where the people seldom saw the daylight; beneath her were the chilling rooms, where the meat was frozen, and above her were the cooking rooms; and so she stood on an ice-cold floor, while her head was so hot she could scarcely breathe. Trimming beef off the bones by the hundredweight, while standing up from early morning to late at night, with heavy boots on and the floor always damp and full of puddles, liable to be thrown out of work indefinitely because of slackening in the trade, liable again to be kept overtime in rush seasons, and to be worked till she trembled in every nerve and lost her grip on the slimy knife, and gave herself a poisoned wound—that was the new life that spread before Marija.[39]

The unspeakably oppressive treatment of other animals and workers driven by monopoly capitalism included pressing children into employment, intensifying a disturbing practice that had been going on for centuries. As two period critics put it, "Extreme insecurity has been the chief economic and spiritual diet of workers' homes. Patently, this would have a direct bearing on sending children to work."[40] Children were employed by slaughterhouses whenever possible, especially after the canning of "meat" began, because they were more easily exploited. Helen Laura Sumner writes:

As early as 1888 a large number of girls were employed in the Chicago stock yards in painting and labeling cans. In some establishments they were paid, it was said, $5 a week, but were expected to paint at least 1,500 cans per day of nine hours. Little girls scoured cans, too, for $3.00 a week. . . . At Armour's packing house girls were paid from 3 cents to 5 cents per hundred for labeling.[41]

Such exploitative, oppressive treatment of workers and children and such hideous treatment of other animals were not primarily motivated by prejudice and hatred but by pursuit of business profit—profit derived from satisfying a taste for the flesh of other animals, a demand promoted increasingly by the "meat" industry and related enterprises.

For instance, "meat" producers induced the privileged to consume more "beef" by increasing its fat content, prompting them to spend more money for the most desirable "cuts." This occurred after vast areas of the western plains were given over to the grazing of cows. It was found that feeding "steers" and cows corn before slaughtering them not only increased their weight, but also the amount of fat in the "beef." Eating the flesh of others became increasingly palatable, and those who could afford it relished the marbled cuts of "beef."[42] (As we shall see later in this chapter and in chapter 4, increased consumption of the flesh of other animals would have deadly consequences—not only for billions of other animals but for thousands of humans in the Third World who have faced military execution after protesting expropriation of their land for cattle production, as well as for countless twentieth- and twenty-first-century humans who have suffered premature death from heart disease, strokes, cancer, and the like.) Increasing consumption of "choice" cuts of flesh was also a way in which more privileged humans distinguished themselves from the "lower" classes, much as "meat" consumption symbolized status in the Middle Ages.

The social class hierarchy spurred by oppressive social arrangements was reflected in other socially cultivated market demands as well. The social divisions based on a group's wealth and status, or lack thereof, were increasingly expressed in consumption patterns, patterns that early twentieth-century critic Thorstein Veblen famously referred to as "conspicuous consumption." Veblen noted that excess consumption of goods and ostentatious displays of wealth go well beyond satisfying individual physical needs and instead become symbols of one's rank, status, and "superior character." Conversely, the "low-grade character" of those who live at subsistence levels is similarly made obvious to all. As Veblen noted, "the failure to consume in due quantity and quality becomes a mark of inferiority and demerit."[43]

Wearing the hair of other animals also has long served as a display of one's superior status in Europe and the United States, and this practice continued under twentieth-century capitalism. Wearing the hair of other animals was particularly promoted as a symbol of elegance for women and of power and success for the men who bestowed such a gift. This status-driven custom exacerbated the objectification of women, who were pictured in ads as being glamorous and sexy when cloaked in "fur." This form of social class distinction and the objectification of women was intertwined with the agonizing deaths of millions of other animals caught in leghold traps and clubbed to death, with the exploitation of Native Americans and with other injustices, as we saw in chapter 2.

The keeping of "pets," particularly pets of distinction, became another symbol of prominent status. "Pedigreed" dogs, for example, were not just companions but indications of an ability to buy the best of everything. The speciesist sense of pride in walking down the street with a purebred dog was not dissimilar to a man's sexist enjoyment of being seen with an attractive woman or a woman's classist satisfaction in walking out with a rich man.

CAPITALIST EXPANSION AND
TWENTIETH-CENTURY WARFARE

While entrepreneurial exploitation and death of humans and other animals were fodder for the continued growth and expansion of monopoly capitalism, as in ages past and as in the U.S. imperialist wars of the nineteenth century, war in the twentieth century also had deep economic roots. Just as war in earlier periods was necessitated by needs for grazing lands, cropland, slave labor and other "resources," twentieth-century world wars were driven primarily by the imperative for capitalist expansion and resultant needs for land, cheap labor, new markets, and assorted resources needed to keep capitalist societies, and particularly large business corporations, growing. Many students are taught that World War I was the result of the assassination of Archduke Francis Ferdinand and that U.S. involvement was caused by the German sinking of the *Lusitania*. However, few are aware of what was really at stake for the competing capitalist powers of England, France, Germany, and the United States: control of the resources—animal, mineral, and vegetable—and markets of Africa, the Middle East, and Asia. What is more, J. P. Morgan and other banking tycoons promoted U.S. involvement in the war to protect investments and loans made to Great Britain, loans that would not be repaid in the event of a German victory. Other industrialists supported direct U.S. involvement because of the potential for lucrative, government-financed wartime contracts, and the capitalist class successfully pressured the government to declare war against Germany, even though many citizens were opposed.

Historian Kenneth C. Davis notes that one of the only members of Congress who dared to speak against the war in the face of such corporate support, Senator George W. Norris of Nebraska, called it a "fight for profits rather than for principles."[44] Quoting a Wall Street memo promoting U.S. entry into the conflict and the "bull" market it would generate, Norris proclaimed:

> Here we have the men representing the class of people who will be made prosperous should we become entangled in the present war, who have already made millions of dollars, and who will make hundreds of millions more if we get into the war. Here we have the cold-blooded propositions that war brings prosperity. . . . Wall Street . . . see[s] only dollars coming to them through the handling of stocks and bonds that will be necessary in the case of war.
>
> Their object in having war and in preparing for war is to make money. Human suffering and sacrifice of human life are necessary, but Wall Street considers only the dollars and the cents. . . . The stock brokers would not, of course, go to war. . . . They will be concealed in their palatial offices on Wall Street, sitting behind mahogany desks.[45]

DuBois also saw the economic motivation at the root of World War I, particularly the desire of powerful capitalists, their well-paid functionaries, and the white, male, skilled laborers to whom they allowed some of the corporate profits to trickle down, to control the resources and markets of the African continent. He wrote:

> The present war is, then, the result of jealousies engendered by the rise of armed national associations of labor and capital, whose aim is the exploitation of the wealth of the world mainly outside the European circle of nations. These associations, grown jealous and suspicious at the division of spoils of trade-empire, are fighting to enlarge their respective shares; they look for expansion, not in Europe but in Asia, and particularly in Africa. . . .
>
> What do nations care about the cost of war, if by spending a few hundred million in steel and gunpowder they can gain a thousand millions in diamonds and cocoa? How can love of humanity appeal as a motive to nations whose love of luxury is built on the inhumane exploitation of human beings, and who, especially in recent years, have been taught to regard these human beings as inhuman?[46]

Working together, industrialists, financiers, and the government launched a massive and crafty propaganda campaign to promote public acceptance of the war, instituted a draft when enlistment calls faltered, and criminalized the practice of speaking out against the war in public.[47]

The cost of the war in human lives was staggering. Roughly twenty-eight million died in fighting or from other war-related causes. The numbers of other animals who perished as a result of the war can only be imagined. Thousands of dogs were used as instruments of war by the British, Belgian, Italian, French, and German armies. It is estimated that 68,682 horses and mules were killed "in service" of the U.S. forces alone.[48]

After World War I ended, the conquering capitalist nations were unable to agree on how to divide the "spoils," particularly the areas of the world previously controlled by Germany. Meanwhile, an unfettered quest for individual wealth continued, not only to motivate the mistreatment of workers and other devalued groups but also to pit powerful national economies against one another. Corporate and Wall Street machinations and greed contributed greatly to the Great Depression, the near-total collapse of both the U.S. and global economic systems in the 1930s. Concerned about the growing power of the political Left, and the consequent possibilities for democratic participation in economic affairs, powerful capitalists in several European nations formed alliances with fascist political-military movements, alliances that successfully quashed Leftist movements by violence and intimidation. Socialists, communists, and intellectuals were targeted for elimination or deportation, while European Jews were scapegoated for economic difficulties.

The U.S. government maintained a position of neutrality as fascist regimes gained increased control in Europe. This policy of nonintervention surely was grounded in part in admiration on the part of the capitalist class in the United States for the way their counterparts in Europe were able to counter Leftist political movements and stifle labor unions. Meanwhile, U.S. corporations found the fascist military machines a lucrative market for goods, especially oil. The U.S. elite remained generally indifferent to the repressive nature of the governments of Germany, Japan, Italy, and fascist Spain after General Franco gained control. Even after disturbing reports of severe anti-Semitic policies in Germany began to reach Washington, the U.S. government largely continued its policy of nonintervention to the point of willful ignorance and inaction. For instance, fearing that a large influx of Jewish refugees, fleeing imminent extermination at the hands of the Nazis, would impair a struggling domestic economy, the State Department stifled reports of death camps and in 1939 even refused to allow an ocean liner full of Jewish refugees seeking asylum, mostly women and children, to come ashore in the United States. Forced to return to Europe, a number of the asylum seekers later were killed in concentration camps.[49] Lamenting the refusal of the U.S. government to assist the refugees, Bishop James Cannon, Jr., of Richmond, Virginia, commented in a 1939 letter to the *Richmond Times-Dispatch,* "The failure to take any steps whatsoever to assist these distressed, persecuted Jews in their hour of extremity was one of the most disgraceful things which has happened in American history and leaves a stain and brand of shame upon the record of our nation."[50]

It was only with the bombing of Pearl Harbor that the United States was pulled directly into the conflict. However, the Japanese attack on the United States was not a total surprise (although the target of the initial attack, Pearl Harbor, probably was). The Japanese had long resented U.S. intervention and economic opportunism in Asia and the unscrupulous treatment of humans of Japanese descent in the States. The growing economic and military power of Japan posed a threat to U.S. corporate interests in Asia—particularly China—and the United States had undertaken embargoes of iron and oil headed for Japanese ports. In his *People's History of the United States,* Zinn cites a State Department memorandum issued a year before the attack on Pearl Harbor:

> [O]ur general diplomatic and strategic position would be considerably weakened—by our loss of Chinese, Indian and South Seas markets (and by our loss of much of the Japanese market for our goods, as Japan would become more and more self-sufficient) as well as by insurmountable restrictions upon our access to rubber, tin, jute, and other vital minerals of the Asian and Oceanic regions.[51]

So, the U.S. involvement in World War II was motivated not so much by opposition to the oppressive practices and policies of fascist nations as by concerns about the future control of global economic resources and markets. Indeed, many policies of the German state that later came to be so vilified—grounded as they were in racism, eugenic philosophy, and contempt for Leftist thought—were not entirely unlike the state-supported practices in the vehemently procapitalist United States at the time.

While U.S. involvement in World War II was motivated in large part by strategic global concerns of the capitalist class, the same class realized that the economic breakdown and depression experienced in the United States in the 1930s would be alleviated by a wartime economy. Indeed, the need for weaponry and war-related supplies revitalized the United States economy, and the 1940s showed greater economic growth than any other decade in U.S. history, with the nation's real gross national product growing by 36 percent in just ten years.[52] The principal beneficiaries of this growth in production were those who owned or had substantial investments in the largest corporations. Historians Charles Beard and Mary Beard write:

> Big business was responsible for much of the expansion in physical output. To get quickly and in fabulous amounts guns, ships, tanks, airplanes, and other implements of war, the Federal Government turned for help to concerns gigantic enough to be able to take huge production orders in their stride. By the close of 1943, for example, some seventy percent of the war business had gone to the hundred largest companies.[53]

Just as the warfare of the ancients was driven by competition for land and resources, and further spurred by the exploitation of the conquered, so was the most devastating war of the twentieth century. Competitive, capitalist nations—under the hegemonic control of large and powerful corporations—struggled for control of markets and parts of the world where large populations and vast resources could be easily exploited.

Again, capitalist-promoted global warfare exacted a tragic cost. In human deaths alone, more than fifty-seven million soldiers and civilians died in World War II, and far more were wounded and disabled. The other animals who were killed, whether directly as weapons or instruments of war and from bombings and other forms of destruction, or indirectly after environmental destruction or from starvation during periods of extreme deprivation, are innumerable. Minimally, it is known that a year after the United States entered the war the government announced plans to use 125,000 dogs as guards, mine sniffers, scouts, and tactical fighters.[54] (Four thousand dogs were used later as instruments of war by the United States in Vietnam. When U.S. forces were pulled out, the dogs were regarded by the military elite as merely war equipment and "abandoned in place"[55]—just like the many South Vietnamese allies of the Americans, mere "others" who were left to face the wrath of the conquering North Vietnamese forces). Of the horses and mules used as tools by the U.S. Army during World War II, more than 243,000 were reported killed.[56]

Moreover, World War II and the casualties it brought—including the six million European Jews and others who were methodically murdered—"had scorched the minds and character of a generation."[57] While the entanglements of the exploitation and oppression of humans and other animals in warfare and violent oppression are numerous and substantial, only one more will be highlighted—the use of barbed wire. First introduced to control the movements of other animals, its use in controlling humans was described at length in a 2000 article by Reviel Netz, who notes:

> If barbed wire now seems so familiar, this is because of the memorial power of the Holocaust . . .
> Barbed wire may seem like a trivial detail in a context of this magnitude. In fact, however, it was the central element in the architecture of the death camps. . . .
> [T]he misery which humans inflict on animals may ultimately be inseparable from the misery which they inflict upon themselves.[58]

At the end of the carnage, with most of the other industrialized nations nearly destroyed, U.S. capitalists prevailed as the most important and powerful agricultural and industrial producers and distributors in the world.

USE OF DEVALUED HUMANS AND OTHER ANIMALS UNDER LATE TWENTIETH-CENTURY CAPITALISM

As a result of its military successes, by the mid–twentieth century the United States was the most significant global supplier of many economic staples as well as luxury goods. This global domination created a period of relative affluence for many in the United States, and the consumption of conspicuous and extravagant commodities spiraled. As in earlier periods, wearing animal skin and hair was one way the "successful" distinguished themselves from those whose labor actually created the wealth.

For instance, by midcentury the "fur" industry was thriving and relied increasingly on mass production methods by breeding and raising other animals on "fur" farms.

Only recently have advocates for other animals worked systematically to enlighten the public about the enormous degree of suffering that underlies the production of such garments. As a result, the market for these items has diminished considerably. Not surprisingly, those most willing and able to carry on the fight to preserve the killing of other animals for their hair are those who profit by it. One of the "fur" industry's primary arguments in favor of its continued existence is that it contributes greatly to the U.S. economy. The industry maintains that in 1990 the "fur" trade "produced a total economic benefit of $4.4 billion and supported more than 100,000 jobs."[59] Industry statistics claim that retail sales in the United States alone in 1998 were $1.27 billion.[60] Similarly, by the beginning of the twenty-first century, the wearing of "leather" (read: skin of other animals) clothing became in vogue and skyrocketed in popularity; many individuals with scant resources sacrificed to get their own expensive clothing fashioned from skin to advertise their social worth.

While some humans benefited from the war-related growth and expansion, many devalued humans and other animals experienced little relief. Following World War II, African Americans continued to experience segregation and other forms of discrimination, including continued acts of violence and terrorism. Many women were forced from wartime jobs and faced high levels of domestic violence and other forms of discrimination, despite winning the franchise so many had struggled for earlier in the century. And many of those with few resources, while lifted somewhat by a war-driven, revitalized economy, continued to enjoy but a small share of the resulting windfall. For example, after nearly two decades of postwar economic growth and expansion, the level of economic disparity in the United States was staggering. The poorest 20 percent of U.S. households received only 4 percent of the annual income in 1967, while the most affluent 20 percent received 43.8 percent.[61] Not surprisingly, the traditionally devalued human groups—whose labor was continuing to produce a great deal of wealth—were disproportionately among those receiving small incomes.

One group that continued to languish in the United States in the mid-1900s was humans with disabilities. Although calls for their forced sterilization abated somewhat during and after World War II, as U.S. policymakers tried to distance themselves from similar discriminatory practices in Nazi Germany, a more complete liberation of those with disabilities was not in the interests of twentieth-century capitalism. In his classic work *The Shame of the States,* Albert Deutsch exposed the treatment of humans with mental illness and other disabilities in the mid–twentieth century. In the following passage, he describes the fate of a young Navy veteran, recently returned from World War II, at the Napa State Hospital in California. Any status the young man might have enjoyed as a returning veteran of the "Great War" clearly was eclipsed by his placement in the category of the "disturbed," as Deutsch describes his treatment at the hospital:

> This patient . . . had been brought in handcuffs to the hospital by four deputy sheriffs.
> He had already had some rough handling by the time he got to the institution.

On arrival at Napa he got some more rough handling in a fracas with four attendants in the admitting ward who had difficulty getting him into a straitjacket. He was later transferred to the disturbed or violent ward, where he got another going-over by another foursome of husky attendants as he again resisted efforts to get him into a straitjacket. He died that night of internal hemorrhages. An autopsy showed 30 bruises on his body. . . .

I discussed the case with Dr. Reginald Rood, assistant superintendent at Napa. . . .

"Were the attendants involved in this incident trained for their job?" I asked.

"No," Dr. Rood answered. "We haven't been able to conduct a training program for any of our attendants. . . ."

"We are short of everything here," Dr. Miller told me. "For years, the state has followed the unwritten policy that the best institution is the one run at the least per capita cost." . . .

California, one of the wealthiest states in the Union, is near the bottom of the list in many categories that make up a modern mental hospital.[62]

Meanwhile, other oppressive and archaic practices flourish even as economic growth under capitalism (read: private profit taking) expands. Many are motivated to exploit humans or other animals in a system characterized by grave disparities and where poverty and lack of resources—although structurally induced—are a mark of disgrace. Many seek to hold, or to develop, an economic niche by exploiting other animals.

For instance, displaying and abusing other animals for entertainment grew in profitability. The rodeo, for example, continues to be a popular spectacle even though its utility to the "beef" industry of the skills displayed has long since faded. Rodeos now are featured programs on some cable networks, particularly those such as ESPN that market to men, with large corporate sponsors such as Anheuser-Busch. The profits from the sale of commercial spots on televised rodeos are paralleled by increased profits from the sales of products such as Budweiser beer. However, smaller entrepreneurs also gain materially from this form of exploitation of other animals. The communities in which rodeos are held see increased patronage for restaurants, motels, convenience stores, and tourist-related businesses. In addition, as Gerald Carson observes:

Also present at the arenas, and a part of the multimillion-dollar economics of rodeo, are stock contractors, who provide the animal raw material, stock foremen, Indian chiefs, beauty queens, sales agents for accessories, hillbilly singers, concessionaires, arena directors, bandsmen, juvenile gunslingers, owners of dog acts, photographers, public relations men, judges, timers, baton twirlers, trick ropers, Roman riders, comedy mules and monkeys—and, of course, the bawling, apprehensive, restless livestock, indispensable yet expendable.

But what ever rodeo is—stirring historical pageant; nostalgic symbol; wholesome, red-blooded entertainment; or commercialized brutality—it is undeniably big business.[63]

From rodeo "queens," to "Indian chiefs," to "hillbilly singers," the spectacle of the rodeo weaves speciesism into various other "isms" and parades them all as "red-blooded" American entertainment. (Interestingly, during testimony before the Balti-more legislature in 1967, opponents to anticruelty legislation stated that the use of the bucking strap, a pain-inflicting device that is strapped against the genitals of rodeo horses and bulls to induce frantic jumping, is "just like fastening a girdle for a couple of minutes on a South Seas maiden." Electric prods, used to torment bulls and horses and to send them wildly bolting from chutes, were defended as minor irritants, "like sticking your wife with a pin."[64] Electric "cattle" prods were also used in the 1960s by police officers in some southern cities against African Americans at civil rights demonstrations.)

Likewise, in the quest for profit, other animals, such as elephants, lions, tigers, and horses, are subjected to cruel treatment in circuses and related entertainment enterprises. Harsh treatment is used to procure submissiveness and to get them to perform tricks and behaviors that are unnatural for them. Writer Amy Blount Achor notes:

> Eye-witnesses report that the training tools at the Ringling Brothers Circus include whips and electric prods. The Washington D.C. Humane Society observed animals traveling with the Ringling Brothers Circus being unloaded and report "callousness and beatings for no apparent reason," "elephants with fresh sores and old scarring appar-ently from hook punctures," "several handlers using their elephant hooks to repeatedly and forcefully beat elephants who were merely walking in line," and animals "appearing frantic for food and water."[65]

Such oppressive training and handling methods are compounded by horrible liv-ing conditions. "Circuses condemn animals . . . to live out their days isolated in tiny, barren cages or, in the case of elephants, shackled in chains for up to 95% of their lives."[66] Many circus owners, seeking to squeeze as much profit from their exhi-bition as possible, keep the "show" on the road forty-five weeks a year.[67]

Many other animals who are confined for long periods, if not a lifetime, and who are forced to live in conditions unnatural to them display abnormal behavior. Such behaviors are frequently in the form of repetitive movements or pacing, referred to as *stereotypies,* and are an indicator of extreme stress resulting from the loss of control over one's environment.[68] (Such behaviors are also common in humans with disabil-ities who are confined to small, barren living quarters in state institutions.)

Like many humans who strive to break free from confinement and deplorable maltreatment—including famous individuals such as Spartacus, Harriet Tubman, Denmark Vesey, Sitting Bull, and countless others—innumerable other animals (like Whitey, the steer mentioned in chapter 2) have attempted their own liberation. However, their efforts, whether successful or unsuccessful, are rarely recorded in his-tory or even come to public attention. One of the few exceptions occurred when writer Eugene Linden decided to write about a number of orangutans who sought to obtain their freedom:

> And then there is Jonathan, an orangutan now at the Cleveland Metropark Zoo and a master escape artist, and his progeny, who have been escaping from zoos across the

country. Rudi, the orangutan's daughter, followed in her father's footsteps right out of exhibits. She spent some time at Lowery Park in Tampa, Florida, but staged so many escapes and attempts that she was sent back to Topeka where she was raised.

Even as I was in the midst of a series of conversations with one of Jonathan's former keepers in December, 1998, he told me that two days earlier Jonathan's son Joseph had staged an escape from the Kansas City Zoo in Kansas City. . . .

Jonathan adapts his strategies to the situation at hand. Some years ago, when Jonathan was at the Los Angeles Zoo, he was let into a new enclosure designed to give the orangutans more free space. One of the features of the new exhibit was a nice tree in the center of the enclosed area. On one of the first occasions he was let into his new home, Jonathan surveyed the surrounding walls . . . ripped the tree out of the ground, placed it against the wall, and climbed out.[69]

Another exception was Tyke, an elephant forced to live as a "performer" for the Great American Circus. After several efforts to escape "her life, her training, and the treatment she got from her caretakers,"[70] Tyke bolted from the circus arena into the streets of Honolulu on 20 August 1994. "There she enjoyed a few minutes of freedom before she was gunned down. Local police fired 86 shots in their pursuit of Tyke. She eventually collapsed of her wounds but she was not dead. Officials then administered what was supposed to be a lethal injection. When the injection did not kill her, police fired three more shots at point blank range. Tyke finally died."[71]

Another tragic example of a break for freedom occurred in Oklahoma in 1982 when five elephants held by the Carson & Barnes circus fled their imprisonment. All were "recovered," except one who ran over a cliff and plunged to his death.

In September 2000, a group of 115 cows to be used in a rodeo exhibition "busted out" of a holding pen at the Franklin County, Ohio, fairgrounds and sought sanctuary in the surrounding, largely suburban, area. Sixty-seven of those fleeing imprisonment were killed by a speeding freight train. Many of those who survived eluded the police (and local *cowboys*) for weeks—some for months. In February 2001, trained dogs were used to track the four remaining cows who had struggled so hard for their liberty. Three were finally flushed out of a thicket, leaving one still clinging precariously to her freedom.[72]

Rodeos and circuses are frequently marketed to appeal to children, and in many cases promoters link the exhibitions with the care of children who are ill. It is not surprising that, under capitalism, rodeos and circuses are promoted as wholesome family entertainment, while children who need health care are portrayed as cute but pitiful unfortunates rather than as individuals with a right to health care—a right not recognized in the United States. The United States is the only Western industrial democracy that refuses to provide health care for all humans. It is important to note that the health care problems of many "crippled" and sick children can often be traced to automobile accidents, lack of prenatal care, malnutrition, exposure to harmful chemicals, and similar consequences of corporate dictatorial control of the economy, social stratification, and systematic exploitation. Real improvement in the overall health of our children would require a significant redistribution of societal resources and a similar adjustment in national economic priorities, shifts that do not benefit the economically powerful. Instead, inadequate funds for "needy children" are supplemented, in part, through admission fees paid to witness abuse and exploitation of other animals. Organizations such as the Elks, Shriners, Jaycees, American Legion, and Lions Club often sponsor rodeos and circuses to raise funds for causes such as children's charities—although these local charities and other causes usually receive a small fraction of circus and rodeo profits. These organizations and their members certainly should not be disparaged for their concern for those without access to health care, but it is unfortunate that the most effective and stable source of revenues they have found under capitalism for these fund drives frequently entails the abuse and exploitation of "others." In this particular variation of entangled oppression, human health care needs are used to help rationalize profit taking from the imprisonment and mistreatment of other animals, while the mistreatment of the latter is accepted as a just means to provide "charitable" contributions for "needy" and "crippled" children.

Such institutional oppression of other animals for entertainment and economic purposes was the topic of a congressional hearing in 1992. A subcommittee of the Committee on Agriculture of the U.S. House of Representatives heard testimony on the treatment of other animals in rodeos, circuses, zoos, movies, nightclub acts, and similar entertainments. The hearings were impelled in part by an audit conducted by the inspector general of the U.S. Department of Agriculture (USDA), which found that relevant government agencies *did not have the funding* to "insure the humanitarian care and treatment of animals" specified by the Animal Welfare Act.[73] The hearing report, more than a thousand pages in length, gave a glimpse of the magnitude and severity of the oppression of other animals by the entertainment industry. In a brief reflection on the problem, Representative Peter H. Kostmayer states:

> Mr. Chairman, let me give you a couple of fairly recent examples. The first unhappily occurred in North Carolina . . . two lions were kept in a menagerie in a cage 8 by 5, barely one-quarter the necessary size.
>
> Another problem is roadside zoos and these small roadside zoos are a real problem. A bear was fed a steady diet of doughnuts and soda pop, forced to stand in its own waste and human trash. Due to a lack of cleaning his cage, the bear developed serious ulcers on the bottom of his feet.
>
> At the San Diego Zoo, elephants were found to be suffering from foot infections called foot scald due to standing on wood floors in pools of urine and excrement. The zoo erected a barrier so the elephants could not be seen by the public.
>
> In the Toby Tyler Circus, employees constantly tossed ice cold water on a caged chimpanzee until the animal became so enraged that it bloodied its hands terribly on the bars of the cage. In the movie "Sheena," horses were tripped on wires in a fast gallop in what is a fairly common undertaking. In a television movie, "Bluegrass," pregnant horses had labor induced for the purposes of filming a live birth. The result was a premature foal who subsequently dies. In a Dove soap commercial, doves had a string, a cord tied around their feet and were yanked through windows. Trip wires and explosions both were used and resulted in the deaths of many horses in a film called "The Charge of the Light Brigade."

> And finally this phenomena of what is called dancing chickens, Mr. Chairman, in which chickens are placed on a surface which has been electrified and they are required to jump up and down, to dance as it is called, for 15 to 20 hours at a time without interruption. If they stop, the board is electrified.[74]

This congressional "dog and pony show," however, produced few tangible results. Laws intended to provide minimal protection for other animals remain seriously compromised by a profound lack of funds for enforcement and implementation.

Weak and underenforced laws also do little to deter those who seek profits by providing entertainment and gambling opportunities from dog fights. While federal law forbids anyone to "knowingly sell, buy, transport, or deliver any dog or other animal for the purpose of having the dog or other animal participate in an animal fighting venture,"[75] such contests are common. For instance, on 28 February 2000, the sheriff in Preble County, Ohio, raided a dog fight involving participants from three states. The dogs forced to fight for their lives were American pit bull terriers. "The sheriff's office seized 14 vehicles and more than $30,000 in cash, drugs and several firearms as a result of the raid."[76] Of the thirty participants arrested in the Ohio raid, all but four were released on their own recognizance.

While breeding and selling "fighting dogs" and the related clandestine contests and gambling remain profitable, the "cockfighting" industry may well be even more lucrative. The federal law that discourages dog fighting exempts "animal fighting ventures involving live fowl unless the fight takes place in a state where cockfighting would be in violation of state or local laws."[77] Pitting roosters against each other for "sport" remains legal in New Mexico, Louisiana, and Oklahoma and is popular in numerous other countries, such as the Philippines, Guam, and Mexico. Again, economic gain plays a central role in encouraging such practices, and profits can be considerable for those who successfully develop a niche in this oppressive "industry."

> Cockfighting classes, instructional videos and books, newsletters and magazines help fuel a subculture and enterprises across the country. More than half the 170 pages of the May [2000] issue of Gamecock, a 62-year-old monthly magazine that claims 16,000 subscribers, are advertisements intended for cockfighters. Breeders from Connecticut to California offer proven winners for $1,000, uncontested cocks for $75 to $300, and a dozen eggs of winners' mother hens for $100 to $200. . . .
>
> Through the advertisements and feedstores, a score of manufacturers sell gaffs and a wide variety of curved, razor-sharp knives, up to three inches long, for mounting on legs. The knives, costing up to $100 . . . rip as well as pierce. . . .
>
> No one knows the full dimensions of this business. Sandy C. Johnson, an Ohio breeder who is director of administration for the United Gamefowl Breeders Association, with affiliates in 33 states, . . . said cockfighting generated hundreds of millions of dollars a year in sales of birds, medicines, feed and breeding and fighting gear.
>
> And Mark Urbanowsky, president of Blue Bonnet Feeds in Ardmore, Okla., said he and his competitors sold fighting-cock feed worth $25 million a year to stores in Oklahoma alone. . . .

[O]pposition to cockfighting has become dicey. Cockfighters contribute to political campaigns, and, like most Oklahoma officeholders, Gov. Frank Keating, a Republican, has been staying out of the dispute.

"He really has not taken a position," said John Cox, a spokesman for Mr. Keating. "I don't think he sees a lot of merit in cockfighting, but there is a lot of business interests in the state that have to be adhered to a little bit."[78]

Another form of economically driven "entertainment" that costs other animals their very lives is hunting. Licensed hunters—about 7 percent of the population—kill roughly 164 million other animals every year.[79] While some forms of subsistence hunting continue to be used by groups of humans around the world, most who hunt other animals in the United States do so for recreation and for trophies, not out of economic necessity. Obviously, speciesist and patriarchal attitudes about other animals play an important role in this appalling form of entertainment; however, a vast "sportsmen's" industry also encourages and fuels both these attitudes and hunting practices. For example, gun manufacturers like Remington, Smith & Wesson, Browning, Barretta USA, and Colt heavily promote sales of their weapons and ammunition. Their products are not confined to killing other animals but are used in the killing of humans as well, a fact that has begun to spawn numerous lawsuits against the gun industry. Countless retail "sporting goods" businesses, such as Cabela's Inc., rely heavily on the sale of guns and other "sportsmen's" accessories. Cabela's even produces and sponsors a nationally syndicated television program designed to promote interest and participation in hunting other animals. The hunting-related industry is so vast that 1,400 companies participated in the 1999 Shooting, Hunting and Outdoor Trade (SHOT) Show, filling the 950,000-square-foot World Congress Center in Atlanta. According to one hunting enthusiast, "An outdoorsman visiting the . . . SHOT Show for the first time might think he'd died and went to a special place in heaven full of great toys just for hunters and shooters."[80]

Recognizing the profit to be made by promoting and selling guns and hunting accessories, midwestern grocery and retail giant Meijer—which, not incidentally, has built discount superstores that squeeze out smaller competitors and result in greater economic concentration—is seeking to increase its hold on the "outdoorsmen" market by producing and distributing free to its customers its own hunting magazine, *Lake 'n Trail*. Meijer's *Lake 'n Trail* is actually more catalog than magazine. It wraps ads for "sportsmen's" products with "exciting" hunting stories and features on how to hunt successfully.

State departments of wildlife also promote hunting, in part because many such agencies are funded by the sale of hunting licenses and permits.

Like the "fur" industry, some defend hunting on the grounds that it makes substantial contributions to state and local economies. For example, in his book *In Defense of Hunting*, James A. Swan notes the economic benefits hunting brings to northern Michigan. "Each November," he writes, "nearly a million men and women dressed in red and orange . . . pump more than $300 million into the local economy, and their license fees contribute more than $14 million to support the Michigan Department of Natural Resources."[81]

In a 1996 press release, the Ohio Department of Natural Resources similarly touted the impact of deer hunting on Ohio's economy:

> Deer hunting is more than pursuing big bucks through Ohio's woodlands, it's about local retailers attracting big bucks from hunters. From the smallest rural carryout to the largest metropolitan area chain retail stores, hunters spend a lot of money. . . . [Hunting] contributes an estimated $200 million to the state's economy, excluding license fees and permits. Ohio deer hunters this year are expected to spend an average of $380 on hunting equipment, clothing, transportation, gasoline, food, lodging, and other items directly related to deer hunting. In addition to these expenditures, deer hunting helps to support more than 6,000 Ohio jobs.[82]

Under conditions of contemporary capitalism, many areas and communities that suffer unemployment and poverty, due in no small part to the priorities, practices, and development decisions of major corporations, seek income by providing recreational opportunities for the killing of other animals. The following excerpt from a 1999 *Wall Street Journal* article by James P. Sterba punctuates the economically driven nature of human killing of ducks.

> Here at the bottom of a vast North American duck funnel called the Mississippi Flyway, shotguns are booming and so, in unprecedented ways, is the duck business. . . .
>
> The duck boom is nowhere more evident than here in Stuttgart [Arkansas], a rice-farming town of about 10,000 situated in bottom land near the convergence of the Arkansas, White and Mississippi rivers. At Bust-a-Duck, Dux-R-Us and other area guide services, the phones are ringing and date books are filling at $125 a morning and up. Pintail Peninsula Lodge, a new $1.2 million "Taj Mahal of duck hunting" over by Bayou Metro about nine miles away, is selling out fast at $350 a day.
>
> This new breed of hunter wants luxury and is ready to pay for it, says Scott Drummond, the owner of Pintail Peninsula. . . . "My customers don't want to sleep in a bunk room for six," he says, showing off his 13,700-square-foot lodge that holds 30 hunters in 16 rooms. Next year his rates are going up to $425 or $450 a day per hunter. Many locals think he's loco.
>
> Stuttgart is a poor region in a poor state. But it has always been rich in Mallards, the most common duck species. And the fortunes of Stuttgart . . . have often mirrored the ups and downs of the North American great duck migrations. . . .
>
> Nationwide, hunters of migratory birds (including ducks, geese and doves) spent about $1.3 billion on hunts in 1996. . . . Since then, the market for waterfowling gear and trips has surged as a brisk economy has thickened hunters' wallets.[83]

Jason Perry, a hunter and entrepreneur from Little Rock, developed a line of upscale duck hunting clothing after seeing privileged humans with disposable income turning to "outdoor sports."[84]

The public generally disapproves of recreational hunting but acquiesces to such killing because they believe some need the "food." The exorbitant prices many "yuppie" hunters are willing to pay to kill ducks, however, belies this assumption. Furthermore, the favorite "quarry" for most hunters in the United States is the deer.

However, by the time a hunter's costs for license, weapons, clothing, and other accessories are tallied, the actual price per pound of deer "meat"—for those who actually eat the deer they kill—is far greater than the price for "meat" at retail stores.

The public also acquiesces to legalized and state-promoted stalking and killing of millions of other animals every year because state officials maintain it is necessary to keep populations of other animals "under control." In the case of deer, for example, state officials claim hunting and killing them is necessary to avoid crop damage, deer–vehicle collisions, and deer starvation. This public position is deceptive and manipulative. Like many other animals who were annihilated in the face of human expansionism, deer would largely have disappeared from the modern landscape were it not for the efforts of state officials who manage deer populations and deliberately cultivate their large numbers to increase opportunities for hunters. Through their management of tens of thousands of acres of *game* preserves—euphemistically called *wildlife* preserves—the states create and nurture the habitat required to support large deer populations. State wildlife officials cultivate deer food plots in these regions, and some permit farmers to plant and harvest crops in wildlife areas, provided they leave a sizable portion for the deer. When hunters' plundering of deer decreases the populations, state wildlife officials will set conservative "bag" limits for a few years to permit the regeneration of large populations. Motivated by the need to generate hunting license fees that fund their agencies and by a perceived need to promote hunting-related businesses, seasonal tourism revenues, and related economic activity, state wildlife officials cultivate not only large deer populations but also misinformation when they purport to manage animal populations in other animals' and the public's interest. Meanwhile, millions of deer are ruthlessly stalked and killed each year, and many humans are disabled or killed when their automobiles strike deer. In Ohio alone, more than 40 humans were killed and 23,196 injured in deer/automobile accidents between January 1988 and December 2000.[85]

Just as an enormous number of other animals are killed by hunters in the United States each year, killing encouraged and promoted in large part to enhance profit taking, many millions more are killed in, or for use in, classrooms and university, military, and corporate laboratories. Additionally, like hunting, profit taking underlies the tortured deaths of countless other animals, all for a cause that provides very little material benefit to most humans.

Estimates of the number of other animals used as tools of research vary widely. In 1986, the United States Congress's Office of Technology Assessment estimated the number used just for experimentation was roughly 19.5 million yearly.[86] However, Andrew Rowan of the Tufts University School of Veterinary Medicine estimated that approximately 71 million other animals are used each year.[87]

These other animals, relegated to the position of "lab animal" or "experimental subject," are confined in tiny, barren cages for most, if not all, of their lives and are deprived of the activities that are natural to them. Most never breathe fresh air or experience sunlight. Their profound and torturous deprivations are frequently compounded by painful, invasive surgical procedures, electrical shocks, intentional burns, extreme heat and cold, exposure to toxic substances, deliberately imposed injuries including crushed skulls and vertebrae, and countless other cruelties. Experimentation on other animals is so commonplace that practically anything can be done to other animals as long as the activities ostensibly serve science and humanity—no matter how trivially.[88] The attitudes of many twenty-first-century vivisectionists, their staffs, and their suppliers are not dissimilar from those of the notorious nineteenth-century vivisector, François Magendie.[89] Most are not sadistic individuals; rather, like most others who oppress, they are primarily driven by a desire for professional or financial gain. Amy Achor Mickunas bserves, "Many careers are based on animal research and people in those careers understandably are reluctant to lose their livelihoods. According to the federal Office of Management and Budget, approximately 70% of the millions of dollars allocated for research grants goes towards salaries."[90]

Reflecting on the broader economic and institutional basis of vivisection, Achor writes, "An estimated 100 million animals are used in research every year. That translates into a lot of dollars for suppliers [like Carolina Biological Supply and Wards Biological]. Vested interests such as animal breeders, animal dealers, equipment suppliers, and animal food suppliers obviously have a lot to lose when animal research goes the way of the horse and buggy."[91]

Many animals die in order to test the level of toxicity in new consumer products, products that are often gratuitous and that exist only to satisfy unnecessary and artificial consumer "demand" generated by glossy Madison Avenue advertisements. Philosopher Herbert Marcuse calls this manufactured demand "false needs."[92] As monopoly capitalism began to generate an extraordinary number of unnecessary and wasteful commodities, manufacturers began to test the toxicity level of various chemicals and consumer products, in part to protect themselves from product liability lawsuits. Two of the most nefarious of these product tests, and the underlying economic basis of their use, are described by Lawrence Finsen and Susan Finsen.

There are different kinds of product tests that use animals. Perhaps the best known are the "Draize" and the "LD50." In the Draize (in use since 1944, and named after its inventor) a product is tested for irritability by placing it in the eyes of rabbits (who have been immobilized) and then charting the progressive deterioration of the eyes over three to four days. The irritancy of a prospective product is shown by comparing the degree of deterioration of the eye after a certain number of hours with the known degree of deterioration . . . for such substances as lye, ammonia, and oven cleaner.

The LD50 is a test of "acute toxicity"—it is used to identify substances that have a dramatic poisonous effect in a short time. In use since 1927, the test is conducted by forcing a group of animals—dogs, cats, rodents, and occasionally even primates—to ingest the substance in question in increasingly large doses until the dosage at which 50 percent of the test animals die is determined ("LD50" stands for "lethal dose 50 percent"). Under such circumstances animals do not simply die but suffer enormously beforehand. In product safety testing it is standard practice to withhold analgesics or anesthesia, in case these might interfere with the effects one is attempting to observe.

Both of these tests have been widely regarded for years as essentially worthless in protecting consumers. . . . Neither of the tests provides information about long-range effects or interactive effects of substances with other products or substances. . . . Companies continue to perform the tests in the hopes that this will protect them in cases where consumers are injured by a product and sue the company.[93]

Almost all experiments on other animals purport to produce some educational, safety, or medical benefit for humans, but the necessity and effectiveness of these oppressive practices are highly contested.[94] For decades, antivivisectionist societies have argued against such cruelty, and today advocates and scientists urge alternative education and research activities.[95] Several organizations, such as the Physicians' Committee for Responsible Medicine and the Medical Research Modernization Committee, maintain that animal research is largely inapplicable to human disease and therefore is wasteful and misleading. In a 1997 article in *Scientific American,* physicians Neal D. Barnard and Stephen R. Kaufman argue for more useful methods:

> Researchers have better methods at their disposal. These techniques include epidemiological studies, clinical intervention trials, astute clinical observation aided by laboratory testing, human tissue and cell cultures, autopsy studies, endoscopic examination and biopsy, as well as new imaging methods. And the emerging science of molecular epidemiology, which relates genetic, metabolic and biochemical factors with epidemiological data on disease incidence, offers significant promise for identifying the causes of human disease.[96]

Due to different physiologies of humans and other animals, some chemicals and drugs that may have a therapeutic effect for one species may have deadly consequences for others, including *Homo sapiens.*[97] Vivisectionists working for corporate interests frequently promote a chemical or drug as safe for human consumption when it appears benign in tests on other animals, but then they brush off research findings that indicate *harmful* potentials of drugs and chemicals on other animals as not generalizable to humans.[98]

Once again, such corporate tactics exploit both humans and other animals, and the increased mistreatment of one group compounds the mistreatment of the other. Numerous social critics also argue that the overall approach to health care in the United States is primarily reactive and largely ignores ways to prevent many serious ailments. Indeed, many illnesses of modern life, including some forms of cancer, heart disease, hypertension, diabetes, and even some forms of mental illness, stem in no small part from conditions created and cultivated under twentieth-century capitalism—stressful, overscheduled work lives, polluted air and water, pesticide- and herbicide-laden food, and a diet high in sugar and the flesh of other animals that is pushed relentlessly by the likes of McDonald's, Burger King, and Wendy's. Rather than provide a comprehensive national health care system that focuses on preventative care and healthful lifestyles and diets, corporate-driven biomedical and pharmaceutical industries devote enormous research—and the lives of countless other animals—to finding profitable *treatments.*

The use of dissection and vivisection is defended vigorously by the multibillion-dollar "medical-industrial complex."[99] The industry, of course, asserts that the health and well-being of humans must come before concerns about the treatment of "mere animals." However, the basic motivation of the industry is not to serve humanity, but rather to benefit stockholders. This point is illustrated by way of several examples of the practices, and the human victims, of the pharmaceutical industry—which accounts for approximately 30 percent of all the testing on other animals in the United States.[100]

DEADLY EFFECTS OF THE
PHARMACEUTICAL INDUSTRY

For decades, practices of the pharmaceutical industry have victimized not only millions of other animals subjected to drug and chemical testing but also unwary human consumers. Take, for instance, the case of Marilyn Malloy. In 1973, Marilyn was a seventeen-year-old high school senior, an enthusiastic honors student looking forward to college. The following year, however, while her friends celebrated their commencement, Marilyn died. In 1955, on the advice of her physician, Marilyn's mother had taken the prescription drug diethylstilbestrol, or DES, to avert a possible miscarriage. Considerable evidence suggests that the pharmaceutical firm promoting DES, Eli Lilly, was aware the drug was carcinogenic and posed a danger to fetuses.[101] Nonetheless, DES was aggressively marketed to physicians.[102] Marilyn Malloy died from adenocarcinoma of the vagina (which spread to her lungs), a cancer commonly found in daughters of mothers who used DES. While thousands of lawsuits were filed against Eli Lilly for "enormous psychological damage, profound reproductive abnormalities, cancer, and premature death,"[103] no criminal charges were ever filed.

Such egregious episodes, with their deadly consequences, have been common occurrences in corporate capitalism, and the history of the pharmaceutical industry is rife with instances of the pursuit of profit at almost any cost. As another example, in the 1960s more than eight thousand babies in the United States and Europe whose mothers had taken thalidomide were born with serious visible deformities.[104] Thalidomide, distributed in the United States by Richardson-Merrell pharmaceuticals, was prescribed as a tranquilizer for pregnant women. While the drug was never approved for sale in the United States, it was sold in Europe and physicians in the U.S. were encouraged to give samples to their patients. Reflecting on the production of thalidomide, and similar dangerous drugs, sociologist David O. Friedrichs notes that there was considerable evidence that the company

> had early indications of the drug's [thalidomide] dangers (as well as its limited effectiveness), but the company continued to promote it as an over-the-counter drug until the enormous scope of the harm being done had been widely publicized and they were forced to withdraw it from the market. . . .
> Many other dangerous drugs and pharmaceutical products have been inflicted on an unwitting public. Drugs such as Clioquinol, MER/29, Oraflex, and Selacryn, all devel-

oped since the 1930s for the treatment of such conditions as diarrhea, excessive cholesterol, arthritis, and mild blood pressure, were widely marketed, and in each case
thousands of people suffered devastating side effects, from blindness and paralysis to
death.[105]

Women seem to be disproportionately affected by the unscrupulous practices of
the pharmaceutical industry. In the 1970s Upjohn promoted the use of Depo-
Provera, an injectable birth control drug that prevents conception. After evidence
emerged suggesting the drug was a carcinogen and produced numerous serious side
effects, huge quantities of the drug were dumped on Third World women.[106] Similarly, although A. H. Robbins pharmaceuticals had over four hundred reports of
serious health problems and injuries stemming from use of the Dalkon Shield, an
intrauterine birth control device, the company did not disclose this information to
physicians they had convinced to promote the product. It was not until seventeen
women had died as a result of the Dalkon Shield that it was recalled. A. H. Robbins
then dumped its inventory on women in forty Third World countries.[107] In the
1990s, lawsuits alleged that silicone gel breast implants produced by Dow Corning
(used by more than two million women in the United States) could rupture and
cause serious illness, and that Dow Corning was not forthcoming about the possible
risks to women. According to a 2001 report by the U.S. General Accounting Office,
"more women than men were hurt by dangerous medications pulled off the market
since 1997."[108]

Interestingly, Congress launched a probe in 2000 into "whether drug manufacturers are encouraging consumers to dispose of drugs that remain effective for years
beyond the date stamped on the bottle" (suggesting that the expiration dates "have
as much, if not more, to do with marketing as with science"[109]), while drugs that
actually have expired are frequently sold to the Third World. What is more, many
pharmaceutical companies actually manufacture drugs in countries with minimal
regulation, like Guatemala, where "product registration is rapid and really only a
formality,"[110] in effect creating a vast number of human research subjects only after
the product is on the market. Reflecting on the general nature of the pharmaceutical
industry, David O. Friedrichs observes, "The common element in all these pharmaceutical product cases was that the corporations put the pursuit of profits ahead of
scrupulous concern for the health and safety of the users of their products. Despite
fines, civil damages, and negative publicity experienced by the pharmaceutical companies, they have typically suffered no lasting damage and have continued to operate
profitably."[111]

The pharmaceutical industry thus builds profit on other animals, women, and
humans in the Third World—and increasingly on children. Some medical experts
are calling attention to the "troubling" and growing practice of prescribing "stimu-
lants, antidepressants and other psychiatric drugs" for both preschoolers and older
children.[112] Critics of this growth in prescription drug use maintain "the increase is
disturbing . . . because research on the safety and efficacy of the medications, scant
for older children, is virtually nonexistent for preschoolers."[113] In 2001, Senator

Christopher Dodd characterized the situation in these terms "Only a fraction of the drugs on the market have been tested for safety to children. It's a lot like playing Russian roulette with our kids."[114]

While drug companies aggressively market and promote products that purport to have some therapeutic value for populations who are affluent or have health insurance, they all but ignore the tens of millions of United States citizens who are uninsured or underinsured, as well as the masses of humans around the world with few resources and little power. For example, because of the enormous demand for medicine in Africa (due in no small part to colonialist and imperialist-based disruption and poverty), prices for drugs are higher there than in the United States and Europe. According to Kirsten Myhr, a pharmacist who worked in Botswana and headed a major study on the availability and cost of drugs in Africa, medicines for tropical ailments like malaria "are often available only at exorbitant prices." "Pharmaceutical pricing is about the law of the jungle where might is right. . . . Profit maximization seems to be the only objective of the industry."[115]

Ironically, drugs for tropical diseases such as malaria are vastly cheaper in Europe, where the diseases are virtually nonexistent, than in Africa. According to a United Nations report, even painkillers are scarce in many Third World countries, and "many are left to die in agony from cancer and other diseases."[116] The report noted that the "great disparities" in access to painkillers among the nations, and also within individual countries, were due in large part to "economic reasons."[117]

Furthermore, while drug companies will defend research on other animals as necessary to fight diseases such as AIDS (although advocates of other animals, progressive physicians, and gay rights groups like ACT-UP in San Francisco dispute the efficacy of AIDS research using other animals), the companies are little interested in getting their anti-AIDS products to the millions around the world, particularly in Sub-Saharan Africa, who are infected but are cash poor. In an article written for *The Nation,* John LeCarré, who might be thought to be unfazed by tales of intrigue, corruption, and scheming, describes the real-life pharmaceutical industry's "pitch-dark underside, sustained by huge wealth, pathological secrecy, corruption and greed."[118] "Big Pharma," he writes, "charged whatever they thought an AIDS-desperate Western market could stand: $12,000 to $15,000 a year for compounds that cost a few hundred to run up. Thus a price tag was attached and the Western world, by and large, fell for it. Nobody said it was a massive confidence trick. Nobody remarked that, while Africa has 80 percent of the world's AIDS patients, it comprises 1 percent of Big Pharma's market."[119]

LeCarré also notes that "Big Pharma" prompted the U.S. State Department to threaten Third World governments "with trade sanctions in order to prevent them from making their own cheap forms of the patented lifesaving drugs that could ease the agony of 35 million men, women and children in the Third World who are HIV positive."[120]

Not only has the Western drug industry kept its own AIDS-related products out of reach of those in the Third World who cannot afford them, but it has aggressively defended patent rights to forestall Third World companies from developing generic forms of these drugs. Only recently did thirty-nine drug companies drop a lawsuit in South Africa that sought to block the distribution of generic AIDS drugs, and then only after it had become a "public relations disaster."[121]

On 11 May 2000, in an uncharacteristic, if long-delayed, move,[122] President Bill Clinton issued an executive order to make AIDS drugs available and more affordable in Sub-Saharan Africa. In essence, the order declared that the "United States government will not seek to interfere with countries in that region that may violate American patent law in order to provide AIDS drugs at lower prices."[123] The pharmaceutical industry was strongly opposed to President Clinton's decision and just a few days earlier had successfully lobbied to have a similar statement removed from an African trade bill before Congress.[124] Hoping to recoup the potential loss of profit to be gained from those in the Third World stricken with AIDS, several drug companies then reduced the price of their antiretroviral products for Third World nations in order to increase sales there. "But even with the price cut, a year's supply of drugs still would cost about $1000—more money than most Africans earn in a year."[125]

Humans of color in the United States also have limited access to prescription drugs, particularly painkilling drugs. In a study of pharmacies in New York, only 25 percent of pharmacies in neighborhoods "more than 60 percent nonwhite" said they maintained "enough pain medication derived from opium on hand to fill a typical prescription for a cancer patient." However, 72 percent of pharmacies in areas that are more than 80 percent white could immediately fill such prescriptions. The most frequent reason given by pharmacists for not having enough supplies of the drugs on hand was that there was not enough demand for the "pricey drugs."[126]

Even for the privileged and those with access to health care, the exorbitant price of prescription drugs has become one of the most public health care and political issues of the early twenty-first century. Early in his presidency, Bill Clinton chastised the pharmaceutical industry for the high cost of prescription drugs in the United States; drug prices are higher here than in Europe, despite the fact that many drugs are developed by research subsidized by U.S. taxpayers. Pharmaceutical companies, however, have shown little inclination to hold down the price of their products for those who have subsidized their development with tax dollars. By 2000, consumers in the United States were spending more than $120 billion a year on drugs, and it is estimated that "prescription drug spending will rise 15% to 18% a year for the next five years, doubling the USA's current tab for drugs."[127] In the 2000 presidential campaign, Democratic candidate Al Gore charged that drug companies hurt many in the United States by their "ridiculously high prices for prescription medicines."[128]

In the face of such criticism, the industry responded with more congressional lobbyists and an unending public relations campaign created to counter the negative image the industry has developed with its gluttonous appetite for profit. For instance, in a May 2000 full-page advertisement in the *New York Times,* bought by the Pharmaceutical Research and Manufacturers of America, the industry relied on the clichés and threats of doom long used by big business in response to widespread calls for change. The industry cautioned the public against any government action that could create "more bureaucracy" and argued that proposed price controls "would have a chilling effect on research and development of new medicines."[129] The political advertisement stated that the pharmaceutical companies "vigorously oppose any proposal that would inhibit our ability to discover and develop life-saving, life-enhancing medicines."[130]

Such a statement of concern for humanity is hypocritical at best, in light of the malevolent practices of the pharmaceutical industry just discussed. Moreover, Le-Carré observes that the industry's "excuse that they need to make huge profits on one drug in order to finance the research and development of others" is inconsistent with the fact that they "spend twice as much on marketing as they do on research and development."[131]

Its emphasis on "new medicines" is also misleading, as a great deal of current research and development focuses on the afflictions of the world's privileged populations and as many "new" drugs are simply slightly altered variations of existing products.[132] These drugs are still tested on countless other animals before the manufacturer strikes out in an effort to secure some share of an existing market. A spokesperson at Bristol-Meyers remarks, "If I look at the marketing activities of many of the major companies the trend is to go for large markets such as the treatment of hypertension [high blood pressure] and to say that even if we get one or two percent of that market that is probably the best way to get a return on investment."[133]

Following the capitalist imperative for expansion and growth, many already-gigantic pharmaceutical companies are pursuing mergers, a trend that will result in increased concentration and higher profits for the fewer, even larger firms that ultimately control the industry. For example, in 1999 American Home Products announced its intention to buy Warner-Lambert for $72 billion, to become the world's largest pharmaceutical company. The deal, however, was challenged and thrown into litigation when industry giant Pfizer proposed to buy Warner-Lambert for $80 billion. Pfizer prevailed, finally acquiring Warner-Lambert for $90 billion.[134] Such colossal pharmaceutical corporations, with large shares of the $335 billion global drug market, stand to reap windfalls as long as they can keep democratically supported governmental actions from interfering with their profit taking.[135] In the United States the industry obviously believed its interests would be advanced by the election of George W. Bush, as it poured "millions into his campaign, more than twice the sums it gave the Democrats."[136]

As huge, private, profit-seeking entities in twenty-first-century capitalism, one of the ways in which the pharmaceutical companies have sought to grow still further is by increasing the demand for prescription drugs among those who have some means to afford them. Within the United States, direct-to-consumer advertising has gone a long way toward expanding sales of expensive prescription medications. Although it was once illegal for drug manufacturers to advertise their products unless their ads listed all the possible side effects, recently the Food and Drug Administration relaxed those standards—after vigorous lobbying by pharmaceutical firms. The United

States is now one of only two countries in the world "where prescription drugs are hawked in prime time."[137] Spending $1.7 billion on TV advertising alone in 2000, "Big Pharma" is seeking to repair any damage to its public reputation while exhorting any citizen with the wherewithal to "ask your doctor" for the latest miracle drug. Notably, the fifty prescription medicines most advertised to consumers accounted for nearly half of the $20.8 billion increase in drug spending in 2000.[138] "The remainder of the spending increase came from 9,850 prescription medicines that companies did not advertise or advertised very little."[139] Lisa Belkin writes:

> Direct-to-consumer advertising has paid off handsomely for the pharmaceutical companies—often turning solid earners into blockbuster drugs. After spending nearly $80 million on [allergy drug] Prilosec advertising in 1999 (up from $50 million in 1998), AstraZeneca saw sales rise 27 percent, to $3.8 billion. Pfizer, in turn, upped consumer advertising for its cholesterol drug, Lipitor, by more than $45 million in 1999, and sales of the drug jumped too—56 percent, to $2.7 billion.[140]

Many physicians facilitate the growing trend of "prescription drug abuse"[141] with their acquiescence to the pressures and enticements of pharmaceutical companies. Chris Adams, in an article for the *Wall Street Journal,* reports:

> As the drug industry reaches new extremes in its courtship of prescribing doctors, the giveaways are flowing freely. Nowhere is this on display more clearly than here in New Orleans, where local doctors have lately been given everything from Christmas trees to Valentine's Day flowers, books, CDs, manicures, pedicures, car washes, bottles of wine and cash. . . . And there is the food, offered at the best places in the city famous for its cuisine.[142]

While total direct-to-consumer drug advertising in the United States was estimated at $2.5 billion in 2000 (up from $1.8 billion in 1999),[143] marketing directly to physicians cost the industry more than $4 billion the same year—an increase of 64 percent from 1996.[144] Many doctors do not research the best use of the drugs they are pressured to use, but instead "they have taken a salesman's word for it."[145] Millions in the United States are now paying for expensive drugs they do not need, are using drugs inappropriately or are using medications without full knowledge of the potential side effects. As countless patients become addicted to some of these drugs, and while many even die from their use or misuse, profits for Big Pharma soar.[146]

What is more, pharmaceutical companies and drugstore chains have successfully resisted government monitoring of the distribution of addictive and dangerous prescription drugs. Due to decades of lobbying by drug manufacturers and sellers, only fifteen states have such programs, and those tend to be underfunded and ineffective.[147] As a result, drugs such as the potent painkiller OxyContin (a synthetic morphine), for instance, are overprescribed and abused. Misuse of OxyContin alone resulted in countless overdoses and almost three hundred deaths in the United States between January 2000 and December 2001.[148]

Even in times of crisis, the pharmaceutical companies cannot resist the temptation to promote expensive drugs, no matter how exploitative and even alarmist their efforts may be. After the anthrax scare in the United States following the 11 September 2001 attacks on the World Trade Center and the Pentagon, the manufacturer Bayer A. G. of Germany and its U.S. subsidiaries aggressively promoted the antibiotic Ciprofloxacin (Cipro) as the primary cure; it often was portrayed in the media as the sole treatment for what was feared to be a potential epidemic of anthrax infection. In fact, other, more affordable antibiotics are also effective in the treatment of anthrax—which, even with the bacteria's apparent terrorist use in 2001, remained rare in the United States. The much more expensive Cipro is simply used as an alternative antibiotic for patients allergic to penicillin.[149] Marc Siegel, a physician who volunteered his services during the 11 September 2001 rescue effort in New York, observed, "Bayer, the Cipro manufacturer, is stoking this frenzy and playing into public hysteria by promoting the drug. . . . With the drug industry . . . [continuing] what it knows best, parasitism, we find our dread exploited by a monolith that can't resist an opportunity to make more money."[150]

Largely out of sight—confined to the "dark underside" of Big Pharma—are millions of other animals used by the drug industry, whose existence and suffering are eclipsed by Madison Avenue advertising, their agony entangled with the exploitation of consumers as each form of mistreatment fuels the other.

The pharmaceutical industry's profitable exploitation of the relatively affluent, and the agony it inflicts on other animals and ignores among those in the masses of the impoverished, are actually promoted by the U.S. government. For instance, government agencies support animal experimentation by "funding it to the tune of approximately $7 billion a year."[151] Government grants are a source of both financing and prestige for most research laboratories and individual vivisectionists, who benefit both fiscally and professionally. In addition, the Department of Defense (DoD) itself is one of the largest users of other animals experiencing pain or distress. In a particularly egregious form of entangled oppression, unknown numbers of other animals are killed during routine military exercises,[152] and millions die at the hands of military vivisectionists—killed in experiments and projects in the race for ever more lethal forms of destruction, all to thwart any significant obstacle to capitalist growth and expansion. Writer and activist Phil Maggitti describes some of the government's military experiments:

> The animals in DoD gulags are burned, shot, bled, irradiated, dosed with biological, nuclear, and chemical weapons, assaulted with cannonades of noise, exposed to deadly viruses, and, to add ineptitude to injury, frequently neglected by their keepers. Indeed, says the Physicians Committee for Responsible Medicine (PCRM), "military experiments are as grim as animal experiments can get."[153]

While numerous other economically motivated uses of other animals could be discussed—from dog and horse racing to the tourist-drawing imprisonment of other animals in zoos and aquariums (not to mention the profits derived from the "black market" in rare and exotic species in which zoos participate)[154]—only one more will be discussed in this chapter: the breeding and selling of other animals as "pets."

PETS: PROFITABLE AND DISPOSABLE

Whether it is breeding and selling "purebred" other animals in a family garage or the operation of large "puppy mills" to supply corporate "pet store" chains, the treatment of other animals as a commodity is a familiar sight. Most every discount chain "superstore" has a "pet" department and regularly runs advertisements for birds, fish, turtles, and hamsters, while "pet stores" in malls and shopping centers profit from impulse purchases as expensive—and frequently sick—other animals are charged to credit card accounts. Classified advertisements in almost every local newspaper include columns of dogs, cats, and horses for sale. While many other animals such as dogs and cats are treated as mere commodities, paraded as "registered" and thus extravaluable, today countless other species are captured and bred for fast profits. Most who are captured will suffer and die due to their confinement and ill care. Writing on the economic foundations of the trade in other animals branded "exotics," author and activist Jim Mason writes:

> Thanks to the expanded trade in exotic animals, people who lack the sense to care for dogs or cats are now able, throughout most of the country, to purchase, keep, breed, and sell just about any animal they fancy. Down-and-out farmers, cringing in the shadows of agribusiness giants, are hoping to meet the mortgage by raising ostriches, emus, and rare breeds of sheep, goats, cattle, and horses. Hustling animal trainers and profit-hungry operators of roadside zoos, drive-through game parks, canned hunts, trophy farms, and horn farms are stocking up on lions, tigers, camels, zebras, elk, deer, ibex, eland, and other large, spectacular mammals. Indeed, no form of life is sacred in the exotic animal business, where only two absolutes prevail—profit and the claim of a constitutional right to own whatever animal one pleases—and where every sort of animal is grist for the commercial mill. . . .
>
> Fad breeders operate on the pyramid-scheme principle: those who get into the game early make big money selling breeding pairs to hobby breeders and others with dollar signs for eyes. Once the suckers and dreamers have "invested" their money in animals, the breeders' market dries up, prices fall, and fad animals that once sold for thousands or tens of thousands of dollars are available dirt cheap at auctions. Breeders then move on to create the next hot animal, and so it goes, species after unfortunate species.
>
> Meanwhile, rampant greed has summoned into existence countless numbers of animals no longer wanted by hobby breeders or no longer cared for by sullen owners who have been misled by promises of the perfect *pet*. These animals fall into a "cycle of hell," says Pat Derby of the Performing Animal Welfare Society. Their lives and well-being are threatened by isolation and social deprivation, unsuitable climates, poor diets, inept handling and frequent abuse, and general deterioration. . . .
>
> Although exotic-industry trade journals make a joyful noise about the money to be made in rare and unusual animals—and articles in the mainstream press often read like press releases from breeders' associations—industry officials are sensitive to outside criti-

cism. Presently there is a public-relations effort to legitimize the exotics trade. Industry leaders, in the kind of semantic shell game favored by movements everywhere, are replacing the term "exotics" with "alternative livestock"; and the industry is attempting to counter criticism and reposition itself in the marketplace by claiming to promote conservation and wildlife education. But, says zoological expert and consultant Sue Pressman, people in the exotic animal trade "are to wildlife education as pornographers are to sex education."[155]

While the trade in other animals termed "exotic" is an estimated $100 million-a-year industry,[156] most trade in other animals to be kept as "pets" still revolves around the status-enhancing "purebred" dog and cat. While selective breeding increases the other animals' market value, it also results in a great deal of suffering. Like many others concerned about such practices, veterinarian Michael W. Fox cites some of the health-related implications:

[P]urebred dogs and cats have fundamental genetic defects. These defects can result in lifelong suffering, sickness, and physical handicap—what I have termed domestogenic diseases, or diseases inflicted upon animals by humans.

Certain handicaps may be *deliberately created* by selective breeding and become breed "standards" in purebred cats and dogs. The pushed-in (brachycephalic) face of the bulldog and persian cat are dramatic examples. This deformity makes it extremely difficult for the animals to breath normally. Their protruding eyes and facial skin folds easily become infected. The bulldog's disproportionately large soft palate sets up a negative pressure so that the animal's windpipe may actually constrict, or sometimes even collapse, and the dog is partially and chronically or suddenly completely asphyxiated. . . .

Some of the genetic problems in purebred dogs include dwarfism, giantism, epilepsy, deafness, cataracts, glaucoma, progressive blindness, muscular weakness, progressive renal disease, increased incidence of various forms of cancer and brain tumors . . . hemophilia, hip dysplasia, hysteria, extreme fearfulness, hyperactivity, auto immune diseases, and reduced resistance to infection and disease.[157]

All the while, as entrepreneurs raise large and small breeds and market other animals as profit-making commodities, millions of other animals who once were pets are killed each year because they are no longer wanted or their companion humans were not able to attend to their daily needs.

Finally, many other animals kept as pets die prematurely as a result of a diet of processed "pet foods." Most of these foods, dry and canned, are primarily slaughterhouse "by-products," that is, they contain "4-D" meat, from the bodies of other animals who are "defined by the U.S. Department of Agriculture as dead, dying, disabled, and diseased."[158]

Unwilling to miss an opportunity to squeeze profit from such "resources," corporations package them inside bags and cans with glossy photographs of healthy dogs and cats. James A. Peden observes, "Whole mammal bodies (cows, sheep, pigs, etc.) by the hundreds of thousands, millions of their major parts, and thousands of tons of bird flesh end up in a reject pile. Much of this waste is diseased, and often cancerous. . . . This reject pile is soon on the move as it magically changes into "meat meal" and "by-products" on pet food labels."[159]

In sum, millions of humans and billions of other animals have been cruelly treated and killed because their existence somehow hindered, or their exploitation furthered, the accumulation of private profit—particularly for the affluent and powerful. The level of this mistreatment has grown for other animals under capitalism. The expansionist imperative inherent in capitalism has led to the appropriation of the homelands of other animals, and an anthropocentric and environmentally unsound transportation system has left hundreds of millions as roadside "debris." Countless other animals are fodder for the entertainment, biomedical, and hunting and gun industries.

At the same time, innumerable humans have become inextricably connected casualties of modern capitalism—as exploited workers, scapegoats, unwary and manipulated consumers, and casualties of corporate-promoted warfare. While some advances in human and civil rights have been gained for some groups of devalued humans in some countries, many reforms are far more impressive on paper than they are in real life, where underfunded enforcement reflects the continuation of a group's devalued status. Many have been largely left out of the prosperity that has been achieved in the twentieth and early twenty-first centuries. Indeed, many continue to be used as fodder for capitalist expansion—particularly in the Third World.

The unjust and often terrible fates of most other animals and millions of devalued humans under capitalism have been woven tightly together. For instance, the killing of countless cows, steers, and pigs—cruel killing that was also unsanitary and careless due to the rapidity of slaughterhouse operations, producing "tainted meat"—came at the expense of exploited workers including children and caused sickness and death in many who consumed it, particularly soldiers. "Meat" packers endorsed war because it increased demand for their "products." The increased demand led to increased suffering and death for other animals who were used as food. Thousands were also used as tools of war, as were thousands of human combatants, and both humans and nonhuman animals suffered tragic and horrible deaths, mere pawns in the struggles between economic elites over control of the economic system and the state.

Millions of other animals suffer and die horrible deaths in laboratories as vivisectionists search for more lethal weapons to kill humans or as they test the toxicity of ingredients in products, many of which are unnecessary or redundant. Drug companies hypocritically cite the "public interest" to defend testing on other animals while they knowingly sell dangerous products, sell discredited drugs to the Third World, price questionable medicines so high as to be unaffordable to many, and virtually ignore the need for affordable basic medications of tens of millions throughout the world.

Vivisectionists also need many other animals to test often-unnecessary products that are aggressively and seductively marketed to create and continuously increase consumer demand (further destroying what little remains of the consumer-driven, market economy advocated by Adam Smith). The ever-increasing and unethical manipulation and exploitation of consumers to purchase more and "new" commodities drives even more vivisection and animal testing, much of which functions primarily as insurance against product liability suits. Such oppression of humans and other animals is interdependent, each practice of exploitation enabling the other.

It is too bad Adam Smith is not around to denounce the corporate-dominated global economy, in which multinational business elites essentially have taken on the role of the former monarchical and aristocratic elites whose control of the economy he so criticized. (For that matter, it is unfortunate Karl Marx is not here to critique those systems that have claimed to be built on his visions.) Smith seemingly did not foresee how a largely unregulated drive for personal profit could pervert the system he believed would best serve humankind. The endless, spiraling, and egotistical drive for profits, expansion, greater profits, and even more expansion—while creating some enormous technological capabilities and potentials (which might well have been developed anyway, through a far less oppressive and even humane and just social and economic order)—has come at a devastating price for countless humans and other animals, past and present. Meanwhile, growing ever larger and stronger in the midst of this labyrinthine and intertwined oppression of the twenty-first century is corporate-dominated agribusiness.

NOTES

1. Farley Mowat, *Sea of Slaughter* (New York: Bantam, 1974), 90.
2. Interestingly, that same city council member was a supporter of public transportation when she suggested that the city's homeless population be placed on buses and sent out of town.
3. Gerald Carson, *Men, Beasts, and Gods: A History of Cruelty and Kindness to Animals* (New York: Scribner's, 1972), 89.
4. Carson, *Men, Beasts, and Gods,* 90–91.
5. See J. Allen Whitt and Glenn Yago, "Corporate Strategies and the Decline of Transit in U.S. Cities," *Urban Affairs Quarterly* 21, no. 1 (September 1985): 37–65.
6. Whitt and Yago, "Corporate Strategies and the Decline of Transit," 55.
7. Whitt and Yago, "Corporate Strategies and the Decline of Transit," 57.
8. Amy Blount Achor, *Animal Rights: A Beginner's Guide* (Yellow Springs, Ohio: Write-Ware, 1992).
9. An exception to this trend can be seen in the cases of urban revitalization where government-subsidized efforts are undertaken to "bring back" a "declining" area or neighborhood. In most instances, however, these efforts produce substantial displacement of residents with lower incomes as buildings are rehabbed and then occupied by the more affluent, a process called gentrification.
10. Michael Harrington, *Socialism* (New York: Saturday Review, 1972), 313.
11. Harrington, *Socialism,* 313–14.
12. Douglas F. Dowd, *The Twisted Dream: Capitalist Development in the United States since 1776* (Cambridge, Mass.: Winthrop, 1974), 36.
13. Howard Zinn, *A People's History of the United States: 1492–Present,* rev. ed. (New York: HarperPerennial, 1995), 301.

14. Zinn, *A People's History,* 301–2.

15. Cited in John A. Garraty and Robert A. McCaughey, *The American Nation: A History of the United States to 1877,* vol. 1, 6th Ed. (New York: Harper and Row, 1987), 244.

16. Matthew Josephson, *The Robber Barons* (New York: Harcourt, Brace & World, 1962).

17. Paul A. Baran and Paul M. Sweezy, *Monopoly Capital: An Essay on the American Economic and Social Order* (New York: Monthly Review, 1966).

18. Mary Beth Norton, David M. Katzman, Paul D. Escott, Howard P. Chudacoff, Thomas G. Patterson, William M. Tuttle, Jr., and William J. Brophy, *A People and a Nation: A History of the United States* (Boston: Houghton Mifflin, 1991), 203.

19. Ben B. Seligman, *The Potentates: Business and Businessmen in American History* (New York: Dial, 1971), 136.

20. The largely untold story of U.S. history from the vantage point of the vast majority of humans involved in it is full of examples of the oppressed who have heroically resisted exploitation and organized for justice. See, for example, Samuel Yellen, *American Labor Struggles* (New York: Russell, 1936); and Richard O. Boyer and Herbert M. Morais, *Labor's Untold Story* (New York: United Electrical, Radio and Machine Workers of America [UE], 1974 [1955]).

21. Dowd, *The Twisted Dream,* 137–38.

22. Boyer and Morais, *Labor's Untold Story.*

23. Noam Chomsky, *Class War: The Attack on Working People;* from a lecture given at the Massachusetts Institute of Technology in Cambridge, Massachusetts, 9 May 1995.

24. See Walter Lafeber, "McKinley, the Business Community, and Cuba," in *American Expansion in the Late Nineteenth Century: Colonialist or Anticolonialist?* ed. J. Rogers Hollingsworth (New York: Holt, Rinehart & Winston, 1968), 59–67.

25. Zinn, *A People's History,* 303.

26. Kenneth C. Davis, *Don't Know Much about History: Everything You Need to Know about American History but Never Learned* (New York: Crown, 1990), 223.

27. Ronald Takaki, *A Different Mirror: A History of Multicultural America* (Boston: Back Bay, 1993).

28. Paul Popenoe and Roswell Hill Johnson, *Applied Eugenics* (New York: Macmillan, 1927 [1918]), 192.

29. John Dollard, *Caste and Class in a Southern Town* (New York: Doubleday, 1957 [1937]), 99 and 107.

30. Dollard, *Caste and Class in a Southern Town,* 115.

31. Richard Wright, "Uncle Tom's Children; The Ethics of Living Jim Crow: An Autobiographical Sketch," in *Bearing Witness: Selections from African-American Autobiography in the Twentieth Century,* ed. Henry Louis Gates, Jr. (New York: Pantheon, 1991 [1937]), 41 and 42.

32. Leonard Beeghley, *The Structure of Social Inequality in the United States* (Needham, Mass.: Simon & Schuster, 1996), 83; see also Carey McWilliam, *A Mask for Privilege: Anti-Semitism in the United States* (Westport, Conn.: Greenwood, 1975 [1947]).

33. Bob McCubbin, *The Roots of Lesbian and Gay Oppression: A Marxist View* (New York: Norton, 1993 [1976]), 35.

34. James J. Dowd, *Stratification among the Aged* (Monterey, Calif.: Brooks/Cole, 1980), 72, 67, and 74.

35. See, for example, Robert W. Friedrichs, *A Sociology of Sociology* (New York: Free Press, 1970).

36. Upton Sinclair, *The Jungle* (New York: Penguin, 1988 [1905]), 39–40.

37. Jeremy Rifkin, *Beyond Beef: The Rise and Fall of the Cattle Culture* (New York: Plume, 1992), 122.

38. Rifkin, *Beyond Beef,* 123.

39. Upton Sinclair, *The Jungle* (paperback edition), (New York: New American Books: Signet Library, 1960 [1905]), 107 and 108; cited in Barbara Mayer Wertheimer, *We Were There: The Story of Working Women in America* (New York: Pantheon, 1977), 224–25.

40. Katharine DuPree Lumpkin and Dorothy Wolff Douglass, *Child Workers in America* (New York: International, 1937), 167.

41. Helen L. Sumner, *History of Women in Industry in the United States* (New York: Arno, 1974 [1910]), 190.

42. See Rifkin, *Beyond Beef,* 93–99.

43. Thorstein Veblen, *The Theory of the Leisure Class* (New York: Penguin Books, 1979 [1899]), 84.

44. Davis, *Don't Know Much about History,* 245.

45. Nebraska Senator George W. Norris, cited in Davis, *Don't Know Much about History,* 245.

46. W. E. B. DuBois, "The African Roots of War," in *W. E. B. DuBois: A Reader,* ed. Meyer Weinberg (New York: Harper & Row, 1970 [1915]), 366 and 367.

47. See, for example, chapter 14 of Zinn, *A People's History,* 350–67.

48. Cindy Myers McNeely, "The War Horses," *The Animals' Agenda* 14, no. 1 (January/February 1994): 29.

49. Arthur D. Morse, *While Six Million Died: A Chronicle of American Apathy* (New York: Ace, 1968).

50. Morse, *While Six Million Died,* 228.

51. Zinn, *A People's History,* 402.

52. Lester C. Thurow, *The Zero Sum Society: Distributions and the Possibilities for Economic Change* (New York: Penguin, 1983 [1980]), 8.

53. Charles A. Beard and Mary R. Beard, *The Beards' New Basic History of the United States* (Garden City, N.J.: Doubleday, 1968), 440.

54. Richard Ben Cramer, "They Were Heroes Too," *Parade Magazine,* 1 April 2001, 5.

55. Cramer, "They Were Heroes Too," 6.

56. McNeely, "The War Horses," 29.

57. John A. Garrity and Peter Gay, eds. *The Columbia History of the World* (New York: Harper & Row, 1981), 992.

58. Reviel Netz, "Barbed Wire," *London Review of Books* 22, no. 14 (20 July 2000): 34 and 35.

59. Fur Information Council of America, *The Fur Industry,* 1998; www.fur.org/furind.html.

60. Fur Information Council, *The Fur Industry.*

61. Harold R. Kerbo, *Social Stratification and Inequality: Class Conflict in Historical, Comparative, and Global Perspective* (Boston: McGraw-Hill, 2000), 23.

62. Albert Deutsch, *The Shame of the States* (New York: Harcourt, Brace, 1948), 81–83.

63. Carson, *Men, Beasts, and Gods,* 57.

64. Carson, *Men, Beasts, and Gods,* 168.

65. Achor, *Animal Rights,* 168.

66. Achor, *Animal Rights,* 169.

67. Laura Dempsey, "Circus Comes to Town: 3 Rings, Clowns and All," *Dayton Daily News,* 26 February 2000, 1B and 4B.

68. Donald M. Broom, "Stereotypies in Animals," in *Encyclopedia of Animal Rights and Welfare,* ed. Marc Bekoff and Carron A. Meaney (Westport, Conn.: Greenwood, 1998), 325–26.

69. Eugene Linden, *The Parrot's Lament: And Other True Tales of Animal Intrigue, Intelligence and Ingenuity* (New York: Dutton, 1999), 139–40.

70. Performing Animal Welfare Society (PAWS), *Everything You Should Know about Elephants* (Galt, Calif.: PAWS, 1995), 30.

71. PAWS, *Everything You Should Know about Elephants,* 30.

72. Jim Woods, "Lone Heifer Still Roams, 5 Months after Escaping," *The Columbus Dispatch,* 10 February 2001, A1 and A2.

73. United States House of Representatives, *Review of U.S. Department of Agriculture's Enforcement of the Animal Welfare Act, Specifically of Animals Used in Exhibitions,* Serial No. 102–75 (Washington, D.C.: U.S. Government Printing Office, 1992), 2.

74. House of Representatives, *Review of U.S. Department of Agriculture's Enforcement,* 22–23.

75. Clifford J. Sherry, *Animal Rights: A Reference Handbook* (Santa Barbara, Calif.: ABC-CLIO, 1994), 135.

76. Margo Rutledge Kissell, "Dog Fight Busted; 30 Nabbed," *Dayton Daily News,* 28 February 2000, B1.

77. Sherry, *Animal Rights,* 135.

78. Peter T. Kilborn, "In Rural U.S. Enclaves, Cockfights are Flourishing," *New York Times,* 6 June 2000, A1 and A28.

79. Achor, *Animal Rights,* 136.

80. Jerry Chiappetta "What's New in '99: A Special Report on Shooting, Hunting and Outdoor Products," *Lake 'n Trail Magazine,* Fall Edition (Grand Rapids, Mich.: Meijer, 1999), 137.

81. James A. Swan, *In Defense of Hunting* (San Francisco: HarperCollins, 1995), 73.

82. Ohio Department of Natural Resources, "Deer Hunting Contributes $200 Million," 1996; www.dnr.state.oh.us/odnr/wildlife/news/archive/deer/deer5.html.

83. James P. Sterba, "Fowl Ball: The Flyaway Is Packed and Revenues Soar in the Duck Business," *Wall Street Journal,* 29 December 1999, A1 and A6.

84. Sterba, "Fowl Ball," A6.

85. Statistic provided to the author by the Public Information Office of the Ohio Department of Public Safety, 1970 Broad Street, Columbus, Ohio 43223, September 2001.

86. Peter Singer, *Animal Liberation,* rev. ed. (New York: Avon, 1990), 37.

87. Singer, *Animal Liberation,* 37.

88. For a brief but well-crafted account, see "Tools for Research," chapter 2 in Singer, *Animal Liberation.*

89. For an example of the treatment of other animals in such settings, see Arnold Arluke and Clinton R. Sanders, *Regarding Animals* (Philadelphia: Temple University Press, 1996), 109–14.

90. Achor, *Animal Rights,* 96.

91. Achor, *Animal Rights,* 96.

92. Herbert Marcuse, *An Essay on Liberation* (Boston: Beacon, 1969).

93. Lawrence Finsen and Susan Finsen, *The Animal Rights Movement in America: From Compassion to Respect* (New York: Twayne, 1994), 17–18.

94. See Robert Sharpe, *The Cruel Deception: The Use of Animals in Medical Research* (Wellingborough, England: Thorsons, 1988).

95. Neal D. Barnard and Stephen R. Kaufman, "Animal Research Is Wasteful and Misleading," *Scientific American* 276, no. 2 (February 1997): 80–82.

96. Barnard and Kaufman, "Animal Research Is Wasteful and Misleading," 81.

97. Achor, *Animal Rights,* 106–7.

98. See Sharpe, *The Cruel Deception.*

99. Finsen and Finsen, *The Animal Rights Movement,* 161.

100. Jerrold Tannenbaum and Andrew N. Rowan, "Rethinking the Morality of Animal Research," *Hastings Center Report* 15, no. 5 (1985): 32–43.

101. David O. Friedrichs, *Trusted Criminals: White Collar Crime in Contemporary Society* (Belmont, Calif.: Wadsworth, 1996), 76.

102. Amanda Spake, "The Drugging Industry," in *The Big Business Reader: Essays on Corporate America,* ed. Mark Green and Robert Massie, Jr. (New York: Pilgrim, 1980), 131–39.

103. Friedrichs, *Trusted Criminals,* 76.

104. Friedrichs, *Trusted Criminals,* 76.

105. Friedrichs, *Trusted Criminals,* 76.

106. John Braithwaite, *Corporate Crime in the Pharmaceutical Industry* (Boston: Routledge, 1984), 258.

107. Braithwaite, *Corporate Crime in the Pharmaceutical Industry,* 258.

108. Lauran Neergaard, "More Women Than Men Were Harmed by Risky Drugs," *Dayton Daily News,* 11 February 2001, 20A.

109. *Wall Street Journal,* "FDA Is Asked How the Expiration Dates For Drugs Are Set," 23 May 2000, B18.

110. Braithwaite, *Corporate Crime in the Pharmaceutical Industry,* 259.

111. Friedrichs, *Trusted Criminals,* 77.

112. Erica Goode, "Sharp Rise Found in Psychiatric Drugs for the Very Young," *New York Times,* 23 February 2000, A1.

113. Goode, "Sharp Rise Found in Psychiatric Drugs for the Very Young," A13.

114. Associated Press, "Pediatric Drugs to Get New Scrutiny," *Dayton Daily News,* Monday, 7 May 2001, 3A.

115. Donald G. McNeil, Jr., "Prices for Medicine Are Exorbitant in Africa, Study Says," *New York Times,* 17 June 2000, A6.

116. Barbara Crossette, "Pain Relief Underused for Poor, Study Says," *New York Times,* 23 February 2000, A5.

117. Crossette, "Pain Relief Underused for Poor," A5.

118. John LeCarré, "In Place of Nations: Big Pharma's Dark Underside," *The Nation* 272, no. 14 (9 April 2001): 12.

119. LeCarré, "In Place of Nations," 12.

120. LeCarré, "In Place of Nations," 12.

121. Molly Ivins, "Pharmaceuticals Adopt Polluters' Tactics," *Dayton Daily News,* 12 May 2001, 10A.

122. L. J. Davis, "A Deadly Dearth of Drugs," *Mother Jones* (January/February, 2000): 31–33.

123. Neil A. Lewis, "Clinton Tries to Expedite AIDS Drugs into Africa," *New York Times,* 11 May 2000, A7.

124. Lewis, "Clinton Tries to Expedite AIDS Drugs into Africa," A7.

125. Jeffrey Goldberg, "Epidemic Proportions," *New York Times Magazine,* 4 June 2000, 27.

126. Denise Grady, "Little Access to Pain Drugs in Some Areas," *New York Times,* 6 April 2000, A24.

127. Julie Appleby, "Drug Spending Will Rise, Study Says," *USA Today,* 14 April 2000, 3B.

128. Peter Marks, "Drug Costs Are Focus of New Democratic Ads," *New York Times,* 8 June 2000, A22.

129. Paid advertisement in the *New York Times,* 23 May 2000, A27.

130. Paid advertisement, *New York Times,* A27.

131. LeCarré, "In Place of Nations," 12.

132. See Sharpe, *The Cruel Deception.*

133. Sharpe, *The Cruel Deception,* 123.

134. "Merck and Schering-Plough to Work Together on Drugs," *New York Times,* 23 May 2000, C10.

135. Daniel McGinn, "Barbarians at the Rx: A Takeover Battle Erupts in the Drug Industry," *Newsweek,* 15 November 1999, 66.

136. LeCarré, "In Place of Nations," 13.

137. Lisa Belkin, "Prime-Time Pushers," *Mother Jones* (March/April, 2001): 32.

138. Melody Petersen, "Increased Spending on Drugs Is Linked to More Advertising," *New York Times,* 21 November 2001, C4.

139. Petersen, "Increased Spending on Drugs," C1.

140. Belkin, "Prime-Time Pushers," 33.

141. Associated Press, "Prescription Drug Abuse Dangerous New Trend," *Dayton Daily News,* 20 May 2001, 6A.

142. Chris Adams, "Doctors on the Run Can 'Dine 'n' Dash' in Style in New Orleans," *Wall Street Journal,* 14 May 2001, A1.

143. Petersen, "Increased Spending on Drugs," C1.

144. Adams, "Doctors on the Run Can 'Dine 'n' Dash' in Style," A1.

145. Jennifer Steinhauer, "That Prescription Drug Trap," *New York Times,* Business Section, 12 May 2001, 12.

146. See, for example, Barry Meier and Melody Petersen, "Sales of Painkiller Grew Rapidly, but Success Brought a High Cost," *New York Times,* 5 March 2001, A1.

147. Melody Petersen and Barry Meier, "Few States Track Prescriptions As a Method to Bar Overdoses," *New York Times,* 21 December 2001, A1 and A14.

148. Petersen and Meier, "Few States Track Prescriptions," A1.

149. Marc Siegel, "Profits of Fear," *The Nation* 273, no. 14 (5 November 2001): 6.

150. Siegel, "Profits of Fear," 6.

151. Finsen and Finsen, *The Animal Rights Movement,* 161.

152. *Dayton Daily News,* "Kennedy Joins Protest in Sea," 19 April 2000, 10A.

153. Phil Maggitti, "Prisoners of War: The Abuse of Animals in Military Research," *Animals Agenda* 14, no. 3 (1994): 21.

154. See Alan Green, *Animal Underworld: Inside America's Black Market for Rare and Exotic Species* (New York: Perseus, 1999).

155. Jim Mason, "The Booming Trade in Exotic Animals," *Animals' Agenda* 14, no. 4 (1994): 20, 22, and 23–24.

156. Mason, "The Booming Trade in Exotic Animals," 20.

157. Michael W. Fox, *Inhumane Society: The American Way of Exploiting Animals* (New York: St. Martin's, 1990), 156–57 and 159.

158. James A. Peden, *Vegetarian Cats and Dogs* (Troy, Mont.: Harbingers of a New Age, 1995), 32.

159. Peden, *Vegetarian Cats and Dogs,* 32.

4

The Growth of Agribusiness and Global Oppression

The United States has the most efficient system of agricultural production in the world. But let me tell you. I sure am glad that I'm not a chicken.

—Ohio "farm animal" veterinarian, 2001

"Let me out! . . . Let me out!" terror-stricken and panicked workers screamed as they pounded and kicked on the padlocked doors and blocked exits of the Imperial chicken-processing plant in Hamlet, North Carolina. On 3 September 1991, a deadly fire broke out during the morning shift, with almost two hundred employees inside. Twenty-five workers, mostly women of color, died in the fire, and another forty-nine were injured.

The morning of the day of the fire began as most mornings in Hamlet, where downtown red, white, and blue banners proclaimed it the "All-American City." Indeed, as in many cities around the United States, decent jobs for members of oppressed groups were hard to come by. Some in Hamlet had found work in the growing "poultry" industry, the largest farm industry in North Carolina. The Imperial plant "processed" chickens for fast-food outlets and restaurants, including Shoney's. According to former Hamlet mayor Tom Smart, "Chickens are very important to us. . . . Chickens have helped us keep going here in Hamlet."[1] However, many of the workers at the Imperial plant loathed their jobs because of the "gore," the "noxious odors," the "heat," the "faulty machinery," the "harassment by white supervisors," and the "unrelenting pace."[2]

Bob Hall, director of the Institute for Southern Studies at the University of North Carolina, termed the poultry industry in the state as "very dangerous and out of control." He said the competitive nature of the industry drove companies to press their workers to work faster in tandem with mechanized equipment.[3] Imperial

101

employees also lamented rigid company rules, particularly those restricting access to lavatories. Mary B. W. Tabor writes:

> Company policy allowed two 15-minute breaks and a half hour lunch break each day. Absence, tardiness or taking extra breaks to go to the bathroom resulted in a warning or "occurrence," said the workers and a policy statement to new employees. If a worker accumulated five "occurrences," it meant dismissal, with no chance of being rehired.[4]

However, workers learned not to make waves, since the area afforded limited employment opportunities and "there were always plenty of other poor people in town who would work the poultry assembly lines if they got the chance."[5]

One of those killed in the fire was Cynthia Chavis Wall. Mrs. Wall was fired from a previous job, one she had held for thirteen years, because of absenteeism when her daughter became sick with pneumonia. Out of desperation she took the $4.90 per hour job at Imperial, but she suffered there—due in part to the strict bathroom rules and "occurrence" policy.

> "[S]he hated it," her daughter said. "She came home with her fingers cut all the time and she said the doors were locked and it was so hot she couldn't stand it." She said her mother's clothes and hair were usually drenched in sweat when she returned to their trailer home each afternoon. "Her pants would be wet all the way down."[6]

The September 1991 fire, caused when vaporized fluids from a ruptured hydraulic line were ignited by a gas-fueled fryer, spread quickly. The plant had only one fire extinguisher, below-standard safety exits, no evacuation plans, no fire drill practice, and several blocked and padlocked exits—ostensibly out of fear that an employee might be tempted to take one of the *half billion* chicken bodies "processed" each year. Most of the dead were found at locked or blocked exits.

As we will see, this tragic incident dramatizes the ways in which the exploitation and hazardous conditions experienced by workers are tightly linked with myriad other harmful and deadly practices of contemporary agribusiness.

THE CONCENTRATION OF AGRICULTURE

In the early 1920s, agriculture in the United States was well on the path toward mechanization and industrialization. Millions of small, diverse, self-sustaining family farms had already been replaced by specialized, commercially driven operations. Tractors began to relieve horses and mules as the primary tools for plowing and hauling. The use of tractors freed tens of thousands of acres of land, once used to produce oats to feed laboring mules and horses, for the cultivation of corn, soybeans, and other marketable crops. By the late 1920s, the United States had a substantial grain surplus, lowering the market value of these plant-based agricultural commodities. As a result, many families were unable to keep afloat financially and were forced to abandon their farms. Meanwhile, relatively inexpensive grain was used increasingly by the "meat" industry as feed for other animals raised for "food," particularly "cattle," as Western grazing lands were becoming depleted. Grain-fed cows and other "livestock" became an important market for grain producers, and the affordable price of feed led to increased consumption of "meat."

Those farmers who did survive fared better with the advent of World War II and the increased demand for food from the U.S. military and war-ravaged countries. Following the war, however, most of those remaining were driven from the land by the economic effects of the rapid increase in farm production known as the "Green Revolution." This "modern miracle" of U.S. agriculture, as agribusiness today touts it, came at a perilously high cost, in terms of not only the suffering of other animals and farm families but also damage to the soil and water needed to produce food.

The goal of steadily increasing production while reducing labor costs—goals set by growing agribusiness corporations and supported by government officials and agricultural scientists—set off a juggernaut of irrational and ultimately destructive developments. Expanded farm operations increased productivity resulting in surpluses that reduced profitability per acre. Farmers responded by further increasing their acreage and striving to maximize yields. However, unlike traditional farming methods, there were now few incentives for soil conservation. Expanded operations required the purchase of large, expensive, oil-guzzling (and polluting) equipment. Enormous modern agricultural equipment is unwieldy and suited for only large fields with straight rows. Use of such equipment, while efficient in the short term, is inconsistent with known soil conservation techniques, such as contour plowing, which are more easily done with smaller, more maneuverable equipment.

Use of large-scale farm equipment contributed to a dramatic increase in topsoil erosion. To further maximize acreage productivity, most farmers also began to plant only the most profitable crops—such as corn and soybeans—and sharply curtailed the traditional, soil-conserving practice of crop rotation. As a consequence, the nutrient-rich and root-friendly topsoil needed to sustain healthy crops has disappeared at an alarming rate. It takes roughly five hundred years for natural processes to create one inch of topsoil. Through contemporary agriculture practices, topsoil is being lost in some areas at the rate of one inch every fifteen years and in other areas at the rate of one inch *every eighteen months.*

Farmers and corporations have held off facing the inevitable consequences of exhausted top soil by using increasing amounts of chemical-based and petroleum-driven fertilizers. Petrochemical fertilizers emit nitrous oxide, which contributes to global warming.[7] Use of chemical insecticides, nematocides (chemicals that kill small worms), and herbicides, as part of the Green Revolution, also relieved farmers of the need for crop rotation and similar practices inconsistent with the short-term pressures to maximize annual yields. In addition to the high cost of these chemicals (usually a farmer's second largest expense, after interest payments), many pesticides and herbicides in use today likely pose physical dangers that are still largely unknown. (That is, the risks are "unknown" in the sense that even though many such chemicals have been associated with illness, birth defects, and deaths, manufacturers and users deflect responsibility and continue to market their products by pointing to the lack of a "scientifically proven" causal linkage between the use of specific chemicals and specific harms.) Of course early generations of the chemicals that fueled increased agricultural production, such as DDT, were eventually recognized as extremely dangerous and pulled from the U.S. market. Other chemical products were rushed to the market to replace them, with little known about their immediate and long-term effects—and almost nothing is known about the compound effects of multiple farming agents on humans and other animals and the environment. Many of the consequences of the questionable use of "miracle" chemicals during the twentieth century have yet to be fully realized.

For example, even though the pesticide DBCP, or dibromochloropropane, was banned from agricultural use in the United States in 1979 due to its links to cancer and birth defects (DBCP is considered the most powerful testicular toxin ever made[8]), the chemical was found in more than two thousand freshwater wells in California by 1984. In 1999 it was found in tap water in nine California counties in concentrations "well above levels considered safe by the state for other cancer causing compounds."[9] "In nineteen communities, bottle-fed infants fed formula mixed with tap water receive a lifetime's "safe" dose of DBCP by their first birthday."[10]

This example points to another monumental cost of the practices prompted by the Green Revolution and the path of agribusiness, the pollution and depletion of rapidly dwindling supplies of fresh water. Contamination of underground water supplies in the United States and around the world, as chemical-based fertilizers, pesticides, and herbicides seep into underground waterways and aquifers, is compounded by agricultural squandering of existing sources of freshwater. Agricultural irrigation, the single largest use of freshwater in the United States and a practice increased by the Green Revolution, consumes an average of 134 billion gallons of freshwater a day.[11] Writer Jacques Leslie observes:

> We face an unassailable fact: we are running out of freshwater. In the last century we humans have so vastly expanded our supply of water to meet the needs of industry, agriculture and a burgeoning population that now, after thousands of years in which water has been plentiful and virtually free, its scarcity threatens the supply of food, human health, and global ecosystems. . . .
>
> The world's supply of freshwater remains roughly constant, at about 2½ percent of all water, and of that, almost two thirds is stored in ice caps and glaciers, inaccessible to humans; what must change is how we use the available supply. . . .
>
> The Ogallala Aquifer, one of the world's largest stores of groundwater, covers 225,000 square miles beneath parts of eight U.S. states, from Texas to South Dakota, and feeds a fifth of the nation's irrigated lands. . . . [I]t is being depleted so rapidly that many farmers who once relied upon it now must rely on rainwater, significantly lowering yield.[12]

In many parts of the world today, fresh water is a *commodity* "more precious than oil."[13] "[N]early a billion people around the world do not have access to clean drinking water,"[14] and countless other animals cannot survive as their homelands dry up. Entire species are threatened with extinction as vast bodies of fresh water disappear.[15] Sensing opportunities for profit, some transnational corporations are pushing for the privatization of control and distribution of the Earth's supply of fresh water.[16]

What is perhaps most dreadful is that a large part of the Green Revolution's dramatically increased agricultural output in the United States and around the world and the accompanying use of freshwater for irrigation have gone into producing "meat." At least 70 percent of the grain produced in Western industrialized countries is sold as feed for "farm animals,"[17] as is more than 70 percent of the grain grown in the United States.[18] The great majority of the fields of corn and soybeans that cover the North American countryside today are used to feed "livestock." The planet's most basic resources, earth and water, are being poisoned and depleted to near-crisis levels in the process of raising billions of other animals solely as agricultural commodities—which are consumed disproportionately by the affluent.

All the while, striving to remain competitive as this cycle spiraled, many farmers borrowed heavily to purchase new equipment, chemical fertilizers, pesticides, herbicides, and more cropland. The increase in production they achieved helped maintain a substantial agricultural *surplus,* beyond what was demanded by the market (i.e., those who could pay for it). The lower prices associated with the surpluses, coupled with periodic downturns in farm commodity values, left many of the remaining farm families unable to repay their debt, forcing many into bankruptcy and vastly reducing the number of family farms. Small farms were replaced by large, capital-intensive agricultural operations, increasingly under corporate control and ownership.

The development of "scientific" (read: "corporate-friendly") farm practices and the growth of giant agribusinesses these practices facilitated reduced the number of farms in the United States from 7 million in 1930 to 1.9 million in 1994.[19] Of the 1.9 million farms remaining by 1994, only 6 percent—125,000—produced the bulk of U.S. food.[20] Seen another way, "in 1900, 50 percent of all Americans lived and worked on a farm. A century later, it's less than 1 percent."[21] The enormous reduction in the number of farms in the United States, caused by the Green Revolution and the inherent necessity of large, for-profit capitalist firms to expand (described by Douglas Dowd in the previous chapter), forced millions of families from their farms into the ranks of the un- and underemployed and devastated countless individuals with businesses in farm towns. Many rural communities were impoverished by the loss of population and economic infrastructure. As one observer put it, "The result is a WalMart-ization of farms. . . . [S]mall farms consolidate into bigger ones, or are bought out or leased by large agribusiness corporations, whose economies of scale put a further squeeze on small family farms."[22] For instance, with the advent of capital-intensive factory farming, the number of pig "producers" in the United States declined from 750,000 in 1974 to 157,000 by 1997.[23] By 1997, only 3 percent of pig "producers" provided 51 percent of all pig "meat" produced in the United States.[24]

Many of the family "growers" of pigs, chickens, and turkeys still in business have been forced to enlarge their operations and are now usually under contract with corporate processors. Most "growers" who raise these other animals do not "own" them "but produce and raise them on a contract basis for fees set by a handful of corporations that dominate the industry."[25] "Growers" must supply the land, pay for the construction of large confinement facilities and assume all the financial risks. According to journalist Mary Lee Kerr, "Many growers have mortgaged their farms to stay in business. When growers complain, the company simply cuts off their contracts, or rigs supplies and prices to drive them out of business."[26]

"Growers" charge that they are often swindled by "food-processing" companies.[27] In Florida, for example, humans who raise chickens for slaughter charged industry giant Cargill with "underweighing birds to cheat them of income" and with threatening retaliation "against growers who organize, take legal action, or contact government agencies with grievances."[28] When "growers" in Texas under contract with Tyson Foods attempted to organize, Tyson "used every word they could think of that would scare farmers" and warned that the effort was the work of "a network of shady characters and organizations."[29]

Such practices are consistent with the reliance of corporate agribusinesses on "efficient" and "cost-effective" ways to raise and "harvest" not just crops but also billions of other animals—*intensifying* the heinous conditions and oppressive treatment of "farm animals." The twentieth-century escalation of the suffering experienced by other animals who are raised to become or to produce "food" first began in the 1950s with the mass production of chickens and the more "efficient" use of "dairy cows." The "intensive production" process is now ubiquitous in all areas of "animal farming." Specially bred, genetically altered and chemically treated to *maximize production,* today billions of these victims of modern capitalist "food" production are tightly packed, row after row, in "confinement sheds" in industrialized facilities called concentrated animal feeding operations (CAFOs). The conditions the other animals are forced to endure in such "total confinement systems" produce severe pathological conditions and behaviors and virulent diseases.[30] Amy Blount Achor writes, "Within the confines of factory farms, animals understandably suffer extreme stress. Overcrowding and the inability to fulfill even basic instincts result in stress-induced behaviors such as cannibalism and self-mutilation. Since these behaviors hurt profits, factory farmers must address them."

To reduce financial costs of stress-induced aggression in chicken and pigs, for example, Achor notes that "farmers instituted the practice of *debeaking,* cutting off the chickens' upper beaks. . . . To prevent pigs from biting off each others' tails—a stress-induced behavior—farmers eliminated the target; they simply cut off the pig's tails."[31]

"Life" in these total confinement systems, so profoundly unnatural and harmful for other animals that it goes far beyond cruelty, results from a quest for profit. For instance, the following passage by Erik Marcus describes the pecuniary calculations involved in decisions about space allotments for pigs.

> Pigs are raised in as little space as possible. For young 250-pound pigs, operators are advised to allow a little more than one square yard of floor space for each animal. The crowding is not just to save space—crowding also reduces feed costs. What most people would consider healthy and natural movement is, to today's pig farmer, expensive and undesirable. A modern pig farmer wants his pigs to stay as motionless as possible—when

a pig walks, the farmer sees costly feed wasted to provide the energy for movement instead of being stored as flesh. . . . When researchers cut floor space given to piglets from .22 to .14 square meters, feed expenses dropped by 10 percent.[32]

It is not unusual for some huge corporate "farms" to hold as many as 60,000 pigs or more than a million chickens, with more than 125,000 chickens in a single building. Many birds and pigs die agonizing deaths as avarice and greed lead to greater crowding, stress, and disease.

Hundreds of thousands of others die trapped in their oppressive quarters when fires, floods, tornadoes, and hurricanes strike. (Some "laboratory animals" experience the same fate. For example, flooding caused by Tropical Storm Allison in the Houston area in June 2001 drowned thousands of caged other animals in a vivisectionist laboratory there.)[33] In September 2000, a tornado touched down on twelve hen barns housing one million chickens at the Buckeye Egg Farm in Ohio. Hundreds of thousands of birds who survived the initial disaster went weeks without food, water or medical care. A small band of rescuers managed to save several thousand individuals and transport them to a sanctuary before Buckeye Egg bulldozed the rubble, crushing hundreds of thousands of birds alive. The rescuers who witnessed this awful tragedy were consoled at least somewhat by seeing the lucky few victims of the tornado—and of Buckeye Egg—experience liberation. Cayce Tracy, cofounder of the sanctuary, commented:

> The moment we witnessed the hens touch the ground at our sanctuary was incredible. It was the first time the hens felt the earth beneath their feet, instead of wire. It was the first time they realized they had wings to flap. To see them enjoying life and celebrating freedom somehow dulls the pain and the horror we experienced while rescuing them from such a horrific tragedy. The several thousand birds we saved are going to enjoy health, happiness, and freedom.[34]

The oppressive, industrialized production of "meat" and other products facilitated recent mass outbreaks of bovine spongiform encephalopathy (BSE), or "mad cow" disease, and "foot-and-mouth" (FMD) disease in Europe, diseases that led in turn to the mass killing of millions of other animals. Contaminated feed (which included slaughterhouse "meal" given to captive other animals to increase their rate of growth) is believed to have caused the outbreak of mad cow—an infection that is lethal to both other animals and to many humans who consume them. Foot-and-mouth disease is not harmful to humans and is not lethal for adult other animals, although it can be for very young other animals; however, the 2000–2001 outbreak in Europe still led to mass killings of other animals infected or possibly exposed to it because the disease reduces the economic productivity of the other animals who are infected.[35] For instance, cows with the disease produce less milk, and pigs tend to lose weight. (Notably, the highly contagious foot-and-mouth disease is spread even more rapidly through modern farms' concentrated living conditions and the national and global economies where farmed other animals and their "products" are shipped long distances rather than being produced and consumed in local communities.)

The outbreak of FMD produced a major constraint on the international trade of other animals and the products derived from their bodies. Hundreds of thousands of other animals in Europe were killed to contain the outbreak and restore consumer confidence in European "meat" and dairy products. Other animals in the position of "wildlife" also fell victim to the disease, which was facilitated by human activity and which is much more of an economic than a health problem. In Ireland, army special forces were called upon to search out and shoot free-living deer and goats who were believed to be potential carriers of FMD.

The mass killing of so many other animals in Great Britain failed to arouse the public, or perhaps simply numbed their sensibilities, until it was reported that a single calf, thought killed in a mandatory "culling," was found alive next to her dead mother five days after her herd was slaughtered. The widely publicized story of the calf, who was named Phoenix, put a face on and made real for many Britons what had been merely a recital of hundreds of thousands of other animals killed. Many rallied in defense of the calf and demanded that her life be spared. The government responded by relaxing the policy of killing other animals on farms that were near infected sites.

The devastating effects of modern agribusiness on other animals, small farms, and farm communities produced huge profits and stimulated the phenomenon known as "vertical integration." By 1980 a relatively small number of conglomerates (business corporations comprising a number of different companies) had gained control of the operations that produced "farm" animals, grain and other "food" resources, the facilities that "processed" these "resources," and many of the businesses and restaurants that sold them. According to Eric Ross:

The degree of vertical integration characterizing not only the meat industry . . . but food processing in general is staggering. Swift and Armour are themselves now subsidiaries of highly diversified corporations—a reflection of the accelerating trend toward corporate concentration, the result of which is that "control of manufacturing assets is lodged in a relatively few hands today." . . . In every specialized sector of food processing, for example, whether bread, cereal, canned goods, or meat, four or fewer companies control 55% or more of the market. . . . Thus, farmers find themselves compelled to deal with a few conglomerates that control seed, fertilizer, farm machinery, and the marketing of grain and livestock. Two companies, for example, DeKalb AgResearch and Pioneer Hi-Bred International, dominate the seed industry; Deere and International Harvester command some 57% of the U.S. tractor market; and Ralston Purina and Cargill, Inc., control the animal feed industry. . . .

The degree of integration in the food industry is partly a matter of conglomerates that have branched out into the diverse phases of food production. Thus, Pillsbury and General Mills have entered the restaurant business (with Burger King and York Steak House, respectively). . . .

[T]he food industry has . . . proven to be a lucrative field for investment by large corporations. In particular, meatpacking and processing, the country's biggest food industry . . . has been so profitable that most major packers have been bought up by conglomerates whose interests are far wider than food alone. Thus, Swift is owned by Esmark, Armour by Greyhound, MBPXL by Cargill, Wilson by Ling-Temco-Vought (which also owns Braniff), Iowa Beef processors—the number one meat packer . . .—by General Electric.[36]

Many humans who do the day-to-day work of agricultural production (like the women at the Imperial chicken-processing plant) and the "caretaking" of the meticulously imprisoned and scientifically tortured other animals frequently are victimized by the same forces and arrangements that have contributed to the unspeakable treatment of the other animals. Many of these workers are now employed by large agribusinesses such as Buckeye Egg, a company that, while bulldozing and crushing chickens at one Ohio facility, was found to be employing thirty-six "illegal" and easily exploitable workers from Mexico and Guatemala at another.[37]

Humans who work in the extraordinarily high-density CAFOs are subjected to hazardous conditions that cause a variety of health problems. The most common are respiratory ailments caused by dust composed of decomposing feces, urine, dander, hair, and feed. Such airborne bacterial dust, called *bioaerosols,* causes ailments of the nose, throat, and sinuses and can contaminate the lungs. According to Kelley J. Donham, a specialist in preventative medicine and environmental health:

> Bioaerosol particles absorb ammonia and possibly other toxic or irritating gases, compounding the potential hazards of inhaled particles. Of the more than 40 gases generated in decomposing manure, hydrogen sulfide, ammonia, carbon dioxide, methane, and carbon monoxide are potentially hazardous gases. . . . Bioaerosol and gas concentrations increase in winter when facilities are tightly closed and ventilation rates are reduced to conserve heat. . . . During the cold season, should the ventilation systems fail for several hours, carbon dioxide from animal breathing and carbon monoxide from heaters and manure pits can rise to deadly levels.[38]

"Growers" commonly dig manure pits, some the size of small lakes, under or immediately adjacent to their confinement facilities. These pits are routinely emptied, a practice that agitates the contents and causes rapid release of lethal levels of hydrogen sulfide. "Numerous cases have been reported of workers and animals dying or becoming seriously ill when hydrogen sulfide levels increased from agitated pits."[39] Accumulated methane gas has even caused explosions.[40]

Studies on humans who work in confinement sheds for pigs found major chronic respiratory problems at two to four times the rate found in control populations.[41] Twenty percent of workers in such facilities experience organic dust toxic syndrome, an acute influenza-like illness, and many have developed debilitating and degenerative obstructive lung disease.[42]

All the while, residents of communities near these huge confinement facilities endure overpoweringly repugnant odors, groundwater contamination, and reckless—and frequently unlawful—dumping of waste. It is estimated that the "poultry" industry alone pollutes fields, streams, and groundwater around the nation by dumping an estimated fourteen billion tons of manure and twenty-eight billion tons of waste water each year.[43] (This high level of contamination compounds the pollution from pesticides, herbicides, and chemical fertilizers discussed earlier.) High levels of nitrogen in this waste kill fish, and streams and wells are contaminated with "bacteria and other pathogens, cancer-causing pesticides such as heptachlor, and residues of arsenic used to control parasites in the chickens."[44] Not only do those living around such facilities experience a major decrease in their quality of life, but many also report "breathing difficulties, burning sensations in their noses and throats, nausea, vomiting, headaches, and sleeping problems."[45]

One resident of an area developed by owners of "mega-livestock facilities" sums the situation up in these terms:

> Many farmers who are hurting financially think that if they contract with corporate agri-business they will be able to make a good living. Many find out too late that they are more like sharecroppers, barely making enough money to cover their overhead costs. Farmers in the past would not raise more livestock than what their acreage would allow for proper manure disposal; in addition, they lived on their farm. Now, most of these mega-livestock facilities are owned by people who do not live nearby. They already know what the smell, and environmental impact is, and they don't want their families to live near it.[46]

Food conglomerates have located slaughterhouses in these same areas, to save transport costs and take advantage of the same "business-friendly" conditions and vulnerable communities and workforces that are already being subjected to their high-density industrialized production methods. Corporate giants such as Smithfield Foods, Tyson Foods, and Cargill respond to worker and citizen complaints in much the same way as they do protests from "growers." They threaten the communities—almost invariably small, rural and economically marginal—with closing the facilities and laying off workers. This tactic was used effectively, for instance, by Tyson Foods in 1988 after residents of Green Forest, Arkansas, complained of groundwater contamination.[47] Of course, such corporate giants also exert powerful control over local and state governments, and lawmakers and government officials are often disinclined to intervene (as we will see in the next chapter).

Corporate cupidity has intensified the abominable treatment of other animals inside slaughterhouses. In the one hundred years since Upton Sinclair exposed to the nation the atrocities of "meat packing," the horrific practices he described have actually worsened. Today, however, the horrors are largely invisible, hidden far from public view in well-guarded facilities, behind barbed-wire fences. Activist and writer Gail Eisnitz gained a rare look at contemporary slaughter practices through interviews with dozens of slaughterhouse workers in the waning years of the twentieth century. She recorded numerous accounts of the monstrous treatment of other animals—from skinning live cows, to sawing off the legs of live pigs frozen to the sides of transport vehicles—with reports of atrocities repeated again and again. One worker described the process:

"It begins at the lead-up chutes when the hogs are brought in from the yards. Two or three drivers chase the hogs up. They prod them a lot because the hogs don't want to go. When hogs smell blood, they don't want to go.

"I've seen hogs beaten, whipped, kicked in the head to get them into the restrainer. One night I saw a driver get so angry at a hog he broke its back with a piece of board. I've seen hog drivers take their prod and shove it up the hog's ass to get them to move. I didn't appreciate that because it made the hogs twice as wild by the time they got to me."

"Don't the hogs get stunned before they go to the sticker?" I asked.

"Management was constantly complaining to us about blown loins," he replied. "They claimed that when the stunner voltage was set too high it tore up the meat. The supervisors always wanted it on low stun no matter what size hogs we were stunning. Then when you got big sows and boars in the restrainer, the stunner wouldn't work at all.

"I yelled so much about having to stick live hogs, the stun operator would double stun them. I'd watch him hitting them two and three times, and still they'd come through conscious. . . . It's amazing the willpower these animals have."[48]

Another slaughterhouse worker told a similar story:

"So the managers knew all about the stunning problem." I said. "Did they ever do anything about it?"

"They'd say, 'That's just muscle reaction, nerves. It's not alive.' I'd say, 'Then why's the damn hog trying to *bite* me? Just how stupid do you think I am?'

"It got to the point where if I had a live hog come at me and I had time, I'd take a lead pipe and beat it over the head until it was knocked out enough for me to stick it. . . ."

"What happens after you stick them?" I asked.

"After they left me, the hogs would go up a hundred-foot ramp to a tank where they're dunked in 140 degree water [a standard procedure in pork processing]. That's to scald their hair off," he explained. "Water any hotter than that would take the meat right off the bones. You stick a live hog, it tightens up the muscles around that slit and holds the blood in. There's no way these animals can bleed out in the few minutes it takes to get up the ramp. By the time they hit the scalding tank, they're still fully conscious and squealing. Happens all the time."[49]

The abhorrent treatment to which slaughterhouse workers are forced to subject cows, pigs, horses, chickens and others induces insensitivity and depravity. Another slaughterhouse worker recalls:

"Sometimes," he said, "when the chain stops for a little while and we have time to screw around with the hog, we'll half stun it. It'll start freaking out, going crazy. It'll be sitting there yelping."

Other times, when a hog would get loose outside the catch pen, he said, he and his co-workers would chase it to the scalding tank and force it to jump in.[50]

Work inside slaughterhouses is horrific and "ghoulish,"[51] and at some plants employee turnover is as high as 43 percent a *month*.[52] According to one observer,

"A meatpacking plant is like nothing you've ever seen or could imagine. It's like a vision of hell." Serious accidents are daily occurrences, such as this story recounted by a former slaughterhouse worker to Eisnitz:

> "How'd you cut your face?" I asked.
>
> Again he touched the scar. "One night I went to stick a hog and it was alive so I let it go. Figured I'd catch it later after it calmed down a little," he explained. "So I stick the next hog, bend down and put my arm on its belly, and suddenly the first one's front leg catches my arm. I didn't think to drop my knife, and when I hit my face, it was just like I stuck another hog. I was wearing a white shirt, suddenly its a red shirt, and my apron's completely bloody.
>
> "The nurse starts wrapping gauze around my face, and about four boxes of gauze later, another worker comes in and tells her he's called an ambulance. She says, 'Get over here and put pressure on his face, we can't stop the bleeding. He hit an artery in his face.'
>
> "The knife cut across my mouth and nose, up the left side of my face, under my eye, and through my eyelid. It took four hours of surgery and a hundred twenty-five stitches to close it up," he said. "That night I asked the nurse for a mirror to see my face. She said no, the doctors said I'd go into shock. When I woke the next day I unhooked the drip from my arm, walked over to the mirror and looked at my face. That was the first time in two years I'd cried about anything."[53]

Agribusiness giants have frequently located their production and slaughterhouse operations in the South. These moves help them to avoid unionized workforces and the modest but still potentially profit-reducing regulations that have been enacted in Northern and Plains states. One group of African Americans in Tillery, North Carolina, formed an organization called Halifax Environmental Loss Prevention (HELP) to resist the growing numbers of confinement facilities established in their community by Smithfield Foods. HELP charges that large agribusinesses such as Smithfield deliberately locate huge confinement facilities in poor, rural communities with large black and Native American populations, groups who have little political clout and whose mistreatment and endangerment are less likely to generate significant public outcry.[54]

Politically weak populations also produce highly exploitable workforces. Just as Armour, Swift, and other "meat" industry giants did one hundred years ago, large agribusinesses today prefer to hire workers who have had little opportunity for quality education, as well as migratory workers and immigrants who are more likely to accept low wages and to tolerate deplorable conditions and less likely to organize into unions, become whistle-blowers, or otherwise make trouble. These corporations shrewdly establish huge slaughtering facilities in areas where poverty levels are high and racism is entrenched. Then they recruit workers from Mexico and other Central American countries, as well as recent Asian immigrants, to intensify division among the workers. Once employed, these workers are exploited by the employers and often also subjected to harassment, threats, and violence by local neo-Nazi or white supremacist organizations.[55]

Perhaps no corporation is more savvy at killing millions of other animals and exploiting devalued humans than Smithfield Foods. Smithfield is the number one killer of pigs in the world, killing nineteen million a year and accounting for 20 percent of the pigs consumed as food in the United States.[56] Smithfield opened a slaughterhouse in one of the poorest regions in North Carolina, an area with an "uneasy racial mix . . . nearly 40 percent . . . Lumbee Indian, 35 percent white and 25 percent black."[57] Then Smithfield recruiters began to "comb the streets of New York's immigrant communities," and word of available work at Smithfield reached to "Mexico and beyond."[58] Some coyotes (immigrant smugglers) delivered undocumented Latino workers directly to the region. Smithfield's profits grew as the company fanned the flames of ethnic conflict within its workforce. Supervisors created stress and tension by keeping the "disassembly line" moving at an impossible pace and then humiliating any worker who could not keep up. Moreover, Smithfield created a workplace ethnic hierarchy by assigning employees' jobs by their "race"— whites get the least stressful and dangerous jobs, while Latinos get the most undesirable.

The divisiveness cultivated by Smithfield naturally helps prevent communication and solidarity among the workers. Recruiting Latino immigrants also deliberately limits the possibility that the workers will organize, as many immigrants are reluctant to support labor organizing efforts for "fear that a union would place their illegal status under scrutiny and force them out."[59] When the United Food and Commercial Workers tried to organize the Smithfield workers in 1997, the effort failed, due in no small part to company intimidation. "When workers arrived at the plant the morning of the vote, they were met by Bladen County deputy sheriffs in riot gear. 'Nigger Lover' had been scrawled on the union trailer."[60]

Suffering, anguish, exploitation, and hatred can produce big profits. In 1999 Smithfield Foods reported sales revenues of $3.8 billion and a net income of $95 million.[61]

Today it is estimated that at least 25 percent of the "meatpacking" workers in the Midwest alone are illegal.[62] "Meat" production in the United States is so entwined with exploitation of devalued workers that a crackdown on the hiring of undocumented workers would, in the words of rural sociologist William Heffernan, "really cripple the system."[63]

THE PROMOTION OF "MEAT"
AND ITS CONSEQUENCES

The focus of agribusiness giants on highly profitable sales of "meat," milk, and egg "products" is based on a longstanding manipulation of cultural practices and consumer preferences.

Earlier in U.S. history, "meat" consumption was much lower than it is today,[64] and pigs were the most widely consumed "meat." However, in the late nineteenth century, large "meat" producers like Armour and Swift greatly increased their production of more profitable "beef. Fat from pigs' bodies, once used as lubricants and illuminants, was being replaced by petroleum, and by-products derived from the skin and other body parts of cows—such as "cowhide"—could fetch far more revenues than pig corpses. Much U.S. "beef," however, was exported for consumption by the privileged in Europe.

In the post–World War II period, when the United States enjoyed economic domination of the Western world, the increased incomes of many in the United States facilitated increased domestic consumption of "beef." New businesses were created, such as White Castle and McDonald's. The industry boosted market demand—through relentless advertising—and capitalized on the increasing consumption of "steers" and "unproductive" cows, particularly in the form of "hamburgers." By 1977, nearly 40 percent of all "beef" consumed in the United States was in the form of "ground beef." Unlike "steaks" and other "choice cuts" of flesh, hamburgers are largely derived from the bodies of grass-fed "steers," as opposed to grain-fed "steers" who produce more desirable "cuts." Much of the grass-fed "cattle" raised in Central America is exported to North America.[65]

Consumption of other animals as food in the United States grew, especially in the latter half of the twentieth century, as agribusiness aggressively marketed the growing supply of "goods." Between 1950 and 1976, the U.S. per capita consumption of "beef" alone more than doubled, from 63.4 to 129.4 pounds annually.[66] Profitable fast food chains flourished as they promoted the growth and expansion of the "hamburger culture." With greater production and consumption of "farm" animals facilitated by the Green Revolution—other animals increasingly being fed grain to facilitate rapid weight gain and reduce "production" time—the use of agricultural land shifted, until about 80 percent of the grain crops were raised to be used as feed for the hundreds of millions of other animals who were exploited for their milk or eggs or slaughtered for their flesh. Today an enormous amount of land in the United States alone, more than 302 million hectares, is used to produce food for the billions of other animals relegated to the social position of "livestock"; of this land, about 272 million hectares are pasture and 30 million are used for cultivation of various "feed" grains.[67]

Increased exploitation of billions of other animals as food is deplorable not only because of the misery of the other animals and the exploitation of agricultural workers but also because agribusiness's self-interested pursuit of short-term profits prevents the development of a rational, sustainable, and ethical form of food production. Jacques Leslie is among those who see the link between escalating "meat" consumption and the destruction of land and depletion of water. He writes:

> Livestock have already grown so numerous that 20 percent of the earth's rangeland has lost productivity because of overgrazing. . . .
>   A ton of potatoes . . . needs 500 to 1,500 tons of water, while a ton of chicken needs 3,500 to 5,700 tons of water, and a ton of beef needs 15,000 to 70,000 tons of water.[68]

A report by a panel of scientists whose work appeared in a 2001 article in the journal *Science* projects an increase in the human population from six billion in 2000 to nine billion by 2050. This increase will "double the world's food demands by mid-century, partly because people in wealthy countries will want diets rich in meat, which takes more resources to produce."[69] The report states that "the projected 50 percent increase in global population and demand for diets richer in meat" by the wealthier world "are projected to double global food demand by 2050." They suggest that, if contemporary forms of agriculture persist, by 2050 the global agricultural land base will have to increase by at least 10^9 hectares of land, resulting in the worldwide loss of forests and "natural ecosystems" in a total area larger than the United States. The displacement, destruction, and death brought on by appropriation of so much of the remaining homeland of devalued humans and other animals would be cataclysmic. The panel writes, "Because of regional availabilities of suitable land, this expansion of agricultural land is expected to occur predominantly in Latin America and sub-Saharan Africa. This could lead to the loss of about a third of remaining tropical and temperate forests, savannas, and grasslands and of the services, including carbon storage, provided by these ecosystems."[70]

Feeding a vastly increasing human population, especially under contemporary agribusiness with its emphasis on "meat" production, would require even greater levels of deforestation, increase desertification (the destruction of soil, rendering it infertile and desert-like), add to air pollution (caused in no small part by the vast amounts of methane gas generated by huge populations of other animals, particularly hundreds of millions of cows), exhaust freshwater supplies, and compound already-critical levels of water pollution. Such wide-scale environmental havoc in the name of food production is likely to leave a large segment of the increased global population undernourished (and leave few life-sustaining resources for future generations of humans and other animals) as long as the agricultural production under capitalism exists to make profits rather than to feed the world.[71] Recall E. P. Thompson's observation on the spirit that sparked agricultural improvements in the eighteenth century under conditions of early capitalism: "[T]he spirit of agricultural improvement in the 18th century was impelled less by altruistic desires to banish ugly wastes or—as the tedious phrase goes—to 'feed a growing population' than by the desire for fatter rent-rolls and larger profits."[72]

Precisely the same observation can be made of agriculture after two centuries of capitalist-based social development. It is as sad as it is ironic that, despite the suffering and social and environmental costs of modern agribusiness methods, there has been little compensating lessening of hunger for hundreds of millions of humans around the world. Indeed, the Green Revolution and capitalist-controlled food production have exacerbated hunger. Modern agribusinesses produce food for everyone who can afford it, not for everyone who needs it.

For example, seeking increasing supplies of low-cost "beef" and "feed," giant U.S. agribusinesses turned increasingly to Central American countries where many "cattle" are now raised and from which "feed" grains are imported at low cost—that is, at low cost to the corporations. Jeremy Rifkin writes:

The increasing demand for beef in post-World War II Europe and the United States spurred renewed interest in the land of Latin America. In the 1960s, with the help of loans from the World Bank and the Inter-American Development Bank, governments throughout Central and South America began to convert millions of acres of tropical rain forests and cropland to pastureland to raise cattle for the international beef market. . . . Much of Central America was turned into a giant pasture to provide cheap beef for North America. In South America the Amazon rain forests were cleared and burned to make room for cattle grazing, largely to supply the beef needs of England and Europe. . . .

At the same time, countries like Brazil are using more and more land to produce feed for livestock. When the land is seeded with soy, far less corn is available for human consumption, resulting in higher grain prices. . . .

Mexico is devoting an increasing amount of its agricultural production to sorghum to feed cattle and other livestock. . . . This in a country where millions of people are chronically malnourished.[73]

Millions of humans in those nations have been forced from their homes and off small, subsistence farms by the economic elite in their countries, who appropriated huge areas of land and supplies of freshwater for cultivating feed crops and the flesh of other animals for export to wealthier nations rather than producing food for their own populations. Frances Moore Lappe and Joseph Collins note:

[M]any of the countries in which hunger is rampant export much more in agricultural goods than they import. It is the industrial countries, not third world countries, that import more than two-thirds of all food and farm commodities in world trade. Imports by the 30 lowest-income countries, on the other hand, account for only 6 percent of all international commerce in food and farm commodities.[74]

Increasingly, then, Third World masses are no longer able to produce food for themselves, and they find it extremely difficult to afford food from countries like the United States. Modern agribusinesses produce food for those who can afford their products, not for those who need them. *Estimates of world hunger range "from 550 million to 1.3 billion,"*[75] *and those affected are disproportionately women and children.*

Interestingly, advocates for both humans and other animals frequently urge that, if privileged humans would only eat "meat" less often, enough food would be available to feed all the hungry humans in the world.[76] Such pleas are laudable; however, they are symptomatic of justice movements that downplay, or are not aware of, the structural forces underlying varying forms of oppression and its effects, including world hunger. Food is produced in capitalist society to generate profit. Unless the millions of hungry and malnourished have the resources to "demand" (i.e., to afford) the surplus food, it would likely be considered a "glut," and production simply would be scaled back accordingly in order to keep prices at profit-producing levels.

The "solution" to global hunger that agribusiness promotes is biotechnology. Biotech-produced crops are genetically altered to do such things as resist weed-killing chemicals and even to release their own insecticides, measures designed to increase yield per acre. Consumer groups and health organizations are deeply concerned about the "long-term health consequences of eating foods that are armed with insecticides and foreign genes."[77] Critics of genetically modified organisms, or GMOs, suspect that agribusiness has deliberately inundated the world market with genetically altered seeds to "pre-emptively settle the question of whether or not to accept biotechnology."[78] (Few, however, are complaining loudly about feeding other animals GMO grain; "the bulk of U.S. grain sold for domestic and international use goes into animal feed.")[79] The plethora of critical problems thrust upon the world by agribusiness practices are thus to be "solved" by further expansion of chemical-based agriculture and genetically modified food (with little known about their long-term effects). Humans and other animals are increasingly left with little choice but to ingest biotech food. Still unanswered, however, is how the hundreds of millions around the world with few resources will be able to "demand" their share of the "brave new" food.

Many humans in the Third World, displaced from land now used to raise other animals or feed crops, have migrated to urban areas to look for jobs—a common historical pattern. There, those lucky enough to find employment are exploited by businesses, including many U.S.–based multinational corporations seeking low-cost laborers, often to work in sweatshops. Ironically, apologists for the exploitation of these workers speak of the much-needed assistance multinational corporations are contributing to the "underdeveloped" economies of the Third World.

Poverty and "underdevelopment" in Third World countries, scholar and activist Michael Parenti observes, is not "an original historic condition" but, rather, the result "of the pillage they have endured."[80] Many in the United States are not aware that the "Communist threats" to the United States from Central and South American "guerilla movements" they have occasionally heard about were, and continue to be, largely efforts by masses of dispossessed humans to regain land that had been expropriated by elites in their countries. The elites used much of the land to raise "cattle," "livestock" feed, and other "cash crops" that are sold to multinational corporations. Such U.S. corporations as Borden, United Brands, International Foods, Cargill, Ralston Purina, and Weyerhaeuser have invested heavily in Latin American "beef" production.

While U.S. corporations had expropriated resources and raw materials, such as cotton, coffee, and bananas, from Central America for decades, the increase in "cattle" raising in the latter half of the twentieth century required much more land and motivated the expropriation of marginal agricultural areas in which countless humans had maintained subsistence plots and tiny farms. Robert G. Williams observes:

> Beef's contribution to instability in Central America was less subtle than cotton's. The beef boom placed greater stress on the rural population than cotton or any other export boom. Coffee, sugar, bananas, cotton, and other export crops had very definite geographical limits outside of which production on a commercial basis was unprofitable. In contrast, cattle could be raised practically anywhere.

With very little starting capital and relatively little effort, ranchers could claim large expanses of land. Physical barriers to cattle ranching were temporary: forests were felled and roads were built. Cotton placed stress on peasants by claiming high-yielding lands from corn production, but cattle competed for the marginal lands as well. Moreover, cattle ranching differed from other export activities in that it offered very little employment for the evicted. . . .

The removal of peasants from lands they had cleared was not always easy. . . . The peasantry did not accept slow death through starvation as inevitable but struggled against the ranchers at every step of the way.[81]

Seeking to protect the United States' "national interest" (read "corporate interest"), the U.S. military and the Central Intelligence Agency (CIA) helped, indeed encouraged, corporate-anointed Central American dictators to ruthlessly smash efforts by tens of thousands of the displaced for political democracy and social and economic justice. Take, for instance, Guatemala, where "less than 3 percent of the population owns 70 percent of the agricultural land, much of it used for cattle ranching."[82] Sociologist Daniel Faber describes the "brutal oppression" that occurred there:

Between 1950 and 1964, . . . Zacapa, Izabal and Chiquimula experienced heavy deforestation and peasant displacement by large cattle ranchers. During this period, pasture acreage tripled in Izabal and nearly doubled in Zacapa. Deforestation was particularly severe along a road running eastward from Guatemala City through the richly forested Motagua River Valley to Puerto Barrios and Matias de Galvez, major beef ports on the Caribbean.

Discontent quickly ripened into rebellion at the edge of the rainforests. By the mid-1960s, as in Matagalpa, Nicaragua, a guerilla organization emerged. Rebel Armed Forces (FAR) formed widespread alliances with desperately poor peasant villages in Zacapa and Izabal to resist the appropriation of their land. . . .

In 1966, at the urging of the U.S. State Department, the Guatemalan government declared these eastern districts a counterinsurgency zone, launching a series of merciless attacks on peasant communities to break the resistance. U.S. supplied-and-piloted helicopter gunships, T-33 fighter jets, and B-26 "invader" bombers armed with napalm and heavy bombs assisted the Guatemalan army in the carnage, killing some 6,000 to 10,000 people between 1966 and 1968.[83]

By 1972, the number of Guatemalans resisting the appropriation of their land and the exploitation of their labor who were killed was estimated to be over thirteen thousand, and by 1976 (the year of the highly celebrated marking of the United States bicentennial of liberation from British tyranny—millions in the United States observed the occasion by barbecuing "steaks" and "hamburgers") the count in Guatemala exceeded "20,000, murdered or disappeared without a trace."[84] Daniel Faber writes:

The "success" of these military campaigns quickly opened up the farms and rainforests found on the "agricultural frontier" to huge cattle ranches owned by landed oligarchs, local and national government officials, and paramilitary personnel. The U.S. trained commander of the counterinsurgency, Colonel Carlos Arana, known as "The Butcher of Zacapa," became one of the largest ranchers in northeast Guatemala and later president of the military government.[85]

Former State Department official (turned journalist) William Blum expands on the nature and extent of U.S. involvement in the extermination of those who were "impediments" to capitalist expansion and profitable "beef" production.

The U.S. Agency for International Development (AID), its Office of Public Safety (OPS), and the Alliance for Progress were all there to lend a helping hand. These organizations with their reassuring names all contributed to a program to greatly expand the size of Guatemala's national police force. . . . Senior police officers and technicians were sent for training at the Inter-American Police Academy in Panama, replaced in 1964 by the International Police Academy in Washington, at a Federal School in Los Fresnos, Texas . . . and other educational establishments, their instructors being CIA officers operating under OPS cover. . . .

The glue which held this package together was the standard OPS classroom tutelage, similar to that given to the military, which imported the insight that "communists", primarily the Cuban variety, were behind all the unrest in Guatemala; the students were further advised to "stay out of politics", that is, support whatever pro-U.S. regime happens to be in power.[86]

Continued expropriation of land by ranchers and would-be ranchers in the late 1970s formed the context of the ruthless massacre in Panzos, Guatemala, described in chapter 1. As Robert G. Williams observed, countless families were forced into marginal agricultural areas after being displaced by the military to make way for "cattle" ranchers. As "cattle" depleted the ill-acquired rangelands, ranchers expropriated the newly settled lands, and thousands of again-dispossessed subsistence farm families—including the Quiche—were subjected to violent and murderous displacement.

The Quiche villagers sent to Panzos by Guatemalan soldiers were confronted by the area's largest ranchers, who joined the military in trapping and slaughtering them at the town plaza. Like the other animals in Hinckley, the inhabitants of the area were obstacles to profitable use of the land under capitalist arrangements. (In much the same way, the quest for cheap "wool" resulted in the murder and displacement of the Native American inhabitants of the Ohio territory in the eighteenth and nineteenth centuries and the subsequent massacre of the other animals at Hinckley; similar incidents have been repeated again and again.) The massacre at Panzos permitted greedy ranchers and military leaders to accumulate more wealth by acquiring or expanding grazing lands to raise "cattle" for export to North America, where McDonald's and Burger King could sell affordable "quarter pounders."

After the massacre at Panzos, many indigenous Guatemalans joined resistance movements, but their overt and ruthless repression continued well into the 1980s, exemplified in the following horrific statement given to Amnesty International in 1982 by a seventeen-year old Quiche woman:

> The soldiers came; we went to the mountains; there we found tree trunks and stones where we hid. A group of soldiers came from behind us. They seized three of us; they took them to the mountains; they tied them up in the mountains and killed them with machetes and knives. There they died. Then they asked me which ones were the guerrillas, and I didn't tell them, so they slashed me with the machete; they raped me; they threw me on the ground and slashed my head; my breasts, my entire hand. When dawn came, I tried to get home. By then I could hardly walk. I came across a girl from our village and she was carrying some water. She gave me some and took me to her house.
>
> The army also seized my 13-year-old brother Ramos and dragged him away and shot him in the foot and left him thrown on the ground. My brother and my parents and my other brothers and sisters had been in the house. The soldiers said "They are guerrillas, and must be killed." My brother saw how they killed my parents, my mother, my brothers and sisters and my little one-year-old brother; the soldiers machine-gunned them to death when they arrived in the village. Only my brother Ramos and I are alive. Our friends are giving us injections and medicines. We can't go to the hospital in Coban. I think they would kill us there.[87]

The calamity visited upon just *one* Third World country, during a single period, represents only a bare glimpse at the international machinations of the U.S. government in the service of corporate interests, in this case in the practices used to acquire cheap "beef."

Much of the horrific violence perpetrated in Guatemala and throughout Central and South America is unquestionably entangled with the oppression of other animals; the more cows raised to be slaughtered for food, the more humans were forced from the land. Ironically, and tragically, some of the tens of thousands driven off their lands in Central America, and their descendants, are recruited for and exploited in slaughterhouses and other "food-processing" operations in the United States. Once here, they are frequently snubbed and harassed by resentful locals, threatened by white supremacists, and sexually exploited by supervisors and managers.

For example, in 2000 W. R. Grace and Company agreed to pay twenty-two women workers from Central America $850,000 to settle a lawsuit alleging egregious sexual harassment at Grace Culinary Systems (a restaurant food-processing plant specializing in soup and "poultry dishes") in Laurel, Maryland. Plant managers and supervisors "engaged in systemic harassment that included exposing themselves, demanding oral sex and touching workers' breasts, buttocks and genital areas."[88] Women who rejected the advances were fired. An Equal Employment Opportunity Commission (EEOC) attorney stated that the harassment had lasted four years and "was one of the worst sexual harassment cases we've seen."[89] In 1999, a major California agribusiness, Tanimura & Antle, agreed to pay $1.85 million to a group of Latino women who complained they were pressured to submit to sexual acts.[90] In 2001, the EEOC filed a lawsuit against DeCoster Farms in Iowa, alleging that Latino women egg packers were raped by supervisors "who threatened to have them fired or killed if they didn't submit."[91] Meanwhile, the EEOC was investigating allegations of egregious sexual harassment of African American women line workers at a Birmingham, Alabama, chicken "processing" plant.[92]

It is important to note that the U.S. food and restaurant industries are deeply grounded in, and profit from, racist, sexist, and classist traditions and practices.[93] The restaurant industry continually uses its considerable political clout to resist any initiatives that would decrease access to "affordable" immigrant labor, to forestall increases in the minimum wage and to fight efforts to expand health care coverage for their employees.[94] Not surprisingly, the industry has been a big advocate of "welfare reform." For example, between 1997 and 2000 Burger King alone has hired more than ten thousand humans subjected to "welfare-to-work" initiatives.[95]

DISEASES OF THE AFFLUENT

While few are aware of the tragic and lamentable costs of the hamburger culture on Third World nations, some have begun to take notice of repeated reports of the consequences to humans' own health of consuming other animals, their milk, and their eggs. Speaking to the increasing level of "meat" and "dairy products" consumed by humans in the United States in this century, Benjamin Miller, Lawrence Galton, and Daniel Brunner write:

> About the year 1900 the average American diet appears to have been composed of 50 percent carbohydrates, 20 percent proteins, 30 percent fats. By 1950, this had changed greatly. Luxury foods were in great supply. As some observers have noted, with dairies churning out vast amounts of milk, cream, butter, and cheese, and with the American youth's taste for them, our youth diet had become "one big milk shake." A little later in life the diet had become "one big beef steak." Thick, marbled steaks had become a status symbol. By 1950, fats made up 40 to 50 percent of the diet.
>
> [Heart attacks were] supposed to be an accompaniment of aging and therefore unassailable. But the age-association notion was exploded during World War II. During the war, physicians began to note heart attacks in relatively young men in the armed forces. They gathered data on 866 cases of heart attack in men aged eighteen to thirty-nine. Most of the men had been in seemingly good health until the very moment of sudden death. Sixty-four of them were less than twenty-four years old; more than 200, all told, were under twenty-nine. Autopsy studies showed typical changes in the coronary arteries. They helped to provide convincing evidence that heart attacks were not matters of advancing age but of advancing disease.
>
> During the Korean War, physicians went a step further. They performed postmortem studies on many soldiers killed in battle. They found clear evidence, when the coronary arteries were opened, that disease was present in these men with an average age of twenty-two. Despite seeming good health, artery disease had begun; in ten percent of these very young men, the atherosclerotic process had already narrowed by 70 percent or more the channel in one or both coronary arteries.
>
> Another fact emerging from more recent autopsy studies carried out on men of all ages is that fatty deposits in the coronary arteries are more common and more severe

than 25 years ago. At age thirty, for example, men have more coronary artery disease now than forty-year-old men did a quarter of a century ago.[96]

More recent studies of children who have died accidentally revealed that "many of them already had some blockages forming in their coronary arteries, especially if their cholesterol levels were elevated."[97]

Numerous agencies and organizations, including the Office of the U.S. Surgeon General, the National Academy of Sciences, the National Cancer Society, and the American Heart Association, have linked high levels of "meat" consumption to such conditions as diabetes, high blood pressure, arteriosclerosis, stroke, and certain forms of cancer.[98] Nonetheless, agribusiness giants continue to promote other animals and their body secretions as food because it is enormously profitable; some of that profit is used to influence public information about the staples of a "nutritious diet" and thus continue high levels of consumption. Physician Edward Taub writes:

It may be hard for you to digest the fact that our basic, earliest learned beliefs about food contribute to the weight and health problems we suffer. . . . In school, one of the first things children learn about food is the story of the four food groups. . . . [A]s interpreted for us by the U.S. Department of Agriculture (USDA), the four-food-group philosophy emphasized heavy meat and dairy intake. These foods, once the image of optimal nutrition, now embody all of our worst eating habits. Our belief in the need for daily doses of meat and dairy in our diets is literally making us sick.

[T]he four food groups were . . . promoted vigorously by the National Dairy Council. We now understand that the four-food-group campaign was more a strategy to bolster the public's view of the dairy and meat industries than a public health message.

In 1991, under pressure . . . by the Physicians Committee for Responsible Medicine, the USDA launched a new campaign based on the Food Pyramid. Although the revised recommendations do emphasize eating more vegetables, fruits, and grains than the original four food groups, the USDA still advocates two to three servings of meat and two or three servings of dairy products daily! . . .

Because of the amount of saturated fat they contain, whole milk and cheese are two of the worst foods to drink and eat. . . . [P]eople whose diets contain little or no meat have notably lower rates of heart disease, hypertension, obesity, lung cancer, coronary artery disease, diabetes, and gallstones. Studies also have shown that a virtually meat free diet lowers cholesterol significantly and, when combined with exercise and stress reduction, can actually reverse artery damage.[99]

According to the USDA, in 1999 total "meat" consumption in the United States amounted to 197 pounds per person (20 pounds above the 1970 level and 91 pounds above the average level for the 1930s).[100] Cheese consumption in the United States increased 250 percent between 1970 and 1999.[101]

The increasing consumption of "meat" and "dairy" products is also linked to the growing problem of obesity in the United States.[102] A 1998 national survey conducted by the Centers for Disease Control and Prevention (CDC) found that 53.8 percent of U.S. respondents reported being overweight.[103] A 1999 CDC study found that the number of citizens considered obese—defined as being more than 30 percent over ideal body weight—was one in five, up from one in eight in 1991.[104]

The U.S. hamburger culture is a plague on the nation's youth. In 1998, the Surgeon General stated that childhood obesity was epidemic. According to the CDC, the number of overweight children increased more than 50 percent during the last two decades of the twentieth century, and the number of extremely obese children nearly doubled during the same period.[105] As Miller, Galton, and Brunner observe, diets based largely on the consumption of "meat" and "dairy" products have serious effects for the young. Children's health care providers are taking notice, particularly of the health problems associated with rising rates of obesity in children. Writer Charles W. Schmidt notes:

> Pediatricians are worried not only about the rising number of obese children but also about the increase in health problems often linked to obesity. William Dietz, M.D., director of the division of nutrition and physical activity at the CDC, says that up to 65% of obese American children ages 5 to 10 now have at least one additional risk factor for coronary heart disease (such as high blood pressure, elevated insulin levels, or increased cholesterol) and 25% have two. New data also shows an alarming increase in the number of children with Type II diabetes, an illness that until recently was unheard of in anyone under age 40 but now is increasingly found in children under the age of 14. Other health concerns potentially faced by overweight kids include asthma, bone problems, and sleep apnea, which is a sudden cessation of breathing for 10-second periods while sleeping.[106]

Meanwhile, the food industry relentlessly strives to increase the consumption of "meat." Many fast-food chains are expanding their sales by offering "supersized" meals. "A traditional McDonald's burger with a sixteen-ounce Coke and a small order of fries carry 627 calories and 19 grams of fat."[107] The new McDonald's "Big Xtra! with cheese" and a supersized Coke and fries carry 1,805 calories and 84 grams of fat.[108] Corporations like McDonald's are increasingly targeting the poor and humans of color—groups least likely to have access to health care or to life-sustaining treatments when they become seriously ill from consuming this "food." Greg Critser writes, "[F]ast food companies . . . have grown more aggressive in their targeting of poor inner-city communities. One of every four hamburgers sold by the good folks at McDonald's, for example, is now purchased by inner-city consumers who, disproportionately, are young black men."[109]

Due to corporate machinations driven by an economic system characterized by greed and an incessant drive for profit maximization, the Worldwatch Institute's 2000 report estimated that 1.2 billion humans, *the largest number they ever reported,* are "underfed and undernourished," while another 1.2 billion are "eating too much or too much of the wrong food."[110] Accordingly, it has been observed that the citizenry of the United States has become the "most overfed, undernourished, and overweight people in the world."[111] Not surprisingly, some vivisectionists are inflicting harm on thousands of other animals in their search for drugs to ameliorate the "diseases of affluence," including drugs that will inhibit the storage of fat in the human body.[112] Such a treatment would enable health-conscious humans in affluent nations to continue, and even to increase, their oppression-based, destructive and poisonous high-"meat" and -cheese diets—so long as they can afford the "antidote."

The USDA (the same government department charged with insuring the humane treatment of other animals in slaughterhouses) combines its harmful dietary recommendations with lax inspection of "meat" products, as we will see in the next chapter. Another health effect of eating "meat" thus stems from the consumption of diseased "food." It is estimated that, in the United States alone, seventy-seven million get sick and five thousand die every year from contaminated food.[113] Activist and writer Micah L. Sifry notes, "The *E. coli* 0157:H7 bacterium alone sickens about 70,000 people a year. Yet Congress continues to turn back efforts to address this grave threat to public health. Since the beginning of 1995, individuals and PACS connected with the meat and poultry industry have given nearly $6.9 million to Congressional candidates and party committees."[114] *E. coli* 0157:H7 infection is especially grave for children, older humans, and those with immune system deficiencies; many of those infected have suffered horrible deaths.[115]

One of the reasons that "beef" is so frequently associated with *E. coli* infections is that many cows are fattened in feedlots on grain diets to speed their growth and increase "productivity." According to a 2001 *Science* article:

> When cattle were fed hay, the concentration of fermentation acids in the colon was low, and virtually all of the *E. coli* were killed by a pH 2.0 acid shock that mimicked the human gastric stomach. However, when cattle were fed an abundance of grain, fermentation acids accumulated in the colon, colonic pH declined, and 10,000- to 1,000,000-fold more *E. coli* survived the acid shock. . . .
>
> Most strains of *E. coli* are harmless, but enterohemorrhagic *E. coli* (e.g., O57:H7) can cause acute human illness. When cattle are slaughtered, carcasses can be contaminated with fecal matter, and hamburger is a source of *E. coli* O57:H7.[116]

Meanwhile, new research suggests that food contaminated with a drug-resistant strain of *E. coli* may well be a new source of urinary tract infections in women.[117]

Growth hormones, antibiotics, and other chemical substances used to facilitate the production of manageable and efficient "biomachines" (a new social position created by agribusiness that renders other animals into an inanimate status)[118] are believed by many critics to pose serious health risks for humans who consume them. For example, due to the concentrated and rapid production of other animals raised as "food," the spread of disease is intensified. Almost half of all antibiotics produced today are used to prevent disease in "livestock";[119] this use accounts for more than twenty million pounds of antibiotics annually.[120] It is believed that, when humans consume the flesh or secretions of other animals, they are consuming antibiotic residues that compromise their own bodies' immune systems and increase the risk of the development of antibiotic-resistant strains of bacteria. Moreover, there is a risk that new bacteria in other animals that are resistant to existing antibiotics could be passed on to humans.[121] According to a 2001 article in the *New England Journal of Medicine*:

The use of antimicrobial agents in any environment creates selection pressures that favor the survival of antibiotic-resistant pathogens. According to the infectious-disease report that was released by the World Health Organization in 2000, such organisms have become increasingly prevalent worldwide. The routine practice of giving antimicrobial agents to domestic livestock as a means of preventing and treating disease, as well as promoting growth, is an important factor in the emergence of antibiotic-resistant bacteria that are subsequently transferred to humans through the food chain. Most infections with antimicrobial-resistant salmonella are acquired by eating contaminated foods of animal origin.[122]

Increasing fears of *E. coli* and similar infections and at least some increased awareness of the health risks associated with "red meat" in particular led to a general decline in the consumption of "beef" in the United States in the latter part of the twentieth century. "Beef" producers responded with an aggressive, pervasive advertising campaign ("Beef: It's What's for Dinner") to boost domestic consumption. Launching a slight remake of its campaign slogan ("Beef: It's What's for Dinner, Tonight"), the National Cattlemen's Beef Association spent an estimated $10 million on the creation and production of two new television spots developed by a Chicago-based advertising firm, the Leo Burnett Company. The commercials feature the voice of actor Sam Elliot and the music of composer Aaron Copland and are aimed at "women 25 to 54, considered by the industry to be the 'gatekeepers' of dinner tables."[123] Between 1994 and 1995, the annual per capita consumption of "beef" in the United States increased by nearly three pounds.[124]

With an eye to the future, corporate retailers blanket both prime-time and children's television programming with hamburger ads. The plethora of hamburger advertisements directed at children are intended both to spark additional profits immediately—families tend to eat where the children will be happy—and to ensure future profits by promoting lifetime consumption patterns. Moreover, the "beef" industry is seeking to increase exports by creating and expanding the hamburger market, and its ill effects, to include the affluent in the Asian Pacific, Third World, and former Soviet bloc nations. Although exports represented only 8 percent of total U.S. "beef" output in 1997, they still generated more than $4.7 billion in sales.[125]

While the consumption of cows as food decreased somewhat in the United States over the past decade, the consumption of pigs has remained solid—due in part to advertising by the National Pork Board and affordable "pork" prices (made possible by capital-intensive corporate farming operations; exploitation of "growers," workers, and communities; and the horrific treatment of millions of pigs every year). In 1987 the National Pork Board pressed its signature campaign, "Pork: The Other White Meat," on the public. In 1996 those raising pigs as food spent more than $15 million on "product" promotion and foreign expansion, with the goal of "continued growth during the next ten years."[126] Indeed, from 1987 to 2000 the production of pigs for food increased 37 percent.[127]

When "pork" prices fell in the mid-1990s, some who raised and sold pigs for a living threatened to shoot the pigs before they would sell them at prevailing rates.[128]

(The financial hardships were suffered largely by contract and family "growers," as many giant agribusinesses posted record profits during the same period.) However, demand for pigs as food picked up considerably in 2000, partly as a result of restaurants increasing the choices for "pork" products on their menus. Sixty-four percent of U.S. consumption of pigs takes place in restaurants.[129]

Prodigious advertising also has helped increase the consumption of chickens and turkeys as "food" in the United States over the past few decades. Since 1960, the per capita consumption in ready-to-cook pounds of chickens and turkeys increased dramatically, from 34.0 to 90.3 per year.[130] Speaking to the increased consumption of turkeys, industry analyst and cheerleader Edward Lotterman gives further insight into agribusiness reality:

> Marketing was key in this process. The high degree of vertical integration in the industry allowed processors to procure birds that were bred with the specific characteristics needed for the new processed products. At the same time, this high level of integration and quality control allowed for the branding, trademarking and advertising of specific turkey products. Unlike beef and pork, where most output is marketed as generic ground beef, chops or roasts, most turkey is now sold under a specific label, one that may be highly advertised. Such trademarking and labeling also lends to marketing efforts for new products, to existing consumers through on-package coupons.
>
> Overall, turkey producers and processors are the home run kings of American meat production. No other meat has experienced such an expansion of per capita consumption or efficiency in production, while maintaining profitability for the now relatively few producers in the sector.
>
> There is only one area where turkey producers may feel some sense of failure—the fast food market. While some turkey is sold as an ingredient at sandwich shops, turkey, like lamb and pork, has yet to achieve a fast food presence on the scale of hamburger, fried chicken or chicken nuggets. But given the stakes, and the ingenuity of the turkey industry, the Big Turk sandwich or its equivalent may soon make an appearance.[131]

Finally, the National Fluid Milk Processor Board has saturated the cultural landscape with the "milk moustache" campaign, in which famous humans—ranging from movie stars to sports heroes—all sport a milk moustache to promote the "wholesome" and "healthy" quality of cow's milk. The campaign was created in part to counter the trend of sugary and adulterated-sugar-substitute-based soft drinks eclipsing milk in the marketplace. "U.S. milk consumption peaked at 32 gallons per person in 1970. In 1999 . . . it was less than 24 gallons."[132] Key to increasing the consumption of cow's milk is boosting its consumption among young people, and "teenagers are considered a critical market for the dairy industry."[133] One of the marketing strategies of the dairy industry is placing flavored milk products in school vending machines, alongside soda machines. The vending machines are decorated with photos of such celebrities as the Backstreet Boys and the Dixie Chicks. The milk products—chocolate, strawberry, and coffee flavored—are high in fat (especially saturated fat) and have as much sugar as the soda.[134]

Consumer groups continually express concern about the safety of cow's milk, particularly the milk produced in today's factory farms. In particular, they are concerned about the hormones used to increase milk production and antibiotics to control related bacterial infections, as these substances are passed through the cows in their milk. Monsanto, for example, sells recombinant bovine growth hormone, rBGH, a substance injected into approximately 30 percent of cows confined and exploited to produce dairy products. Recombinant bovine growth hormone is touted by Monsanto as the "largest selling dairy animal drug in this country."[135] Journalist Jean Akre, writing about an investigative report on rBGH milk for television that was sidetracked by a lawsuit threatened by Monsanto, states:

> I soon learned that millions of Americans and their children who consume milk from rBGH-treated cows unwittingly have become participants in what amounts to a giant public health experiment. Despite promises from grocers that they would not buy rBGH milk "until it gains widespread acceptance," I discovered and carefully documented how these promises were quietly broken. I also learned that health concerns raised by scientists around the world have never been settled, and indeed, the product has been outlawed or shunned in every other major industrialized country.[136]

Recombinant bovine growth hormone is allegedly linked to dead and deformed calves, creates mastitis in cows requiring antibiotic treatments, and is believed to increase the risk of breast and colon cancer in humans.[137]

Aggressive agribusiness promotion of "meat," dairy (including the "Ah, the Power of Cheese" campaign), and egg products ("The Incredible, Edible Egg" campaign) is overwhelming and eclipsing the publicity for reports by the U.S. Surgeon General, the Centers for Disease Control, and other public health organizations warning about the risks of these same products. A report by the USDA notes that humans in the United States "are consuming record-high amounts of caloric sweeteners and some high-fat dairy products, and near record amounts of added fats, including salad and cooking oils and baking and frying fats."[138] According to the Food Marketing Institute, public concern in the United States about fatty diets and cholesterol levels is on the decline.[139] An institute spokesperson suggests that consumers have been "deluged" with conflicting information about proper nutrition and many have reacted by "tuning it out."[140] An Associated Press article quotes a man, munching on a "meat"-and-cheese-stuffed, "croissant-like pocket," who states, "I don't watch my fat intake at all. I like what I buy and I eat it and enjoy it."[141]

THE NEW GLOBAL CAPITALISM: INCREASED OPPRESSION AND DISPARITY

Modern corporate capitalism's imperative for expansion and increased profit prompted the Green Revolution and has greatly concentrated U.S. agriculture and expanded the use of other animals as food—while intensifying their horrific treatment. The expansion and concentration also have depleted and polluted life-sustaining natural resources, increased the exploitation of agricultural and "meat" production workers, encouraged the expropriation of land (and the unmerciful crushing of dissent) in Third World nations, increased world hunger, and indoctrinated millions to consume diets that cause illness, debilitating conditions, and premature death. What is more, contemporary capitalism steadily has increased disparities in income and wealth, both in the United States and around the world. How has capitalism managed to compound already extreme levels of inequality?

As capitalism developed in the twentieth century, expanding corporations began acquiring smaller enterprises or pushing them out of business. As a consequence, people came to rely increasingly on corporations for jobs and goods. Writing in the early 1950s, the sociologist C. Wright Mills observed:

> In the early 19th century . . . probably four-fifths of the occupied population were self-employed enterprisers [many as small farmers]; by 1870, only about one-third, and in 1940, only about one-fifth, were still in this old middle class. Many of the remaining four-fifths of the people who now earn a living do so by working for the 2 or 3 percent of the population who now own 40 or 50 percent of the private property in the United States. Among those workers are the members of the new middle class, white collar people on salary. For them, as for wage workers, America has become a nation of employees for whom independent property is out of range. Labor markets, not control of property, determine their chances to receive income, exercise power, enjoy privilege, learn and use skills.[142]

In his influential book, *The Other America,* scholar and socialist activist Michael Harrington notes that in the early 1960s, between forty and fifty million citizens of the United States were poor, suffering from hunger, inadequate housing and education and enjoying little access to health care.[143] The presence of the "other Americans" was masked in part by media coverage that focused on those who were able to indulge in the "good life," by economic segregation that allowed rich and poor to lead nearly separate lives and even by highway systems that circumvented, if not destroyed, the neighborhoods and communities of the poor—so much so that it took "an effort of the intellect and will even to see them."[144] The masses of the poor, Harrington notes, were disproportionately those who have endured oppression and privation over the centuries—women, humans of color, children, and agricultural workers.

The economic expansion that was created in the United States by World War II (discussed in chapter 3) and its aftermath eventually diminished by the 1970s, as the war-ravaged economies of Europe and Japan realized their inevitable recovery and emerged as global competitors. Many large corporations adjusted to this new age and sought to maintain high profit levels by deindustrializing in this country—moving operations to nations with low wages and poor environmental and health standards—and by merging and downsizing. The effects on the "new middle class" and on workers of these global changes and corporate decisions were profound, producing economic instability and lowered standards of living.

It was in this context that an insecure and dazed public—many of whom were watching their paychecks shrink or even disappear—vented their resentment at taxes. The ensuing tax revolutions of the 1980s, however, largely worked to the advantage of the same affluent segment of the population that benefited from corporate restructuring. Personal income tax rates for those in the top bracket dropped from 70 percent to 28 percent between 1980 and 1987.[145] By 1983, federal receipts from corporate income taxes dropped to an all-time low of 6.2 percent of all tax revenues, down from 12.5 percent in 1980 and 32.1 percent in 1952.[146] And the top rate for taxes on capital gains was reduced to 20 percent, down 29 percentage points since 1978.[147] At the same time, the government drastically cut domestic social programs, including those that provided food, health care, affordable housing, and income supports.

In the face of capital flight and shrinking treasuries, state governments became fiercely competitive with one another (and with Third World countries) for economic development and jobs, offering corporations huge tax abatements and subsidies. Such federal and state policies proved to be a bonanza for the affluent but a disaster for millions of working and economically marginalized citizens. According to Pulitzer Prize–winning investigative reporters Donald L. Barlett and James B. Steele, such pro-corporate government efforts further "rigged" the economy to favor the rich.[148] As a result, between 1977 and 1989, 60 percent of newly created income in the United States went to the wealthiest 1 percent of the nation's families.[149] By the beginning of the twenty-first century, the poorest 20 percent of the U.S. population received only 3.6 percent of money income, while the more affluent upper 5 percent took 20.7 percent;[150] the wealthiest *1 percent* of U.S. households controlled more wealth than the poorest 90 percent of the population.[151] Journalist James Lardner further observes, "In 1979, average family income in the top 5 percent of the earnings distribution was more than 10 times that in the bottom 20 percent. A decade later, the ratio had increased to nearly 16 to 1; by 1999 it stood at 19 to 1. That's the biggest gap since the Census Bureau began keeping track, in 1947."[152] Journalist Shannon McCaffrey writes, "Researchers attributed the widening gap to Wall Street's long running bull market, which favors wealthy investors; lower-paying service jobs replacing manufacturing jobs; and the largely stagnant minimum wage."[153]

The affluent segment of the U.S. population that is the primary beneficiary of the corporate-orchestrated boom economy of the late twentieth and early twenty-first centuries is defined, according to essayist Christopher Lasch, "apart from its rapidly rising income, not so much by its ideology as by a way of life that distinguishes it, more and more unmistakably, from the rest of the population. This way of life is glamorous, gaudy, sometimes indecently lavish."[154]

Meanwhile, many households in the United States have stayed afloat financially with the expansion of two-income households and the widespread use of credit cards and loans. While the average household debt as a percentage of after-tax income in the early 1950s was approximately 33 percent, it climbed to almost 95 percent in 1997.[155] Much of today's consumer debt is in the form of high-interest credit card accounts.[156] In 2000, citizens in the United States owed their creditors $1.43 trillion, not including home mortgages.[157] That debt is more than $5,200 for every human child and adult in the nation, and when the Federal Reserve boosts interest rates, "a growing number of families are likely to face the financial equivalent of drowning."[158]

Decent affordable housing remains an elusive aspiration for many in the United States. Millions pay more than half their incomes for housing or live in dilapidated or substandard structures, and the number without decent and affordable housing has increased since 1991.[159] Concomitantly, in 1997, 16.1 percent of people in the United States, amounting to 43.4 million people, had no health insurance for the entire year.[160] An estimated 108 million have no insurance coverage for dental care, creating what the U.S. surgeon general calls a "silent epidemic" of oral disease, which disproportionately affects oppressed groups due to "economic and social barriers to getting care."[161] Twenty-six million children alone in the United States have no dental insurance—which is not surprising, since nearly one in five children in the United States lives in poverty.[162]

Social activists and scholars concerned about increasing *global* inequality have attempted to alert the public to the plight of many around the world who are victims of twentieth-century economic arrangements. For example, in 1974 a distinguished team of scientists called the Club of Rome issued a report that called attention to global food shortages, human population growth, and disparity in global economic development. They noted:

> Two gaps, steadily widening, appear to be at the heart of mankind's present crises: the gap between man and nature, and the gap between "North" and "South," rich and poor. Both gaps must be narrowed if world-shattering catastrophes are to be avoided; but they can be narrowed only if global "unity" and Earth's "finiteness" are explicitly recognized.[163]

It is not in the nature of capitalism, however, to narrow these gaps, and it has not done so. By 2000, the global population living in poverty had climbed to 1.5 billion—750 million of whom are children.[164] Approximately 3 billion humans around the world do not have access to sanitation facilities, one billion do not have access to safe drinking water and, in 1998, two-fifths who died in the world died prematurely.[165] As noted in chapter 1, these and pages of similar tragic statistics prompted authors of a 1999 United Nations report to declare that "global inequalities in income and living standards have reached grotesque proportions."[166] Such conditions are not the result of "underdevelopment" but of capitalist, colonialist-imperialist policies and practices, arrangements that will only worsen under the "new world order."

Recent changes in global economic organization, couched in such institutions as the North American Free Trade Agreement (NAFTA) and the World Trade Organization (WTO), have further rigged the global capitalist order to the advantage of powerful transnational corporations. Called "the most fundamental redesign of the planet's political and economic arrangements since at least the industrial revolution,"[167] these agreements among the economic elite essentially pry open national economies and coerce them to maintain policies and practices that do not hinder global trade. Nations that establish legal protections for other animals, workers, consumers and the environment are finding that many of these acts conflict with international trade agreements. Ralph Nader and Lori Wallach write:

> Under the new system, many decisions that affect billions of people are no longer to be made by local and national governments but instead, if challenged by another WTO member nation, would be deferred to a group of unelected bureaucrats sitting behind closed doors in Geneva. The bureaucrats can decide whether or not people in California can prevent the destruction of their last virgin forests or determine if carcinogenic pesticides can be banned from their food; or whether European countries have the right to ban the use of dangerous biotech hormones in meat. Moreover, once these secret tribunals issue their edicts, no external appeals are possible; worldwide conformity is required. A country must make its laws conform or else face perpetual trade sanctions. . . .
>
> Best described as *corporate globalization,* the new economic model establishes supranational limitations on any nation's legal and practical ability to subordinate commercial activity to the nation's goals. The objective is to overrule democratic decision making on matters as intimate as food safety or conservation of land, water, and other resources.[168]

This new economic and political order holds little promise for the oppressed. The growing profits of transnational corporations theoretically are supposed to "trickle down" to the "less fortunate" members of humanity––a ruse that apparently is infinitely reusable even as U.S. and global disparities widen. Meanwhile, hard-fought legislative reform efforts (not the least of which have been obtained by advocates for other animals) in all certainty will be challenged and weakened, if not entirely rejected, by the WTO. For example, nations that restrict certain methods of trapping or capturing other animals for sale find that such restrictions are being challenged as obstacles to "free trade." Speaking at a 1996 World Congress for Animals, Patricia Forkan, a vice president of the Humane Society of the United States (HSUS), cited a few examples.

> In 1993 the United States threatened to challenge a Canadian regulation . . . to prohibit our puppy-mill puppies from coming into Canada. The U.S. said wait a minute, that is an unfair trade barrier and Canada backed off. . . . The European Union has a law preventing the use of steel jaw leghold traps in the EU. They also have a law . . . preventing the importation of animal pelts caught in those traps. What's happened? The United States and Canada, in the name of free trade, are pressuring the EU to repeal that law. . . . They want to allow these inhumanely caught pelts to go back into Europe. So the Canadian and United States trade representatives have warned the EU that if they don't change their laws, saying they can't bring these pelts in, they're going to go to GATT. . . . Milk produced with genetically engineered hormones, the EU doesn't want it in, Clinton says if you don't let this milk in, we're going to go GATT. . . . It goes on and on.[169]

Another conference participant, Michael W. Fox, also an HSUS Vice President, gave an impassioned commentary on these new arrangements.

[T]ransnational corporations are using the United States as their operational base. . . . From this base . . . these transnational conglomerates are seeking a monopolistic control over the markets, labor and natural resources of third world countries. The rape and plunder of the earth, and annihilation of indigenous cultures has been given a new name—sustainable development—and it has been sanctified by an entity called GATT (The General Agreement on Trade and Tariffs). GATT has given birth to the World Trade Organization. This new world order of trade and commerce, that Presidents Bush and Clinton worked so avidly to establish, without any environmental or animal protection considerations or concern for human rights, is obviously as nonsustainable as it is socially unjust.[170]

While the new order produces affluence for those who benefit from the system's rapacious drive for expansion and elevated profits, it also ensures the continuation and growth of oppression well into the twenty-first century.

The entangled oppression of groups of devalued humans and other animals is the material fodder for existing and emerging global disparities, exploitation, and violence. What is more, new structurally imposed austerity is prompting millions of individual humans to continue, if not increase, the exploitation of other animals. Countless humans supplement their incomes by trapping, exhibiting, breeding, slaughtering, stuffing, smuggling, and poaching other animals. For example, commercial hunting is on the rise in the world's tropical forests, as other animals are relentlessly pursued, killed, and sold as "bushmeat." As affluent populations in Third World nations are encouraged by transnational corporations to eat "meat," and as the cost of such "meat" increases in these areas, "the international market for food made from wild animals is large, and getting larger."[171] Although all the other animals that live in the tropics are at risk, primates—including gorillas, chimpanzees, and monkeys—are especially imperiled. Suppliers of "bushmeat" frequently are indigenous people who now supplement what is left of their subsistence practices by supplying local markets with "meat." As large oil, mining, and timber companies increasingly invade their homelands, and as more and more land is cleared to raise cows or crops for export to affluent nations, hunting "bushmeat" is—in the words of a timber company executive—"a way for the guy with no income to pick up a buck or two."[172] Moreover, workers employed by mining and timber companies find that "they can make extra money adding carcasses to the cargo."[173] Such practices at the individual level are inevitable in a selfish and profit-driven global economic system that has fostered the Green Revolution, megamergers, corporate flight, sweatshops, child labor, and other problems of the new century.

By the summer of 2001, as many capitalist economies around the world deteriorated, systemic mismanagement and greed pushed the U.S. economy into recession. Predictably, corporations responded by laying off both blue- and white-collar workers by the tens of thousands. Homelessness and hunger increased, especially among the working poor. And, in the aftermath of the 11 September attacks on the World

Trade Center and the Pentagon, the economy faltered even further as countless businesses and workers suffered.[174] Seeing an opportunity to further promote and protect the expansion of global capitalism (with its highly concentrated distribution of wealth and highly centralized control), President George W. Bush and his advisers proclaimed that the goal of the attacks was to weaken the world economy and bring about a collapse of world markets.[175] Congress responded by giving Bush his requested "fast-track" authority to negotiate "free trade" agreements. The House of Representatives promoted an economic stimulus package that, according to a *New York Times* editorial, "was top-heavy with giveaways to corporations and tax cuts to the wealthiest 30 percent of Americans. . . . At a time when the country is being urged to make sacrifices for the common good, the idea of well-to-do Americans lining up for a tax break is appalling."[176]

The powerful government forces being used to promote the interests of the affluent in the wake of the 11 September 2001 attacks are complemented by powerful private institutions. For example, according to the *New York Times,* immediately after the attacks of 11 September, private bankers for Chase Manhattan and J. P Morgan "raced" to contact and advise their wealthy clients. The *New York Times* article, titled "Making Sure the Rich Stay Rich, Even in Crisis,"[177] does not disclose the nature of the advice, but, judging from history, one would surmise that it would include shifting investments to the weapons industry. Indeed, in January 2002 the Defense Department requested a $20 billion increase in its next budget to stockpile new weapons and to replenish arsenals conveniently depleted by the bombings in Afghanistan.[178] Shortly thereafter President George W. Bush proposed a $48 billion increase in the military budget, more than double what the Pentagon itself had requested.[179] This new buildup will obviously benefit defense contractors and their shareholders. In a capitalist system, the response of the elite to virtually every problem or crisis involves an increase in their wealth and power.

CONCLUSION

In sum, the imperative of modern capitalism for growth and expansion has perhaps affected human and other animals most deeply by way of corporate agribusiness. Food, especially "meat," is very abundant in most Western capitalist nations today, an availability that encourages overeating. Vast quantities of food are discarded thoughtlessly because "there's more where that came from, right?"

Few are aware of the terrible costs associated with the food abundance experienced by those in advanced capitalist nations, and of the inherent unsustainability of their culinary opulence, particularly their consumption of "meat."

Even when scientists report on the costs of the Green Revolution and predict the further effects of agribusiness practices, they usually voice their warnings using such terms as "further reductions in biodiversity," "further destruction of ecosystems" and "Third World population migrations." Such abstract and arcane expressions do not make real or visible to the public the pain, suffering, and death for countless humans and other animals which both underlie and result from the current abundance.

The oppression of humans and other animals associated with corporate agribusiness—from the terrible confinement and slaughtering of *billions* of other animals, a practice whose form and consequences are now beyond the macabre, to the abusive treatment of "food-processing" workers; from the killing of those in the Third World who resist the expropriation of their land for use as new grazing land to the production of more "grass-fed beef"; from the expansion of global hunger to the "diseases of affluence" caused by largely other-animal-based diets—such practices and conditions are entangled and mutually reinforcing.

Corporate agribusiness is a creation of powerful capitalists and their agents, in pursuit of their private, material interests. Capitalism not only drives oppressive practices but also builds ideologies such as speciesism, racism, sexism, and classism that both legitimate oppression and reduce resistance to it—as in the case of Smithfield Foods's cultivation of an ethnically diverse and divided workforce. Public resistance to practices and conditions linked to machinations by the pharmaceutical industry and agribusiness is largely suppressed by glitzy and manipulative advertising that extols the virtues of these corporate leviathans, their "products," and capitalism in general.

However, in a nation that is supposed to be the epitome of capitalist progress, "nearly half of Americans suffer at least one chronic disease," and that number is expected to grow by thirty million within the next twenty years.[180] Preventive care is inconsistent with the production of food under modern capitalism and with the profitable "treatment" of the diseases linked to its consumption. Meanwhile, the vast majority of the oppressed—with rare exceptions, such as Phoenix, the calf who came to symbolize the foot-and-mouth disease massacres—are faceless, nameless, and invisible.

Chapters 2 through 4 have emphasized the material and social structural forces underlying oppression and pointed to the deep entanglements that characterize these arrangements. The theory of oppression also illuminates the importance of power in protecting the interests of those who profit from these arrangements. Much of this power comes through control of the state—a powerful part of the social structure and a primary social institution. The first part of chapter 5 will bring the nature of the state into historical focus, particularly looking at how it has been used as a tool to maintain elites' control of their societies. Then we will examine how the U.S. state has been used to blunt efforts for social change, with an emphasis on legislation and court decisions pertaining to other animals. An analysis of congressional hearings will serve to further illuminate the awful treatment of other animals in the United States and how state processes and practices largely protect the corporate interests that are responsible for the abuses.

As noted in chapter 1, after publishing his *Theory of Ethnic Stratification,* Don Noel was criticized for underemphasizing the key role of economic factors. In response, Noel suggested that future research should examine the relative importance of both prejudice and economics in spurring racism and racist practices by examining historical materials, particularly legal documents. He writes, "Within the context of the legal institutions the rationale for decisions pertaining to certain issues might be especially enlightening. . . . Hence, it is important to ascertain the rationale which lies behind discriminatory decisions and practices. An ideology is not revealed nearly so well by what people do as by why they do it."[181] Exploring congressional testimony, then, will also help examine the supposition that economic interests, not individual prejudices or amorality, are the primary forces driving institutionalized, oppressive practices.

It is important to understand the nature of the state not only because it is an essential factor in the theory of oppression but also because it is in this area that most human liberation activists, and some advocates of other animals, place their hopes and spend their energy working for social change.

NOTES

1. B. Drummond Ayres, Jr., "Factory Fire Leaves Pall over All-American City," *New York Times,* 5 September 1991, D25.

2. Ayres, "Factory Fire Leaves Pall," D25.

3. Ronald Smothers, "25 Die, Many Reported Trapped as Blaze Engulfs Carolina Plant," *New York Times,* 4 September 1991, B7.

4. Mary B. W. Tabor, "Poultry Plant Fire Churns Emotions over Job Both Hated and Appreciated," *New York Times,* 6 September 1991, A17.

5. Tabor, "Poultry Plant Fire Churns Emotions," A17.

6. Tabor, "Poultry Plant Fire Churns Emotions," A17.

7. See, for example, David Tilman et al., "Forecasting Agriculturally Driven Global Environmental Change," *Science* 292 (April 2001): 281–84.

8. www.ewg.org/pub/home/reports/dbcp/dbco.html.

9. www.ewg.org/pub/home/reports/dbcp/dbco.html.

10. www.ewg.org/pub/home/reports/dbcp/dbco.html.

11. Associated Press, "World Tapping Out of Water," *Dayton Daily News,* 14 May 2001, A12.

12. Jacques Leslie, "Running Dry: What Happens When the World No Longer Has Enough Freshwater," *Harper's Magazine* 301, no. 1802 (July 2001): 37, 39.

13. Timothy Egan, "Near Vast Bodies of Water, the Land Still Thirsts," *New York Times,* 21 August 2001, A1.

14. Egan, "Near Vast Bodies of Water," A16.

15. Egan, "Near Vast Bodies of Water," A16.

16. Egan, "Near Vast Bodies of Water," A16.

17. Tilman et al., "Forecasting Agriculturally Driven Global Environmental Change," 283.

18. Marvin Harris, *The Sacred Cow and the Abominable Pig: Riddles of Food and Culture* (New York: Simon & Schuster, 1985), 21; John Robbins, *The Food Revolution: How Your Diet Can Help Save Your Life and the World* (Berkeley, Calif.: Conaru, 2001), 292.

19. Robert K. Schaeffer, *Understanding Globalization: The Social Consequences of Political, Economic and Environmental Change* (New York: Rowman & Littlefield, 1997), 150.

20. Schaeffer, *Understanding Globalization,* 150.

21. Charles W. Holmes, "In Farm Country, a Way of Life Slowly Withers," *Dayton Daily News,* 22 May 2000, 1A, 4A.

22. Holmes, "In Farm Country, a Way of Life Slowly Withers," 4A.

23. Kendall M. Thu and E. Paul Durrenberger, eds., *Pigs, Profits and Rural Communities* (Albany: State University of New York Press, 1998), 7.

24. Thu and Durrenberger, *Pigs, Profits and Rural Communities,* 7.

25. Robert Morgan, "Legal and Political Injustices of Industrial Swine Production in North Carolina," in *Pigs, Profits and Rural Communities,* 139.

26. Mary Lee Kerr, "Poultry Growers Beat Retaliation," *Southern Exposure* 20, no. 3 (1992): 7.

27. Kerr, "Poultry Growers Beat Retaliation," 7.

28. Kerr, "Poultry Growers Beat Retaliation," 7.

29. Kerr, "Poultry Growers Beat Retaliation," 7.

30. Paul Waldau, "Factory Farming" in *Encyclopedia of Animal Rights and Animal Welfare,* ed. Marc Bekoff and Carron A. Meaney (Westport, Conn.: Greenwood, 1998), 168.

31. Amy Blount Achor, *Animal Rights: A Beginner's Guide* (Yellow Springs, Ohio: Write-Ware, 1992), 78.

32. Erik Marcus, *Vegan: The New Ethics of Eating* (Ithaca, N.Y.: McBooks, 1998), 119–20.

33. National Public Radio, *All Things Considered,* 12 June 2001.

34. Animal Free Press, *One Million—Trapped, Then Crushed* (Vacaville, Calif.: Fund for Animals, Winter 2001), 5.

35. Associated Press, "California Prepares for Disease," *Dayton Daily News,* 23 March 2001, 5A.

36. Eric Ross, "Patterns of Diet and Forces of Production: An Economic and Ecological History of the Ascendancy of Beef in the United States Diet," in *Beyond the Myths of Culture: Essays in Cultural Materialism,* ed. Eric Ross (New York: Academic Press, 1980), 209–11.

37. Associated Press, "Egg Farm Raid Means Deportations," *Dayton Daily News,* 8 November 2000, 3B.

38. Kelley J. Donham, "The Impact of Industrial Swine Production on Human Health," in *Pigs, Profits and Rural Communities,* 78.

39. Donham, "The Impact of Industrial Swine Production on Human Health," 78.

40. David Cecelski and Mary Lee Kerr, "Hog Wild: How Corporate Hog Operations Are Slaughtering Family Farms and Poisoning the Rural South," *Southern Exposure* 20, no. 3 (Fall 1992): 15.

41. Donham, "The Impact of Industrial Swine Production on Human Health," 79–80.

42. Donham, "The Impact of Industrial Swine Production on Human Health," 80.

43. Denise Giardina and Eric Bates, "Fowling the Nest," in *Southern Exposure* 19, no.1 (Spring 1991): 8.

44. Giardina and Bates, "Fowling the Nest," 9.

45. Cecelski and Kerr, "Hog Wild," 15.

46. Roberta Rogers, "Farm Runoff Spoiling Darke County," *Dayton Daily News,* 30 April 2001, 11A.

47. Giardina and Bates, "Fowling the Nest," 8.

48. Gail A. Eisnitz, *Slaughterhouse: The Shocking Story of Greed, Neglect, and Inhumane Treatment Inside the U.S. Meat Industry* (New York: Prometheus, 1997), 68.

49. Eisnitz, *Slaughterhouse,* 69.

50. Eisnitz, *Slaughterhouse,* 98.

51. Jeremy Rifkin, *Beyond Beef: The Rise and Fall of the Cattle Culture* (New York: Plume, 1992), 127.

52. Rifkin, *Beyond Beef*, 127.

53. Eisnitz, *Slaughterhouse*, 73.

54. Cecelski and Kerr, "Hog Wild," 14.

55. Barry Yeoman, "Hispanic Diaspora," *Mother Jones* (July/August 2000): 34–41, 76–77.

56. Charlie LeDuff, "At a Slaughterhouse, Some Things Never Die," *New York Times*, 16 June 2000, A1, A24–A25; this article was sixth in a series titled *How Race is Lived in America*.

57. LeDuff, "At a Slaughterhouse, Some Things Never Die," A24.

58. LeDuff, "At a Slaughterhouse, Some Things Never Die," A24.

59. LeDuff, "At a Slaughterhouse, Some Things Never Die," A25.

60. LeDuff, "At a Slaughterhouse, Some Things Never Die," A25.

61. www.smithfieldfoods.com/invest/body_finhigh.html.

62. David Barboza, "Meatpackers' Profits Hinge on Pool of Immigrant Labor," *New York Times*, 21 December, 2001, A14.

63. Barboza, "Meatpackers' Profits," A14.

64. Benjamin F. Miller, Lawrence Galton, and Daniel Brunner, *Freedom from Heart Attacks* (New York: Simon & Schuster, 1972).

65. The majority of grass-fed cows imported to the United States today come from Australia and New Zealand. However, Mark Edelman observes that "what may seem of minor significance in the United States looks different when seen from Central America, where pasture is often the major land use and beef a key source of foreign exchange." See Mark Edelman, "From Costa Rican Pasture to North American Hamburger," in *Food and Evolution: Toward a Theory of Food Habits,* ed. Marvin Harris and Eric B. Ross (Philadelphia: Temple University Press, 1987), 545.

66. Eric Ross, "Patterns of Diet and Forces of Production: An Economic and Ecological History of the Ascendancy of Beef in the United States Diet," in *Food and Evolution*, 190.

67. Roger Segelken, *U.S. Could Feed 800 Million People with Grain That Livestock Eat* (Ithaca, N.Y.: Cornell University Science News, 1997); www/news/cornell.edu/science/Aug97/livestock.hrs.html.

68. Leslie, "Running Dry," 50.

69. Jill Mahoney, "Environmental Havoc Forecast," *Dayton Daily News*, 16 April 2001, 9A.

70. Tilman et al., "Forecasting Agriculturally Driven Global Environmental Change," 283.

71. Rifkin, *Beyond Beef*.

72. Edward Palmer Thompson, *The Making of the English Working Class* (New York: Pantheon–Random House, 1964), 217.

73. Rifkin, *Beyond Beef*, 147, 148, 149.

74. Frances Moore Lappe and Joseph Collins, *Food First: Beyond the Myth of Scarcity* (New York: Ballantine, 1979), 11.

75. Schaeffer, *Understanding Globalization*, 165.

76. See, for example, Norine Dworkin, "22 Reasons to Go Vegetarian Right Now," *Vegetarian Times* 260 (April 1999): 90–93.

77. David Barboza, "As Biotech Crops Multiply, Consumers Get Little Choice," *New York Times*, 10 June 2001, A28.

78. Barboza, "As Biotech Crops Multiply, Consumers Get Little Choice," A28.

79. Barboza, "As Biotech Crops Multiply, Consumers Get Little Choice," A28.

80. Michael Parenti, *Against Empire* (San Francisco: City Lights, 1995), 7.

81. Robert G. Williams, *Export Agriculture and the Crisis in Central America* (Chapel Hill: University of North Carolina Press, 1986), 158–59, 151.

82. Rifkin, *Beyond Beef,* 193.

83. Daniel Faber, *Environment under Fire: Imperialism and the Ecological Crisis in Central America* (New York: Monthly Review Press, 1993), 127–28.

84. William Blum, *Killing Hope: U.S. Military and CIA Interventions since World War II* (Monroe, Maine: Common Courage, 1995), 232.

85. Faber, *Environment under Fire,* 128.

86. Blum, *Killing Hope,* 234.

87. Amnesty International, *Political Killings by Governments* (London: Author, 1983), 27.

88. Steven Greenhouse, "Companies Pay $1 Million in Harassment Suit," *New York Times,* 2 June 2000, A12.

89. Greenhouse, "Companies Pay $1 Million in Harassment Suit," A12.

90. Cathleen Ferraro and Eric Young, "Huge Ag Sex-Harass Suit Ends: Lettuce Grower to Pay Victims $1.85 Million," *The Sacramento Bee,* 24 February 1999; http://cgi.sacbee.com/news/beetoday/newsroom/biz/022499/biz02.html.

91. Emily Gersema, "Female Workers Raped at Iowa Plants, Suit Alleges," *Seattle Post-Intelligencer,* 23 August 2001; http://seattlepi.nwsource.com/business/36156_assault23.shtml.

92. http://www.eeoc.gov/press/4-10-01.html.

93. See, for example, Glenn Collins and Monte Williams, "In Restaurants with the High Tips, Black Waiters Are Few," *New York Times,* 30 May 2000, A23; Robert Klara, "Don't Ask, Don't Tell," *Restaurant Business* (15 January 2000): 30–36.

94. Victor Wishna, "You've Got Issues: From Capitol Hill to the Town Hall, This Year's Legislative Battles Are Already Brewing," *Restaurant Business* (15 January 2000): 21–27.

95. Wishna, "You've Got Issues," 22.

96. Benjamin F. Miller, Lawrence Galton, and Daniel Brunner, *Freedom from Heart Attacks* (New York: Simon & Schuster, 1972), 50, 20.

97. Dean Ornish, *Program for Reversing Heart Disease* (New York: Ballantine, 1990), 51.

98. See, for example, *Surgeon General's Report on Nutrition and Health,* Pub. No. 88–50210 (Washington, D.C.: U.S. Department of Health and Human Services, 1988).

99. Edward A. Taub, *Balance Your Body, Balance Your Life* (New York: Kensington, 1999), 19, 20, 21, 22, 23.

100. USDA, *Agricultural Fact Book 1999* (Washington, D.C.: U.S. Department of Agriculture, Office of Communications, July 2000), 2.

101. USDA, *Agricultural Fact Book 1999,* 4.

102. Rifkin, *Beyond Beef,* 165–69.

103. Dayton Daily News, "Adults Lacking Enough Exercise," 21 April 2000, 3A.

104. *New York Times,* "Obesity Rate Rising Fastest in the South," 27 October 2000, A21.

105. Charles W. Schmidt, "Too Big, Too Soon?" *Child* (August 1999): 28.

106. Schmidt, "Too Big, Too Soon?" 31–32.

107. Geoffrey Cowley, "Generation XXL," *Newsweek,* 3 July 2000, 43.

108. Cowley, "Generation XXL," 43.

109. Greg Critser, "Let Them Eat Fat: The Heavy Truths about American Obesity," *Harper's* (March 2000): 42.

110. Barbara Crossette, "In Numbers, the Heavy Now Match the Starved," *New York Times,* 18 January 2000, A10.

111. Taub, *Balance Your Body, Balance Your Life,* 20.

112. *Dayton Daily News,* "Bad Gene Keeps Overfed Mice Thin," 28 March 2000, 3A.

113. Micah L. Sifry, "Food Money," *The Nation* 269, no. 22 (27 December 1999): 20.

114. Sifry, "Food Money," 20.

115. See Eisnitz, *Slaughterhouse,* 155–77.

116. James B. Russell and Jennifer L. Rychlik, "Factors That Alter Rumen Microbial Ecology," *Science* 292, no. 5519 (11 May 2001): 1121, 1122.

117. Walter E. Stamm, "An Epidemic of Urinary Tract Infections," *New England Journal of Medicine* 345, no. 4 (4 October 2001): 1055–56.

118. The term *biomachine* was used by Jim Mason and Peter Singer to highlight the objectification of animals in modern agribusiness in their book *Animal Factories,* rev. and updated version (New York: Harmony, 1990).

119. Robert Sharpe, *The Cruel Deception: The Use of Animals in Medical Research* (Wellingborough, England: Thorsons, 1998).

120. Associated Press, "Disease Control Unstable," *Dayton Daily News,* 18 October 2001, 3A.

121. Sharpe, *The Cruel Deception,* 131.

122. David G. White et al., "The Isolation of Antibiotic-Resistant Salmonella from Retail Ground Meats," *New England Journal of Medicine* 345, no. 16 (18 October 2001): 1147.

123. Courtney Kane, "Pork and Beef Producers Are Moving to Freshen Up Their Long-Running Consumer Campaigns," *New York Times,* 27 April 2000, C10.

124. USDA, *Agriculture Fact Book 1999,* 2.

125. www.beef.org/librfacts/fs-statistics.html.

126. Aaron Putze, *1997 Pork Checkoff Dollars to Focus on Markets, New Products;* www.fb.com/iafb/fbnews/check1.htm.

127. Kane, "Pork and Beef Producers Are Moving to Freshen Up Their Long-Running Consumer Campaigns," C10.

128. Scott Elliott, "It's Tough Bringing Home Bacon," *Dayton Daily News,* 29 November 1998, 7B.

129. Michael Pearson, "Hog Farming Becomes Profitable Once Again," *Dayton Daily News,* 22 April 2000, 1E.

130. Texas A&M University, *Per Capita Meat Consumption in Pounds of Ready-to-Cook or Retail Weight,* 1998; http://savell-j.tamu.edu/consum.html.

131. Edward Lotterman "A Turkey in Every Pot?" *Fedgazette* (Minneapolis: Federal Reserve Bank of Minneapolis, April 1998): 2; http://woodrow.mpls.frb.fed.us/pubs/fedgaz/98–04/turkey.html.

132. Associated Press, "Got Milk? Campaign Targets School Vending Machines," *Dayton Daily News,* 5 April 2001, 5A.

133. Associated Press, "Got Milk?" 5A.

134. Associated Press, "Got Milk?" 5A.

135. Jean Akre, "Got Milk? Get Fired," *Impact Weekly* (Dayton, Ohio), 17 May 2000, 8.

136. Akre, "Got Milk? Get Fired," 8.

137. http://weep-cancer-project.org/rgbh.html.

138. USDA, *Agriculture Fact Book 1999,* 1.

139. Associated Press, "Americans Resume Love Affair with Fat," *Dayton Daily News,* 9 May 2000, 5A.

140. Associated Press, "Americans Resume Love Affair with Fat," 5A.

141. Associated Press, "Americans Resume Love Affair with Fat," 5A.

142. C. Wright Mills, *White Collar: The American Middle Classes* (New York: Oxford University Press, 1951), 63.

143. Michael Harrington, *The Other America: Poverty in the United States,* new ed. (New York: Macmillan, 1969 [1962]), 182.

144. Harrington, *The Other America,* 2.

145. Kevin Phillips, *The Politics of Rich and Poor: Wealth and the American Electorate in the Reagan Aftermath* (New York: Random House, 1990), 94–95.

146. Phillips, *The Politics of Rich and Poor,* 78.

147. Phillips, *The Politics of Rich and Poor,* 79.

148. Donald L. Barlett and James B. Steele, *America: What Went Wrong?* (Kansas City: Andrews & McNeel, 1992), 2.

149. Sylvia Nasar, "The 1980's: A Very Good Time for the Very Rich," *New York Times,* 5 March 1992, A1.

150. James Lardner, "The Rich Get Richer," *U.S. News & World Report,* 21 February 2000, 43.

151. Chuck Collins, Betsy Leondar-Wright, and Holly Sklar, *Shifting Fortunes: The Perils of the Growing American Wealth Gap* (Boston: United for a Fair Economy, 1999).

152. Lardner, "The Rich Get Richer," 40.

153. Shannon McCaffrey, "Income Disparity Widens," *Dayton Daily News,* 18 January 2000, 1A.

154. Christopher Lasch, "The Revolt of the Elites," *Harper's* (November 1994), 41.

155. *Left Business Observer,* "Squeezing Debtors," 84 (21 July 1998): 1–2.

156. *Left Business Observer,* "Squeezing Debtors," 1–2.

157. Eileen Alt Powell, "Cost of Debt Is Rising," *Dayton Daily News,* 29 May 2000, 4C.

158. Powell, "Cost of Debt Is Rising."

159. *Dayton Daily News,* "Working Poor Still Lack Housing." 28 March 2000, 7A.

160. Associated Press, *Survey: Many Americans Still Lack Health Insurance,* 1998; http://cnn.com/allpolitics/stories/1998/10/19/hmo.ap/.

161. Karen Gullo, "Report: Millions Lack Dental Care," *Dayton Daily News,* 26 May 2000, 9A.

162. Doug Henwood, "Kids Today," *The Nation* 270, no. 12 (27 March 2000): 8.

163. Mihajlo Mesarovic and Eduard Pestel, *Mankind at the Turning Point: The Second Report of the Club of Rome* (New York: Dutton, 1974), ix.

164. Megan McKenna, "State of the World's Children 2000: An Urgent Call to Action," in *Thursday's Child* 9, no. 1 (Winter 2000): 4 (New York: United States Fund for UNICEF, February 2000).

165. Jim Yong Kim, Joyce V. Millen, Alec Irwin, and John Gershman, *Dying for Growth: Global Inequality and the Health of the Poor* (Monroe, Maine: Common Courage Press, 2000), 4.

166. Kim, Millen, Irwin, and Gershman, *Dying for Growth,* 33.

167. Jerry Mander, "Facing the Rising Tide," in *The Case against the Global Economy: And for a Turn toward the Local,* ed. Jerry Mander and Edward Goldsmith (San Francisco: Sierra Club Books, 1996), 3.

168. Ralph Nader and Lori Wallach, "GATT, NAFTA, and the Subversion of the Democratic Process," in *The Case against the Global Economy,* 94.

169. Patricia Forkan, "Law, Legislation and Politics: Using the System to Defend Ani-

mals," remarks made as part of a panel at the World Congress for Animals, Washington, D.C., 21 June 1996.

170. Michael W. Fox, "A Vision Shared: What We Are Fighting For," presentation at the World Congress for Animals in Washington, D.C., 21 June 1996.

171. John Nielsen, "Bushmeat," *All Things Considered,* National Public Radio (8 July 1999).

172. Nielsen, "Bushmeat."

173. Nielsen, "Bushmeat."

174. See, for example, Aaron Donovan, "For Many, Sliding into Poverty Takes Only a Few Missed Paychecks," *New York Times,* 18 November 2001, A30; John W. Fountain, "On an Icy Night, Little Room at the Shelter," *New York Times,* 5 January 2002, A1 and A9.

175. David E. Sanger, "Bush Calls World Economy Goal of Attacks on U.S.," *New York Times,* 21 October 2001, A8.

176. *New York Times* editorial, "The House Acts Badly," 25 October 2001, A20.

177. Geraldine Fabrikant, "Making Sure the Rich Stay Rich, Even in Crisis," *New York Times,* 7 October 2001, section 3, 1 and 10.

178. James Dao, "Pentagon Seeking a Large Increase in Its Next Budget," *New York Times,* 7 January 2002, 1A.

179. Sonya Ross, "$48B More Sought for Military," *Dayton Daily News,* 24 January 2002, 1A.

180. Associated Press, "Chronic Ills Hit Nearly 1 of 2 in U.S.," *Dayton Daily News,* 1 December 2000, 4A.

181. Donald L. Noel, "Slavery and the Rise of Racism," in *The Origins of American Slavery and Racism,* ed. Donald Noel (Columbus, Ohio: Merrill, 1972), 168.

5

Oppression and the Capitalist State

We are made aware of our constitutional rights, in the Bill of Rights, and other provisions, from the earliest grades in school, with such fanfare and attention as to persuade us that these are the most important parts of our law; when we think of "respect for law" we are likely to think of these benign provisions of law which speak of rights and liberties. But we are told very little—so little as to escape our consciousness quickly—about the vast body of legislation which arranges the wealth of the nation: the tax laws, the appropriation bills (on the local as well as the national level), and the enormous structure of law which is designed to maintain the property system as is—and therefore the distribution of wealth as is.

—Howard Zinn[1]

Until recently, scores of gun enthusiasts gathered in Hegins, Pennsylvania, once a year to massacre thousands of birds. The event, the Fred Coleman Memorial Pigeon Shoot, was one of many such spectacles that have occurred annually in Pennsylvania and around the country. (Many recreational massacres of this type continue to this day.) It was common during the Fred Coleman massacres, which continued through 1998, for several hundred state and local law enforcement officers to be on hand. But, as legal scholar Gary Francione observed, they were not there to enforce Pennsylvania's animal cruelty statutes but, rather, to control protesters.

> Several hundred Pennsylvania state troopers would stand by and watch the carnage year after year. Their job was only to ensure that protesters and locals stayed away from each other, but for the most part, they did nothing if a local person assaulted, battered, or harassed protesters. One year, a shoot supporter sprayed urine on protesters. The state troopers did nothing. If a protester so much as tried to assist an injured pigeon that was lying somewhere on the grounds, however, the troopers arrested the protester and subjected her to demeaning treatment.[2]

The annual Hegins massacre was suspended after 1998 largely because the national attention protesters focused on such an atrocious event helped their efforts to challenge recreation hunting in general; the event was sacrificed lest further anti-hunting sentiment be aroused.

In 1983, largely unbeknownst to the residents of Parma Township, a small community in Jackson County, Michigan, the Michigan Department of Commerce supported the construction of ten five-hundred–pig CAFOs in their township. A number of prominent Michigan attorneys, with ties to the governor's office, invested in the project. State officials maintained that the Jackson County *Hog* [emphasis added] Production Project (JCHP) was good for state economic development and that the project would help alleviate Michigan corn surpluses and keep the state's slaughterhouses operating at peak capacity. The residents of Parma Township were about to experience life next to a giant pig "production" facility. Anthropologist Laura B. DeLind writes:

> Many reported a "horrific stench" that caused nausea, headaches, and respiratory ailments; burned eyes, noses, and throats; prevented sleep; and could be detected up to five miles away. Residents photographed dead pigs "piled up for days along the side of the road." Others reported pools of manure 8 inches deep lying on fields within 150 feet of private property. Airborne particles were thought to contaminate swimming pools. Manure spilled on roadways caused accidents. . . . There were also claims that neighboring wetlands and water resources were being compromised by manure runoff and field drains. Fish no longer swam in Rice Creek.[3]

Parma residents registered complaints and requested help from "the county planning commission, the county health department, the DNR [Department of Natural Resources], the MDA [Michigan Department of Agriculture], individual members of Congress, and the governor's office often on a daily basis."[4] However, county, state, and federal officials largely shrugged off their complaints, discounted their evidence, and insulted their integrity. The experience profoundly changed their perception of government. DeLind notes:

> Prior to the controversy . . . most Parma residents shared a sense that government was there to serve their needs. They were respectful of the law and the processes that created and upheld it. Though few had any political experience or "know how," most felt that they only had to express themselves to get what they wanted. With the introduction of the "hog hotel," they began to sense that the system was reluctant to embrace their interests over those of power and profit. They began to feel collusion, if not outright conspiracy, existed among politicians, government employees, and Sand [company] supporters. "Many high up political persons were invested in the operation. No one wanted to look too closely or to step on toes. It was a case of 'one hand washing the other.' " . . .
>   As this realization grew, so did local anger over the vulnerability of area residents and their loss of real security. . . .
>   Local residents expressed a loss of faith in the state. "Our own state government

really let us down. People who think they can fall back on the state for protection need to wake up."[5]

Elected officials, government employees, and police officers, charged with making and enforcing the law and protecting the public, often do so in prejudicial and discriminatory ways. Official action or inaction is frequently harmful or even lethal for communities or individuals. Take, for example, several notable incidents of police misconduct from the closing months of the twentieth century. A New York City police officer, Justin Volpe, tortured a Haitian immigrant by sodomizing him with a broomstick inside a police stationhouse.[6] Also in New York, Amadou Diallo, an unarmed immigrant from West Africa, was shot at forty-one times by four white police officers.[7] In Riverside, California, police officers shot twelve times Tyisha Miller, a black teenager who was sitting in a locked car with a flat tire, because she had a gun. In March 1999, a federal jury found Salvatore Gemelli, a Nassau County, New York, jail guard, guilty of beating a developmentally disabled inmate with a metal frying pan, an assault so severe it produced broken ribs and multiple spinal fractures.[8] Incidents such as these occur every day throughout the nation. Indeed, in May 2000 the United Nations Committee against Torture admonished the United States: "[T]he number of cases of police ill-treatment of civilians, and ill-treatment in prisons" were matters of concern. This was particularly true, they said, because 'much of this ill-treatment by police and prison guards seems to be based upon discrimination.' "[9]

Those victimized are seldom from the ranks of the affluent but are almost always individuals who have been socially devalued because of the positions they occupy in the social system. In turn, the dispositions and behaviors of lawmaking and enforcement officials are profoundly conditioned by the social positions *they* occupy within an oppressive social structure.

Recall from chapter 2 that, in the absence of ancestral memory, humans must create culture and social structure to facilitate social organization. And, for the social system to come to life, humans create social positions. The ways humans regard and behave toward others are dictated largely by the system of organization of the society and the positions the individuals occupy in that society. As we have seen in the previous chapters, most humans tend to see themselves and the world largely from the vantage point prescribed by their social position.

One of the most persuasive examples of the power of social position occurred during a mock prison experiment conducted in 1973 by Stanford psychologist Philip Zimbardo and his colleagues. Zimbardo launched a two-week study using twenty-one seemingly typical male college students who were carefully screened for physical health, emotional maturity, and respect for the law. The students were then randomly assigned the position of "prisoner" or "guard" in a mock prison. After six days the experiment was terminated due to the outrageously base and cruel way in which the "guards" treated the "prisoners." Not only had a group of college students been swiftly transformed into cruel guardians, but the students who were incarcerated demonstrated extreme depression, with one even breaking out in a psy-chosomatic rash. According to Zimbardo and his colleagues:

> [T]he subjects' abnormal and personal reactions are best seen as a product of their trans-action with an environment that supported the behavior that would be pathological in other settings, but was "appropriate" in this prison. Had we observed comparable reac-tions in a real prison, the psychiatrist undoubtedly would have been able to attribute any prisoner's behavior to character defects or personality maladjustment, while critics of the prison system would have been quick to label the guards as "psychopathic." This tendency to locate the source of behavior disorders inside a particular person or group underestimates the power of situational forces.[10]

Reflecting on the control that society and social positions exert over our lives, sociologist Ralph Dahrendorf comments:

> The fact of society is vexatious because we cannot escape it. . . . For every position a person can occupy—whether it is described in terms of age, family, occupation, nation-ality, class membership, or what have you—"society" has defined certain personal quali-ties and modes of behavior as acceptable. The incumbent of such a position must decide whether or not to behave as society says he must. If he yields to society's demands, he abandons his virgin individuality but gains society's approval. If he resists society's demands, he may preserve an abstract and bootless independence, but only at the expense of incurring society's wrath and painful sanctions.[11]

In contemporary society, then, individual humans filling, for example, manage-ment positions in huge agribusinesses, the pharmaceutical industry, the automobile industry, the guns and munitions industry, and so forth, make decisions that cause harm largely because they are compelled to do so by the corporations that employ them: it is the behavior called for by their social position. If they fail in that regard, they are sanctioned—they are replaced.

In a society that is deeply rooted in oppressive social arrangements, in which the affluent and privileged profit from devaluation and exploitation of the oppressed, many social positions play a significant role in protecting the status quo; lawmaking and enforcement officials are no exception. Unlike the powerful in society who are largely physically and socially segregated from the oppressed, law enforcement offi-cers are on the "front lines," dealing daily with the consequences and manifestations of exploitation and deprivation. Because of the controlling function inherent in the position of law enforcement officials, many of the dispossessed and exploited view them with distrust and resentment. It is predictable, then, that many law enforce-ment officers, especially those with many years on the job, feel less than friendly or respectful toward those they are required to "control" (much like workers' disposi-tion toward other animals in CAFOs and slaughterhouses). Of course, many officers do not harbor the extreme dispositions that were associated with beatings, like the one given to Rodney King in Los Angeles in 1992, or torture, as in the case of the Haitian immigrant sodomized in a New York police station, or excessive use of lethal force, as in the cases of Amadou Diallo and Tyisha Miller. However, the prejudice that precipitated such tragedies is profoundly conditioned by the social, economic, and political organization of an oppressive society—and so it has been throughout much of human history.

Reflection on the previous chapters' glimpse at social history supports the theory of oppression that suggests that exploitation and competition—particularly in pursuit of economic self-interest—are strongly associated with the oppression of humans and other animals. Following the theory, unequal power is an *essential* element in the formation, maintenance, and expansion of oppressive conditions. While various types of power are wielded in society, the power of the state will be the particular focus of this chapter. Obviously, the power of the state is very important to those who benefit from the oppression of humans and other animals, as well as those seeking to challenge oppression. In the contemporary United States, most who occupy state positions are not ruthless individuals who consciously conspire to promote suffering and harm. Rather, they are individuals occupying government positions in a capitalist system, and they occupy those positions because they support existing arrangements and promote (or at least do not hinder) policies that facilitate greater economic concentration and corporate expansion. However, in a society ostensibly characterized by democratic rule, social harms and the will of the public cannot be entirely disregarded, and social critics and protest may force reforms. As we will see, however, such reforms are usually crafted by the powerful; many have only superficial impact, and they are frequently rescinded when protest fades and new economic exigencies arise.

Before we begin our brief examination of how the state has been used to facilitate oppression and fend off substantive reform efforts, it is important to note that, from a sociological vantage point, the "state" is not quite the same thing as the "government." "The state is an impersonal social authority, whereas the government is the collection of individuals who happen to be directing the power of the state" at any given time.[12] In the words of early twentieth-century social critic Randolph Bourne, "Government is the idea of the State put into practical operation in the hands of definite, concrete, fallible men."[13]

THE NATURE OF THE STATE

Most of us are taught that the federal government, and the numerous local governments, impartially and democratically create laws for the benefit of all. Moreover, we are taught that law enforcement officials, including police officers and judges, exercise their authority in a fair and impartial fashion. In the rare instances in which state-inflicted injustices are brought to public attention, they are represented in the media as aberrations. Nonetheless, despite what we are taught, and despite the fact that governmental misdeeds are largely portrayed as exceptional occurrences, some among us still become conscious of the underlying patterns of injustice and come to distrust government. For the most part, though, our misgivings focus largely on individual unscrupulous politicians and officials, while the structure and organization of the state is still viewed as mainly sound and just. However, many activists and scholars view the state as "a device actively developed by powerful elites to establish and maintain their dominance" over others.[14]

As we have seen, expansion of economic production under early agricultural society and the creation of individual wealth was achieved through widespread exploitation and oppression. Humans and other animals and the land and the seas all came to be viewed as personal possessions of emperors and other potentates. The unequal and exploitative arrangements were reinforced by an increasingly formalized political system—the state. The laws of society generally were made by powerful elites and, naturally, reflected their interests. Friedrich Engels put it this way:

> [T]he old wars between tribe and tribe [were] already degenerating into systematic pillage by land and sea for the acquisition of cattle, slaves and treasure, and becoming a regular source of wealth. . . . Riches [were] praised and respected as the highest good. . . . Only one thing was wanting . . . an institution which set the seal of general social recognition on each new method of acquiring property and thus amassing wealth at continually increasing speed; an institution which perpetuated not only this growing cleavage of society into classes but also the right of the possessing class to exploit the non-possessing, and the rule of the former over the latter. And this institution came. The *state* was invented.[15]

The laws developed by the early state formalized some of the unjust but customary practices. As Marc Bloch observes, "through the play of custom, an abuse might always by mutation become a precedent, a precedent a right."[16]

One of the first known written codes of laws was created under the direction of Hammurabi, the eighteenth century B.C. ruler of Babylon. A predictable quality of this early series of laws was its sanctification of socially created classes and its concentration on the protection of personally held property. Crimes against property frequently were capital offenses, deemed to warrant the death penalty.

> If a man has stolen from a temple, or house, he shall be put to death; and he that has received the stolen property from him shall be put to death.
> If a man has broken into a house he shall be killed before the breach [or place where the thief broke through] and buried there.
> If a man has committed highway robbery and has been caught, that man shall be put to death.
> If a fire has broken out in a man's house and one who has come to put it out has coveted the property of the householder and appropriated any of it, that man shall be cast into the selfsame fire.[17]

While these sanctions are obviously severe by today's standards, many might regard the basic prohibitions as sound. But bear in mind that everyone in Babylon did not have a house or valued possessions. Legal scholar Kenneth Cloke observes, "The law of theft dates back from the emergence, on a large scale, of private, movable property and from its unequal distribution, i.e., scarcity. The law, 'Thou shall not steal,' therefore is an expression of the existence of poverty and a social need to steal."[18]

Hammurabi's law also sanctified different rights and obligations for the privileged, the devalued, and the enslaved. If someone assigned to a devalued social position injured someone from the "upper class," severe reprisals were called for. If one from the "upper class," however, injured someone occupying a devalued social position, he was required only to pay fines.

For millennia, similar laws have been made by the ruling class and enforced by state-anointed organizations of humans in the socially created position of "law enforcer." The power of the state cannot be underestimated in its capacity to harness the vast majority of societal members into a system of laws that strongly favors the interests of the privileged. Throughout most of the past ten thousand years, that power has been used largely tyrannically and oppressively. In many instances, women, children, devalued males, and other animals have been viewed as personal property, and the full weight of the state has been used to protect the economic and utilitarian uses of these "others."

Even when a glimmer of enlightened thought regarding political equality emerged with the early Greeks in Athens, women, children, and those enslaved or considered to be foreigners were excluded. Other animals were not considered members of the community—they were property and thus also excepted from social consideration or extension of rights. Moreover, the same ostensibly democratic Athenians gained considerable wealth through the subjugation of other Greek city-states. Tired of Athenian exploitation, other city-states eventually rebelled, and widespread warfare ensued. Weakened by exploitation, political corruption, and warfare, the Greeks were invaded by the Macedonians, and their power eventually was eclipsed by the ascent of the highly stratified and oppressive Roman Empire.

Effective challenges to control of the state are usually made by a disgruntled segment of the elite or by a newly emerging group of powerful individuals seeking elite status and political control. For example, during the early years of the Roman republic, only well-established, land-owning *males,* the patricians ("fathers" of the state), were granted rights to political participation. The remainder of the human population, the plebeians (the multitudes), were made up of a diverse group ranging from the smallest farmers to artisans and traders. In the fifth century B.C., a group of plebeians who had managed to obtain some economic affluence and power led a campaign to obtain political rights for their class. Rallying support among the disenfranchised masses, they threatened to leave Rome to establish their own city unless political reforms were enacted. Eventually they gained the right to have public officials of their own, called the tribunes of the people. However, tribunes were permitted only to observe senate discussions and to voice dissent against unpopular senate actions. The plebeians eventually won the right to hold state office, and they forced the removal of laws that forbid intermarriage between patricians and plebeians. However, the intermarriages of wealthy plebeians and patricians simply created a new class of "nobles." Despite the social mobility acquired by wealthy plebeians, major economic and political inequality continued to plague most of the Roman population.

Just as the Athenians' hunger for wealth and power led to their downfall, the Roman senate was corrupted by riches accrued from imperial expansion, plunder of the conquered and the forced payment of tributes. Officials sent by the senate to govern new provinces amassed riches as opportunities for graft abounded. Such injustice and exploitation were exacerbated during periods of intense military conflict and during the grab for "spoils" (read: land, slaves, women, and other animals) after an adversary had been subordinated. H. G. Wells described the republic in 46 B.C. in this way:

> There can be no doubt that all Italy, all the empire, was festering with discomfort, anxiety, and discontent in the century after the destruction of Carthage; a few men were growing very rich, and the majority of people found themselves entangled in an inexplicable net of uncertain prices, jumpy markets, and debts; but there was no way at all of stating and clearing up the general dissatisfaction. . . . So long as there were no actual violence, the Senate and the financiers kept on in their own disastrous way. Only when they were badly frightened would governing cliques or parties desist from some nefarious policy and heed the common good.[19]

Examples such as this, common through the history of the West, demonstrate not only the importance of the state in maintaining oppressive arrangements but also how avarice can corrupt a social system, even one already organized to substantially favor the elite. Moreover, when a substantive challenge to the established order is made, it is usually forced by groups who have little concern for those beneath themselves in the oppressive socioeconomic and political hierarchy, as seen in the example of the affluent Roman plebeians. If those who have forced change are successful in obtaining rights for themselves, or even control of state power, they are seldom inclined to extend newly acquired privileges to the less powerful and the oppressed. This tendency is noted by sociologist Daniel W. Rossides:

> Many reforms are "revolutions from above"—segments of the dominant oligarchy seeking to oust other segments, to institute "reforms." A characteristic feature of Greece and Rome, for example, is "caesarism"—a reform movement initiated at the top in populist language but which leaves class relations substantially intact and distracts the masses by providing bread, circuses, and moral exhortation as substitutes for equality and justice.[20]

There are countless historical examples of such "revolutions from above." For example, as nation-states began to develop in the late Middle Ages, monarchs' grasps for power and wealth began to infringe upon what had become the traditional rights of the feudal lords. In 1215, the rapacious and churlish actions of King John of England led members of the feudal aristocracy to create the Magna Carta. The Magna Carta was designed to limit monarchial power and to protect feudal rights. However, the nobles' concerns about rights extended little beyond themselves. The principles declared in the Magna Carta—such as "No *freeman* [emphasis added] shall be taken or imprisoned or disseised [having his property taken] or exiled or in any way destroyed, nor will we go upon him or send upon him except by the lawful judgement of his peers and the law of the land"—excluded the vast majority of males who were not free but relegated to involuntary servitude. The devalued social positions and economic conditions of non-"freemen," women, and other groups of "others" cast them as possessions, appendages, and property and stalled the creation and enforcement of laws that might have served their interests.

Revolutions from above frequently are touted as holding out hope for substantially benefiting many of the oppressed. For example, in Europe and what was to become the United States, the emerging capitalist system was producing an economically powerful merchant and business class, a class that wanted freedom from monarchial control over economic matters. This desire to be free from aristocratic rule, and also to gain as much control as possible over the state to protect and enhance their interests, led the capitalist class to form an alliance, albeit a superficial one, with the human masses. It was only with the muscle of an activated populace that the capitalists could gain control of the state. Using ideas developed by eighteenth-century French Enlightenment philosophers, the nascent capitalist elite induced the disenfranchised and deprived masses to take arms against the military forces of the aristocracy. While the goals of *equality, liberty, and fraternity* were promoted publicly, many of the newly privileged class were quite concerned about the actual degree of political participation that should be afforded the mass of the citizenry. As a result, the emerging structure of the modern state and the procedures of political process under capitalism were in many ways variations of "revolutions from above." The new capitalist states were structured in the interests of those in society who were wealthy and successful in commerce. Political and human rights were promoted as universal—but with significant exceptions that, naturally, excluded "others."

THE FIVE POWERS OF THE STATE

State power is usually conceptualized as the right to use physical force—by way of police and military organizations—to uphold the legally sanctified social order. While a virtual monopoly on the right to use physical force is a formidable resource, those who control the state exercise other types of power as well. Writing in 1976, Austin Turk outlined five kinds of power that law can give to those who control it: physical force, economic control, political control, ideological power, and diversionary power.[21] While each type of power can be isolated for theoretical reflection, in reality they are usually tightly woven together and are, as such, mutually reinforcing.

What is more, Turk maintains that while many emphasize the role of law in regulating and resolving conflicts, in many ways law leads "toward instead of away from conflict."[22] Turk's insight into the uses of law is helpful to us, especially since control of law is synonymous with control of the state.

As we have seen, state control of organized police and military forces is key in establishing and perpetuating oppression through sheer physical force. Examples of the second type of power, economic power, can be gleaned from chapters 2 and 3. Those controlling the state can stifle citizen dissent, dispatch military forces to conquer and pillage other societies, and build their wealth from the spoils of their aggressive campaigns. From the Athenian warriors' subjugation of other city-states, to the looting of the Western Hemisphere by the conquistadors, to the United States's economic-based wars with Mexico and Spain, the use of state military and police power has enhanced both state treasuries and personal fortunes. Moreover, those in control of the state can enact laws declaring who can legally hold property, laws establishing systems of taxation and monetary control and similar measures, all of which may come to seem immutable and even consecrated to those who are governed—and all of which serve to enhance the material interests of the powerful.

Third, control of the state brings the ability to create procedures and rules of political participation—rules that protect the system from potential reformers and challengers from within. For example, as we have just seen, starting in the eighteenth century the emerging capitalist elite in the West began to create new constitutions that diminished many of the powers and entitlements previously enjoyed by the old ruling class but that continued to favor the powerful and disenfranchise the masses. For instance, a key provision of the constitution crafted after the French Revolution stated that election to the postrevolution French Legislative Assembly depended on property ownership. Consequently, only about fifty thousand out of a population of twenty-four million were eligible to run for an assembly seat. Similarly, the creators of the U.S. Constitution debated whether the masses should have a voice in government affairs.[23] While some members were in favor of widespread participation, others were strongly against it. Regarding this debate, Charles and Mary Beard write:

> Many members expressed a deep distrust of "the people," a distrust as deep as they felt for the monarchy. Indeed one or two were inclined to prefer a monarchy or an "aristocracy of wealth and talents." The "dangers" of popular rule were portrayed by Elbridge Gerry of Massachusetts in these words: "All the evils we now experience flow from an excess of democracy. The people do not want virtue but are the dupes of pretended patriots. . . . I have been too republican heretofore but have been taught by experience the danger of a leveling spirit." So he thought that the people should have as little to do as possible with government. Others agreed with him and sought to put a brake on the people by allowing them to vote, if at all, for rich men only. Charles Pinckney of South Carolina argued that no one should be elected President who was not worth $100,000 and that members of Congress and federal judges should be large property owners.[24]

Eventually a compromise grew out of the debate. Like the British Parliament of the time, Congress was to be composed of two branches. The House of Representatives would be elected directly by the *eligible* citizenry. The Senate, however, was to resemble the English House of Lords, which served to maintain aristocratic control over the House of Commons. The Senate would be a smaller, more elite group that was to be elected by state legislatures. Additionally, once elected, senators would serve for six years, while House members would serve for only two. The Senate was unmistakably created to serve as a brake on popular elections, a political mechanism to control the "rash" action of more democratically selected representatives. A further compromise on democratic participation resulted in the decision that the president would be elected indirectly by electors, chosen in ways to be decided by state legislatures. Finally, it was agreed that federal judges were to be presidential appointees who met with Senate approval.

In addition to establishing safeguards against political challenges to their control of the state, the framers also made sure they were fortified against rebellions. Noting the link between political and military control, Michael Parenti observes, "The Framers believed the states acted with insufficient force against popular uprisings, so Congress was given the task of 'organizing, arming, and disciplining the Militia' and calling it forth, among other things, to 'suppress Insurrections.' "[25]

And, very importantly, the United States Constitution protected private property. In another passage that illuminates the connection between political and economic control, Parenti writes:

> The Framers spent many weeks debating their differences, but these were differences of merchants, slave owners, and manufacturers, a debate of haves versus haves in which each group sought safeguards within the new Constitution for its particular regional or commercial interests. . . . [Q]uestions of enormous significance, relating to the new government's ability to protect the interests of property, were agreed upon with surprisingly little debate. For on these issues there were no dirt farmers or poor artisans attending the Convention to proffer an opposing viewpoint. The debate between haves and have-nots never took place.[26]

A well-thought-out political structure and process established by those in control of the state can enhance their material interests and thwart substantive reforms and liberation movements for centuries.

As Turk noted, the military, economic, and political power vested in those who control the state are supplemented with two additional powers—ideological and diversionary power. For thousands of years, ruling classes impressed their authority over the rest of the populace through the forced construction of temples, pyramids, and other awe-inspiring monuments. One of the more shocking ideological statements—intertwined with a show of physical force—occurred in response to an insurrection in 73 B.C. Rome. An enslaved human named Spartacus, forced into the position of "gladiator," amassed an army of forty thousand, most of whom were enslaved. For nearly two years his army avoided defeat, but the enormous military power of Rome eventually prevailed. To impress their "supremacy" and power on the populace, the Roman rulers cruelly executed thousands of the dissenters. The members of the Spartacan rebellion were crucified along the Appian Way, the major road to and from Rome, their dead bodies serving as a powerful testimonial to the supremacy of the Roman ruling class and the futility of challenging the status quo for all who saw or heard of the gruesome spectacle.

Finally, with control of the state comes considerable diversionary power. Turk writes:

Human attention and living-time are finite resources—a trite but profoundly consequential observation. Insofar as the rhetoric and the real workings of law occupy men's attention and time to the exclusion of other phenomenon—perhaps of greater import for the probability and quality of life—the law exerts diversionary power.[27]

One example of this diversionary power is seen from the Middle Ages. During this period state power, once held by the Roman ruling class, was assumed in part by the Christian Church. The Church was highly organized and eventually issued its own law and operated its own ecclesiastical courts. The statelike power of the Church enabled it to become one of the largest holders of feudal estates, at one point controlling about a third of the landed property of Europe. Widespread exploitation and vast disparities in the distribution of resources sparked resistance. The Church managed this dissent in part by the Inquisitions, official public spectacles in which, among other atrocities, countless women were tried for allegedly practicing witchcraft and causing great misfortunes to occur in their communities. Other animals were similarly used, as they, too, could be "possessed by demonic forces." When an "offense" by an other animal was alleged, Gerald Carson writes:

> Papers were served on the offending animals by an officer of the court, who read them in a loud voice where the culprits were known to congregate. . . . Thus, if the proceeding was against rats, the defendants were described as dirty, grayish rodents who lived in holes. . . . If they failed [to appear], they were warned to leave the district, or could be consigned to damnation by the dread curse of the Church. . . . If the animals persisted in being obstinate, their contumacy was not attributed to any lack of competence on the part of the court but to the superior power, temporarily, of Satan and his minions.
>
> Condemned animals that were physically in the custody of the law were killed by a variety of methods. They could be lightly singed, then strangled; burned at the stake; buried alive; sometimes tortured before being strung up on a gibbet.[28]

While some Church officials might have taken these criminal proceedings against other animals seriously, it is doubtful that the diversionary power of such events was entirely overlooked. While those promulgating and enforcing these nefarious laws and practices were no doubt deeply imbued with the religious and moral beliefs of their epoch, they likely were also quite aware of the source of their wealth and power, and shrewd about protecting it. As we observed in chapter 2, one of the by-products of the witch trials during this period was appropriation of the land and property of the convicted "witches"; some of the victims, it turns out, were political adversaries of the inquisition and humans of affluence.

So it is that, from the very beginning, the *state* has almost universally been securely under the control of the privileged, and the full weight and powers of the state have long been used against devalued groups of humans. It has been little different in the United States. A survey of the use of just the police and military powers of the state, for example, finds that the government uses physical force to quash rebellions of the enslaved, to displace and exterminate countless Native Americans, to thwart or limit efforts by exploited workers to form unions, and to wage imperial-ist wars against less powerful nations.[29] Strong evidence of the level of powerful capi-talists' control over the state in effect in the late nineteenth century is provided in the words of a former resident of the White House.

In the last quarter of the nineteenth century, President Rutherford B. Hayes became concerned about the increased concentration of economic wealth brought on by business trusts, combinations, and developing corporations and the resulting disparities in living conditions. Hayes, it must be noted, was not particularly known for challenging oppression. Fulfilling a promise to southern Democrats who helped put him in the White House, he had removed federal troops from the South, thus subjecting the formerly enslaved humans to decades of unrelieved violence and ter-ror. However, even Hayes felt compelled to speak out about the growing corporate control of the nation, a position that placed him in opposition to his Republican Party. Following his departure from the White House, a diary entry from 1887 observes:

> [I]t is time for the public to hear that the giant evil and danger in this country, the danger which transcends all others, is the vast wealth owned or controlled by a few persons. Money is power. In Congress, in state legislatures, in city councils, in the courts, in the political conventions, in the press, in the pulpit, in the circles of the edu-cated and the talented its influence is growing greater and greater. Excessive wealth in the hands of the few means extreme poverty, ignorance, vice, and wretchedness as the lot of the many.[30]

As the locus of economic control shifted from powerful individuals to powerful corporations, corporate control of the state grew. In 1888, another resident of the White House, President Grover Cleveland—again, a politician who was not known as a friend to the oppressed, having sent federal troops to break the famous Pullman Strike of 1884—stated in his annual message to Congress:

> We find the wealth and luxury of our cities mingled with poverty and wretchedness and unremunerative toil. A crowded and constantly increasing urban population suggests the impoverishment of rural sections, and discontent with rural pursuits. . . .
> We discover that fortunes realized by our manufacturers are no longer solely the reward of sturdy industry and enlightened foresight, but that they result from the dis-criminating favor of the government, and are largely built upon undue exactions from the masses of our people. The gulf between employers and the employed is constantly widening, and classes are rapidly forming, one comprising the very rich and powerful, while in another are found the toiling poor.
> . . . [W]e discover the existence of trusts, combinations, and monopolies, while the citizen is struggling far in the rear, or is trampled to death beneath an iron wheel. Cor-porations . . . are fast becoming the people's masters.[31]

While legislative bodies created laws that substantially protected and advanced the economic elite and their corporate enterprises, historically the U.S. judiciary buttressed these legislative controls. Rulings from the federal court system have long exemplified the use of the political and ideological power of the state to protect privilege. For instance, when the national debate over slavery was growing in the mid–nineteenth century, the Chief Justice of the Supreme Court, Roger Taney, in the majority opinion in the *Dred Scott* case of 1857 declared that blacks "had no rights which the white man is bound to respect."[32] In 1872, the Illinois Supreme Court refused Myra Bradwell the right to practice law because of her sex. Her case was ultimately heard by the United States Supreme Court, which ruled against her. The Court proclaimed:

> [T]he civil law, as well as nature herself, has always recognized a wide difference in the respective spheres and destinies of man and woman. Man is, or should be, woman's protector and defender. The natural and proper timidity and delicacy which belongs to the female sex evidently unfits it for many of the occupations of civil life. . . . The paramount mission of woman is to fulfill the noble and benign offices of wife and mother. This is the law of the creator.[33]

One of the primary ideological refuges the elite used to combat calls for social reform and change during the early twentieth century was "social Darwinism." This pseudoscientific doctrine essentially placed the responsibility for social ills on the oppressed, due to their alleged "mental deficiencies," while extolling the virtues of the "intellectually endowed" capitalist class. The Supreme Court helped promulgate this ideology in a ruling that upheld the forced sterilization of humans believed to be "defective." Writing for the majority, Justice Holmes stated in 1927, "It is better for all the world if, instead of waiting to execute degenerate offspring for crime, or to let them starve for their imbecility, society can prevent those who are manifestly unfit from continuing their kind."[34]

THE RISE OF POLITICAL CAPITALISM

In 1896, an effort was made to persuade the U.S. government to establish modest regulation over the actions of vivisectionists in the District of Columbia. Proponents of Senate Bill 1552 produced endless, horrific examples of common laboratory practices. The following examples from a vivisector's notes were read into evidence at a Senate hearing on 26 May 1896.

> First experiment.—Large watch dog. Extended on the vivisecting table on its stomach—the four limbs and head fastened, but not too tightly. With a large, empty stone bottle I strike a dozen violent blows on the thighs. The animal, by its cries, more and more violent, indicates the bruise is great, and vividly felt.
>   Second experiment.—Large hound. The animal is fixed like the former. Placing myself at a certain height, that my mallet may strike with greater force on the part to be experimented upon, I give, with all the strength in my right arm, twelve successive blows with a great wooden mallet, some on the deltoid, some on the shoulder, some on

the back, some in front. As in the first case, this dog indicates by his cries that the bruises are very painfully felt, after which he falls into a sort of sleep, broken by moans, for ten minutes. After this again he awakens agitated, and seems to suffer more than the first dog. . . .

Seventh experiment.—Large bitch. We proceed without anesthetics, thinking that they have nullified previous experiments. The animal is fastened on the vivisecting table. I dislocate successfully both her shoulders, doing it with some difficulty. The animal, which appears to suffer much, is kept in a condition of dislocation for about half an hour. It struggles violently in spite of its bonds. The autopsy shows that on the left shoulder there had been a tearing of the small tuberosity and of all the adjoining skeleton.

Eighth experiment.—Poodle dog. . . . I dislocate his two shoulders. The animal utters screams of suffering. I hold him for twenty minutes, with two shoulders dislocated and the elbows tied together behind his back.[35]

The bill, similar to legislation enacted in Great Britain twenty years earlier, would have required the licensing of vivisectors and subjected their laboratories to occasional inspections. While the British law had only a modest effect on vivisection in that country, the proposed law here was resisted strongly by many in the medical and scientific establishment who contended such regulation was unnecessary and would impede the development of scientific and medical knowledge—knowledge to be used in the interests of "humanity." Interestingly, the federal government itself was deeply into the practice of vivisection through the work of the Bureau of Animal Industry, a division of the U.S. Department of Agriculture. The bureau was "charged by law with the duty of investigating and controlling animal diseases . . . for securing a food supply from them uncontaminated by disease."[36] In a letter to the Senate opposing the regulation of vivisection, the acting secretary of the Department of Agriculture, Charles A. Dabney, Jr., declared, "[U]nder no circumstances should local legislation be allowed to interfere with, demoralize, or prohibit the important scientific investigations which are specifically authorized by Congress for the benefit of the great agricultural industry of the whole country."[37]

In this letter, Dabney also sought to protect vivisection by linking it frankly to commonly accepted cruelties against other animals that were accepted for other economic reasons.

Some of these experiments have been painful for the animals operated upon. . . . Such experiments . . . are less subject to the charge of cruelty, even though they cause pain, than are the ordinary practices of emasculation, branding, and slaughtering, all of which are countenanced for economic reasons and cause more pain than scientific experiments. So long as we admit that an animal may be caused to suffer the intense pain of castration in order that it may be more economically raised and better suited for the service of man or for the production of edible meat, and so long as we admit that animals may be killed by painful processes to supply us with food, it is inconsistent to say that they can not be used in experiments necessary for the advancement of knowledge, the relief of suffering, and the saving of property and life.[38]

One opponent of the legislation, the president of the Medical Society of the District of Columbia, stated that the legislation was "based upon sentimentality, old maids having a fondness for cats."[39]

Bill proponents countered that many experiments, purportedly conducted to benefit humanity, were performed rather with an eye to "the commercial value of those who deal in it."[40] One proponent, expressing a concern about the quality of life of millions of members of humanity living in squalor and poverty, implored the medical establishment to resist diversionary, vivisectionist-based cures, urging that, "If our doctors would turn their attention more to sanitation among human beings more cures could be effected, and less disease contracted."[41]

In the end, SB 1552, which would have done no more than effect modest reforms over vivisection in the District of Columbia, did not pass. One potent reason, in all likelihood, was the fear noted by Charles Dabney, Jr., that legislation regulating the treatment of other animals by vivisectionists might establish precedent for similar reforms of other economically motivated activities that cause great suffering—such as the regulation of methods of slaughter. In retrospect, the rejection of the bill was not surprising in a society where great numbers of humans lived in crowded, unsanitary conditions and worked under dangerous circumstances at grossly poor wages. While many members of the medical, scientific, and business establishments offered testimony that their various experiments, practices, and enterprises were in the interest of the human community, few voiced any concern about the widespread poverty, exploitation, and suffering that plagued so many at the beginning of the twentieth century. (Sadly, the same observation can be made more than one hundred years later.)

Few other legislative debates at this time emerged from concerns about the oppression of other animals. Most activists were consumed with the extreme oppression of U.S. workers, including women, humans of color, and children. Early in the twentieth century a considerable amount of corporate energy was spent diluting legislative reforms promoted by social critics and revolutionaries. While historians generally credit the Populist movement with forcing reforms and concessions from big business during this period, there is reason to rethink, and to qualify, this interpretation. In most instances, the committees or commissions that became responsible for regulating troublesome industries were made up of industry representatives or those friendly to industry interests. Moreover, opportunistic big business often used the "reforms" of the Progressive era as vehicles to control or eliminate their smaller competitors. Writing in 1963, Gabriel Kolko reflected on the increasing degree of control big business was exercising over political decisions during the early years of the twentieth century:

> The fact that federal regulation of the economy was conservative in its effect in preserving existing power and economic relations in society should not obscure the fact that federal intervention in the economy was conservative in purpose as well. This ambition was publicly proclaimed by the interested business forces, and was hardly conspiratorial. . . . Political leaders such as Roosevelt and Wilson, and their key appointees, held that it was proper for an industry to have a decisive voice or veto over the regulatory process

within its sphere of interest, and such assumptions filled many key businessmen with confidence in the essential reliability of the federal political mechanism.[42]

One example that supports this thesis takes us back to the 1896 Senate hearings on vivisection. Acting Secretary of Agriculture Charles Dabney had argued that experiments on other animals, especially experiments conducted by the Department of Agriculture's Bureau of Animal Industry, were necessary for the "advancement of knowledge, the relief of suffering, and the saving of property and life." In actuality, the Bureau of Animal Industry was created by Congress in 1884 at the urging of the "meat" packing industry because European nations were refusing to import diseased U.S. "meat." Late in the nineteenth century, many European countries, including Italy, France, Spain, England, Denmark, Austria, and Germany, were banning the importation of contaminated U.S. "meat" products and turning to other suppliers. In a discussion of the response of U.S. "meat" packers, Gabriel Kolko wryly notes, "These packers learned that . . . it was not to their profit to poison their customers, especially in a competitive market in which the consumer could go elsewhere."[43]

The loss of the European market had enormous costs for the largest of the U.S. "meat" packers, who killed millions of other animals every year and exported their bodies as food. One of the basic aims of the Bureau of Animal Industry was to eradicate pleuropneumonia, cholera, and other diseases infecting the other animals bred and slaughtered as profitable exports. The vivisectionist activities thus undertaken by the federal government apparently were motivated more to protect the economic interests of the agriculture industry than to serve the public, Acting Secretary Dabney's idealistic characterizations of this activity notwithstanding. Furthermore, an 1891 federal act that required a post-mortem inspection of "meat" intended for interstate commerce *excluded* "meat" intended for domestic consumption. Thus, industry representatives promoted government regulation of "meat" exports in order to obtain state seals of approval on their exported "products," while they successfully placed the expense for research and inspections on an unprotected public. Vivisectionist research and "meat" inspections were intended largely "to fight European restrictions, not to aid the American consumer."[44] The larger packers also persuaded the federal government to extend inspection laws to smaller slaughter and packing houses as well, an action that eventually forced hundreds of small companies out of business. As Kolko notes, while Upton Sinclair's *The Jungle* is popularly credited with bringing about the reform of the "meat" industry, the need to protect the interests of the large packers played a far more powerful role. Indeed, Sinclair's goal was not to bring reform to "meat" processing but, rather, to bring some relief to the exploited workers inside the slaughterhouses and packing plants. That goal was easily resisted by the "meat" industry.

This example of powerful capitalists crafting regulations that served their interest is characteristic of many such "progressive reforms." The trend in the early twentieth century for the economy to become concentrated, centralized, and monopolistic in nature was accompanied by the trend for the state to move toward what Kolko labeled "political capitalism." Douglas Dowd explains:

The State in the United States has always operated so as to provide an acceptable or favorable context for capitalist development; in the 19th century it did so largely through "non-decisions," that is, unobtrusively. . . . But in the 20th century the State's role became obtrusive, and explicit. The political outlets and institutions of the State had to be and came to be used to attain the desired conditions of stability, predictability, and security.[45]

Hence, the activities of reform- and revolution-minded individuals and the related movements of the period were diluted by political capitalist reforms.

What is more, the reformers' concerns and efforts were eclipsed further by the patriotic fervor that was aroused when the United States entered World War I. While U.S. military power was used to protect the nation's large business interests, and "progressive" legislation was diverting and defusing social change movements, the law enforcement arm of the state was used to discourage and eliminate further domestic calls for change. Forty-five years after Susan B. Anthony was arrested and tried for attempting to vote, women picketing for suffrage outside the Wilson White House during World War I were arrested and beaten while in police custody. A major setback for the Left occurred when the attorney general of the United States, Mitchell Palmer, aided by his young assistant, J. Edgar Hoover, illegally arrested, detained, and deported several thousand socialists and labor leaders in 1919 and 1920.

Meanwhile, government officials did little to protect black communities from rioting groups of white racists or to stem the proliferation of lynchings. Biased judicial proceedings flourished, evidenced by such infamous spectacles as the trial of the Scottsboro defendants and the bogus trial of the killers of Emmett Till.

An important diversionary and ideological exhibition staged by the government was the "anticommunist" McCarthy hearings of the early 1950s. In the 1960s and early 1970s, there was Cointelpro, a covert FBI program created to stifle domestic reform and entailing such activities as the secret surveillance of Dr. Martin Luther King, Jr., and FBI-supported assassinations and framing of Black Panther and American Indian Movement leaders. In these and countless other instances, the various powers of the state were widely used in the twentieth century to maintain oppression and protect privilege while largely suppressing any significant efforts to promote social justice.[46]

This brief glimpse into history helps bring the essential character of the state into focus. Although eventual and hard-fought constitutional reforms, such as public election of senators, expansion of the right to vote, and civil rights legislation, ostensibly made the political process more democratic, the structure and operations of the state continue to abet oppression and to protect and promote privilege. Certainly, such a broad stroke does not acknowledge ways in which the state—especially in the contemporary United States—does serve the public in numerous ways. However, in critical areas of decision making around important economic issues and in the protection of wealth, the operations of the state are largely rigged. Even when efforts to reform political or economic practices are successful, they are frequently "revolutions from above" (e.g., the contemporary "tax reforms" and "welfare reforms") that do relatively little to ameliorate conditions of injustice and exploitation for those who most need it. Such a perspective on the nature of the state raises issues about the possibility of ending oppression through state reform. How are "rights" for other animals to be obtained within a system that is constructed to guard against the imposition of such rights? Examples of how state power has been used to thwart or weaken such efforts are reviewed in the next section.

CONGRESSIONAL "WELFARE" ACTS
FOR OTHER ANIMALS

One of the key points of this chapter is that power in contemporary society—the capitalist state—while ostensibly democratic in nature, is actually designed and used to protect wealth. Those reforms that do occur are usually crafted to a substantial degree by those they attempt to regulate, are relatively modest in scope, are weak in enforcement, and serve to provide social stability and security for the affluent and their corporate enterprises. Many "reforms" divert attention away from the continued, systematic injustice and oppression suffered daily by devalued humans and other animals.

The propensity and ability of those in control of state power to resist or buffer reforms, particularly those that might cut into profit margins, are seen, for example, in U.S. Senate hearing testimony and debate around the issue of "humane slaughter," the specter that Acting Secretary of Agriculture Charles A. Dabney, Jr., had warned against a half century earlier. In May 1956, Senator Hubert H. Humphrey chaired hearings on SB 1636, Humane Slaughtering of Livestock and Poultry, a bill that would have regulated slaughtering methods for "products" intended for interstate or foreign commerce. Although the history of the United States is fraught with illustrations of exploitation and oppression of "others," and although many European countries already had enacted "humane" slaughter acts by this time, Senator Humphrey initiated the hearing with a falsely flattering statement that is typical of the use of the ideological power of the state.

> We Americans are inherently a humane and compassionate people. I think it is one of our great and one of our truly sterling qualities. We abhor cruelty in any form. We dislike to see suffering, whether human or animals. It is therefore in the American tradition to seek to eliminate as much cruelty, hardship and suffering as we can.
>
> Whenever we shut our eyes to cruelty and suffering, whether among people or among animals, we are shutting out part of the spirit that has made America great, and makes us stand apart in the world as a nation that puts moral principles and decency above sheer material value.[47]

At the time, the primary method of killing cows in this "inherently humane" nation's five thousand slaughterhouses was by having "strongmen" strike them on the head with a pole ax. Pigs and birds were still largely killed by the fiendish methods described by Upton Sinclair at the beginning of the century. Speaking in favor of federal legislation that would "reform" slaughtering practices, bill advocate Christian P. Nargord, a representative of the American Humane Association, described one of the problems of killing with a pole ax: The pole axman "often misses and the sledge slides down the faces of the animals and cuts their eyes and their ears, and they bawl and are frightened and hurt."[48]

Fred Myers, executive director of the National Humane Society, submitted a statement that included the following horrific description of killing pigs.

> We doubt that packers will deny that methods of slaughter now used in animal packing plants cause agony to the animal victims. Many packers, indeed, have publicly admitted the fact. It may be well, however, to describe briefly what is being done to animals in packing plants. . . .
>
> Hogs[:] some 50 million go through slaughterhouses every year . . . . Approximately a dozen animals are driven into a shackling pen, a pen about the size of a small house kitchen. There a short length of chain is noosed around one hind leg of each animal. The end of each chain is then hooked to a moving belt or chain which inexorably drags the shrieking animal to one end of the room and then upward, dangling by the shackled leg, to a floor above.
>
> On the upper floor, still writhing and shrieking, the hog is carried before a man who is called a sticker. The sticker is supposed to plunge a broad bladed knife into the big vein in the throat of the hog. It is not desired that the hog shall be quickly killed, the deliberate intent is that the animal shall die slowly so that the laboring heart will clear the body of blood.
>
> Stickers in the big slaughterhouses become quite expert with practice but often the knife fails to strike a struggling hog in the precise spot intended. Hogs frequently are stuck several times in various parts of the face and head, and even in the shoulders before the knife reaches the big vein.
>
> After a hog is stuck, the overhead conveyance moves it still farther to a huge scalding vat. It is intended, one assumes, that a hog should have become unconscious from loss of blood and shock before it is plummeted into the scalding water. Ordinary routine leaves about five minutes between sticking and scalding.
>
> Not all hogs become unconscious in the allotted time, however, and at times the routine is not perfect and the interval between sticking and scalding is considerably less than five minutes.
>
> There is certainly no experienced packinghouse worker in the hog killing department who has not seen agonized animals struggling desperately to swim out of the water that is hot enough to loosen hair. Indeed, the National Humane Association has repeatedly been told by packinghouse workers of hogs that still showed signs of life, and reflex to stimuli, after going through the scalding vat to the big dehairing machines that tumble the animals vigorously about and strip the hair from them.
>
> The method that we have described is used with only minor variations of technique in all but two of the major slaughter houses in America.
>
> Sheep, lambs and calves are killed in substantially the same way, although they are not, of course, scalded.[49]

The "meat" industry did not dispute the tales of horror introduced by the proponents of SB 1636 and did not try to defend itself by defaming the other animals or minimizing their ability to suffer. Rather, the industry generally represented itself as desiring more humane methods of slaughter. For example, R. W. Regensburger, vice president of Swift and Company and a representative of one of the largest industry associations, the American Meat Institute, stated, "The American Meat Institute has constantly favored and sponsored efforts which could secure humane treatment of all livestock under all conditions from farm to packing plants."[50]

> However, the Institute is opposed to S.B. 1636 because . . . [t]here is no practical method that has so far been developed that will bring death to any animal or individual that is pleasant. . . . The livestock dispatched annually in this country is very large—far greater than in European countries with which comparisons are drawn with respect to humane methods of slaughter.[51]

By "no practical method," Regensburger meant none that packers believed was *economically* feasible. When confronted with examples of better European practices, Regensburger maintained it would be unfair to subject large U.S. packers to the standards of smaller packers in Europe when large U.S. packers "processed" so many more other animals per hour.

Speaking for the National Independent Meat Packers Association, Wilbur La Roe claimed, "I would like to say that the small packers are thoroughly in sympathy with the objective here of bringing about humane slaughter. They are not satisfied with present arrangements for slaughter and they welcome improvements, but what scares them to death is these big figures of cost."[52]

L. Blaine Liljenquist, speaking for the Western States Meat Packers Association, summed up the industry position:

> I would like to make it clear . . . that our members are very much in favor of working out the most humane methods of slaughtering livestock and the most humane way of raising and marketing animals. . . .
>
> But our members sincerely believe that we have not yet progressed to a point in perfecting improved methods where it is at all economically feasible to require that livestock be rendered insensible by mechanical, electrical, or chemical means before slaughter. Undoubtedly this desirable objective may someday be reached, but to require it now by legislation would mean economic havoc in the meat packing industry.[53]

R. Harvey Dastrup, claiming to represent 1,623,222 members of the American Farm Bureau Federation, stated, "It is our belief that the greatest progress toward the solution of the problem will come about through the development of voluntary programs by all segments of the livestock and meat industry and those interested in the humane handling of livestock. . . . We would like to suggest, therefore, that great emphasis be placed on an educational program."[54]

Proponents of the legislation attempted to ease the concerns of the packing industry by suggesting that alternative methods of slaughtering other animals would be in their economic interest. For example, the House sponsor of the bill, Representative Martha W. Griffiths of Michigan, stated:

Apart from the compelling considerations to accord humane treatment to the animals involved, the use of humane techniques in slaughtering could have important and beneficial economic opportunities for the meat packing industry.

Perhaps most important would be the reduction in bruised and damaged meat. It is presently estimated that as much as $50 million worth of meat is rendered unsalable annually because of the damage coincident with the slaughtering process. This loss could be reduced substantially if humane methods were employed. An unconscious animal is easy to work with, presents no problem in the subsequent killing process, and thus the prospect of loss in dressing is reduced to an important degree.

Secondly, it should be noted that the meatpacking companies would be entitled to the generous depreciation rate of the internal revenue code in charging off the cost of new installations necessary to accomplish humane slaughtering.

Under the 1954 Revenue Act this depreciation can be accomplished at twice the rate previously allowed.[55]

Representative Griffiths also noted that the proposed legislation would affect only those companies that were engaged in interstate commerce, just 455 out of more than 5,000 slaughterhouses operating throughout the nation. Another appeal to the economic interests of the packing companies was offered by Senator Richard L. Neuberger of Oregon:

[T]he workers in slaughterhouses are not in control of these plants. . . . Once or twice I have had members of the Butcher Workers' Union observe to me:

We realize that cruel ways of slaughter will only hurt the meat industry and promote vegetarianism among Americans. We believe that every possible humane method of killing should be used in slaughterhouses just as soon as it is developed.[56]

Speaking on behalf of the Society for Animal Protective Legislation, Madeleine Bemelmans reacted against the economic basis of the debate by making an ethical appeal for state intervention: "Time and time again people cry 'sentimentality,' and say in the time of world upheaval there are more important things to think about. But what kind of civilization is it which does not recognize any values besides the material ones? I think the qualities of a civilization are evident in the treatment of the weak and powerless."[57]

In a society where money is power, Bemelmans's ethical appeal did not carry the day. It took four more years of "study" and debate before legislation to regulate the slaughter of other animals became law, and the legislation passed only narrowly in the Senate by a vote of 43 to 40. Even then, the 1960 act did not cover all slaughterhouses but was restricted to those companies selling "meat" to the federal government.[58] Moreover, the only enforcement mechanism included in the act was the ability of USDA inspectors to stop the "disassembly line" until compliance was obtained. This hard-fought act did not stop the killing of other animals for food and resources but merely purported to reduce the degree of agony that some endured just before their deaths.

One of the obvious problems with this reform, besides being a largely industry-crafted bill and essentially legitimating the continued oppression of "farm" animals, is that the enforcer of the act is the U.S. Department of Agriculture, the same government body charged with *promoting* agricultural development and sales. While advocates for other animals continually criticize the USDA for its minimal enforcement of the act, the public is officially "assured" that other animals who are converted to "food" are slaughtered humanely—a key ideological benefit. Furthermore, the lengthy and protracted legislative process also served a diversionary function, focusing the passions and energy of animal advocates on this minimal reform. To this day, the act diverts the energy of advocates, who expend great effort to monitor its enforcement and to obtain closely guarded evidence of continued illegal and torturous practices, embroiling them in quixotic political struggles for effective enforcement rather than further change. The economic interests of those profiting from the tortured existence and death of other animals ultimately were protected by the act through the power of the state, as the government's seal of approval was affixed to the nation's largest slaughterhouses.

All the while, the level of suffering and explicit cruelty against other animals in the nation's slaughterhouses today is beyond hideous, as we saw in chapter 4. Due to the deregulation fever of the 1980s, the "meat" industry was able to speed up the disassembly lines of the nation's largest slaughterhouses and neutralize the impact of USDA inspectors. With little change in the gruesome methods of slaughter described in the 1956 Senate testimony, contemporary slaughterhouses continue to inflict agony on ever-greater numbers of other animals who are not effectively stunned or rendered unconscious before they begin their descent down the disassembly line. As Gail Eisnitz documented, many are mercilessly beaten and even skinned and boiled alive.[59] Workers are driven by company supervisors to keep the line moving at all costs. Many USDA inspectors and veterinarians are also pressured to downplay or ignore such practices, as reports to high-level USDA officials—many of whom were recruited from agribusiness corporations—produce few results or consequences, and meddlesome inspectors face the very real possibility of losing their jobs.[60] For instance, twenty public interest groups in June 2000 accused the USDA of "trying to intimidate its own food safety inspectors" and "misrepresenting conditions at two poultry processing plants in Alabama."[61] The groups charged that powerful USDA officials were upset that inspectors at these plants were reporting that "carcasses with scabs, sores and pus were cut up and made into chicken nuggets that the federal government then purchased and distributed to school lunch programs around the nation."[62] In New York, inspectors "claimed they were ignored, or even retaliated against by high-level USDA officials, after reporting possible improprieties involving other inspectors."[63]

STATE PROTECTION OF
LABORATORY OPPRESSION

A similar example of both the economic basis of oppression and the use of state power to quiet public concern and protect the status quo was seen in the 1960s, when the rapacious appetite of vivisectionists for other animals stimulated another congressional act. The capitalist entrepreneurial spirit had motivated some to seek income by stealing other animals kept as "pets," mostly cats and dogs, and selling them to research laboratories. The practice became so pervasive and obvious that public opinion prompted federal action. Legislation proposed at the time would have required licensure both for research laboratories and for "dealers" in dogs, cats, and other animals, required vivisectionists to keep records on the purchase and disposition of other animals, and permitted occasional inspection of laboratories that subject other animals to experiments.

Testifying before a 1966 House hearing on the proposed legislation was Declan Hogan, hired by the Humane Society of the United States to work undercover as an "animal dealer."

[I] traveled more than 32,000 miles covering some 15 states. I saw all kinds of dealer operations with animals, bound for research, suffering from the most appalling conditions. I was particularly shocked at the scope and magnitude of the business and the unscrupulous methods of procuring and handling that are commonplace. The cynicism with which I had undertaken the job soon disappeared as my probe developed.

I found that cruelty, whether by omission or commission, is the general rule among dealers. The dealers consider research animals nothing more than a product with resale value. The principal motivation is profit. There is no thought that animals are living creatures needing food, water and care to survive. I saw hundreds of animals in a condition of semistarvation, many others dead from malnutrition, and still more without water, shelter, or care of any kind. I saw pigeons being devoured alive by raccoons simply because no one had bothered to separate the cages of both. I saw dogs tied with short chains to outside, unheated huts in freezing weather. I saw cats lying listlessly in their own feces which obviously hadn't been cleaned up for months. I saw sick and injured animals dying of hunger and thirst in penned enclosures while healthy animals with them devoured the cattle entrails and slaughterhouse products thrown indiscriminately to all.

Easy money and large profits are the easily recognized causes. Without legal requirements, no dealer will lessen profits by providing heated and lighted buildings, trained personnel, adequate food and water, and veterinary care. . . .

The "no questions asked" attitude of the suppliers and the research organizations has fostered the small time operator dealing strictly for beer and cigarette money. . . . Gentlemen, I need hardly to tell you that the animals handled by this type of character are subjected to extreme cruelty and neglect.

I have found cruelty rampant throughout the entire chain of supply of research animals. The large dealers, last stop for many animals going to laboratories, run their operations for maximum profit and minimum loss. The huge number of animals being handled contributes further to the prevailing indifference and carelessness. . . .

I also applied to the National Institutes of Health in Bethesda, Md., for a contract to supply animals to that institution. I was received by Dr. Cameron and asked my name and address. No effort was made to probe into my background but I was subjected to a lengthy explanation of the idealistic requirements which NIH supposedly wants from animal suppliers. I knew from my investigations that these standards were not being followed and Dr. Cameron's entire attitude toward me indicated that he was in a position of having to, but not wanting to, deal with a seemingly derelict character. Such is the tremendous demand for animals in research institutions.[64]

For the most part, the scientific community and the rapidly growing biomedical industry opposed the legislation. While some opponents of the legislation professed sensitivity to the theft of a "pet," many claimed that the asserted linkage between that activity and "legitimate" laboratory work was scandalous, and they opposed any part of the legislation that sought to regulate laboratory activities. As one might expect, arguments against the proposed legislation cited the expected monetary costs of compliance with the proposed regulations and urged the necessity of unhampered research needed to benefit the "public interest." Speaking before a subcommittee of the House of Representatives, Joseph B. Sprawls, representing the American Association of Colleges of Pharmacy, stated, "[W]e are confident that it is not the intent of the legislation to increase unnecessarily the already heavy administrative burden of the laboratories responsible for the conduct of research. To do so would not only impede the essential work of researchers but, in addition, would increase the cost of the program."[65]

Dr. Frank N. Miller of the National Society for Medical Research maintained:

The requirements in the bills for the licensing and inspection of laboratories and for extensive record keeping in such facilities would not be in the public interest. . . . [P]rovisions for the licensing of research facilities, the charging of license fees, the authorization of the Secretary to set standards for the handling of animals at research laboratories, and the requirements for detailed recordkeeping would impose burdensome restrictions on research workers. Time and money which could be better spent on experimental work for the public good would be wasted.[66]

Due in no small part to public pressure generated by journalistic exposes of incidents of "pet" theft, the Congress enacted Public Law 89–544, known as the Dogs and Cats Act of 1966. However, the act only required "animal dealers" and research facilities to be registered with the secretary of agriculture and for dealers to be licensed. Research facilities were prohibited from purchasing other animals from unlicensed dealers. The Dogs and Cats Act did *not* authorize the USDA to regulate the care or treatment of other animals during actual research or experimentation. With modest reforms seemingly in place, and with public confidence in the scientific use of other animals buttressed, tens of millions of individuals were delivered into the hands of vivisectionists, with both the official approval and the participation of the state. Like the Humane Slaughter Act, the Dogs and Cats Act remains largely unenforced. According to one observer, "[R]esearchers know USDA is not doing its job. If it did, the supply of cheap dogs and cats would diminish and prices would rise."[67]

Eventually, antivivisection forces in the United States did have some impact on the numbers of other animals relegated to the social position of "research subject."[68] However, federal legislation, such as the Animal Welfare Act of 1976 and subsequent amendments that purported to require at least minimal standards of care and use for other animals subjected to vivisection, bolstered public support of vivisectionist activities.[69] As with other legislative "reforms," the industries involved successfully influenced the content of this act, resulting in a weak, minimal set of suggested guidelines—which could be set aside if required by "scientific protocol." Like the Humane Slaughter Act, the Dogs and Cats Act, and most other pieces of key legislation that ostensibly regulate huge, profitable industries, these efforts are significant as uses of state ideological power in ways that largely stifle industry critics and quell public concern.

In response, a small number of activists have turned from these diversionary, almost ritualized attempts at minimal reform; instead, they have opted to obtain evidence of continued atrocities and even to attempt actual rescues of oppressed individuals. For example, in 1984 the Animal Liberation Front raided the laboratory of Thomas Gennarelli at the University of Pennsylvania and found videotapes of experiments on other animals that not only violated the Animal Welfare Act but outraged the public and many members of Congress.

After several similar raids, which provided evidence of the horrors of experimentation on other animals, the mammoth biomedical and agricultural industries sought to use the physical power of the state to protect their economic and professional interests—again, they claimed, the same as the "public interest." These industries, and others with a stake in protecting their "animal enterprises," pressured politicians to support the Farm and Research Facilities Protection Bill, which was created to ban acts of "domestic terrorism." The legislation proposed to make it a federal crime for a person without the effective consent of the owner to acquire or "otherwise exercise control over an animal facility, an animal from an animal facility, or other property from an animal facility, with the intent to deprive the owner of such facility, animal, or property and to disrupt or damage the enterprise conducted at the animal facility."

A primary goal of the bill was to criminalize unauthorized investigative activities in "animal enterprises." Furthermore, it labeled many activists working in the interests of other animals as "terrorists." This labeling would invoke the participation of the Federal Bureau of Investigation and the federal courts and prisons—a tactic not unlike the numerous other instances in which the criminal justice system in the United States has been used to protect systemic oppression and to stifle effective dissent.[70] Despite statements by officials at the Department of Justice that adequate laws and enforcement procedures already existed to deal with the alleged activities of animal advocates, the powerful coalition of biomedical and agricultural industry associations pushed strenuously for enactment of the proposed legislation. However, the attempt to minimize dissent and criticism around the treatment of other animals was obvious and troubling even for some members of Congress. Speaking at a 1990 House hearing on the matter, Representative Dan Glickman of Kansas stated:

> First, the bill, theoretically, would make simple trespass a Federal crime. We ought not to be making simple trespass a Federal crime if it's trespass on an "animal facility." I

mean, what's different from trespass on an animal facility from trespass on a jewelry store or trespass on a clothing store? Our Federal courts are overloaded as it is, so we need to have a focused effort on why we are doing this bill. . . .

Second, this bill is a felony statute. So when you examine a felony statute, you have to make sure that Federal jurisdiction is absolutely required in all contexts of it, and I'm not sure in all contexts that it is required.

Third, it could be interpreted that the prohibited acts of this bill, intending to deprive the owner of a facility and to disrupt or damage the enterprise conducted at the animal facility, could be to prohibit normal first amendment acts of protest, and I don't think that we want to get into that ball game here of saying somebody . . . wanting to protest at an animal welfare facility or at a university would be guilty of this statute. . . .

Fourth, . . . the potential scope of the remedy [is] way beyond the nature of the problem.

. . . [I] think we have to be awful careful in setting precedents which might abridge both first amendment rights to protest as well as creating Federal crimes and things that ought not to be in the Federal courts at all.[71]

In an insightful comment about who might be the real terrorists, Representative Charles Rose of North Carolina stated:

One of the things that concerns me is that everybody has been led to believe that there is very little truth to the fact that terrorism—and I don't even like to use that word, but that's what has been used by the biomedical research community—that terrorism is all against them. Well, last night on "20–20," Hugh Downs had a very enlightening segment on puppy mills or organizations that have been caught stealing from private individuals their pets and selling them to research laboratories.

Now we're opening a can of worms here today. I'm going to offer an amendment at the appropriate time to make it a crime to steal people's pets to give them to research laboratories.[72]

In addition to the concerns about the necessity and purpose of the proposed bill raised by some members of Congress, advocates for other animals also offered insightful comments about the true nature of federal "protection" of other animals in research facilities. William Cotreau read a statement prepared by Christine Stevens of the Society for Animal Protective Legislation that included the following passage:

[The last time I testified] was in 1984, when I presented the preliminary results of a study conducted by the Animal Welfare Institute analyzing reports by USDA's Veterinary Services of 214 registered research facilities. The study was later published as part of the book "Beyond the Laboratory Door."

You will note that 174 of these facilities had one or more deficiencies, some serious or chronic. In only 37 were no deficiencies reported during the 3-year period covered. This 81 percent failure rate to observe the minimum standards established by the Animal Welfare Act shows in numerical terms why there is such a widespread public concern about how laboratory animals are treated. There is a strong consensus among

American voters that these animals must be treated humanely, but so far the public has no assurance that they are.

The Society for Animal Protective Legislation and the Animal Welfare Institute have done their utmost to plead, pressure, and cajole institutions into taking seriously their responsibilities for the animals they use. For example, "Comfortable Quarters for Laboratory Animals," which we provide free to scientists and administrators, shows good examples from facilities where animals are properly housed, but aggressive lobbying by the National Association for Biomedical Research and its constituent organizations has even prevented major sections of the improved standards for laboratory animals amendments, passed as part of the 1985 farm bill, from being made final.

Yesterday, a toothless version of some of the standards was made final. Due to industry pressure, these regulations have two nullifying provisions: a grandfather clause for substandard caging and a discretionary clause whereby the institution can opt not to follow the regulations. . . . Eviscerated regulations do not ensure that the public demand for humane care of laboratory animals is met. . . .

You may not be aware of the acts of aggression coming from the biomedical side or of how they are being used. . . . I know from personal experience how fearful of reprisals are individuals employed by medical schools who dare to criticize abuse of laboratory animals in their own institutions. . . . [T]wo school teachers . . . were sued into pennilessness by a dog dealer. . . . Nor are the victims of commercial biomedical interests limited to nonscientists. Immuno AG, an Austrian multinational pharmaceutical company, has sued some 60 different people and institutions over unfavorable comments on the company's acquisition of endangered chimpanzees. After a 5-year court battle, Dr. Moor-Jankowski . . . has only recently been vindicated by the appellate division of the First District Court of New York and the New York Court of Appeals for having published, as editor of the "Journal of Primatology," a letter on the subject.

Presiding Justice Francis T. Murphy commented, "To unnecessarily delay the disposition of a libel action is not only to countenance waste and inefficiency but to enhance the value of such exercises as instruments of harassment and coercion inimical to the exercise of first amendment rights." It is that same harassment and coercion to eliminate the exercise of first amendment rights that we are fearful this legislation before the subcommittee today would only further. . . .

Since H.R. 3270 actually serves no legally necessary purpose, it would appear that the only reason it was drafted in the first place was to undermine the animal protection/animal rights movement.[73]

While such organizations as the Society for Animal Protective Legislation urged Congress to recognize and act on the problem of the suffering of other animals at the hands of vivisectionists instead of stifling whistleblowers, the American Civil Liberties Union described the proposed 1990 bill as "an official secrecy act for federally funded animal research . . . [and] a sweeping assault on the public's right to know."[74] While opponents of the legislation did modify some of the text, they were unable to resist the force applied by the colossal biomedical and agricultural industries, and a federal law against animal enterprise "terrorism" was enacted. The ideological and police powers of the state were used intensively in corporate efforts to control liberators of other animals.

We see from this example that, when it come to oppressing other animals, corporate control of the state in the United States is not limited to co-opting and neutralizing reform efforts. Its considerable influence has also been used to initiate new federal statutes that criminalize covert activities of some advocates of other animals and to stamp them as "terrorists." Of course, the effectiveness of covert operations is well known to the corporate, congressional, and military elite, and such tactics have been used extensively to protect the interests of those who profit from the "meat" industry.

For example, to the extent they are known to the public, the fierce military campaigns and clandestine operations used throughout the world (representing the physical and ideological powers of the state) are presented as necessary to protect "freedom," "liberty," and the "national interest." From this perspective, many in the Third World resisting appropriation of their lands and homes, including the Quiche villagers massacred at Panzos, are "dangerous communists," and now advocates for other animals are "domestic terrorists"—all so labeled because they threaten the greater accumulation and concentration of capital in private hands. Domestically and abroad, official and semiofficial policies and practices by the FBI and other agencies, policies such as Cointelpro, for decades have involved such tactics as infiltration of groups promoting social change, use of agents provocateurs, fabrication of evidence, assassination, eavesdropping, spreading disinformation, and sending bogus mail. These activities, designed to protect the "American Way of Life" (read: "the capitalist system") from the influence of dissent, are not officially considered "terrorism."[75]

All the while, the day-to-day activities of the nation's criminal justice system continue to "control" the dispossessed. In a time of economic downsizing and increased financial precariousness, the number of citizens labeled "criminal" and imprisoned in the United States is approaching two million, the highest rate ever, almost doubled from a decade earlier. At least one million of those behind bars in 1999 were convicted of nonviolent offenses. Not surprisingly, the vast majority of those incarcerated possess few resources, and members of oppressed groups are decidedly overrepresented. While the U.S. criminal justice system ostensibly works for all citizens, it is rigged to provide substantial advantages to the affluent, not the least of which is ideological.[76] In the words of philosopher Jeffrey Reiman:

> [T]he idea is that the goal of our criminal justice system is not to eliminate crime or to achieve justice, but to project to the American public a visible image of the threat of crime as a threat from the poor. To do this, the justice system must maintain the existence of a sizable population of poor criminals. To do this it must fail in the struggle to eliminate the crimes that the poor commit, or even to reduce their number dramatically. . . .
>
> The value of this to those in positions of power is that it deflects the discontent and potential hostility away from the classes above them and toward the class below them.[77]

Few are aware that for most of the twentieth century, the automobile companies, the pharmaceutical industry, agribusiness, and other powerful industries routinely have violated laws and cost the public countless millions and considerable loss of life by engaging in fraudulent practices and price fixing, selling unsafe products, dumping toxic substances, and ignoring occupational safety regulations—all in the name of making profits.[78] For example, the practices of U.S. oil companies at midcentury were so appalling that even high-level government officials denounced them. Robert Sherrill writes:

> During World War II, Interior Secretary Harold Ickes persuaded President Roosevelt to establish a Government corporation (The Petroleum Reserves Corporation) to buy out the American oil partners—Standard Oil of California and Texaco—in Saudi Arabia. Ickes, who had seen enough profiteering to conclude that "an honest and scrupulous man in the oil business is so rare as to rank as a museum piece," wanted the public to have more control over supplies. The oil companies were powerful enough to kill Ickes' proposal in the cradle.[79]

Reflecting on corporate lawlessness in the twentieth century (which include nefarious activities by the automotive industry, agribusiness, the pharmaceutical industry, and biomedical industries), Ralph Nader made a plea to the corporations that was morally rich but that lacked practical currency, at least in twentieth-century capitalist values. The modern giant corporation, Nader said in 1983, should "stop stealing, stop deceiving, stop corrupting politicians with money, stop monopolizing, stop poisoning the earth, air and water, stop selling dangerous products, stop exposing workers to cruel hazards, stop tyrannizing people of conscience within the company and start respecting the needs and rights of present and future generations."[80]

Almost twenty years after Nader's plea, however, the imperatives of modern capitalism—increased corporate growth and profits—continue to demand "bold" initiatives in the accumulation of profit, frequently at the expense of consumers. For example, one such initiative pursued by Sears, Roebuck and Company was an effort to "force credit card customers who had filed for personal bankruptcy protection to pay Sears their back debts anyway,"[81] in violation of the bankruptcy law. After a two-year criminal investigation, in 1999 Sears pleaded guilty to bankruptcy fraud and paid a fine that a company spokesperson said would have "no effect on Sears' earnings." One financial expert quoted in the *New York Times* shrugged off the conviction. "This scandal has had very little effect on their business. . . . It really hasn't crept into the consciousness of most customers' opinion of Sears."[82]

While such stories appear in newspaper business sections on a daily basis, corporate executives involved in such schemes generally are not viewed as criminals—and when their profits are based on practices that include selling products they know pose a threat to consumer health and safety, they are never stamped as "terrorists." They almost never personally face criminal charges, and most government fines are easily absorbed as a cost of doing business and passed on to consumers. For example, when the Fruehauf Corporation, its chairperson, William Grace, and its president, Robert Rowan, were found guilty of conspiring to evade more than $12 million in federal taxes, the company bankrolled three years of "long and expensive legal maneuverings."[83] In the end, the judge decided against jail time, and Grace and Rowan even retained their jobs. When the vice president and a director of Diamond International, William J. Kolso, was convicted of price fixing in violation of the antitrust laws, he was fined a mere $15,000 and sentenced to seven days of community service. He later was promoted to chairperson and CEO of the company.[84] Even when evidence surfaced that the tobacco industry spiked cigarettes with chemicals that compounded the already-addictive quality of their products, none of the CEOs of these powerful companies—whose pursuit of profits caused countless deaths—were ever stamped as criminals.

Although countless examples of state acceptance of corporate crime exist, just one more will be mentioned here. In June 2001, the Sara Lee corporation, "one of the nation's largest makers of hot dogs and supermarket deli meats," pleaded guilty to producing and selling contaminated "meat." While at least fifteen human deaths, six miscarriages, and scores of illnesses were linked to the tainted "meat," produced in dirty, unsanitary facilities, federal prosecutors brought only a misdemeanor charge against the corporation.[85]

Meanwhile, many humans who struggle financially and who commit desperate, frequently petty, economic offenses are "criminals" confined to jails and prisons. And those who use nonviolent methods to expose violence against other animals or who rescue animals from laboratories or "production" facilities are labeled as dangerous "terrorists."

At the dawn of a new century, abuse of the physical power of the state to preserve the status quo and control those who are exploited and oppressed remains painfully apparent, and police departments around the nation continue to be charged with discriminatory acts and policies against devalued groups. In New York City the police are so blatant in their discriminatory practices that only one out of four New Yorkers believe they treat humans of color fairly. Thousands of humans of color in New York protested police "stop and frisk" tactics in the neighborhoods of oppressed groups.

After a 1999 study by the Associated Press revealed that complaints of civil rights violations were given low priority by the U.S. Department of Justice, the department initiated investigations into practices of "brutality" and racial profiling in police departments with the worst records and reputations. Cities under investigation include New York City; Washington, D.C.; Columbus, Ohio; New Orleans; Los Angeles; and Riverside, California. Investigations into practices of racial profiling in Michigan, New Jersey, and Florida were also initiated.[86] Meanwhile, news of some Los Angeles police officers falsifying evidence that had been used to convict people of color came to public light, and several instances of police shootings of unarmed African Americans sparked an inner-city rebellion in Cincinnati in the spring of 2001.

While state abuse and violence continue against humans of color, others in the ranks of the oppressed, who are ostensibly "protected and served" by the state, endure continued degradation and suffering. For example, although federal law now mandates care and treatment of humans with developmental disabilities (a hard-won legal victory), a lack of serious enforcement of these legislated reforms reflects their place in the states' priorities. Many accounts of emotional, physical, and sexual abuse in state-operated institutions around the nation were presented before a U.S. Senate committee in 1985. Reflecting on the evidence that dangerous abuse and neglect were widespread, Senator Lowell Weicker observed, "If 1/100 of the abuses documented in this Senate report ever related to these hospitals and institutions which serve us and our family members we would be on the ceiling. But let us face that, as a nation, . . . we do not include treatment of the mentally ill and the mentally retarded in that category."[87]

Despite these revelations, the nature of institutional life for tens of thousands remained largely unchanged, as allegations of continued horrors continue to surface. For example, in 1999 six doctors at the Polk Center, a state-run developmental center in Pennsylvania, were charged with such offenses as manslaughter and sewing up wounds sustained by center residents without the use of anesthesia. One doctor "did not treat a man with a blocked intestine for hours—until his body temperature had dropped to 82 degrees—and sent a vomiting, feverish woman whose skin had turned blue for an X-ray."[88] The patient with the blocked intestine died. One of the doctors who was charged claimed that "hospital and state officials were aware that doctors at Polk commonly used surgical staples without anesthesia if an injury needed immediate treatment."[89] Unfortunately, the investigative reports and congressional hearings that document the suffering of devalued groups produce few tangible results. Burton Blatt, an advocate for those with disabilities, writes, "More and more, the legislatures of our country are reluctant to either pass progressive legislation or to fully implement current legislation that would cost the taxpayers money."[90] The "shame of the states" observed by Albert Deutsch continues into the twenty-first century.

Another example of questionable government enforcement of legislated reform again arises through an examination of the contradictory roles of the USDA: in this instance, the department's goal of promoting "meat" production and consumption while administering both health inspection and surplus commodities programs. The agency buys "meat" and other agricultural commodities from producers, particularly in times when prices drop, to support producers' profits and reduce the volume of commodities on the market, thus boosting prices. These commodities are then distributed to schools and social service organizations. In 1998, the USDA bought twenty million pounds of "beef" for a school lunch program from a ConAgra subsidiary, the Northern States Beef Company, even though it had a history of *E. coli* contamination in its products and of violations of federal regulations. In October 1998, "meat" from this subsidiary was sent to a school in Finley, Washington. Twelve children became ill with *E. coli* infections, four so seriously that they were sent to Seattle for blood transfusions and, in one case, kidney dialysis. What the townspeople in Finley never knew was that in the eighteen months before the government's meat purchase, the Agriculture Department's own inspectors found 171 "critical" violations of U.S. food safety regulations at the Northern States Beef plant.[91]

The USDA was financially supporting ConAgra at the same time its own inspectors were producing reports that the ConAgra-produced "meat" was contaminated. Corporate-initiated systems of inspecting "meat" that are "streamlined" and "modernized," together with USDA-endorsed systems that speed the grisly "disassembly line" and reduce the oversight of federal inspectors, have resulted in numerous incidents of public consumption of contaminated "meat," some of which were documented by investigative reports in Cox Newspapers in 1999–2000.[92] In the spring of 2001, after further reports of contaminated "meat"—this time in New York and New Jersey after allegations of unsanitary conditions in slaughterhouses and falsification of inspection records—federal and congressional investigations into "possible lapses and misconduct in meat safety regulations" were initiated.[93] However, one might predict that these investigations are conducted primarily to restore public confidence in the U.S. "meat" industry and will not produce any substantive change or pose a challenge to corporate profit taking.

While examples of corporate influence over the state abound, just two more will be mentioned. As we saw in the last chapter, the Green Revolution and consequent growth of enormous agribusinesses resulted in the failure of countless family farms. However, this process was facilitated by use of state power. Seeking to maintain stable prices for the "meat" industry and other components of agribusiness, the government sought both to reduce the supply of food the nation was capable of producing—so as not to deflate prices and profits—and to expand the market for U.S. agricultural products. In the first instance, the government began a program of paying farmers not to produce. However, these payments were not enough for many farmers to keep up with their debts, and they were driven out of business. Larger businesses could absorb the losses, and they ultimately benefited from reduced competition. Robert K. Shaeffer writes:

> [D]espite large subsidies, or rather because of the way government subsidy programs were designed, one-half of all U.S. farmers were forced out of farming between 1950 and 1970, the number of farms falling from six million to three million in just twenty years. So while the government spent billions of dollars on subsidy programs . . . the program kept half of the farmers in business but helped drive the other half *out* of business.[94]

The use of federal government subsidies to drive smaller farms out of business continues in the twenty-first century. According to a May 2001 article in the *New York Times,* the largest 10 percent of farmers in the United States now receive 61 percent of the billions of dollars spent on farm subsidies. "The subsidies have been a chief source of capital for large operators to expand their holdings, often by buying out their smaller neighbors."[95]

While the power of the state has been used to reduce domestic competition and facilitate concentration of U.S. agribusiness, it also has been used to create overseas markets for agribusiness "products." For example, at midcentury the government sought to increase global demand for U.S. agricultural products by selling them at bargain prices to other nations, particularly those friendly to U.S. corporate interests. While this program served as an outlet for surplus agricultural commodities the government had purchased to stabilize U.S. agribusiness, it also helped other countries cultivate both a taste for and a dependence on imported First World food. However, as domestic food shortages became a problem for what was then the Soviet Union and other nations in the 1970s and demand for food increased, the United States largely discontinued the surplus give-away and began charging increased prices for its products. This change in U.S. policy "forced many poor countries to borrow heavily to pay for food imports,"[96] particularly because many of their more affluent citizens had developed a preference for U.S. agricultural "products." After accumulating enormous debt, in part from these food imports, Third World governments were forced to implement austerity programs, further increasing the privations and misery of tens of millions around the world—and forcing many more desperate individuals into survival practices and enterprises based on the exploitation of other animals.

While such profit-motivated machinations continue, many advocates for other animals continue to pursue efforts for social justice through legislative channels within the capitalist system—with mixed results.

On the state level, many recent legislative acts have focused on enforcing penalties for cruel acts against other animals. Cruel acts against other animals traditionally have been viewed as minor offenses, or misdemeanors. However, by 2000 thirty-one states had made cruelty to other animals a felony.[97] Many state lawmakers have supported the changes largely because of mounting evidence that violence against other animals is linked to violence against other humans.[98] The new legal measures, however, largely exempt entire classes of other animals who are relegated to the position of "farm animal," "research animal," "wildlife," and "pest"; some states also exempt other animals used in rodeos, zoos, and circuses.[99] Moreover, anticruelty laws are "rarely enforced and minimally punished."[100] While no national database tracks cases of cruelty against other animals, legal scholar Pamela D. Frasch uses anecdotal evidence in her report that

> some prosecutors are less likely to charge or prosecute animal cruelty compared to other violent crimes, except in the most extreme cases. This apparent reluctance to prosecute stems from many factors including: real or perceived limited resources; inexperienced staff; incomplete or botched investigations; pressure from the community to focus on other crimes; and personal or political bias against taking animal abuse seriously as a violent crime.[101]

On the federal level, since the enactment of landmark pieces of legislation cited earlier that largely cemented and legitimized economically driven uses of other animals, several recent, if relatively modest, enactments help restore some hope in this arena. In 2000, Congress passed, and President Clinton signed, the Great Ape Conservation Act, a measure that provides funds to protect the natural homelands of great apes. That same year the CHIMP Act also became law, creating and support-

ing sanctuaries for chimpanzees who have survived vivisectionist experiments and
are no longer useful research subjects. A federal law was also enacted to make air
travel safer for other animals (a measure predictably opposed by the airline industry).[102] Such legislative accomplishments at the federal level are relatively minor
when compared to the government sanctioned slaughter of more than eight *billion*
"farm animals" in the United States every year.[103]

Activists struggling with government agencies that regulate the use and treatment
of other animals also recently exerted some influence over important decisions. For
example, on Earth Day in 1999, Vice President Al Gore announced a Chemical
Right-to-Know Initiative, which included the intent to test and publicize the toxicity of chemicals imported or manufactured in the United States at a rate of one
million pounds or more a year. The Environmental Protection Agency (EPA) was
empowered to establish the testing requirements. People for the Ethical Treatment
of Animals (PETA) estimated that toxicity tests required by the initiative would kill
approximately 1.3 million other animals. After strong lobbying by PETA and other
movement organizations and an advertising campaign calling attention to the numbers of other animals to be killed by the program, the EPA and the White House
Council on Environmental Quality reached agreement on a program protocol that
would use approximately eight hundred thousand fewer other animals than did the
original initiative.[104] A report on the agreement in *Animal Law* suggested that "serious commitment towards the development of nonanimal-based testing standards
will allow progression towards a future free of animal-based laboratory testing.
Finally, the recognition of animal welfare groups as significant stakeholders in the
design of Federal testing programs should work to improve their access and influence in future planning of toxicity testing programs."[105]

The USDA has also felt the influence of advocates for other animals. For years,
the agency has exempted rats, mice, and birds from coverage under the Animal Welfare Act (unless vivisectionists experimenting on these other animals were funded by
federal grants). After considerable lobbying and legal pressure by antivivisectionist
organizations and other groups working for rights for other animals, the USDA
agreed to include these previously exempted other animals in their enforcement of
the Act beginning in the autumn of 2001. Critics of the USDA decision claim the
inclusion of rats, mice, and birds will be too expensive to enforce and that the
increased cost of housing and caring for these others will force smaller organizations
to discontinue their vivisectionist activities. Vivisectionists from both academia and
industry continue their efforts to thwart implementation of the USDA's decision.

While some animal advocates see all such efforts to assist other animals as laudable, not all agree. Law professor Gary Francione urges that those working to establish legal protections for other animals should be careful that their efforts do not
merely (and not just ostensibly) ameliorate the suffering of other animals while
accepting their status as "livestock," "laboratory subjects," and other instruments of
production—as has happened, for example, in the Humane Slaughter and Animal
Welfare Acts. Instead, Francione argues purely for abolitionist measures that challenge and reduce the oppression of other animals. Such measures would denounce

the property status of other animals, and their cumulative effects would substantially reduce and eliminate that oppression—not legitimate it.[106] He states:

> If we decide to pursue legislation, we should stop pursuing welfarist solutions to the problem. Animal *welfare* [emphasis added] seeks to regulate atrocity by making cages bigger or by adding additional layers of bureaucratic review to ensure that the atrocity is "humane." We should pursue legislation that seeks to abolish particular forms of exploitation. Animal advocates should always be upfront about their ultimate objective, and use all campaigns as an opportunity to teach about nonviolence and the rejection of all institutionalized animal exploitation.[107]

THE COURTS AND OPPRESSION OF OTHER ANIMALS

While the system of jurisprudence in the United States, as in most other nations, has been used to protect and rationalize privilege (as we saw in the examples of Dred Scott and Myra Bradwell), it is also used in efforts to further social justice. However, that road is long, arduous, and expensive. Moreover, the infrequent and often modest victories are prone to reversal. Speaking to the rigged nature of the United States Supreme Court, for example, Michael Parenti observes:

> Through most of its history "the Court's personnel were recruited mainly from the class of corporate lawyers, so there was no shortage of empathy with the desires of expanding capitalism."[108] The process of legal education and professional training makes it unlikely that dissidents will be picked for the bench—and very few have been. The bar associations and law schools, and the foundations that finance the law journals, endowed chairs and research grants in jurisprudence, are dedicated to fortifying, not modifying, the existing system of ownership and wealth.[109]

Still, some maintain that judicial avenues have led to some victories and progress. There is a great deal of difference between the 1857 *Dred Scott* decision that declared that humans enslaved in the United States had no rights and the 1954 *Brown v. Board of Education* decision that declared "separate but equal" public institutions unconstitutional. Legal scholar Helena Silverstein notes that many find hope in legal strategy, believing that "litigation opens the door for participation and provides the opportunity for social change."[110] However, she observes that some scholars criticize litigation strategies, "arguing that while victory in court may be attained and precedent established, the actual impact on society is minimal."[111] She notes that those who take this position often maintain

> that litigative victories in this realm have largely been hollow since they create the appearance of formal equality but in fact result in minimal implementation . . . [and that] judicial victory often places the responsibility for enforcement and implementation on the victims of discrimination. For them, litigation in antidiscrimination law has

been largely ineffective since the victim must bear the costs of enforcing equal protection laws.[112]

Some legal scholars are of the opinion that, in the last analysis, even the momentous *Brown v. Board of Education* decision has had limited social impact.[113] Indeed, the case can be made that reform legislation, and the related judicial remedies developed over the past fifty years, have promoted justice primarily in those areas least applicable to institutionalized, economic arrangements.

The judicial approach to other animals, based in a long tradition of common law, is to regard them as property. According to law professor Gary Francione:

> [T]he ownership of animal property is, for all intents and purposes, no different from the ownership of other sorts of personal property. . . . [O]ur current system of animal protection, legal welfarism, requires that animal interests be balanced against human interests. The problem is that the law has not developed any doctrines that require that animal property be treated differently because an animal is different from inanimate property, such as a tool. Rather, the law only requires that animal property not be "wasted" or that animals not be killed or made to suffer when there is no legitimate economic purpose.[114]

One example of this approach by the courts is provided by the 1983 case *Fund for Animals v. Mud Lake Farmers Rabbit Committee*. In that case, the Fund for Animals sought to stop the organized practice of encouraging families to club to death rabbits who sought nourishment from cultivated crops. "The trial court . . . found that the purpose of [the state's] anti-cruelty statute was to prohibit unnecessary abuse of animals and that 'when animals threaten the physical or financial survival of man, he is lawfully entitled to strike back and to use such tactics as appear necessary and reasonable.' "[115] The court both protected and legitimated the "rabbit drive."

In a 1991 case, PETA challenged the legality of various experimental protocols approved by Institutional Animal Care and Use Committees (IACUCs) in Oregon. IACUCs are required in some instances of vivisection, as specified by the Animal Welfare Act and the agencies that administer it, to oversee the treatment of other animals subjected to experiments at each affected laboratory or university. The regulations the committees apply, however, are minimal and can be waived if a majority of IACUC members believe such action will enhance the experiment. Not surprisingly, in most instances IACUCs' membership is stacked, and the vivisectionists essentially regulate themselves. In the 1991 case, the Oregon Supreme Court ruled that PETA was not an aggrieved party harmed by the unlawful experiments and thus did not have legal standing to bring the case before the court.[116]

In other cases, however, the question of "legal standing" has been decided in favor of advocates for other animals. These are important legal precedents that have opened the courts to hear cases pertaining to the oppression of other animals. In 1991, a federal judge granted standing to the Fund for Animals in its effort to stop the hunting of buffalo who journeyed outside the boundaries of Yellowstone

National Park. However, the judge did not find sufficient merit in the case to order a halt to the killing of the buffalo.[117]

Some legal scholars, such as Steven Wise (a powerful advocate for the liberation of other animals), still contend that case law is an important avenue in which to pursue legal rights for other animals. He writes:

> This decade, judges who matured alongside the newer animals-rights movement have begun to take their places. Many judges from these slowly filling pools will have watched Jane Goodall respectfully document the lives of the chimpanzees of Gombe on National Geographic, will understand and believe basic principles of Darwinian evolution and ecology, will reject the hierarchy of the Great Chain of Being, and will not be personally invested in the wholesale exploitation of animals or saturated with religious and other arguments against their legal personhood. They will be better equipped to examine the objective data and hear—not just listen to—the supporting arguments. They will begin to rattle the cage.[118]

The cages confining other animals, both literally and figuratively, have been rattled somewhat by custody disputes—cases that force the judiciary (and the larger society) to acknowledge both the deep and meaningful bonds that can form between humans and other animals and the inherent interests of other animals. One such instance is described by Barbara Newell, an attorney for the Animal Legal Defense Fund.

> Courts across the country have begun to adopt the more enlightened view that companion animals are more than mere chattels. Specifically in the context of pet custody, courts in New York recently examined a case in which the plaintiff brought a cat, Merlin, later named Lovey, into a shared housing situation. Plaintiff left the premises and later sought to remove Lovey to a new residence. In a preliminary ruling on the plaintiff's seizure motion, the trial court explicitly deferred to Lovey's best interests, ordering the parties to "work out a visitation schedule" rather than "shift custody of Lovey back and forth." In its final ruling, however, the trial court used a strict bailment of chattels analysis [a traditional property principle] and awarded Lovey to the plaintiff. The appellate court reversed and awarded custody to the defendant, citing "the cherished status accorded to pets in our society" and recognizing the interests of Lovey as an aging individual who for four years had "lived, prospered, loved and been loved" in the residence finally occupied by the defendant alone.[119]

Newell suggests such rulings represent a "growing crack in the 'legal thinghood' of nonhuman animals."[120] (This crack was widened in Boulder, Colorado, in July 2000 when the city council voted to change the city's municipal code to replace "owner" with "guardian" to denominate a person who is responsible for the care of other animals. Comparable changes are now occurring in other parts of the nation.)[121]

Similar challenges to the traditional view of other animals as "property" and "things" have been brought in court cases on the recovery of noneconomic damages for the wrongful killing or injury of companions who are other animals. In a 1994 decision by a Texas appellate court, one judge, supporting the majority opinion, wrote:

> The law must be informed by evolving knowledge and attitudes. Otherwise, it risks becoming irrelevant as a means of resolving conflicts. Society has long moved beyond the untenable Cartesian view that animals are unfeeling automatons and, hence, *mere* property. The law should reflect society's recognition that animals are sentient and emotive beings that are capable of providing companionship to the humans with whom they live. In doing so, courts should not hesitate to acknowledge that a great number of people in this country today treat their pets as family members. Indeed, for many people, pets are the *only* family members they have.
>
> Losing a beloved pet is not the same as losing an inanimate object, however cherished it may be. Even an heirloom of great sentimental value, if lost, does not constitute a loss comparable to that of a living being. This distinction applies even though the deceased living being is a nonhuman. . . .
>
> [T]estimony that an animal is a beloved companion should generally be considered sufficient to justify a finding of damages well beyond the market value of the animal and its yet unborn progeny.[122]

Opinions like this, however, are not embraced by many members of the judiciary. Attorney David J. Wolfson notes that "such opinions are typically viewed by other courts as 'aberrations flying in the face of overwhelming authority to the contrary.' "[123] While litigation to vindicate the interests of other animals and their human companions is growing, Helena Silverstein observes that most lawsuits in pursuit of rights for other animals

> [primarily] have been useful in achieving "negative" movement goals: to delay, limit, or prevent harmful practices toward animals. Litigative actions have prevented the navy from deploying dolphins and from poisoning squirrels. Lawsuits have halted and limited mountain lion hunts, bear hunts, rattlesnake roundups, elk hunts, and more. Injunctions have been successful in delaying animal experiments. . . . [F]or the most part, litigation is deployed to stop rather than to promote action.[124]

Silverstein suggests that the effects of the struggle for the liberation of other animals in the judicial realm are mixed and ambiguous. While "important judgments have been reached in favor of the movement," "direct losses have been experienced at great cost,"[125] particularly in the more deeply entrenched, legalized view of other animals as property.

The past teaches us that the strategies that spring from a hopeful outlook based on popular beliefs about the power of democracy and the state's proclivity for rational decision making need to be tempered by a full realization of the power over the state wielded by powerful capitalists from agribusiness, pharmaceutical, biotech, and related industries. These capitalists will use their considerable power and resources to defend and expand their institutionalized oppression of humans and other animals. This is again to say that the primary obstacle to liberation is not just, or even primarily, one of moral philosophy or legal principle.

While the courts certainly should not be abandoned as a mechanism for social change, for many they have been a source of frustration and, some could argue, a diversionary exercise for many liberation activists. What is more, like state assemblies and the federal legislature, they also have been used by oppressive industries to control and intimidate activists and sympathizers.

Recall the congressional hearing testimony of Christine Stevens pertaining to lawsuits filed by vivisectionists against those who challenged and publicized their practices. Two similar but highly publicized lawsuits warrant brief discussion.

In Great Britain two London Greenpeace activists, Helen Steel and David Morris, were sued for libel by McDonald's for distributing a leaflet titled "What's wrong with McDonald's?" The leaflet charged McDonald's with perpetrating a number of social injuries, including "exploiting children with advertising, promoting an unhealthy diet, exploiting their staff, and being responsible for environmental damage and ill-treatment of animals."[126] To file a libel suit, McDonald's needed to name individual activists who were writing and circulating the leaflets, so the company hired seven individuals to infiltrate London Greenpeace to obtain information necessary to file the suit. Steel and Morris took a courageous stand by attempting to represent themselves (as English law does not provide counsel to those with limited incomes in libel cases) against the power of the largest fast-food corporation in the world. Others recoiled in the face of such intimidation. According to journalist Eric R. Smith:

> Three other Greenpeace defendants chose to recant their statements and apologize rather than take the course of action that has led Steel and Morris through six years of full-time court work—without pay. Other accused parties, including the BBC, the *Guardian,* King George's Nature Conservancy, and Prince Phillip, also apologized and recanted statements to avoid a trial.[127]

The libel suit was filed in 1990 and became the longest civil trial in British history. The judge, reading his decision to a packed courtroom in June 1997, ruled that Steel and Morris had proven a number of their allegations to be true (a heroic act in the face of an extremely well-financed effort by McDonald's, with its virtual parade of expert witnesses). However, Steel and Morris did not have the resources to supply all the evidence needed to prove all their assertions were true. Consequently, the judge ruled that Steel and Morris had libeled McDonald's and ordered them to pay £60,000 in damages. While many claimed a moral victory for Steel and Morris—they had proven that McDonald's exploits children, falsely advertises the nutritional value of its products, risks the long-term health of steady customers, is responsible for the mistreatment of other animals, is antipathetic to unions, and pays low wages to its workforce—the profound and very public detrimental effect of the ordeal on the lives of Steel and Morris, the crucified Spartacans of their day, stands as a lesson to others who may consider public education as a tool of social change.

In the United States in 1996, one of the wealthiest and most influential women in the nation, Oprah Winfrey, was sued by Texas "cattlemen" for airing a TV program that discussed the potential risks of consuming cows slaughtered in the United States. The suit was brought under a Texas food disparagement law created to discourage anyone from saying anything critical about an agricultural product produced in the state. The lawsuit against Winfrey, which also named as a defendant Howard Lyman of the Humane Society of the United States, resulted in dismissal and a victory for Winfrey and Lyman—but only after a time-consuming and emotionally draining ordeal that cost Winfrey millions of dollars in attorney's fees. The Texas "cattlemen" appealed the decision, further spiraling the cost of free speech in a capitalist society. Texas is one of thirteen states whose legislatures, seeking to protect their state's agribusinesses from the harm that could result from consumer decisions made by an informed citizenry, have enacted such "food-libel" laws. Many critics of these laws, like Ronald Collins, director of the FoodSpeak Project for the Center for Science in the Public Interest, claim that such laws are not only unconstitutional but also unnecessary, as legal measures for redressing reckless and false statements have long been in place. However, like the congressional enactment of special "antiterrorist" laws to dissuade animal rights activists from seeking and disseminating damaging information about the treatment and use of other animals in vivisectionist or commercial enterprises, the "food disparagement" laws are intended to discourage discussion and dissemination of information about the ethical problems and potential dangers of contemporary agribusiness practices. While these laws may well be unconstitutional and ultimately defeated in court, those who are targeted by agribusiness face potentially ruinous consequences when forced to defend themselves against legions of corporate attorneys using every tool and procedure at their disposal to deplete the resources of their critics and silence their opposition. Such threats are not to be taken lightly, as few have the resources of Oprah Winfrey. Thus as, Ronald Collins notes, "state food libel laws have a real and chilling effect on book publishers, broadcasters, magazines and newspaper publishers, and on anyone who has a website."[128]

While the court system in the United States offers both hope and peril for those working for social justice, activists for other animals have turned to another mechanism for effecting change—ballot initiatives. Twenty-four states permit ballot initiatives, which allow voters to approve or disapprove a proposed law after a prescribed number of petition signatures are gathered to place it on the ballot. State initiatives advanced by advocates for other animals were largely unsuccessful until 1990; since then, a number of efforts have succeeded due to hard-fought, labor-intensive campaigns waged by many dedicated activists. For instance, in the mid-1990s, citizens in California voted to ban trophy hunting of mountain lions, and successful initiatives in Colorado, Massachusetts, Oregon, and Washington banned bear baiting (described as "setting out a pile of material to attract a bear, then shooting the bear, usually from a blind"—i.e., from a camouflaged or concealed location).[129] Initiatives to ban bear baiting in Idaho and Michigan, however, were defeated.

Between 1992 and 2000, leghold and other body-gripping traps were banned by voters in Arizona, California, Colorado, Massachusetts, and Washington. A similar measure failed in Oregon, while Alaska voters rejected a proposal to ban wolf snaring (a form of trapping in which wolves—and any others who are caught in the snare—are strangled as they struggle to get free).

In 1998, initiatives in Arizona and Missouri banned cockfighting. The Missouri initiative was launched when the Missouri Supreme Court invalidated an existing 112-year-old ban. Similarly, in one recent example of a legislative rather than a ballot initiative created in response to public outrage over the forced fighting of other animals, Congress in 2000 amended the Animal Welfare Act "to prohibit the transportation or sale, in interstate or foreign commerce, of any dog or other animal for fighting purposes."[130] However, the United Gamefowl Breeders Association and the Animal Husbandry Coalition successfully lobbied for a loophole that permits interstate transport of "gamecocks" for fighting from states where cockfighting is illegal to states where it is legal. The cockfighting industry is resisting efforts to remove that loophole.[131]

Realizing the general tendency for the public, most of whom oppose sport hunting, to vote to restrict or ban certain types of hunting and trapping, hunters, trappers, gun manufacturers, "outdoorsmen" equipment producers and retailers, and state divisions of wildlife have developed strategies to forestall such democratic action. First, the interest and industry groups try to out-organize and out-spend the advocates for other animals. For example, in 1995 the Ohio Legislature voted to legalize dove hunting, which had been illegal in the state for most of the twentieth century. Advocates for other animals launched a ballot initiative in 1998 to restore the ban. A highly organized coalition of prohunting organizations and the Ohio Division of Wildlife countered the proposal with a well-financed media campaign that claimed that animal rights activists were harming children and families. The widely seen television advertisements and other ads said almost nothing about doves. (The campaign signs and bumper stickers said only "Issue 2: Bad for Families, Bad for Ohio.") After the ballot initiative failed, several major newspapers in the state observed that most voters had no idea what the measure was actually about.

In addition to outspending advocates for other animals to defeat ballot initiatives, many prohunting groups, such as the Ballot Issues Coalition (BIC), contend that the public should not determine issues of "wildlife" management, which should be "left to wildlife professionals." The BIC and the National Trappers Association "vow to file suits to overturn ballot initiatives in Arizona, California, Colorado, Massachusetts, Oregon, and Washington."[132] Meanwhile, state-based groups, like Utahans for Wildlife Heritage and Conservation (UWHC) (a euphemistically named prohunting group), fearing that ballot initiatives will be used to take away "sportsmen's opportunities," have tightened their influence and control over their state assemblies to thwart the democratic impulse and protect their interests. In 1998, UWHC successfully promoted a state constitutional amendment to restrict citizen-initiated ballot issues regarding "wildlife." An analysis of the ballot initiative in the journal *Animal Law* notes:

> The new amendment requires that any citizen-initiated drive to "allow, limit, or prohibit the taking of wildlife or the season for or method of taking wildlife" be approved

by a two-thirds majority of the voters in an election. The proposition was approved by both houses of the state legislature by the required two-thirds vote before being submitted to the voters, and passed by fifty-six percent to forty-four percent on election day.

The amendment was formed as a preemptive strike against pro-wildlife and animal public interest groups.[133]

Groups that supported the proposal included the National Rifle Association, gun manufacturers, and the sporting goods industry; they outspent advocates of other animals in advertising by a margin of ten to one.[134] Wildlife Heritage ran advertisements stating that the proposition would preserve "Utah's wild landscapes, conserve its wildlife, and uphold its hunting traditions. The advertisements made no mention, however, of how it would change the constitution or reduce the power of citizens to check their government."[135]

State assemblies in Arizona and Alaska approved "right to hunt" constitutional amendments but did not obtain the voter approval necessary to change the constitutions in those states. However, prohunting alliances in four other states, Alabama, North Dakota, Minnesota, and Virginia, succeeded in gaining such constitutional protections. For example, North Dakota's constitutional amendment reads, in part, "[h]unting, trapping, and fishing and the taking of game and fish are a valued part of our heritage and will be forever preserved for the people."[136] Further evidence of the willingness of "the sportsmen's industry" to use the powers of the state to defend its interests is seen in a January 2000 announcement by the National Shooting Sports Foundation that it intended to raise millions of dollars "to support candidates and to lobby at all levels of government to fight greater gun restrictions."[137] The organization, which represents 1,700 manufacturers and distributors of handguns, rifles, telescopic sites, camouflage clothing, and related "sportsmen's" goods, has decided to join the National Rifle Association in trying to turn back gun control laws and efforts by local and state governments to sue the industry for the harms caused by its products.

THE STATE AND THE POTENTIAL FOR INSTITUTIONAL CHANGE

The state in contemporary capitalist society is, ironically, both a crucial avenue for progressive social change and liberation for humans and other animals and, at the same time, one of the biggest obstacles to that change. From its inception the state has been used largely to protect and enhance the interests of the powerful and affluent, and so it is used today.

The economic underpinnings of oppression of humans and other animals, and the complex web of entanglements among oppressed groups, are tightly wrapped and meticulously cloaked by those who control the various powers of the state. From the creation of early laws that institutionalized the characterization of women and other animals as property, to state-sanctioned witch trials that scapegoated women, cats, and others in the ranks of the devalued for social ills caused by tyrannical social systems; from the protection of horrific treatment of other animals cast as agricultural commodities and laboratory subjects, with a government seal of approval on their use and consumption, to the displacement of family and subsistence farms in the United States and the Third World, to the abusive treatment of workers and consumers—the physical, political, economic, ideological, and diversionary powers of the state support and build such entangled oppressions while giving such atrocities legal and social respectability.

Schemes, machinations, and abusive activities, lawful and unlawful, when committed by corporations and those in the position of business executive, are seen as natural parts of the market system. The damaging and sometimes even deadly consequences are simply business costs or an inevitable part of "progress." Certainly, corporate perpetrators are rarely labeled as criminals. Meanwhile, two million humans, disproportionately from the ranks of the oppressed, are incarcerated, often for relatively minor economic or drug offenses that are tied inextricably to the social conditions in which they are placed. Those committed to nonviolent liberation of other animals—others who are experiencing unrelieved suffering—are stamped as terrorists.

Few in society challenge this state of affairs. The "respectable" social positions available for occupancy in contemporary capitalist society provide very little incentive or opportunity to contest oppressive arrangements.

Nonetheless, the spirit of humans and other animals can be robust, and many have risked their reputations and personal safety to struggle against oppression and injustice. Informed and impassioned citizens have fought for and won changes, as in women's successful eighty-year struggle for the vote or the ongoing fight of humans of color for full civil rights. Such concessions are acceptable to the capitalist elite only because the changes have but limited effect on the structure and capitalist control of the economic system and the distribution of wealth. Such hard-earned changes in the law admittedly have opened the doors of the capitalist system to many who once had little or no opportunity for education and social mobility. However, women, humans of color, the aged, and those with disabilities are still disproportionately in the ranks of the poor and the economically marginalized and now face further privations due to growing economic disparity. These groups also are still far more likely to be victims of prejudice, discrimination, and violence. These facts show the limitations of the reforms achieved thus far in the United States.[138]

What is more, the increased but still insufficient opportunity for some members of devalued groups to achieve economic security and even political and social power—that is, the opportunity to compete more equally with privileged white males for a limited number of desirable positions within capitalist society, in a competition that has created considerable backlash—has led many to believe that vestiges of innate privilege have been eliminated and that the United States is now largely a society of equals. Political and social criticism—particularly in the form of participation in demonstrations and protest marches—now is viewed by many as an anachronism, an outlet only for "kooks" and fanatics. Such perceptions lay the groundwork for social, economic, and political backsliding. For example, many of the reforms that advanced the quality of life in the United States in the post–World War II period, not just for devalued groups but for most of the middle class as well, were rescinded or weakened during the 1980s under the corporate-capitalist-friendly Reagan administration. During the Reagan years, the drive to "get government off our backs" by reducing taxes and government oversight of corporate practices led to deep cuts in federal spending for education, health care, housing, child care, child abuse prevention programs, senior citizen centers and programs, urban rejuvenation, and entitlement programs.[139] The federal government retreated from affirmative action and from many hard-won regulatory policies established to keep major industries operating in ways that, ostensibly at least, helped protect the health and safety of the public. All the while, the president and his administration waged a major offensive against organized labor.[140] The tax cuts, which favored wealthy individuals and substantially reduced corporate tax rates, were accompanied by huge increases in military spending, causing an enormous growth in national debt.[141]

Following the first Bush presidency, Democratic president Bill Clinton did little to restore the reforms and programs that were decimated in the 1980s. Indeed, Clinton pressed for the North American Free Trade Agreement (NAFTA) and the latest General Agreement on Tariffs and Trade (GATT)—agreements made by the world's economic elite that have been decried by social justice and liberation activists around the world. (As we saw in chapter 3, under this new capitalist order often hard-fought domestic protections for workers, consumers, other animals, and the environment may be abolished if they are determined to be obstructions to free trade.) The modest environmental and workplace reforms and "wildlife" restoration programs that were achieved under the Clinton administration were almost immediately delayed or rescinded in 2001 by President George W. Bush.[142] This President Bush also successfully promoted a new round of Reaganesque tax cuts amounting to an estimated $1.3 trillion, reductions that again largely favored the wealthiest families. George W. Bush's cabinet, in the words of Molly Ivins, looks like a corporate *Who's Who*. For instance, his secretary of agriculture, Ann Veneman, is a lawyer who came to the USDA from a firm "specializing in representing agribusiness giants and biotech corporations."[143] Bush further demonstrated his indebtedness to powerful capitalists, for example, by withdrawing the United States from international accords intended to reduce global warming; that decision angered most of the nations of the world, including strong U.S. allies. To fend off any challenges to U.S. global domination, Bush has increased military spending to fund a controversial missile defense system while repudiating the 1972 Anti-Ballistic Missile (ABM) treaty and nixing a draft agreement, six years in the making, to enforce an international treaty banning germ weapons[144]—decisions that also dismayed all those around the globe working and hoping for a better world.

Tragically but predictably, the response of the U.S. government to the attacks on the World Trade Center and the Pentagon was to launch a "war" on terrorism. The quick decision to respond to the attacks with an overwhelming display of military might eclipsed thoughtful reflection. The immediate calls for a violent response, and the portrayal of any dissent as unpatriotic, prevented any real public discourse about the underlying causes of the attacks (which should have included discussion of the role of Western elite-driven colonialist and imperialist practices, past and present) and about ways to create a safer and more secure world for all. Much like the long-running "Cold War" against the "communists" of the twentieth century, the "new war against terrorism" in the twenty-first century, according to George W. Bush, "may take years."[145] Certainly, it will provide enormous additional ideological and diversionary power for capitalist elites in the United States and around the world.

As with previous wars in U.S. history, the ideological power of the state, in conjunction with the elitist control of the mass media, was used to exhort the public into a patriotic fervor after the 11 September attacks. The general climate of fear, combined with strong progovernment feeling, also created opportunities to increase state control in other ways. President Bush promoted repressive "antiterrorist" legislation and policies that provided for indefinite detention of noncitizens, limits on attorney–client privilege, and reduced rights to privacy, while announcing his intention to utilize secret military tribunals to try noncitizens accused of involvement in terrorist activities. The *New York Times* called these efforts "a travesty of justice" and an attempt to do "an end run around the Constitution."[146] The FBI's public harassment of both citizens and noncitizens of Middle Eastern descent increased their "other" status and fueled hate crimes. (This practice was so blatant and unjust that numerous police departments around the country refused to assist the FBI in questioning and detaining those of Middle Eastern ancestry.) Meanwhile, many believe that the changes in the law—often buried in the hundred-plus-page U.S.A. Patriot Act rushed into law in the autumn of 2001—will make it easier for the government to stifle dissent by U.S. citizens. *Time* magazine reports:

> Critics fear that the new legal rules will wind up being used against all Americans, not just suspected al-Qaeda members. The "domestic terrorism" provisions of the law could have very broad reach . . . [that could include] getting into a heated fight with a police officer at an antiglobalism protest. . . . Many of the new rules could easily be applied to conduct surveillance on ordinary Americans. The act gives the government broad new power to conduct "sneak and peak" searches—to go into Americans' homes when they're out and look around without telling anyone.[147]

Meanwhile, sensing opportunities, large corporations (e.g., Cipro manufacturer A. G. Bayer) sought increased profits in the aftermath of the 11 September attacks, and entire industries (e.g., the airline and energy industries) sought government bailouts and relaxation of existing regulations. For example, longtime proponents of lifting restrictions on drilling for oil in Alaskan "wildlife" refuges persuaded President Bush to urge the Senate to set aside the restrictions—in the interest of "national security."[148]

It is in the context of such blatant control of the state by powerful capitalists that many advocates of other animals maintain the time has come to grant to other animals legal personhood and some of the basic rights accorded to humans. However, the reality is that basic rights established for humans, both around the world and in the United States, although passionately and eloquently stated on paper and in political and popular rhetoric, are mostly eclipsed by the realities of modern capitalism. The inclination and ability of powerful capitalists to stifle and buffer reform measures (many of which are "revolutions from above" used to shield corporate interests, as we saw in examples of congressional hearings), and to promote candidates committed to rescinding enacted reforms (or undermining their enforcement), should be well understood by all liberation activists.

Put differently, under modern capitalism many legal reforms achieved by activists for humans and other animals are the equivalent of the decision to suspend the pigeon shoot in Hegins, Pennsylvania. The elite may call a halt, if temporarily, to the worst deeds and permit some minor reforms in order to preserve public acceptance of industrialized and highly profitable oppressive practices. For example, while cockfighting and bearbaiting may be banned in many areas, increasingly the general practice of hunting is protected by state constitutional amendments. Even in the case of hard-fought abolitionist victories that have stood for decades, such as the bans on cockfighting in Missouri and shooting doves in Ohio, monied interests have proven themselves capable of turning back reforms and resurrecting these horrific practices.

Fully aware of the limitations and obstacles to real and lasting change under capitalism, strategists for liberation of humans and other animals should continue to pursue liberation through political measures, but they must also challenge the control of the capitalist elite over the various powers of the state while striving to change the structure of the state to one that is responsive to public, not monied, interests. Continued efforts to oppose oppression through legislation, litigation, and ballot initiatives (efforts that must be abolitionist rather than welfarist) have the potential to save many others from pain and suffering while serving as *one part* of a strategic formula for the creation of a truly democratic, benevolent, and sustainable system—free from oppressive practices.

Another important reason to pursue liberation efforts in the legal arena is that it helps make oppressive arrangements more visible to the general public. The capitalist elite do not desire such visibility, and ideological control is an important tool for them to maintain and expand their control. They know that enough democracy exists in the U.S. state to permit some popular influence over the powers of the state. The elite must exert considerable control over public perceptions and opinion, disparaging those most victimized by oppressive arrangements and portraying them as somehow deserving of their fate. The theory of oppression points to the role ideology plays in creating and perpetuating oppressive conditions. Ideology both reflects and perpetuates deeply rooted ideas that legitimate the poor quality of life and mistreatment of devalued others in a society. The role of such ideology in the oppression of devalued humans and other animals, viewed with examples of the pervasive and insidious nature of contemporary social, political, and economic indoctrination, is the subject we shall turn to next.

NOTES

1. Howard Zinn, "The Conspiracy of Law," in *The Rule of Law,* ed. Robert P. Wolff (New York: Simon & Schuster, 1971), 24.

2. Gary Francione, *Animals, Property and the Law* (Philadelphia: Temple University Press, 1995), xiv.

3. Laura B. DeLind, "Parma: A Story of Hog Hotels and Local Resistance," in *Pigs, Profits, and Communities,* ed. Kendall M. Thu and E. Paul Durrenberg (Albany: State University of New York Press, 1998), 27.

4. DeLind, "Parma," 27.

5. DeLind, "Parma," 32–33, 35.

6. "Graphic Details as Trial Opens in Torture Case," *New York Times,* 5 May 1999, A1, A24.

7. "After Shooting, an Eroding Trust in the Police," *New York Times,* 19 February 1999, A1, A21.

8. "Guard in Nassau Jail Beat a Mentally Retarded Inmate in 1993, Jury Finds," *New York Times,* 2 March 1999, A19.

9. Elizabeth Olson, "Geneva Panel Says U.S. Prisoner Restraints Amount to Torture," *New York Times,* 18 May 2000, A11.

10. Philip Zimbardo, Curtis W. Banks, Craig Haney, and David Jaffe, "The Mind Is a Formidable Jailer," *New York Times,* 8 April 1973; cited in Beth B. Hess, Elizabeth W. Markson, and Peter J. Stein, *Sociology,* 4th ed. (New York: Macmillan, 1991), 109.

11. Ralph Dahrendorf, *Class and Class Conflict in Industrial Society* (Stanford, Calif.: Stanford University Press, 1959), 31.

12. Ian Robertson, *Sociology,* 3d ed. (New York: Worth, 1987), 479.

13. Randolph Bourne, "War as the Health of the State," *The Annals of America: 1916–1928, World War and Prosperity* (Chicago: Encyclopedia Britannica, 1968), 136.

14. Robert L. Kidder, *Connecting Law and Society: An Introduction to Research and Theory* (Englewood Cliffs, N.J.: Prentice Hall, 1983), 83.

15. Friedrich Engels, *The Origins of the Family, Private Property and the State* (New York: Penguin, 1986 [1884]), 223.

16. Marc Bloch, "The Rise of Dependent Cultivation and Seigniorial Institutions," in *Cambridge Economic History of Europe: Vol. I. The Agrarian Life of the Middle Ages,* ed. Michael M. Postan (New York: Cambridge University Press, 1966), 269; quoted in Immanuel Wallerstein, *The Modern World-System: Capitalist Agriculture and the Origins of the European World-Economy in the Sixteenth Century* (New York: Academic Press, 1974), 28.

17. T. Walter Wallbank and Arnold Schrier, *Living World History,* 3d ed. (Glenview, Ill.: Scott Foresman, 1969), 39.

18. Kenneth Cloke, "The Economic Basis of Law and State," in *Law against the People: Essays to Demystify Law, Order and the Courts,* ed. Robert Lefcourt (New York: Random House, 1971), 67.

19. H. G. Wells, *The Outline of History: Being a Plain History of Life and Mankind* (Garden City, N.J.: Garden City, 1949 [1920]), 457.

20. Daniel W. Rossides, *Social Stratification: The American Class System in Comparative Perspective* (Englewood Cliffs, N.J.: Prentice Hall, 1990), 30.

21. Austin Turk, "Law as a Weapon in Social Conflict." *Social Problems* 23, no. 13 (1976): 276–91.

22. Turk, "Law as a Weapon," 288.

23. For a more developed critique of the class biases inherent in the United States Constitution, see Michael Parenti, *Democracy for the Few* (New York: St. Martin's, 1990).

24. Charles Beard and Mary Beard, *History of the United States* (New York: Macmillan, 1930), 170–71.

25. Michael Parenti, *Democracy for the Few,* 2d ed. (New York: St. Martin's, 1977), 55.

26. Parenti, *Democracy for the Few,* 54.

27. Turk, "Law as a Weapon," 281.

28. Gerald Carson, *Men, Beasts and Gods: A History of Cruelty and Kindness* (New York: Scribner's, 1972), 27, 30.

29. See, for example, Alan Wolfe, *The Seamy Side of Democracy: Repression in America* (New York: Longman, 1978); Vincent Pinto, "Soldiers and Strikers: Class Repression as State Policy," in *The Capitalist System,* 2d ed., ed. Richard C. Edwards, Michael Reich, and Thomas E. Weisskopf (Englewood Cliffs, N.J.: Prentice Hall, 1978); Michael Parenti, *Against Empire* (San Francisco: City Lights, 1995).

30. Rutherford B. Hayes [1886], "Wealth in the Hands of a Few," in *The Annals of America,* ed. William Benton, vol. 11 (Chicago: Encyclopedia Britannica, 1968), 125.

31. Harold L. Wilensky and Charles N. Lebeaux, *Industrial Society and Social Welfare: The Impact of Industrialization on the Supply and Organization of Social Welfare Services in the United States* (New York: Free Press, 1965), 84.

32. Haywood Burns, "Racism and American Law," in *Law against the People: Essays to Demystify Law, Order and the Courts,* ed. Robert Lefcourt (New York: Random House, 1971), 45.

33. Karen DeCrow, *Sexist Justice* (New York: Vintage, 1974).

34. *Buck v. Bell,* United States Supreme Court Reports 247 (1927): 207.

35. Senate Report No. 1049 (54-1) 3366, submitted to the United States Senate to accompany S. 1552 on 26 May 1896 by the Committee on the District of Columbia.

36. Letter to the United States Senate from Charles W. Dabney, Jr., acting secretary of the Department of Agriculture, dated 20 May 1896 (Senate Document No. 3354, Fifty-fourth Congress, First Session).

37. Letter from Dabney, Fifty-fourth Congress, 6.

38. Letter from Dabney, Fifty-fourth Congress, 1–2.

39. United States Senate, *Vivisection.* Hearing on the Bill (S. 1552) for the Further Prevention of Cruelty to Animals in the District of Columbia (1896), 104.

40. Senate Report No. 1049 (54-1) 3366, submitted to the United States Senate to accompany S. 1552 on 26 May 1896 by the Committee on the District of Columbia, iii.

41. United States Senate, *Vivisection.* Hearing on the Bill (S. 1552) for the Further Prevention of Cruelty to Animals in the District of Columbia (1896), 41.

42. Gabriel Kolko, *The Triumph of Conservatism: A Reinterpretation of American History, 1900–1916* (New York: Free Press, 1963), 282–83.

43. Kolko, *The Triumph of Conservatism,* 99.

44. Kolko, *The Triumph of Conservatism,* 100.

45. Douglas F. Dowd, *The Twisted Dream: Capitalist Development in the United States since 1776* (Cambridge, Mass.: Winthrop, 1974), 264.

46. See Mary Francis Berry, *Black Resistance, White Law: A History of Constitutional Racism in America* (New York: Appleton-Century-Crofts, 1971); Ward Churchill and Jim Vander Wall, *Agents of Repression: The FBI's Secret Wars against the Black Panther Party and the American Indian* (Boston: South End, 1988).

47. U.S. Congress, Senate, Committee Hearings, Eighty-fourth Congress, Volume 1198-1, *Humane Slaughtering of Livestock and Poultry* (Washington, D.C.: U.S. Government Printing Office, 1956), Senate Library, 2.

48. U.S. Congress, *Humane Slaughtering*, 46.

49. U.S. Congress, *Humane Slaughtering*, 82–83.

50. U.S. Congress, *Humane Slaughtering*, 16.

51. U.S. Congress, *Humane Slaughtering*, 16.

52. U.S. Congress, *Humane Slaughtering*, 33.

53. U.S. Congress, *Humane Slaughtering*, 35.

54. U.S. Congress, *Humane Slaughtering*, 132.

55. U.S. Congress, *Humane Slaughtering*, 74.

56. U.S. Congress, *Humane Slaughtering*, 64.

57. U.S. Congress, *Humane Slaughtering*, 138.

58. In 1978, Congress amended the Humane Slaughter Act to include all slaughterhouses inspected by the USDA.

59. Gail A. Eisnitz, *Slaughterhouse: The Shocking Story of Greed, Neglect, and Inhumane Treatment Inside the U.S. Meat Industry* (Amherst, N.Y.: Prometheus, 1997).

60. Eisnitz, *Slaughterhouse*.

61. Elliot Jaspin, "Groups Criticize USDA over Alabama Chicken Plants," *Dayton Daily News*, 1 June 2000, 7A.

62. Jaspin, "Groups Criticize USDA," 7A.

63. Christopher Drew and Bud Hazelkorn, "U.S. Officials Investigating Meat Safety," *New York Times*, 22 March 2001, A21.

64. United States House of Representatives, *Regulation of the Transportation and Sale and Handling of Dogs and Cats Used for Research and Experimentation*, Report No. 1418 to accompany H.R. 13881, Eighty-ninth Congress, Second Session (1966), 88–89.

65. United States House of Representatives, *Regulation of the Transportation and Sale*, 226.

66. United States House of Representatives, *Regulation of the Transportation and Sale*, 73.

67. Judith Reitman, *Stolen for Profit*, rev. ed. (New York: Kensington, 1995), 38.

68. "Legislative Review," *Animal Law* 6 (2000): 172–78.

69. For a good summary and evaluation of these regulations, see Gary Francione, *Animals, Property and Law* (Philadelphia: Temple University Press, 1995).

70. Lefcourt, *Law against the People.*

71. United States House of Representatives, hearings on H.R. 3270, the Farm Animal and Research Facilities Protection Act, 17 July 1990, 17–18.

72. U.S. House, Farm Animal Protection, 19.

73. U.S. House, Farm Animal Protection, 30–34.

74. Cited in Judith Reitman, *Stolen for Profit* (New York: Kensington, 1992), 180.

75. See, for example, Churchill and Vander Wall, *Agents of Repression.*

76. See, for example, Jeffrey Reiman, *The Rich Get Richer and the Poor Get Prison: Economic Bias in American Criminal Justice* (Boston: Allyn & Bacon, 1996).

77. Reiman, *The Rich Get Richer and the Poor Get Prison*, 1, 4.

78. See, for example, M. David Ermann and Richard J. Lundman, eds., *Corporate and Governmental Deviance: Problems of Organizational Behavior in Contemporary Society* (New York: Oxford University Press, 1992).

79. Robert Sherrill, "The Case against the Oil Companies," in *The Big Business Reader:*

Essays on Corporate America, ed. Mark Green and Robert Massie, Jr. (New York: Pilgrim, 1983), 23.

80. Ralph Nader's introduction to Green and Massie, eds., *The Big Business Reader,* 5.

81. Leslie Kaufman, "$60 Million Fine for Sears in Bankruptcy Fraud Case," *New York Times,* 10 February 1999, C2.

82. Kaufman, "$60 Million Fine," C2.

83. Milton Moskowitz, Michael Katz, and Robert Levering, *Everybody's Business, an Almanac: The Irreverent Guide to Corporate America* (New York: Harper & Row, 1980), 620.

84. Moskowitz et al., *The Irreverent Guide,* 620.

85. David Barboza, "Sara Lee Corp. Pleads Guilty in Meat Case," *New York Times,* 23 June 2001, A7; and Associated Press, "Sara Lee Pleads Guilty to Selling Tainted Meat Linked to 15 Deaths," *Dayton Daily News,* 23 June 2001, 3A.

86. Human Rights Watch, *World Report 2000: The United States,* http://www.hrw.org, 2.

87. U.S. Senate Committee on Labor and Human Resources, *Care of Institutionalized Mentally Disabled Persons,* pts. 1 and 2 (Washington, D.C.: U.S. Government Printing Office, 1985), 3.

88. Associated Press, "Doctors Accused of Abusing Patients," *Springfield* [Ohio] *News-Sun,* 27 February 1999, 8.

89. Associated Press, "Doctors Accused," 8.

90. Burton Blatt, *The Conquest of Mental Retardation* (Austin, Tex.: Pro-Ed, 1987), 230.

91. Elliot Jaspin and Scott Montgomery, "Unsafe Plants Supply Schools," *Dayton Daily News,* 28 March 1999, 1A, 15A.

92. Scott Montgomery, "Court Rules Feds Must Continue Meat Inspections," *Dayton Daily News,* 1 July 2000, 1A, 7A.

93. Drew and Hazelkorn, "U.S. Officials Investigating Meat Safety."

94. Robert K. Schaeffer, *Understanding Globalization: The Social Consequences of Political, Economic, and Environmental Change* (New York: Rowman & Littlefield, 1997), 157.

95. Elizabeth Becker, "Far from Dead, Subsidies Fuel Big Farms," *New York Times,* 14 May 2001, A1, A12.

96. Schaeffer, *Understanding Globalization,* 158.

97. Joseph G. Sauder, "Enacting and Enforcing Felony Animal Cruelty Laws to Prevent Violence against Humans," *Animal Law* 6 (2000): 1–21.

98. Sauder, "Enacting and Enforcing"; Randall Lockwood, "Animal Cruelty and Violence against Humans: Making the Connection," *Animal Law* 5 (1999): 81–87.

99. Pamela D. Frasch et al., "State Animal Anti-Cruelty Statutes: An Overview," *Animal Law* 5 (1999): 69–80.

100. Sauder, "Enacting and Enforcing," 2.

101. Frasch, "State Animal Anti-Cruelty Statutes," 70.

102. "Legislative Review," *Animal Law* 7 (2001): 154.

103. David J. Wolfson, "Steven M. Wise: Rattling the Cage—Toward Legal Rights for Animals," *Animal Law* 6 (1999): 262.

104. "Legislative Review," *Animal Law* 6 (2000): 172–78.

105. "Legislative Review," (2000): 177–78.

106. Gary Francione, *Animals, Property and the Law* (Philadelphia: Temple University Press, 1995); Gary Francione, *Rain without Thunder: The Ideology of the Animal Rights Movement* (Philadelphia: Temple University Press, 1996).

107. Gary Francione, "Animal Rights and the Future," speech delivered before the World

Vegetarian Congress at the University of Pittsburgh at Johnstown, 3 August 1996; www.aeinc-online.org/gary96.html (visited 26 June 2001).

108. Parenti cites Russell Galloway, *The Rich and the Poor in Supreme Court History, 1790–1982* (Greenbrae, Calif.: Paradigm, 1982), 163, 180–81.

109. Michael Parenti, *Democracy for the Few,* 6th ed. (New York: St. Martin's, 1995), 290.

110. Helena Silverstein, *Unleashing Rights: Law, Meaning, and the Animal Rights Movement* (Ann Arbor: University of Michigan Press, 1996), 131.

111. Silverstein, *Unleashing Rights,* 131.

112. Silverstein, *Unleashing Rights,* 131.

113. Silverstein, *Unleashing Rights,* 131.

114. Francione, *Animals, Property and the Law,* 35.

115. Francione, *Animals, Property and the Law,* 151.

116. Francione, *Animals, Property and the Law,* 156.

117. Silverstein, *Unleashing Rights,* 140.

118. Steven M. Wise, *Rattling the Cage: Toward Legal Rights for Animals* (Cambridge, Mass.: Perseus, 2000), 77.

119. Barbara Newell, "Animal Custody Disputes: A Growing Crack in the 'Legal Thinghood' of Nonhuman Animals," *Animal Law* 6 (2000): 180.

120. Newell, "Animal Custody Disputes," 184.

121. Newell, "Animal Custody Disputes," 183.

122. 886 S. W. 2nd 368, 376–78 (Tex. App.), Andell, J., concurring. Cited in Sonia S. Waisman and Barbara R. Newell, "Recovery of 'Non-Economic' Damages for Wrongful Killing or Injury of Companion Animals: A Judicial and Legislative Trend," *Animal Law* 7 (2001): 55.

123. David J. Wolfson, "Steven M. Wise: Rattling the Cage—Toward Legal Rights for Animals," *Animal Law* 6 (2000): 264.

124. Silverstein, *Unleashing Rights,* 157.

125. Silverstein, *Unleashing Rights,* 156.

126. www.mcspotlight.org/case/trial/story.html.

127. Eric R. Smith, "McLibel," *Z Magazine* (September 1996): 20.

128. Ronald K. L. Collins, *Congress Must Address Food-Disparagement Laws* (1999); www.cspinet.org/foodspeak/oped/balsun2.htm.

129. "Ballot Initiatives Review," *Animal Law* 7 (2001): 99.

130. "Legislative Review," *Animal Law* 7 (2001): 147.

131. "Legislative Review," *Animal Law* 7 (2001): 147.

132. Ted Williams, "Management by Majority," *Audubon* 101, no. 3 (May–June 1999): 47.

133. "Ballot Initiatives Review," *Animal Law* (1999): 109.

134. "Ballot Initiatives Review," *Animal Law* (1999): 110.

135. "Ballot Initiatives Review," *Animal Law* (1999): 109–10.

136. "Legislative Review," *Animal Law* (2001): 145.

137. Michael Janofsky, "Gun Producers, under Assault, Turn to Politics," *New York Times,* 19 January 2000, A1.

138. See for example, Ruth Sidel, *Women and Children Last: The Plight of Poor Women in Affluent America* (New York: Penguin, 1992).

139. Alan Gartner, Colin Greer, and Frank Riessman, *What Reagan Is Doing to Us* (New York: Harper & Row, 1982).

140. Gartner et al., *What Reagan Is Doing to Us.*

141. See Kevin Phillips, *The Politics of Rich and Poor: Wealth and the American Electorate in the Reagan Aftermath* (New York: Random House, 1990).

142. Cox News Service, "Bush Laying Siege to Clinton Regulations," *Dayton Daily News,* 1 April 2001, 5A.

143. Molly Ivins, "Corporations Have Taken over U.S.," *Dayton Daily News,* 12 February 2001.

144. Michael R. Gordon and Judith Miller, "U.S. Germ Warfare Review Urges Pullback from Talks," *New York Times,* 20 May 2001, A1.

145. David E. Sanger, "Bush Calls World Economy Goal of Attacks on U.S.," *New York Times,* 21 October 2001, A8.

146. "A Travesty of Justice," *New York Times,* 16 November 2002, A22.

147. Adam Cohen, "Rough Justice: The Attorney General Has Powerful New Tools to Fight Terrorism. Has He Gone Too Far?" *Time* 158, no. 25 (10 December 2001): 37.

148. Katharine Q. Seelye, "Bush Promotes Energy Bill as Security Issue," *New York Times,* 12 October 2001, A12.

6

The Social Construction
of Speciesist Reality

Would you like to swing on a star
Carry moonbeams home in a jar
And be better off than you are
Or would you rather be a mule?

A mule is an animal with long funny ears
Kicks up at anything he hears
His back is brawny but his brain is weak
He's just plain stupid with a stubborn streak
And by the way, if you hate to go to school
You may grow up to be a mule

—"Swinging on a Star," circa 1943 (Johnny Burke and Jimmy Van Heusen)

[I]f members of the family—especially children—. . . object to the idea of butchering an animal, it may be a good idea to explain that livestock which are raised for food are the same as vegetables in the garden.

—Phyllis Hobson[1]

In October 1987, eighteen-month-old Jessica McClure became a household name when she was trapped in the bottom of an abandoned residential water well in Midland, Texas. The nation and the world watched from their living rooms as rescuers struggled to save "Baby Jessica." After three days of frantic activity and the aid and assistance of countless volunteers, Jessica McClure was freed.

The efforts to rescue Jessica McClure were heroic, and the outpouring of assistance to the family was tremendous—and necessary: the girl's young parents did not have health insurance. Jessica's injuries required surgery, and she was hospitalized for almost a month. Gifts and support poured in from around the country, and

President George H. W. Bush and the First Lady visited her in the hospital. Paradoxically, though, most of the same caring people who had responded so strongly to Baby Jessica's plight remained indifferent to the fact that roughly thirty-seven million of their fellow citizens also were without health insurance (by 2000, that number had grown to forty-five million) and faced similar distress when they had emergencies and tragedies of their own. This situation prompted commentary from one of the leading socialists in the United States, the late Michael Harrington, who observed that people in the United States were capable of "collective cruelty and individual generosity."[2]

Similarly, after the success of the film *Free Willy,* Keiko, a whale used by the filmmakers, became known to tens of millions around the world. They learned about his poor health and endangered condition resulting from years in captivity. After an outpouring of public concern, millions of dollars were spent in an effort to save Keiko, and tens of thousands of well-wishers came out to greet him as he traveled from Mexico to a specially constructed tank in Oregon, where thousands more visited him. Meanwhile, the plight of other captive whales and the continued commercially motivated killing of whales, particularly by Japan and Norway, move relatively few members of the public.

This chapter will suggest that the entangled nature of the oppression of humans and other animals not only has deep economic roots, supported by a powerful state apparatus, but also has considerable public support among a citizenry raised in a society in which powerful corporations exert extraordinary control over beliefs and values. Certainly, corporate attempts to legitimate oppressive practices are not thoroughly successful in controlling public opinion. However, enough corporate control exists to keep institutionalized oppression intact. The conflict between most people's urges toward decency and a social system rooted in oppression leads to the widespread ambivalence about various oppressed "others."

Such ambivalence can be seen in the fact that while children are cherished in the contemporary United States, at least in popular culture and political rhetoric, one in six lives in extreme poverty. Millions of children around the world suffer from hunger and malnutrition, and thousands starve to death. The poor within the United States are simultaneously pitied—and made the object of charity during the holidays—while held in contempt for their alleged laziness and sloth. Similarly, the traditional view of womanhood that many still espouse is that of a sanctified and revered status warranting chivalry, respect, and protection, as described in the Supreme Court's ruling in the *Blackwell* case. However, domestic violence, femicide, exploitation of women's labor, and sexual objectification abound, while the rate of sexual assault on women in the United States is higher than in any other industrialized nation in the world.[3]

Humans who are older are, ideally, esteemed, honored, and respected; in reality, old age is widely viewed in the United States as an undesirable status. Older individuals are largely invisible in the mass media; when they do appear, they tend to be portrayed in uncomplimentary and stereotypical ways. Tens of thousands of older humans are confined in nursing homes, where they are vulnerable to neglect and abuse and consumed by boredom and loneliness. Many in the United States also voice support for the concept that humans with disabilities should receive appropriate care, but they ignore the harshness of institutional life, form citizen groups to keep group homes out of their neighborhoods, and laugh at the "morons" and "idiots" who are the brunt of jokes on prime-time television. State and local legislation protecting gays and lesbians from discrimination that may be passed one year is rescinded the next. In the past century, many abolitionists struggled passionately against human enslavement but did not welcome humans of color into their neighborhoods, schools, and communities—as many do not to this day. In 1944, the Swedish sociologist Gunnar Myrdal characterized the treatment of humans of color in the United States as "An American Dilemma"; that dilemma continues to characterize the ideas about, and treatment of, all of the oppressed in the United States as we pass into the early stages of the twenty-first century.[4]

The inconsistent ideas about, and treatment of, devalued humans and other animals are not manifestations of a natural human tendency toward malevolent dissonance. Indeed, humans have a great capacity for caring and empathy, for "equality" and "fraternity." But that capacity is compromised and neutralized by economic, political, and belief systems that glorify private wealth and promote egotism. Thus, the "dilemma" arises from the contrasts between what we can be and profess to be and what we actually are. (Consider the platitudes about America's compassion in Senator Hubert Humphrey's opening statement for the 1956 hearings on proposed legislation on "humane slaughtering" and the testimony in his hearings about the horrible suffering in slaughterhouses.) Inconsistencies, paradoxes, and contradictions are inevitable, and cultivated, in societies such as the United States that strive for "civilization" while continuing to build great wealth and privilege for some upon a deep and extensive foundation of exploitation and oppression of "others."

The inherent unnaturalness of many of our relations with other animals and with each other, and the relationship of this state of affairs to highly concentrated, privately held wealth and corporate power, are obscured by the way we are programmed to see the world. Social systems with deep economic roots in the oppression of devalued others are safe for the elite, economically, politically, and socially, if devaluation of the oppressed is widely accepted and deeply felt. Thus, if oppression is primarily motivated by economic interests and the interests of elites are well protected by the powers of the state, beliefs that justify social arrangements—ideologies—play the most important role in legitimizing oppression by rendering it invisible. Oppression must be accepted as normal, natural, and necessary. As Michael Harrington observed in *The Other America,* it takes a considerable will power to *see* it, much less to understand the structural arrangements that compel it. Invidious ideologies (classism, racism, sexism, speciesism, etc.) are manufactured by the powerful to legitimate their wealth—and these ideologies spawn individual prejudice.

Ethnocentrism/anthropocentrism[5] is essential to this process. If the masses are taught to discount the oppressed as "foreign," "alien," "uncivilized," "unclean," "stupid," "inferior," and so on, they become socially distanced from the devalued others, thus precluding both opportunities and tendencies for empathetic response.

Many humans who are deeply situated in the status quo, through indoctrination, social position, and self-interest, even express indignation at any suggestion that "others," particularly other animals, are oppressed.

Actually, ambivalence about other animals has roots deep in human history, and such cultural conditioning has been around a long time. Living in close cohabitation with other animals and observing their families and social relations likely engendered in many humans a substantial level of sensitivity, understanding, and respect. As human animals cultivated the ability to capture and kill other animals, such treatment of other animals spurred an anxiousness in humans, an uneasiness that found its way into religious belief and ritual. James Serpell notes:

> The idea that animals are fully conscious beings who possess spiritual powers is widespread among hunting and gathering societies. Not surprisingly, it also appears to engender considerable anxiety and guilt about killing animals for food. Most of these cultures engage in complex rituals and taboos designed either to relieve the guilt arising from hunting or to honor the spirits of the deceased animals.[6]

Examples of several such beliefs are taken from the writings of R. A. Marchant:

> Eskimos also believed that because seals and whales lived in the sea they were unable to drink and so suffered from a continual and intolerable thirst. They therefore allowed themselves to be caught, knowing that the Eskimos would end their agony by giving them an offering of fresh water. If a hunter neglected to put this water into the mouth of his victim, the other seals or whales would know of his treachery and would never again allow themselves to be caught by him.
>
> Polar bears were envious of [human] possessions and so their skins had to be hung up in the house alongside the tools they coveted—knives and bow drills if the animal was male and needles and skin scrapers for a female. The soul of the animal stayed in the skin until it was driven out in a special ceremony four or five days later. It then departed, taking with it the spirits of the proffered tools.[7]

Thus, some ideologies have justified and naturalized the killing of other animals by making such killing a sacred activity, one that transcends other mundane, daily activities, and, thus, more acceptable. The sacred nature of an activity, however, can be eroded if the once-disturbing activity becomes a routine and ordinary aspect of day-to-day existence, particularly as the numbers of other animals being mistreated and killed increases. Writing about this process, and providing yet another insight into the entanglement of the oppression of humans and other animals, Elizabeth Fisher notes:

> [H]umans violated animals by making them their slaves. In taking them in and feeding them, humans first made friends with animals and then killed them. To do so, they had to kill something in themselves. When they began manipulating the reproduction of animals, they were even more personally involved in practices which led to cruelty, guilt, and subsequent numbness. The keeping of animals would seem to have set a model for the enslavement of humans, in particular the large scale exploitation of women captives

for breeding and labor, which is a salient feature of the *developing civilizations* [emphasis added].[8]

The eventual domestication of various groups of other animals surely rendered their exploitation and death a mundane matter for their captors. The perceived naturalness of such treatment grew with the expansion of agriculture production in various parts of the world, an economic practice that facilitated growth in the populations of other animals such as sheep, goats, cows, pigs, and others held captive. Imprisonment and "domestication" of other animals diminished humans' ability and willingness to see the nature and abilities of other animals. Writing in 1754, for example, Jean-Jacques Rousseau observed, "The horse, the cat, the bull . . . are for the most part larger and all have a more robust constitution, more vigour, more strength and more spirit in the forest than under our roofs; they lose half those advantages on becoming domesticated, and one might say that all our efforts to care for and feed these animals have only succeeded in making them degenerate."[9]

A servile and listless demeanor follows when an individual is stripped of self-determination and liberty or has never experienced them. The confinement of other animals in small or tiny areas, where they were unable to behave in ways that were natural to them or even to distance themselves from mud and excrement, to clean and groom themselves, and to seek comfortable bedding, also unquestionably contributed to their devaluation and fostered the "lower" status that had been ascribed to them. For the most part, recognition of the individuality and personality of confined other animals waned as their numbers grew.

Thus, as other animals became more deeply integrated into the day-to-day organization of agricultural society, their "inferior" status, relative to human animals—especially those human animals perceived as intrinsically important and valuable—came to be viewed as natural. The powerful and compelling forces that diminished human recognition of the significance and individuality of other animals also subverted recognition of and sensitivity to the individuality and suffering of devalued humans who were cast into such positions as slave, peasant, and harem possession.

The political, educational, religious, and familial institutions of these societies were shaped and molded by the economically motivated oppression of humans and other animals. Through custom and practice, the "rightful" place of both the powerful and the oppressed were engraved in the collective and, accordingly, individual consciousness. The power of this ideological force can be so compelling that it is common for oppressed humans to accept the "naturalness" of their own devalued position. For example, reflecting on his experience growing up African American in the southern United States early in the twentieth century, Amzie Moore recounted, "for a long time, I had the idea that a man with white skin was superior because it appeared to me that he had everything. And I figured if God would justify the white man having everything, that God put him in the position to be the best."[10]

Meanwhile, those who do not suffer oppression, and may even reap some benefits from the oppression of others, similarly are steeped in a social reality that presents the arrangements as natural. Again, drawing an example from the pervasiveness of racism in the southern United States, civil rights activist Virginia Durr recalled:

> If you are born into a system that's wrong, whether it's a slave system or whether it is a segregated system, you take it for granted. And I was born into a system that was segregated and denied Blacks the right to vote, and also denied women the right to vote, and I took it for granted. Nobody told me any different, nobody said it was strange or unusual.[11]

Powerful ideological and social forces frequently produce distorted outlooks and dispositions that naturalize oppression, a process social theorist and educator Paulo Freire referred to as "domestication" of the human animal.[12]

However, no matter how strong the ideas that rationalize and promote oppression, there are always some in every society, like Virginia Durr, who nonetheless perceive that something is wrong. Some find they are unable to look indifferently at the suffering experienced by others—especially if they do not have vested interests in the oppression they observe. If these individuals set their ideas down in political tracts or travel speaking out against the particular social arrangements to others similarly situated in the social order, they have the potential to cast doubt upon the perceived naturalness of oppressive practices, in turn perhaps challenging the economic practices from which many powerful individuals derive wealth.

As a result, throughout the ages it has been necessary for many philosophers, system apologists, and, later, "scientists" to expound ideas that counter such dissension and reinforce acceptance of oppressive practices.[13] Plato, for instance, in his most famous work, *The Republic,* maintained that some humans were more useful to society than others. Using a metallurgic metaphor, Plato asserted that some humans were "gold," some were "silver," some were "iron," and that each had a specific service to provide. Workers produced, soldiers protected the state, and philosophers—the "golden humans"—ruled. Pythagoras expressed concern about human treatment of other animals in ancient Greece around 500 B.C., but ideas such as those of Aristotle that legitimized privilege carried the day—or rather, the epoch. Aristotle defended the oppression of other animals against those who questioned the naturalness of those arrangements, as seen in the following passage from *Politics:*

> Plants exist for the sake of animals, and brute beasts for the sake of man—domestic animals for his use and food, wild ones (or at any rate most of them) for food and other accessories of life, such as clothing and various tools.
>
> Since nature makes nothing purposeless or in vain, it is undeniably true that she has made all animals for the sake of man.[14]

Similarly, while some Christians throughout the ages expressed concern about the suffering imposed on other animals, the views expressed by Saint Thomas Aquinas largely reflected the church's position that animals were placed on earth solely to serve "man." Explicitly restating the position set forth by Aristotle, Aquinas wrote, "There is no sin in using a thing for the purposes for which it is. Now the order of things is such that the imperfect are for the perfect. . . . Things, like plants which merely have life, are all alike for animals, and all animals are for man. Wherefore it is not unlawful if men use plants for the good of animals, and animals for the good of man, as the Philosopher states (Politics I, 3)."[15]

The power of the Christian Church and the ideological defense it provided against challenges to the oppression of other animals expanded during the early Middle Ages after the fall of Rome in Europe. The demeaning social positions assigned to other animals and their exploitation and oppression in the Western world were sanctioned as the will of God.

The oppression of human animals received the same ecclesiastical support. For example, Saint Paul instructed humans who were enslaved to "Be obedient to them that are your masters, with fear and trembling, as unto Christ." Similarly, the patriarchy and misogyny that characterized the ancient world continued, with Church authorization, into the agrarian-based, war-afflicted world of the early Middle Ages. Del Martin, author of *Battered Wives,* writes:

> In Europe during the Middle Ages, squires and noblemen beat their wives as regularly as they beat their serfs. The peasants faithfully followed their lords' examples. . . . The habit of looking upon women as a *species* apart [emphasis added], without the same feelings and capacity for suffering that men have, became inbred during the Middle Ages. . . . During medieval times the law of the land was the law of the church, and the civil courts were puppets of the ecclesiastical hierarchy. Judeo-Christian doctrine, which espoused the inferiority of women and the supremacy of men, gave its stamp of approval to domestic violence.[16]

Another way to buttress ethnocentrism and ideological support for oppression, and to protect the status quo, is to scapegoat devalued others for the structural problems that beset the populace. As we have seen, women were scapegoated for the myriad ills that plagued the corrupt system of social arrangements of medieval society, and the "witch" hunts emerged. Both Protestant and Catholic churches in the late Middle Ages persecuted women, mostly peasant women, as witches. Church officials created handbooks that aided the inquisitors by instructing them in various forms of torture that could be used to extract "confessions" from witches. As noted earlier, cats and others thought to be closely aligned with "witches" also were blamed for the ills of the period, resulting in their torture and death as well.

Church-based ideologies also legitimized and supported the disastrous exploits of Europeans in the Western Hemisphere. In 1493, after European adventurers "discovered" the existence of new pillagable lands and conquerable humans in the Western Hemisphere, Pope Alexander VI issued the *Bull of Donation,* which purported to grant the rulers of Spain most of the Western Hemisphere, "so that the Abandoned heathen could be drawn to embrace the Catholic faith and be trained in good morals."[17] Although some concerned advocates for enslaved indigenous humans challenged the ideas that legitimized their oppression, the philosophies of the system apologists were given the force of law. Tragically, after a few decades of a frenzied grab for wealth, the actions of the Spanish elite "had exterminated almost the entire native population of the Caribbean."[18]

The economically motivated oppression that grew dramatically with the development and expansion of agricultural society no doubt seemed to many as natural. Philosophical and religious-based ideologies (ideas that were backed by the various powers of the state) were created and ethnocentrism fanned to reduce intellectual challenges to oppressive economic arrangements.

IDEOLOGY OF CAPITALIST DEVELOPMENT

The advent of capitalism brought about dramatic changes not only in the form and scale of oppression but also in the justification and rationalization used to support it. Powerful merchants, striving to create social systems more conducive to the creation of commercial profit and wealth, began to challenge existing social arrangements. Nascent capitalists needed an ideology to undermine the control of the church and the monarchies that long had dictated what economic goods would be produced, who would produce them, and how they would be distributed. Philosophers and writers created new rationalizations and explanations about what was natural and just. These emerging ideas shunned long-held metaphysical ideas about the divine rights of rulers and the rightful places of their "subjects" and sought to replace the troublesome existing theological explanations of the world with mathematical and scientific ones. These new ideas purported to represent the interests of the "common man" and to signal the birth of a new era—one with increased sensitivity to human rights. In truth, these new ideas largely supported the transfer of political, social, and economic power to a new elite, doing relatively little to stem oppression. The emerging new ruling class in capitalist society was wary of any true political empowerment of the masses, lest the masses push for economic empowerment and a more equitable distribution of resources. As we saw in the last chapter, in the United States the "founding fathers" were very concerned with such a prospect and created a constitution and system of government that would protect the interests of the affluent.[19]

Nonetheless, some philosophers and moralists were serious about the development of equitable and just human societies, free of oppression and poverty; several also discussed the interests of other animals in their treatises. Enlightenment-era writers such as David Hume, Jean-Jacques Rousseau, Jeremy Bentham, and François-Marie Voltaire advocated, in varying degrees, for a change in humanity's view and treatment of the oppressed, including other animals. Once again, however, the ideas promulgated by the advocates of the oppressed were eclipsed by the demands of dominant material arrangements—in this case, by the social, economic, and political organization that grew out of the unfolding capitalist system. One eighteenth-century philosophical apologist for the emerging system and its various forms of oppression, Immanuel Kant, promoted the view that other animals were not self-conscious but simply represented means for human ends, while René Descartes declared that other animals were unfeeling, machinelike robots who should be used to serve human interests.

While writers like Kant and Descartes effectively deflected philosophical challenges to the oppression of other animals, by necessity, a general consensus emerged regarding the importance of establishing "liberty, equality, and fraternity" for humans. Such ideas were important in enlisting public support for the "revolution from above" staged by the rising capitalist class. However, by the late nineteenth century, these egalitarian and democratic ideas were clearly incongruent with the advancement of modern capitalism. Nonetheless, in the United States idealistic philosophical tenets were brandished by reformers and revolutionaries who charged the new elite class with perpetuating and profiting from widespread poverty and misery. In response, the U.S. elite found ideological refuge in "science." Having diluted metaphysical justifications for privilege and rule by divine right, the capitalist elite rationalized their power, control, and privilege by virtue of their alleged intellectual superiority. As the twentieth century approached, pseudoscientific social Darwinist philosophy had become an important tool with which to defend against challenges to oppression. Poverty, disease, hunger, and other social problems existed, according to social Darwinists, because immigrants, humans of color, and those living in poverty were "intellectually inferior" to the "successful." The ideas underlying social Darwinism were seductive in their simplicity and easily promulgated. The perspective this theory offered was easily accepted, as the long-held devaluation of humans with disabilities and the stereotype of the "dumb" animal had for centuries supplemented religious legitimation of their exploitation. With the ascent of science, the alleged lack of intelligence of an individual or group became a more powerful justification for oppression. The place and treatment of the oppressed continued to be presented as natural and normal and to be used to rationalize various unjust arrangements, such as institutionalized racism. For example, in 1940 L. L. Burlingame, professor of biology at Stanford University and an apologist for ethnic oppression, wrote, "In proportion to their numbers, Negroes contribute far too few persons of high ability and far too many who are low normal or deficient in ability. . . . Mexicans are the second most serious race problem. They are apparently of distinctly low mental caliber, have not yet produced eminence and do contribute heavily to various dependent classes."[20]

Similarly, oppression of other animals has frequently been defended by accentuating their alleged deficiencies as well. For instance, in a 1968 book titled *Sportsman's Guide to Game Animals*, Leonard Lee Rue III justified hunting opossums by virtue of their "stupidity."

[The opossum's] tiny brain case indicates it is one of the stupidest animals alive. . . . The opossum is rather slow-moving and dim-witted. . . . The animal can stand more physical abuse than any other creature I know of. I have seen people beat opossums with clubs, attempt to drown them and even hang them, and although the opossums certainly didn't enjoy this treatment, they frequently were able to survive.[21]

The notion that other animals were low in a natural hierarchy of living beings due to their alleged lack of intelligence was further buttressed by *behaviorism,* a school of "scientific" thought that maintained that the lack of empirical laboratory proof of the existence of consciousness—especially in other animals—required that scientists regard them as only mechanically responding to environmental stimuli. This twentieth-century version of Descartes's view provided further "scientific" defense for the oppressive practices on other animals.

Thus, in the age of "liberty, equality, and fraternity," many oppressed groups were disparaged for their alleged "low mental caliber" and consequently scaled low in a hierarchy of worth. The measurement of an individual's or group's value was based on the purported level of intelligence, measured or attributed in ethnocentric, anthropocentric ways. In addition, ecofeminists[22] have observed that ideas about the hierarchy of worth are deeply entwined with patriarchy, a system of social organization in which masculinity is valued over femininity (both being social constructions).[23] Ecofeminist Janis Birkeland put it this way:

> In the dominant Patriarchal cultures, reality is divided according to gender, and a higher value is placed on those attributes associated with masculinity, a construction that is called "hierarchical dualism." In these cultures, women have historically been seen as closer to the earth or nature. . . . Also, women and nature have been juxtaposed against mind and spirit, which have been associated in Western cosmology with the "masculine" and elevated to a higher plane of being. . . . [I]t is clear that a complex morality based on dominance and exploitation has developed in conjunction with the devaluing of nature and "feminine" values.[24]

General acceptance of the existence and naturalness of such a hierarchy continues to legitimate oppression of other animals, women, humans of color, humans with disabilities, and other devalued groups. The denigration of some groups, generated to a large degree by cupidity, is increased by high levels of socially cultivated egocentrism and is woven into both the culture and individual psyches in a way that shapes personal identities. Those who perceive themselves to be superior to others sometimes display their socially induced prejudice by acts of discrimination, frequently by creating physical, social, and emotional distance between themselves and the devalued. At times, discriminatory acts are perpetrated only for the amusement value in denigrating and harming the "lowly other" and to display the perpetrator's power—or, put more correctly, to reassure one who is insecure about his or her possession of personal power.

Such circumstances underlie the attack by the boys on bicycles on Willow Grear, the woman with a vision disability, and Cassidy, the dog. A dog, a woman, a human with a disability, and a human with limited monetary resources, all combined in the forms of Cassidy and Willow Grear, can be an irresistible target for a group of adolescent boys in the United States. Most would not commit or condone their cruelty. But the prevailing beliefs and values required to legitimize widespread institutionalized oppression, such as that practiced by agribusiness and the pharmaceutical and chemical industries, shape the reality and cultivate the general personality types of human members of society. In an often predatory system, in which the prevailing ideology glorifies wealth and power, more humans will be inclined to accept or tolerate, if not practice, violence against those "others" who are perceived as poor, weak, or powerless. The widespread acceptance of the general concept of the hierarchy of worth of living beings both rationalizes oppressive acts and arrangements and thoroughly entangles the various beliefs that arise from a hierarchical worldview. Only the rejection of the entire notion of such hierarchy can remove the ideological support for oppression of any group and begin to make all groups secure.

The indoctrination of the masses of humans is achieved mainly through their daily experiences in a stratified and hegemonically controlled society. (*Hegemony,* as used here, refers to the process in which a relatively small number of powerful humans and corporations exert an enormous influence over cultural beliefs, values, practices, and institutionalized arrangements.) As the early twentieth-century critical theorist Antonio Gramsci observed, humans develop what seems to be "common sense" through their daily experiences.[25] After one is taught successfully that a "natural hierarchy" exists in the world, one's worldly task is perhaps not so much to make it to the top of the social order as it is to distance one's self from the "bottom"—for those at the bottom suffer derision, deprivation, and violence. This socially created hierarchy is deeply rooted in the social fabric and is embedded in individual consciousness, so much so that, for many, challenges to the existence of oppression appear "stupid."

Sociologists frequently speak of *agencies of socialization*—that is, those forces such as the mass media, the schools, the state, and other powerful social institutions that serve to program or indoctrinate humans with the socially constructed reality of their society. We will look briefly at what several of these agencies teach about the "true nature" of the world and the place in it of the oppressed, particularly other animals.

MASS MEDIA: OUR FILTERED VIEW OF THE WORLD

Before the twentieth century, entertainment, news, and information were provided mainly by public gatherings and town meetings and through the distribution of pamphlets and tracts. By the nineteenth century, magazines and newspapers grew in number and readership, permitting the publishers to share their views of the world—and their prejudices—with the literate of the time. For example, widely circulated magazines such as *Judge* and *Puck* routinely disparaged oppressed groups through stereotyped and disparaging portrayals in cartoons and graphics.

The twentieth century brought movies and newsreels that continued to present the oppressed in ways that legitimized their status and treatment. Oppressed groups have frequently been portrayed in films either as dangerous threats to "civilized" society or as comic buffoons with obvious intellectual deficiencies. For example, one

of the first widely viewed feature films, *Birth of a Nation,* told a story of how granting voting rights to humans once enslaved in the United States would corrupt the
country. At the same time, many black actors, like Step 'n Fetchit, were restricted to
playing "fools," amusing white audiences with their "moronic" behaviors. Overall,
however, the countless others who experienced oppression were largely invisible in
films. Such invisibility rendered them unimportant, if not nonexistent. They had
few stories, experiences, or struggles worthy of telling about; when they did appear,
their devaluation was represented in the positions in which they were cast—adjuncts
to the important and worthy central characters. They appeared as servants, assis-
tants, drivers, and were vehicles of transportation, laborers, and other roles that
implicitly, but powerfully, portrayed their lowly positions. Michael Parenti observes
that this "invented reality" was largely the product of wealthy film producers and
distributors.[26] While a few films presented notable exceptions to this rule, they were
usually not widely distributed, and they rarely connected the oppression and suffering directly to the capitalist system.[27]

With the advent of radio and television, the ability of powerful capitalists to exert
influence over popular culture and the day-to-day perceptions and experiences of
the citizenry increased enormously. The capitalist-controlled mass media became a
powerful ideological force, arguably the greatest instrument of propaganda in modern society.

However, when radio first emerged, few beyond the ranks of educators seemed
aware of its enormous potential. Early radio broadcasts were largely informative and
public-service oriented until a jittery capitalist class—fending off considerable
threats, especially from organized labor, to their oppressive ways—recognized the
potential of the new medium. The elite began to fear radio as a tool of insurrection
and came to recognize its value as an instrument to manipulate and control consumer behavior. Using their considerable political power—and sidestepping democratic participation—capitalists expropriated the airwaves for their own political and
commercial interests. Communications scholar Robert W. McChesney writes,
"With the passage of the Telecommunications Act of 1934 and the creation of the
Federal Communications Commission . . . the profit-motivated basis of U.S. broadcasting was politically inviolate forever after."[28]

As with radio, capitalists quickly appropriated television broadcasting rights and
obtained the ability to reach into nearly every household that could afford electricity
and a secondhand radio or television. Commercial broadcasting transformed the
human population of the United States into a "mass"—that is, a population largely
receiving one-way communication, with little or no way of questioning or holding
a dialogue with those creating and disseminating the programming.

Just as film has been used as an ideological tool to legitimize oppression, so have
radio and television (and, increasingly, the Internet).[29] For instance, humans with
disabilities have been plagued by stereotypical portrayals in films that are made for,
or eventually make their way to, television. It is common for villains and monsters
in films to be characterized by some form of physical or mental disability, from the
"insane" killer to the evildoer with a disfigurement or hooklike prosthesis.[30] While

our society frightens itself at the expense of people with disabilities, it amuses itself as well.

> The Three Stooges, Laurel and Hardy, Step 'n Fetchit, Jerry Lewis and numerous other comedians have made careers out of portraying characters that have an apparent intellectual deficiency. The latest generations have been repeatedly exposed to such caricatures through cable television networks. . . .
>
> Some of the most popular contemporary television comedies, such as *Wings* with its Lowell character, also get laughs at the expense of the "slow-witted," while on *Roseanne* the Conners often perform caricatures of "defective hillbillies." On a[n] . . . episode of *Seinfeld*, a shot of novocaine by the dentist left Kramer with a contorted face and slurred speech; the running gag was based on his treatment by strangers who took him for a person with a developmental disability.[31]

Gays and lesbians have been portrayed as, at best, presenting problems and uncomfortable situations for heterosexuals on television programs,[32] and humans who are older are frequently "infantized" and represented in stereotypical ways when they appear in television programs and commercials.[33] Similarly, despite years of activism, women are still sexually objectified and widely represented in stereotypical ways.[34] While some programs may occasionally counter such defaming images, these efforts have yet to dilute significantly the oppressive ideology propagated through the mass media.

Likewise, media portrayals of other animals also reflect the assumed naturalness of their lowly social status. Like the other oppressed groups, other animals are frequently portrayed as dangerous and largely deserving of violent treatment.[35] Contemporary examples of the former and its potential entanglement with the tradition and escalation of interpersonal violence in the United States are described in the *UCLA Television Violence Report for 1997*, which expressed particular concern about representations of "dangerous animals" on television.

> A new section [of the report] was added last year because of a worrisome trend that started to develop in that season. . . . *The World's Most Dangerous Animals I* and *II* on CBS and *When Animals Attack* on Fox were heavily promoted and achieved respectable ratings. It was our fear that this was the beginning of a trend that could escalate in the 1996–97 television season. Unfortunately, our fears were well founded. . . .
>
> These specials contain some of the most graphic and terrifying images to be found anywhere on network television. . . . There are still many examples of this programming in the current season. This season saw the airing of programs like *The World's Most Dangerous Animals III*, *When Animals Attack II*, and *When Animals Attack III*. . . .
>
> An argument could be made that shows of this variety could potentially inspire unreasonable fear of certain animals. To varying degrees, *The World's Most Dangerous Animals Part III*, *When Animals Attack II* and *When Animals Attack III* all exploit viewers' fears in the way they present these violent attacks. One noteworthy instance of this effort concerns an attack by a housecat. When it aired on *The World's Most Dangerous Animals III*, the attacking cat was portrayed as vicious and deadly. Interestingly, the

exact same footage was shown on a different program as a comedic moment when it aired on NBC's *TV Censored Bloopers.*[36]

In 1994, the Ark Trust, an animal rights group that monitors media portrayals of animal issues, commissioned a study of the portrayals of other animals on television. The researcher, George Gerbner, dean emeritus of the Annenberg School of Communication at the University of Pennsylvania, spent two years examining samples of television programs that aired on the four major broadcast networks from 1972 to 1993. The principal findings of the study were as follows:

> Violence toward animals is rampant in Saturday morning children's programs, even more so than in prime-time programming.
>
> Compared to humans, animals are over-represented as perpetrators of violence.
>
> Wild animals are treated worse than other types, especially when in their own habitat.
>
> Compared to humans, animals are more frequently cast as villains.
>
> Animal activists are depicted as violent most of the time they are shown, and disapproval of animal rights activists is much more frequent than approval.[37]

If they are not being represented as dangerous, just as other oppressed groups are, other animals are also used to amuse with their antics. From the ever-popular gag of dressing other primates in animal clothing (mirroring the equally comical appearance of men in women's clothing), as evidenced in *The Chimp Channel,* a weekly Turner Broadcasting/Time Warner television program, to David Letterman's "Stupid Pet Tricks," the "natural inferiority" of other animals is strongly suggested.

Other animals are represented in largely disparaging terms and rarely portrayed as worthy individuals (with infrequent exceptions that may appear from time to time in documentaries or on some of the programs broadcast on Animal Planet—a cable channel that is otherwise largely "welfarist" and "pet" oriented). Indeed, in the vast majority of novels, stories, and films, the virtual invisibility of other animals—similar to that of devalued groups of humans—teaches that their lives and experiences are irrelevant and insignificant. Reflecting on the results of his study, George Gerbner maintains that the portrayals of other animals mirror the views of corporate America. He specifically cites the influence of the interests of agribusiness. "Agriculture and the meat industry have a very strong investment in the types of portrayals we get." Even when the influence is indirect, "there's a very active censorship in the [entertainment] industry to avoid material that offends advertisers."[38]

The renowned Harvard zoologist Stephen Jay Gould described the anthropocentric tendency of U.S. society by noting, "Everything we know about animals we see in our terms."[39] This insightful observation needs one important correction. Since much of what we see and learn is filtered through, if not directly propagated by, powerful capitalists, we should acknowledge that everything we know about animals we see primarily in *corporate* terms.

The control of the mass media by the capitalist class is used not only to disparage the oppressed but also to create a growing demand for products. With the development of almost total corporate control of the mass media during the twentieth century, a relatively informed and active citizenry has been largely transformed into a "mass" of consumers.[40]

Corporate control of the media and ever-increasing efforts to use that control in the manipulation of consumer behavior have resulted in a highly concentrated handful of media conglomerates. Such companies dominate "the entirety of U.S. mass media, ranging from newspapers, books, and magazines to film, radio, television, cable and recorded music" and have used that power and control to usher in a era of "hyper-commercialization."[41] Robert McChesney reports that the "first tier" of media conglomerates includes

> Time Warner, Disney, Viacom, Seagram, Rupert Murdoch's News Corporation, all connected to the big six film studios. . . . [C]onsider the holdings of Viacom to get a sense of how one of these giants looks. Viacom owns Paramount Pictures, Simon and Schuster book publishers, Spelling Entertainment, MTV cable network, VH1 cable network, Nickelodeon cable network, TV Land cable network, Showtime cable network, eighteen U.S. television stations, the UPN network, the Blockbuster video rental chain, five theme parks, retail stores, and a vast movie theater empire outside the United States.[42]

The power of these media conglomerates, not only to manipulate consumers but also to influence cultural beliefs, values, norms, and standards, is enormous. And those with the economic power to purchase vast advertising time and space in such a highly concentrated system of mass media hold a "crushing advantage" over those who hold different ideas (e.g., the need for a democratic, sustainable, oppression-free social system) but have fewer resources.[43]

It is in this context, then, that the masses of humans are incessantly exhorted to eat "meat" and to consume other products derived from the oppressive treatment of other animals (not to mention to increase their use of pharmaceuticals, purchase new automobiles, smoke cigarettes, consume alcohol, see new Hollywood films created by Disney, Viacom, AOL Time Warner, and other media conglomerates, etc.). If, as many would have us believe, eating the flesh and body products of other animals is so "natural" to humans, why are billions of dollars spent just to ensure the continuation and expansion of this genocidal,[44] destructive, and debilitating consumption pattern?

As we saw in chapter 4, to maintain and boost sales, organizations such as the Cattlemen's Association, the Pork Producers Council, and America's Dairy Farmers saturate the airways with "Beef: It's What's for Dinner," "Pork: The Other White Meat," "Ah, the Power of Cheese," and "Got Milk?" commercials. Television commercials for hamburgers, cow's milk, and various "foods" derived from the bodies of other animals are not only ubiquitous but also so well produced that a number of them were included in a list of the "50 Greatest Commercials of All Time," generated by a poll undertaken by *TV Guide*.[45] Included was Wendy's "Fluffy Bun" ad in which Clara Peller, described by *TV Guide* as a "dainty little" older woman, bellows out, "Where's the beef?" The campaign, which reduced cows to "beef" and stereotyped older women as discourteous and ill-tempered while plying consumers with saturated fat, boosted Wendy's sales by 30 percent in 1984.[46] Also included on the list was Wendy's 1985 "Russian Fashion Show," a piece that hyped the company's products while contributing to the anti-Russia Cold War mentality of the Reagan era. Also worth noting from the list was McDonald's "Showdown," a 1993 ad that featured sports icons Michael Jordan and Larry Bird in a "wild hoops competition." If such role models as Bird and Jordan support and eat McDonald's products, what could be wrong with them? It also should be noted that, while many programs and commercials on television make use of stereotypes of oppressed groups of humans to interest or amuse viewers, the entertainment value of these stereotypes has not escaped the retailing component of the "meat" industry. Another glimpse at the entangled nature of oppression is seen not only in Wendy's portrayal of older women as rude and socially embarrassing but also in a McDonald's campaign that portrayed older humans as childlike. Sociologists Arnold Arluke and Jack Levin note, "Posters in a popular chain of fast-food restaurants urge customers to 'have a senior birthday party at McDonald's.' For the 'birthday kid' who is 'young at heart,' McDonald's offers to provide the cake, hats and party favors."[47]

Those behind the mass media campaigns to promote the eating of "meat," "dairy products," and bird eggs have long been aware of the necessity of reaching and indoctrinating young children. It is no secret that corporations seek to establish consumer patterns in children, habits the advertisers hope will last a lifetime. In the age of hypercommercialization, the level of advertising directed at children in the United States is absolutely unprecedented—and, unlike in many other nations, virtually without regulation. Robert W. McChesney writes:

> By age seven, the average American child is watching fourteen hundred hours and twenty thousand TV commercials per year, and by age twelve his or her preferences are stored in massive data banks maintained by marketers of consumer goods. In the 1990s commercial television for children may well have been the most rapidly growing and lucrative sector of the U.S. industry, with 1998 ad revenues pegged at approximately $1 billion. Each of the four largest U.S. media giants has a full-time children's cable TV channel to capture the thirty-nine million viewers aged two to eleven.[48]

The explosion of hypercommercialization in the last ten years has been advanced in part by the development of *synergies*—that is, the process of taking a product brand and promoting it for all the profit possible by thoroughly hyping it through a firm's multiple corporate holdings. Disney, McChesney writes,

> is the master of synergies. . . . With some 660 Disney retail stores worldwide as well as merchandising and licensing deals with numerous manufacturers and retailers, Disney is evolving into what one industry observer characterizes as "the ultimate global consumer goods company." . . .
> As one observer noted, Hollywood films now have so many promotional tie-ins and deals that their competition "extends from theaters to fast-food chains to grocery aisles."

Disney and McDonald's have a ten-year exclusive agreement to promote each other's products in 109 nations, a relationship so detailed that the *Wall Street Journal* termed the two firms "McDisney."[49]

Today, Hollywood films not only underrepresent and perpetuate largely stereotypical views of "others" (with some occasional exceptions usually coming from the ranks of independent filmmakers), but their capitalist-friendly story telling also increasingly shows central characters using or consuming products with clearly identifiable corporate brand names, a practice that further roots the "invented reality" in profitable and oppressive practices. For instance, in the recent popular and enormously hyped children's film *Spy Kids,* the central child characters are shown selecting a McDonald's meal.

The direct promotion of "meat" and "dairy products" permeates most children's programming in the United States. For example, the following lines from a Burger King commercial, taken from daytime Nickelodeon programming for young children, not only urged consumption of Burger King hamburgers but also took the opportunity to disparage a group of other animals.

If you were a goldfish you'd swim around a bowl eating soggy fish flakes. If you don't like soggy fish flakes, tough, you don't have a choice. But you're a kid. You can go to Burger King. No mustard, no problem. You don't like choices, be a goldfish. You want it your way, you can go to Burger King.

Burger King routinely participates in joint advertising projects with Nickelodeon, such as sponsorship of the annual Nickelodeon "Kids' Choice Awards." Children are urged to frequent Burger King to acquire toys based on popular films and cartoon characters. Many mothers can been seen at lunchtime on weekdays breaking their isolation in one of the few "public" venues friendly to young children—Burger King and McDonald's "playscapes"—feeding their young children high-fat, nutrient-deficient hamburgers, fries, and sodas and securing the latest massively hyped toy based on such popular characters and films as Pokémon, the Rugrats, and SpongeBob SquarePants—"One with every Tasty Kids Club Meal you buy."

McDonald's, the largest fast-food company in the world and the one that does by far the most commercial advertising, every day draws millions of families whose children have been literally programmed to pester parents for the latest hyped Happy Meal toy, often tied to the latest Disney film. For decades now, McDonald's with its highly recognizable Ronald McDonald character has sought to secure children as lifetime consumers of its various "products." Furthermore, while the nation becomes increasingly concerned about the level and intensity of violence in children's entertainment, fast-food firms like McDonald's ultimately "go with what sells," with advertisements that banalize, if not encourage, violence. For instance, a 1999 commercial, broadcast during daytime programming on Nickelodeon, combined burger promotion with a troublesome scene of children engaged in make-believe violence. A young child, cloaked in a pretend suit of armor and waving a sword, yells to a group of similarly dressed children, "We will do what we must for a Mystic Knights Happy Meal at McDonald's!" The visual then switches to four figurines, all similarly cloaked in armor and brandishing weapons in striking positions as a narrator says, "Now, there is one Mystic Knights figure in every Happy Meal that you buy." The picture then switches back to the children, happily seated in a McDonald's establishment eating burgers. "Ah, the sweet, sweet taste of victory," says a child, and Ronald McDonald appears repeating the latest slogan, "Did somebody say McDonald's?" The 2001 summer release of the Disney film *Atlantis: The Lost Empire*—which television commercials referred to as "the best family movie of the year"—was accompanied by the hyping of *Atlantis* toys at McDonald's. One reviewer, however, cautioned that the film "offers intense battle sequences and a remarkably high body count. . . . Given the violent nature of its brisk action sequences . . . *Atlantis* really isn't suitable for very young viewers."[50]

As their young customers grow into teenagers, McDonald's promotes continued patronage by associating the corporation with teen idols, such as Britney Spears and 'N Sync, who license sales of their "Number 1 Request CDs" "only at McDonald's." Not to be left out, Dairy Queen solicits purchase of both "meat" and "dairy products" by enticing children with collectible "Scooby Doo Toys." On some days on children's television, scarcely a commercial break passes without at least one Burger King, McDonald's, or Wendy's commercial. Sometimes the same one is repeated over and over, becoming imprinted on the consciousness of young viewers. Furthermore, the American Dairy Farmers' "Got milk?" campaign also invades children's daytime Nickelodeon programming with such spots as "How to trap a monster stealing your milk." (The "monsters" are really Mom and Dad who are surreptitiously helping themselves to the child's milk.) The animated host of Nickelodeon's daytime programming, the popular "Face," encourages the consumption of milk with the following between-programs filler.

> It's me, Face, with a big glass of milk. I drink a glass of milk every day. Milk makes you grow big and strong. And it makes your teeth nice and bright too. But most of all, it's delicious. And look, I have a milk moustache.

These commercials, which impose a self-centered, "meat"-eating, violence-prone reality on impressionable minds and which help form patterns of consumption, are intermixed with ads that strongly promote gendered behavior. Despite gains made by feminists and social scientists during the 1960s and 1970s in raising awareness of the problems of sex-role stereotyping for both women and men, corporate cupidity has pushed such concerns to the margins of both parenthood and society. Today, commercials for Barbies, baby dolls, homemaker items, play jewelry, and adornments and the like, with only female models and actors and lots of pink, obviously targeted to girls, proliferate on commercial children's television. At the same time, advertisements for items often involving violence, from machine-gun water toys to fighting robots and sports toys, clearly are directed at boys.

Both programming and commercials often encourage violence in various forms.

The tired and troublesome (but cheaply recycled) "Looney Tunes" cartoons, for example, amuse children with characters that continually insult and assault one another. Going even further, 1998 Nickelodeon daytime programming included a commercial for "Aviation Camp," a camp that trains children to be "jet fighter pilots." A portion of the commercial's narrative was as follows:

> Welcome to Aviation Challenge, a totally unique camp, with simulators so real, fantasy becomes reality. Aviation Challenge, where you spend five days *toasting something besides marshmallows* [emphasis added]. Where you don't just make friends, you depend on them. It's a place where you hop out of bed in the morning, and hop into your cockpit. A camp where you'll train to be a jet fighter pilot, just like the real jet fighter pilots. And where poison ivy just might be the least of your worries.

All the while, many children's programs reflect children's fascination with, and interest in, other animals. The shows feature anthropomorphized caricatures of other animals, a representation referred to as "Disneyfication."[51] These characters are frequently presented as having the same reality as human animals—living in houses, going to school, riding bikes—and thus have value mostly because of their anthropomorphized nature. A child's eventual recognition that other animals do not talk or live as human animals may well mute further empathetic responses and lead children to eventually see other animals in the ascribed social positions that best serve capitalist arrangements. Indeed, in many instances the "humanized" other-animal characters actually eat other animals, go to zoos and circuses, and otherwise devalue other animals in their anthropocentric existence. Such is the case, for example, in the popular public television series *Arthur*. Arthur—a barely recognizable aardvark—and his friends of various species share an anthropocentric reality that includes pony rides, burger cook-outs, and a family's planned treat of a lobster dinner. Although the show attempts to promote positive, cooperative values, the producers also frequently portray the main characters insulting one another using such words as *idiot, stupid,* and other terms that devalue and defame humans with disabilities.

Another popular children's program on public television, *Barney,* occasionally takes young viewers out to "visit the farm," showing "calves gamboling in green pastures with their mothers, smelling the flowers and enjoying the fresh air and sunshine."[52] The presentation not only leaves children feeling good about the treatment of "farm animals" but also creates the perception that the very purpose of the existence of cows is to provide humans with milk and cheese.

Reflecting on the hegemonic use of mass media, Edward S. Herman and Noam Chomsky maintain that a primary function of mass media in capitalist society is to "manufacture consent": to disseminate a reality to the masses that has largely been created by the elite. They write:

> The mass media serve as a system for communicating messages and symbols to the general populace. It is their function to amuse, entertain, and inform, and to inculcate individuals with the values, beliefs, and codes of behavior that will integrate them into

the institutional structures of the larger society. In a world of concentrated wealth and major conflicts of class interest, to fulfill this role requires systematic propaganda.[53]

HIDDEN CURRICULUM OF SCHOOLS AND MUSEUMS

Scholars have long recognized the general role of public education in Western society to generate acceptance of the status quo and to perpetuate stratification. For instance, Samuel Bowles and Herbert Gintis observe in their seminal book, *Schooling in Capitalist America,* that the capitalist elite promoted public education to supply them with an indoctrinated, disciplined, and docile workforce.[54] In such a context, the "education" received by the young in many ways mirrors the content of the mass media. For instance, the history of women, humans of color, humans with disabilities, and other devalued groups has been told primarily from the vantage point of the privileged. Even with the current day's increased emphasis on multiculturalism, schools rarely address, or address seriously, the role of capitalism in creating and perpetuating prejudice and social ills.

As children enter the world of organized education, they learn to see other animals through the official and "scientific" lens—that is, as our inferiors and as tools for learning. From preschool through graduate and professional training, the educational system largely teaches that other animals are unimportant and insignificant except for serviceable purposes.

For many children, other animals are brought into the classroom in cages as "mascots," "pets," and "science projects." Chick-hatching projects, for example, are still widely used in preschool and elementary school classrooms. Defenders of such projects contend the activity fosters an appreciation of "the beauty and wonder of life" and "respect for all living things" and promotes consideration of "how wonderful life and living creatures are." These goals, however, are utterly inconsistent with the realities of hatching projects. Children are taught that it is acceptable to deprive baby animals of their mothers and for animals to be kept in unnatural, stark environments. Moreover, the children are deceived about the ultimate fate of the chicks—for most, a "disposal" that would horrify the children and adults who briefly come to know them. Male chicks are killed shortly after their sex is determined because they have little economic value. The most common ways of killing male chicks are crushing, suffocation, or decapitation. Female chicks, or "pullets," are channeled into one of two forms of "livestock" production. Some will be confined in tiny, cramped battery cages—now banned in many European countries—as "layers." When their ability to produce eggs is reduced by the stress of such awful confinement, they will be killed. Other female chicks will be reared in a dark, crowded "broiler house" for six weeks before they are cruelly rounded up and sent to slaughter. Thus, postproject "care" of the chicks is far from beautiful, wonderful, and respectful. Bringing animals into the world just for the amusement of children and then subjecting them to this treatment is ethically bankrupt, as is the practice of deceiving the children about their fate.

The "naturalness" of the exploitation of other animals is further instilled in children through other projects, ranging from making collections of small living creatures to participation in dissections. One particularly egregious such "project" occurred in May 2001 when "T-Bone," a cow raised by students at a Christian school in Brea, California, was killed in front of an assembly that included students as young as five. The project was intended as a lesson in physiology as well as "where meat comes from." T-Bone was immobilized with a stun gun and then cut apart, skinned, and eviscerated. Although a small group of students tried to stop T-Bone's murder, they were turned back by local police. After the grisly event, a science teacher at the school lauded the activity as "an excellent lesson."[55] Such "projects"—which teach powerful lessons, including the necessity of abandoning friends and of accepting oppression as one prepares to enter the "adult" world of contemporary capitalism—also are undertaken every year by tens of thousands of children who are prompted by parents and 4-H clubs to raise other animals for competition in county and state fairs. Such lessons are often deeply painful, as evidenced by a newspaper account of a nine-year-old boy's trauma at sending his friend off to the slaughterhouse.

> After the applause and handshakes . . . Thomas urged his pig out of the ring and toward a waiting livestock trailer, then turned on his heel and walked out of the show barn for a few minutes.
>
> "He spent the whole morning with his pig. He couldn't eat this morning," Thomas's mother . . . said. "He asked me if it was okay if he cried."[56]

Such newspaper accounts, however, are part and parcel of the legitimizing process. They depict the guilt and heartbreak young people experience when they must abandon beloved friends and see them sent to the slaughterhouse as a necessary rite of passage to adulthood, as a natural part of learning the ways of the world. Media accounts also banalize these practices with attempts at humor. The story of Thomas and his friend (whom the reporter was careful not to personalize with a name), for example, ended by noting that, after his friend was sent to his death, Thomas was treated to pork chops.

Meanwhile, back at school, slaughtered "others" are served up in school lunchrooms as children are taught not only where "meat" comes from but also that eating other animals is both natural and necessary. Biological conceptions of a natural "food web" are largely distorted to promulgate the myth of the *food chain*, a claim of the existence of a fixed and hierarchical feeding protocol in which the animals allegedly "most evolved" naturally eat their "inferiors." This widely held idea is compounded by the notion that humans must eat other animals if they are to be healthy, an idea widely promoted by the "meat," "dairy," and "poultry" industries and government-endorsed "food group" lessons, as we saw in chapter 4.

The capitalist imperative to maintain and expand markets has led to more intense corporate efforts to establish and increase the "natural" tendency for children to eat other animals. Such overt corporate indoctrination is now conducted directly inside the classroom. For example, the "news" on Channel One, now an institution in many classrooms throughout the country, is viewed by many as a mere diversion from the myriad commercials it shows. According to one observer, "many spots for candy, chewing gum, tacos, cereal, and burgers are the most successful ads on Channel One."[57] Even some textbooks now incorporate positive references to consumer products, including Burger King and McDonald's, amounting to what some critics call "a collection of advertisements."[58] All the while, even relatively favored other animals, such as cats and dogs, are not welcome and are usually banned from school grounds—further lessons on the unworthiness of other animals.

The biological-scientific view of other animals is most profound in colleges and universities. This level of education is frequently where "childish" and "sentimental" attitudes about other animals are finally laid to rest as young adults are prepared for successful integration into the capitalist workplace. Reflecting on her experiences in secondary education, biologist and feminist scholar Lynda Birke writes:

> I found it peculiar that the love of nature that, in part, drove me to want to study biology seemed to be at odds with the scientific methods in which I was trained. Loving nature meant a respect for its complexity, yet, to do science means to accept its reductionism. Books from my undergraduate days testify to the ways in which the living animal becomes coded as an assemblage of parts, as machine-like; "Living Control Systems," "Nerve, Muscle and Synapse," "The Ovary," among others. Doing science often meant awe at the wonderful ways that such "systems" worked; nature was, indeed, very clever. But it also seemed to mean denying the awe at the marvelous creatures that exist in the world, in all their complexity and individuality.[59]

As we saw with the Columbus Center of Science and Industry, mentioned in chapter 2, children's museums are yet another powerful socialization device about the role of devalued others in society. The Boonshoft Museum of Discovery in Dayton, Ohio, introduces children to the range of species of animals "that are native to the state" by way of a miniature zoo. Animals ranging from a coyote and a bobcat to an opossum to a squirrel are imprisoned in tiny spaces and viewed through thick glass while photographic images of the Ohio landscape line the backs of their stark cubicles. Decapitated and mounted "trophy" heads of numerous species of animals are displayed in another area of the museum, juxtaposed with exhibits on indigenous humans and "other cultures"—now all relegated to the status of "natural history." Similarly, the Indianapolis Children's Museum's exhibit on U.S. history teaches how other animals have contributed to the "development of Western civilization," naturally serving as food, clothing, and other resources. From hanging a killed and stuffed deer by her front legs in a model human settlement to displaying the bodies, or body parts, of numerous other animals in a display of a "butcher" shop, the message sent about the worth and place of other animals is profound. Of particular significance is an exhibit that re-creates an entire "French Fur Trading Post" filled with actual "pelts" of other animals. (In a summer 2001 travel advertisement titled "Family Adventure Package," readers were invited to stay at Indianapolis-area Holiday Inns while they took their children to the Indianapolis Zoo and the Children's Museum, both venues more geared to tourism and indoctrination than to the development of enlightened views about self and others.)

While museums with such awful anthropocentric displays dot the nation, perhaps nowhere is such ideological manipulation more powerful than in Chicago's famous Field Museum of Natural History. Thousands of other animals, most of which were killed, stuffed, and mounted for the museum, are displayed. At this major tourist attraction and field trip destination, particularly for young students, one can spend an entire day wandering the endless halls and rooms displaying thousands and thousands of other animals—all dead. In many exhibits other animals are surrounded by their babies, frequently posed in positions depicting youthful frolic and playfulness—as they well may have been before they were stalked, killed, and relegated to the position of "specimens." "Oh, look at the ba-a-a-bies" is a common exclamation made as continuous streams of humans file past the appalling exhibits—as though the other animals were still alive but simply motionless. During one observation in the Field Museum, I heard a boy proclaim to his parents, "They're easier to look at 'cause they can't move." In only one instance during my observation in the museum did I hear any empathetic comments generated by the enormous display of dead "others." That remark was made by an obviously distressed teenage girl who exclaimed, "A baby giraffe. They killed a baby giraffe!" A woman with her said, "Maybe they didn't. Maybe it was already dead when they found it." An occasional disclaimer from the museum management was seen noting that, while many of the "specimens" were secured for the museum, more recent acquisitions of some other animals were secured after they had perished in captivity.

The poses in which many of the other animals are placed and the descriptions that accompany them accentuate just one aspect of their character, one amplified by biologists and traditional ethologists—aggression. This scientific cultivation of public consciousness of the alleged viciousness of the other animals is powerful in its effect, evidenced by comments of museum visitors. One man was overheard saying to his children, "How would you like to run into that in a dark alley?" while another asked his son, "How would you like to shoot that?" Special signage directed visitors to exhibits featuring "man eaters." This experience, which objectifies and demonizes other animals and promotes anthropocentrism, is topped off by a visit to the huge fast-food restaurant located in the heart of the museum—McDonald's. The public, especially children, are given a powerful lesson about other animals and humans' "natural" relationship to them—the power of the lesson punctuated by the palatial, awe-inspiring setting of the museum, which further legitimates this lesson in "natural science."

The lessons of the Chicago Field Museum of Natural History do not stop with the profound devaluation of other animals. The museum, which stands across from a huge statue of Christopher Columbus, also features a rich assortment of artifacts once used by indigenous humans of the Western Hemisphere whose societies were decimated by Columbus and those who followed his trail. Their early twenty-first-century descendants are suppressed and rendered largely invisible, as if Native Americans now exist only in artifacts and photographs.

If visitors tire of looking at mounted corpses and cultural remnants of human societies decimated by European-conveyed disease and genocide, they can walk next door to the Shedd Aquarium, where countless living but also captive others are displayed to attract tourist dollars. Finally, if one were to have looked out from the elevated position of the museum between 15 June and 31 October 1999, one would have seen many cows—life-size, fiberglass cows. Intended as an art display with a comic flair, the cows' bodies essentially were canvases decorated by local artists in another tourist draw for the city. The sight of children hugging the fake cows and adults posing next to them for photos was ironic in a city where hundreds of millions of real cows were cruelly transported and suffered ghastly deaths through the repeated blows of axmen. Meanwhile, looming ominously over the Field Museum, the Shedd Aquarium, and most of Chicago's highly stratified community, with its mix of enormous wealth and devastating deprivation, rose the skyscrapers of Chicago's financial district. Like the inhabitants of the sacred temples and monuments of centuries past, the city's most powerful and affluent inhabitants are safe and secure. Such landscapes, and the economic, political, and social realities that cultivate them, are largely characteristic of most cities across the United States and throughout the Western world.

LIABILITIES OF LANDSCAPES AND LANGUAGE

Writing of the invisibility of those who are poor in the United States, Michael Harrington states, "[T]he very development of the American city has removed poverty from the living, emotional experience of millions upon millions of middle-class Americans. Living out in the suburbs, it is easy to assume that ours is, indeed, an affluent society."[60]

In most large cities, the neighborhoods of those who are poor, most of whom work hard but for low wages and without benefits or pensions, are largely by-passed by interstate highways that veil their existence. Humans with privilege are able to speed by on their way to more desirable locations—shopping malls and neighborhoods in the "good" parts of town.

For the generations growing up in the post–World War II era, with its emphasis on highway construction and suburban life, well-manicured and sanitized parks have largely constituted their outdoor experiences. Asphalt spread with plaguelike speed across the United States, a disease carried by growing numbers of automobiles. Endless miles of shopping malls and strips, huge retail outlets, multiplex cinemas, fast-food restaurants, and more expensive restaurants for those who can afford the more desirable "cuts" of meat stretch as far as the eye can see. The humans, especially the young, who swarm these venues see nothing unusual or wrong with the landscape. The fact that the pavement covers what once was forest, pasture, and homes to both countless other animals (and the remains of many who were killed in the razing of their homes) and humans who were displaced by this "progress" never enters their consciousness. The asphalt-covered landscape, with its "virtual nature"—strategically placed trees, bushes, and flowers surrounded by neat piles of mulch—is normal and natural. Remaining woods and pastures are seen as merely "undeveloped" lands waiting to be formed into homes and new malls and shopping areas when the existing ones grow dated—or become too accessible to those from the "bad" parts of town. And, as one familiar with the entanglement of oppression can predict, once this occurs, the remaining "wildlife" will be transformed into "pests" to be displaced or exterminated. It is not surprising, then, that when humans see other animals only in "pet" stores and zoos or in cages in museums and classrooms, "common sense" dictates that is where they belong.

Language is yet another powerful force that both reflects and conditions human perceptions and attitudes toward devalued humans and other animals. The devaluation of other animals is reflected and perpetuated by their common use as derogatory device. Writing in 1974, the late Cleveland Amory observed:

> There is no better place to begin an examination of our treatment of our fellow creatures than with our language.
>
> Take the word "animal." One of the dictionary definitions for "animal" is "a bestial person; a brute." . . .
>
> Television is a particular offender. "He's an animal," says a character on one program. "He deserves to be killed." Meanwhile, on another program, a woman shouts to another, in utter contempt, "You're an animal!" Later in the same episode, when she learns she has misjudged that particular person, she apologies, and then points to someone else. "He's an animal," she says. And if this weren't enough, another program—an interview show—is promoted as follows: "A Tough Judge Says 'Don't Coddle Criminals. They're Punks, Vermin and Animals.' " . . .
>
> As for man, of course, he doesn't even consider himself an animal—which, considering the way he considers them, is probably, all things considered, the only considerate thing about him.[61]

One way in which humans anthropocentrically distance themselves from others is in the "deanimalized" description of our bodies and our social activities. For example, humans have "hair" while others have "fur," humans have "skin" while others have "hide," and deceased humans are "corpses" while deceased others are "carcasses." Associated humans are called "groups," while associations of some other animals are "herds." Humans "have sex," while other animals "mate," "rut," or "reproduce."

Humans are commonly called "dog," "pig," "cow," "jackass," "weasel," "ape," "turkey," and other names with the intent to insult and disgrace. This process defames other animals, who are regarded as bad, while encouraging humans to see themselves as distinct and superior to the lowly, offensive other. Similarly, another way to put someone down is to call them "stupid," "dumb," "numbskull," "pea-brain," "bonehead," "idiot," "moron," "imbecile," and numerous other words that denigrate them by suggesting they have a developmental disability—a defamation of humans with disabilities that plays a profound role in their social marginalization and victimization. Similarly, males frequently seek to slight and humiliate one another by calling other males "girls," "ladies," "panty-waists," "sissies," "bitches," and other more obscene phrases that equate them with the apparently inferior female. The parallels in these linguistic patterns illuminate not only the common motivations for the subjugation of others but also the hierarchical and ideological entanglements of these various forms of oppression. Some terms of denigration, such as "dumb ass" and "stupid bitch," are intended to injure another by comparison to two or more devaluated groups.

While comparison to the devalued and "vile" other serves to naturalize the "others'" oppressed status, other words are used to mask the actions and processes that are based in abusive and even torturous treatment of the oppressed. For example, the practice of stalking and killing other animals is sanitized by referring to other sentient beings as "game"; terms such as *culling, harvesting,* and *taking* are used instead of the words *killing* or *murdering.* Within the increasingly mechanized processes of late twentieth-century factory farms, pigs, cows, sheep, chickens, and other groups of other animals are referred to in the industry as "food-processing units" and "protein harvesters." After they are slaughtered, dismembered, and processed for consumption, they are symbolically sterilized and presented not as cows and pigs but as "meat," "hamburgers," "bacon," "sausage," and "poultry" in a form of verbal and ideological sleight of hand. Ecofeminist theorist Carol J. Adams observes, "Through butchering, animals become absent referents. . . . Animals are made absent through language that renames dead bodies before consumers participate in eating them. Our culture further mystifies the term 'meat' with gastronomic language, so we do not conjure dead, butchered animals, but cuisine."[62]

From the popularity of the cable Food Network to daily tips by Martha Stewart, "tasty" and "creative" ways of preparing and serving "meat" are presented daily on television cooking programs as well as in countless magazines and newspapers; other animals are presented as being synonymous with food. The festive and celebratory tone of these programs and pieces obscures the pain and suffering of billions of other animals, the exploitation of agribusiness workers and adjoining communities, the horrific oppression of humans striving for justice and land reform policies in Central America, environmental spoilage, and so forth. In a society in which the current overabundance of "food" carries disastrous costs, those with fewer resources have access to affordable hamburgers, fried chickens, french fries dripping with saturated fat, and soda packed with sugar, while the more affluent are urged to indulge themselves conspicuously. For example, in 1999, the weekly "Lifestyle and Food" section of the *Dayton Daily News* featured a piece titled, "Veal Cuts on the Bone Have a Fuller Flavor." The piece maintained that "the elegant, thin veal scallops of years past are out of favor, replaced by giant veal chops served on the bone. The thick chop, served with its long frenched bone (the upper third stripped of meat) is the darling of diners and chefs alike."[63] The piece includes a recipe for "Veal Chops with Olives and Capers." The story makes no mention of the horrendous treatment of calves who are separated from their mothers, forced to live in crates so tiny that they cannot turn around, and deprived of iron and fiber in their food; they experience unimaginable physical and mental distress, all so their flesh is an "elegant" pale color when served to the privileged.[64] Henry the VIII would have loved it.

On a different day the same newspaper featured a piece titled "Tiny Cornish Game Hens Rock Palates." A recipe for "Game Hens Braised in Apple Brandy" was promoted as "a charmingly upscale main course."[65] A later piece exhorted readers to dine on rabbit and included recipes for "Deviled Rabbit," "Smothered Rabbit," and "Rabbit in Shiitake Mushroom Sauce," along with a guide to "rabbit cuts."[66] Even those who do not routinely read the food sections cannot miss the advertisements stuffed into the newspaper in which giant supermarket chains feature pictures of various types of "meat" at special prices.

As Cleveland Amory notes, humans do not consider themselves to be "animals." This is a notable consequence of a hegemonically constructed reality that promotes anthropocentrism. This transcendence of the obvious human connectedness with other animals is furthered by capitalism with the unending flow of products—such as cosmetics, deodorants, creams, and colognes—that disguise the body of the human animal and reduce any ponderings of human connectedness with the rest of the Earth's inhabitants. Our physical and cultural environment exerts profound control over our view of ourselves and the world, including the other inhabitants of the planet.

IT'S THE *LAW*

As we saw in the previous chapter, those who control the state have considerable power at their disposal. Not only do they possess great political and economic power by virtue of their control of the process of lawmaking and use of military forces, but they also have considerable ideological control. This is because, in part, once a bill is enacted, "the law is the law"—that is, the law becomes naturalized. This is particularly true in contemporary capitalist society where theological legitimation of reality has been substantially replaced by "science" and "rationality." Summarizing relevant research on the metaphysical aspect of law, sociologist Robert Kidder writes:

> [L]aw has become a modern substitute for gods or spirits, whose existence has fallen into doubt and whose authority has disappeared from political life. With church and state separated, and science and rationality taking over the dominant ideology, the name of God carries little weight in a world of secular politics. To fill the void left by the loss of religious mystery, we have elevated LAW to a level of mystical significance.[67]

For many, the law is perceived as an omnipotent force that must be followed strictly—with little understanding of how the affluent create and use the law to their advantage. As we saw in the last chapter, those with economic interests in oppression exercise substantial control over the federal government, and the same process occurs on the level of state governments—as the residents of Parma Township, Michigan, and countless other communities invaded by intensified "farm" animal production have learned the hard way. Because those who control the state have such an enormous ideological advantage, a further look at the ideological power vested in the state is in order.

A good example of this power is seen in the way vested interests pursued the reinstitution of state lotteries and made them acceptable to the public. For most of the twentieth century, lotteries were widely recognized as an unfair practice that debauched the public, a regressive form of taxation that swindles those with low and fixed incomes and, disproportionately, humans of color. Many states and the federal government banned lotteries. However, state governments in the late twentieth century faced financial deficits due in part to the loss of tax revenues after layoffs and other effects of corporate downsizing and deindustrialization and the costs of offering tax abatements and other corporate welfare benefits to both attract and keep business. States were also squeezed by reductions in funds from the federal government, which had cut taxes to protect corporate interests in the emerging "new economic order." Desperate state government officials used their considerable ideological power to promote and relegitimize state-sponsored gambling to fund basic services. Prodded by lobbyists from gambling and lottery industries, and "flanking themselves with local beauty queens and bands playing the Star Spangled Banner,"[68] state officials altered public beliefs and values about gambling.

As we saw in the last chapter, such reversals in law and social policy are one of the problems with struggling for rights and reforms within the margins of the capitalist system. Lamenting the efforts to reinstate lotteries in the twentieth century, one writer observes, "Discredited institutions of one century, thought to have been permanently abolished after a long struggle, are revived in later centuries and the battle has to be fought all over again."[69]

Just as endless stretches of asphalt and small areas of manicured green space now constitute much of the physical landscape, state lotteries are now a widely accepted part of the cultural landscape.[70] For many younger humans, the reemergence of state lotteries and associated gambling opportunities predate their birth, and the "games" are viewed as a normal part of reality. Importantly, the lotteries' existence is further "naturalized" because it is "legal."

Similarly, when humans encounter another animal labeled as "wildlife" or a lost "pet" near their homes, they frequently call county "animal control" authorities who almost always "destroy" "pesky wildlife" and routinely kill unclaimed "pets." Indeed, in most states it is illegal to rescue or harbor "wildlife" in need of assistance or to keep "farm animals." Such legal rules unquestionably communicate other animals' lack of importance and help keep human interaction with these others to a minimum—keeping human advocacy on their behalf under control.

State government exercise of its ideological power can also be seen by a further look at some of the policies of state departments of "wildlife."[71] State government officials not only promulgate laws and regulations that continue the oppression of other animals but also actively seek to inculcate children with the ideas underlying these laws. Wildlife officers, in official state uniforms, make regular visits to schools and libraries to teach children about "wildlife" and "nature" in presentations that are laden with anthropocentric and speciesist ideas. Recently, such agencies have adopted an aggressive public policy created to turn children into gun-toting killers of other animals. Hunting classes and special youth hunts are now practiced in forty states striving to turn children into hunters "while they are at an impressionable age," according to the deceptively named New York Department of Environmental Conservation.[72] This effort by state governments to teach children to objectify other animals and kill them for sport is aided by campaigns such as the Youth Hunter Education Challenge (YHEC), which, according to *Petersen's Hunting Magazine,* "is just one of the many important programs that the NRA [National Rifle Association] Foundation funds to insure the future of hunting and wildlife conservation." *Petersen's Hunting Magazine,* which maintains that the "heart and future of sport hunting is kids," further reports:

> In addition to funding YHEC, the Foundation invests in many of today's leading youth shooting sports programs that are developed and conducted by the NRA: Youth Sports-fest, Shooting Sports Camps, Air Gun Program for Schools and the Marksmanship Qualification Program. Additionally, support goes beyond these important NRA programs. Using fund-raising events, thousands of additional grants have been awarded to leading organizations that educate America's youths about firearms and involve them in hunting and shooting sports. These organizations include Boy and Girl Scouts, 4-H, U.S. Jaycees, Salvation Army and JROTC.[73]

State divisions of wildlife, which count the NRA and prohunting organizations as their "partners," are out of step with the vast majority of the public, who do not support sport hunting. As we saw in chapter 3, they are also involved in a campaign of public deception about the necessity of hunting.

State government promotion of youth hunts and numerous other policies that objectify and devalue other animals, as noted in chapter 3, are prompted—and largely financed—by a multimillion-dollar industry. Not only does hunting contribute to state and local coffers through license fees, hunting-related businesses, seasonal tourism revenues, and related economic activity, but also hundreds of millions of dollars are spent on hunting-related consumer items. Ads for such products as "game callers," which play recordings of the vocalizations of other animals ($250); night-vision binoculars ($480); satellite-connected global-positioning systems ($130); spotting scopes ($240); endless varieties of rifles, shotguns, and handguns; and countless other accessories saturate advertising inserts into local newspapers as well as the pages of hunters' magazines and fill hundreds of pages of "outdoorsmen" catalogs.[74] Any store that sells magazines usually has from a few to more than a dozen "hunter" magazines, which also litter waiting rooms in car repair shops, barber shops, doctors' offices, and hospitals and can be found in public libraries around the country. Stories in these publications frequently quote officials from state divisions of wildlife or cite their reports. It is further troubling to notice that bookstores frequently display magazines as *Fur-Fish-Game, Outdoor Life, Trophy Hunter, Wing and Shot, Primitive Archer,* and *Field and Stream* next to, and even mixed with, publications like *Soldier of Fortune, Combat Handguns, American Survival, Shooting Times, Guns and Ammo, Autopistols,* and *Gun World*—a juxtaposition that illuminates the closely knit economic and ideological association between violence against humans and against other animals. Yet, hardly a single magazine presenting an "animal rights" position can be found. They are few in number and generally are available only by subscription or through membership in an animal rights organization; thus, they are largely invisible to the public.

Driven in large part by economic considerations, state divisions of wildlife and the vast "sportsmen's" and gun industry are a substantial part of the cultural obsession with guns and killing, and they are actively recruiting the young into this "way of life." It therefore does not strike many members of the public as bizarre that state governments exhort tourists in summer to visit their parks to observe "the wonder of woodland animals" and then in the autumn entice hunters to come to the state parks to stalk and kill these same wondrous individuals.

This brief examination of how socially created (although profoundly hegemonic) social beliefs and values are dispersed, particularly those that legitimize oppression of humans and other animals, will end with but a glance at two additional agents of socialization and social control—organized religion and the family.

Historically, as we have seen, organized religion largely has justified and legitimized oppressive arrangements, and to a substantial degree it continues to do so today. However, as in almost all recognizable social patterns, there are exceptions. Religion also has been used as a tool to challenge oppression, as in the work of Desmond Tutu in South Africa and of Martin Luther King, Jr., and the Southern Christian Leadership Conference in the U.S. South and in the prevalence of liberation theology in Central America. And notable advocates for other animals have come from the ranks of the clergy or have had their struggle against oppression both motivated and informed by deep religious conviction. Generally speaking, however, organized religion remains a largely conservative force in Western society, substantially supportive of the status quo and conspicuously silent on the deep and pervasive social ills caused by capitalism, past and present. Organized religion largely accepts and legitimizes institutionalized forms of oppression of other animals, usually grounding that support in dominionist arguments. Members of the clergy may seldom use the pulpit to devalue or denigrate other animals. However, the social and fund-raising activities of the church and its congregation, such as fish fries, chicken barbecues, and pig roasts, are powerful, day-to-day ideological statements.

Such daily activities permeate the profound lessons that most parents impart to their children. Almost all parents want their children to be successful in life, and they strive to teach their children appropriate beliefs, values, and practices. An important measurement of a child's success is whether she or he "fits in." And the power parents exert over the views about the world internalized by their children, while certainly not without rival in the mass media age, is dramatic. Writing in 1966, the scholar Everett Wilson observed:

[When] the child enters the human group, he is quite at the mercy of parents and siblings. They determine what he shall eat and wear, when he shall sleep and wake, what he shall think and feel, how he shall express his thoughts and feelings, . . . what his political and religious commitments shall be, what sort of vocation he shall aspire to. Not that parents are ogres. They give what they have to give: their own limited knowledge, their prejudices and passions.[75]

Few parents, who themselves were raised within the capitalist system and who have been indoctrinated with the beliefs that legitimize oppressive practices, particularly at the institutional level, are likely to challenge such oppressive arrangements. While most children are taught to share and "be fair," everyday family life tends to accept, if not replicate, the "commonsense" social hierarchies.

While families, broadly defined, can be havens of loving and nurturing relationships, they are also frequently locales of cruelty and violence. Violence against women, children, those with disabilities, and those who are older within families is so common and widespread in the United States that it can be characterized as a social epidemic. It is in this regard that another powerful entanglement of the oppression of humans and other animals should be noted. A growing body of evidence has confirmed the relationship among domestic violence, child abuse, and abuse of other animals.[76] It is so common for households investigated for alleged family violence to reveal evidence of violent treatment of other animals who live in the household that social service agencies and those who work for the protection of other animals increasingly are sharing information and reports.

ECONOMIC OPPORTUNITIES AND EMPATHY

While the culture of the United States does relatively little to encourage understanding of and empathy for devalued humans and other animals, there is a closely related element of life in capitalist society that also inhibits a positive relationship with "others"—privation. The United States has wider disparities in the distribution of wealth than any other industrial nation.[77] Exploitation and extreme disparities in the distribution of resources result in widespread deprivation. Deprivation creates stress, and, when under stress, most every species of animal will exhibit aberrant, if not pathological, behavior. Material deprivation and the demeaning treatment of those with few resources generally blunt their tendency toward human concern and empathy for "others" as day-to-day activity for the deprived is largely focused on survival. No doubt the oppression and violence done to countless humans and other animals throughout recorded history have been accepted in part because the human potential for empathy has been suppressed by extensive experiences of oppression and violence.

The human potential to be sensitive or respond to the suffering of others is explained in part by Abraham Maslow's theory of the hierarchy of needs.[78] Essentially, Maslow maintained that humans have various types of needs, ranging from basic physiological ones to emotional needs for love and affection. He held that, once one's conscious concerns about food, shelter, safety, and security are calmed, one is much more inclined to respond to overtures of love and affection and to return these emotions. That is, if one has adequate food, shelter, and security, one is more likely to share love, affection, and goodwill for others. In Maslow's words:

> To some extent, the higher the need the less selfish it must be. Hunger is egocentric; the only way to satisfy it is to satisfy oneself. But the search for love and respect necessarily involves other people. Moreover, it involves satisfaction for these other people. People who have enough satisfaction to look for love and respect (rather than just food and safety) tend to develop such qualities as loyalty, friendliness, and civic consciousness, and to become better parents, husbands, teachers, public servants, etc. . . .
>
> Better environmental conditions (familial, economic, political, educational, etc.) are all more necessary to allow people to love each other than merely to keep them from killing each other.[79]

Material deprivation, insecurity, and fear can profoundly reduce the capacity to be empathetic toward "others," particularly if they are disparaged in the popular culture and relegated to a devalued status. While there certainly are exceptions to this tendency, generally such has been the case over the course of the past ten thousand years for countless humans who were exploited and relegated to the position of peasant, serf, or slave, as it is for many today who suffer the effects of economic stratification and the aggressive advancement of global capitalism. The oppression of devalued humans and other animals, then, continues into the new millennium in part because empathy and compassionate thought are muted by an economic system that continues to rely on exploitive arrangements—arrangements sanctified and naturalized by a hegemonically controlled popular culture and state—and by the poverty, economic insecurity, and privation that characterize life for many in the United States and around the world.

Importantly, however, the powerful ideological indoctrination that naturalizes oppression was countered somewhat in the twentieth century by an increased ability of many workers in industrialized nations to achieve a somewhat stable material existence. Wealth generated by capitalist oppression facilitated the growth of a middle class in the nineteenth century, and socialist and worker struggles in the twentieth century contributed to social reforms such as the minimum wage and other labor protections and the creation of the welfare state (reforms, as we have seen, that are subject to reductions and elimination). Still, it was not simply the forging of reforms and modest entitlement programs, especially Social Security, that created a basic level of subsistence for many workers and retirees. The increased ability of workers in the United States to obtain adequate food, shelter, and safety was also due to a self-interested scheme promoted by none other than Henry Ford, who not only perfected assembly-line production but successfully advocated a practice known today as Fordism. Michael Harrington explains:

> Ford understood that his technical breakthroughs required a transformation of the society, not just the factory or even just the economy.

"In underpaying men," Ford said, "we are preparing a generation of underfed children who will be physically and morally undernourished; we will have a generation of workers weak in body and spirit who, for this reason, will be inefficient when they come into industry. It is industry which pays the bill." But Ford did more than simply talk about the necessity of decent wages. He paid five dollars a day in his own plants and was attacked by some of his fellow capitalists as a "socialist" for doing so.[80]

But Ford's real interest and his ability to persuade other capitalists to increase wages were based on more than a concern for efficient workers: he needed to sell cars. Again Harrington notes:

> Mass production, Ford understood, could not exist unless there was mass consumption. The enormous increase in output made possible by the new technology that he had perfected—the assembly line—simply could not be absorbed by an economy of low-paid workers. . . . Ford tried to convince his fellow industrialists that, in their own interest, they should increase the pay—and the buying power—of their "hands" just as he had done. He succeeded in winning over converts, usually when there was a crisis—the Rockefellers joined the movement when their hired guns outraged the nation by killing strikers' wives and children in Colorado—and mainly in the ranks of big business.[81]

Motivation notwithstanding, the grudging increases in workers' wages and resulting improvement in their material circumstances under capitalism increased the possibility for many humans to experience empathy and enhance their capacity to help others. Ironically, the *potential* for empathy, especially for other animals, was improved by another, less salutary capitalist development as large agribusiness came to dominate agricultural production in the twentieth century. Forced to give up family farms, millions saw their day-to-day economic dependence on the direct exploitation of other animals diminish as they moved to urban areas and took up blue- and white-collar jobs, some of which provided for a reasonable level of economic comfort. Possibilities for empathy for oppressed others grew, so long as the oppression was not directly related to one's own economic aspirations or other self-interested pursuits. Consequently, the capacity for many humans to be moved by the suffering of others has increased, as evidenced by demonstrations of concern and charity when the public is presented with individual situations of suffering or distress. This is particularly true when the individual in distress is personalized and strong empathetic responses are encouraged, as in the cases of Jessica McClure, Keiko the whale, and Phoenix the calf. This supposition that financial and social security facilitate empathetic response and action of course does not suggest a fixed or deterministic relationship but rather a general pattern, particularly in Western society.

Examples from Western history lend support to this proposition. For example, the abolitionist movement in the United States and Western Europe found public support largely in a growing middle class, as the spoils of commercial and industrial capitalism in the nineteenth century began to "trickle down." The ability of a growing middle class to meet its physical needs facilitated empathetic responses and prompted civic action. While some members of devalued and dispossessed groups surely joined the antislavery movement, on the whole their privations and insecurity likely prevented both an empathetic response and an ability to spend time and energy for another's liberation. Reflecting on one such group, the Irish, who faced intense exploitation and discrimination in the nineteenth-century United States, sociologists Joe R. Feagin and Clarece Booher Feagin note:

> As early as the 1840s, Irish competition with black Americans in northern cities engendered substantial distrust and hostility between the two groups. Between the 1840s and 1860s Irish workers attacked black workers in several cities in the North. During the Civil War Irish hostility toward black Americans increased, for the two groups were competitors in the struggle for the low-paying jobs at the bottom of the employment pyramid.[82]

Similarly, contemplating the sentiments of northern laborers in general, economic historians Susan Previant Lee and Peter Passell write:

> Free labor in the North had a stake in the continuation of slavery. . . . Slavery was an impenetrable barrier for blacks who might otherwise have migrated north to the cities and competed for jobs with whites. Thus, northern white workers could—and some did—see emancipation as a threat to their livelihoods. In the relatively competitive, rapidly growing economy of the antebellum North, it is unlikely that emancipation would have created chronic white unemployment, but it is likely that it would have meant lower competitive wages and living standards for white workers.[83]

In addition, as the theory of oppression would suggest, many Southern whites who had vested interests in the continuance of slavery were not abolitionists and were not predisposed to respond empathetically to enslaved others.

Similarly, historical changes in attitudes toward other animals have also been affected by changing economic circumstances and the improved conditions experienced by beneficiaries of capitalist expansion. James Serpell and Elizabeth Paul write:

> Despite criticism, pet-keeping continued to be popular among the wealthy and powerful, but it did not acquire more widespread respectability until the late seventeenth century. This coincided with the gradual rejection of the narrow, anthropocentric ideas of the previous centuries, and a growing "enlightenment" enthusiasm for science and natural history, on the one hand, and concern for the welfare of animals on the other. This change in cultural attitudes can be attributed, at least in part, to increasing affluence resulting from the growth in foreign and colonial trade, as well as to the steady migration of Europeans out of rural areas and into towns and cities. Both helped to distance growing sectors of the population from any personal involvement in the slaughter, subjugation or maltreatment of animals, and removed the need for belief systems designed to justify or reinforce such practices. Although socioeconomic forces probably initiated this change in attitudes to animals, circumstantial evidence suggests that pet-keeping may have helped to accelerate the process.[84]

Just as with the emergence of a sizeable antislavery movement, the emergence of a movement for animal protection was associated with the period of rapid capitalist growth and expansion.[85] Regarding changing attitudes toward other animals, Joyce E. Salisbury writes:

> In the nineteenth century, . . . [p]eople began to define humans as creatures of feeling and passions, rather than just intellect. This they shared with animals, and thus animals might be treated with care for feelings. When people began to see themselves in their animals, they increasingly began to have a different relationship with them. Animals became the source of and outlet for affection as people emphasized their relationship with their pets.[86]

What is more, Serpell and Paul note that "middle-class pet owners were in the forefront of many Victorian debates on animal cruelty."[87]

Evidence from the late twentieth century provides further support for the thesis that rising standards of living and the development of empathetic response brought a reduction of societal interests in the direct oppression of other animals. For example, reviewing the findings of their study of public attitudes toward research on other animals, Linda Pifer, Kinya Shimizu, and Ralph Pifer note:

> [T]here is some linkage between a nation's level of industrialization and urbanization and attitudes toward animal research. Within the European community, the two least industrialized and urbanized countries had the lowest level of opposition to animal research. The chickens one cares for will yield eggs, the next generation of layers, and finally dinner when the birds are done laying. In more developed countries people may never come into contact with the animals they eat and that clothe them.[88]

Finally, studies of animal rights activists and sympathizers have found that they are far more likely than the average U.S. citizen to have a college education,[89] suggesting that most of them likely have a level of economic security. The majority consider themselves politically liberal or leftist,[90] indicating a concern for the life experiences of devalued groups of humans as well as other animals.

Members of the general public with some measure of economic security can be moved by the plight of those subjected to the institutionalized practices of oppressive industries. For example, in 1998 two pigs escaped from a slaughterhouse near Malmesbury, England, and eluded pursuers in a drama that "captivated Britain" and "resulted in a wave of public sympathy." The pair was purchased by a British tabloid that ceremoniously turned them over to a sanctuary. According to an Associated Press report, "Their adventure may also have converted some meat-eaters. The Vegetarian Society said it received three times the normal level of calls . . . , a surge it attributed to compassion for the pigs."[91] It is this potential for public consciousness to be so aroused that causes agribusiness, the pharmaceutical and biomedical industries, and similar enterprises with interests grounded in oppression to try to exert control over popular culture while shielding their practices from public view.

Many individuals are able to transcend their social and cultural indoctrination, some because of particular personal experiences. Humans frequently develop empathetic responses and concern for devalued others when their lives directly converge, and humans are capable of developing deep relationships with other animals if there are opportunities for meaningful interaction. (As mentioned previously, many such opportunities are precluded by laws that prohibit most human contact with "wildlife" and "farm animals," not unlike former laws prohibiting "miscegenation.")[92]

Over the years, numerous books, articles, and stories have been written by those who have experienced such relationships. From *Rascal,* to *Arnie, the Darling Starling* to *Born Free,* humans have demonstrated the capacity for strong empathetic responses and relationships with other animals. For example, Margaret A. Stanger eloquently detailed her friendship with a quail in the 1996 book, *That Quail, Robert.*

> Much of her charm and many of the enchanting things she did were reserved for times when we were by ourselves. I would expect this to be true, as indeed it was, of her periods of showing affection, getting on my shoulder and rubbing against my neck with little coos of endearment; but I was a little surprised by "the game." She usually entertained herself well, or busied herself, when I was working. But at times she wanted to be amused. This most often happened over a bit of lettuce. Instead of eating it, she would come running to me, holding the lettuce in her beak. Then, pushing my ankle with her tail and looking up at me with a real gleam in her eye, she let me know that she wanted to play "Chase Me."
>
> I usually stopped what I was doing and, bending over her, saying, "I'll get you! I'll get you," would start the chase. Off she would run, with me after her, across the kitchen, through the living room, across the hall and through the bedroom back to the kitchen. Round and round we went, sometimes for as long as five minutes. Sometimes I doubled back and met her face to face in the hall, at which point she would brake to a stop, pivot in a flash and reverse the path. It was definitely a game; if she had been trying to get away from me, all she had to do was disappear under a table or a bed. The chase continued until she was tired, at which time—*gulp-gulp,* the lettuce was swallowed and the game was over.[93]

Such relationships as these, as well as public response to the plight of Jessica McClure, Keiko, and Phoenix, and publicized, individualized stories about sweatshop workers, victims of rape or violence, and other individual emergencies and tragedies, speak to the potential of humans for empathy and justice. However, while stable and secure economic conditions may permit many to feel concern for the welfare of devalued humans and other animals, this possibility is still mostly hindered when the "mass" is profoundly steeped in a "commonsense" reality that is speciesist, racist, sexist, classist, homophobic, and ageist and that devalues humans with disabilities. In such a society, many who achieve economic security, if not success, are exhorted to display symbols of their social worth and status conspicuously in a hierarchical society. Those with vested interests in oppression, particularly in the oppression of other animals, encourage the comfortable and successful to eat "upscale" preparations of "meat" and wear the finest clothing, frequently fashioned from others' hair and skin. Great efforts are made to see that those with enhanced potential for empathy and action are limited to acting on behalf of the "deserving poor" and the "good" other animals—dogs and cats. The possibility for empathetic response to "others," then, does not automatically lead to its actuality.

This chapter opened with a recognition of the widespread ambivalence about the treatment of oppressed humans and other animals. This ambivalence can be understood in part as the product of an enhanced possibility of some for empathy when they are made aware of unjust practices, when they see the faces and learn the identities of the oppressed but live within the context of the capitalist system with its ideological and legal bases of support for oppression. Liberation activists face a formidable task in making visible to all the existence and consequences of oppression. Economic security will help the public to see, hear, understand, and embrace the message.

NOTES

1. Phyllis Hobson, *Raising a Calf for Beef* (Charlotte, Vt.: Garden Way Publishing, 1976), 63.

2. Michael Harrington, "The New American Poverty," lecture given at Rosemont College, Rosemont, Pennsylvania, 29 October 1987.

3. Albert J. Reiso, Jr., and Jeffrey A. Roth, eds., *Understanding and Preventing Violence* (Washington, D.C.: National Academy Press, 1993).

4. While I appreciate Gunnar Myrdal's highlighting the dilemma—that is, the inconsistencies between conflicting values and beliefs in the United States—I do not embrace his analysis, which places the root of the problem in the "American Creed." As stated earlier in this text, analysis of oppression that overemphasizes the importance of ideas and diminishes the powerful forces of economic arrangements serves to present capitalism as a largely benign force. One of the recurring ideas in this book is that, while the power of values and other ideas should not be minimized, the importance of economic arrangements frequently are. In reality, the relationship between ideas and material conditions is interdependent; however, in most cases, the economic circumstances dominate the formation of practices, customs, and laws.

5. This revised version of Donald Noel's theory of ethnic conflict alerts us to the importance of ethnocentrism in the oppression of both human and other animals. Ethnocentrism is present when one believes that one's own group is the center of everything, and all others are scaled and rated with references to it. Ethnocentrism, then, encompasses anthropocentrism.

6. James A. Serpell, "Pre-Christian Attitudes," in *Encyclopedia of Animal Rights and Animal Welfare*, ed. Marc Bekoff and Carron A. Meaney (Westport, Conn.: Greenwood, 1998), 76.

7. Ronald A. Marchant, *Man and Beast* (New York: Macmillan, 1968), 3–4.

8. Elizabeth Fisher, *Woman's Creation: Sexual Evolution and the Shaping of Society* (New York: McGraw-Hill, 1979), 197.

9. Jean-Jacques Rousseau, *A Discourse on Inequality* (New York: Penguin, 1984 [1754]), 85–86.

10. Amzie Moore, interviewed in "Awakenings, 1954–1956," *Eyes on the Prize* (video-recording), Blackside Productions, Inc. (Atlanta: Turner Home Entertainment, 1987).

11. Virginia Durr, interviewed in "Awakenings."

12. Paulo Freire, *Pedagogy of the Oppressed* (New York: Seabury, 1970).

13. For a more extensive history of some of the ideas used to devalue animals and justify their oppression, see Peter Singer, "Man's Dominion: A Short History of Speciesism," chapter 5 in his *Animal Liberation,* rev. ed. (New York: Avon, 1990), 185–212.

14. *Politics, Everyman's Library* (London: Dent, 1959), 10; cited in Singer, *Animal Liberation,* 189.

15. Singer, *Animal Liberation,* 193–94.

16. Del Martin, *Battered Wives* (San Francisco: Glide, 1976), 29.

17. James E. Falkowski, *Indian Law/Race Law: A Five-Hundred-Year History* (New York: Praeger, 1992), 8.

18. Falkowski, *Indian Law,* 13.

19. See, for example, Michael Parenti, *Democracy for the Few* (Belmont, Calif.: Wadsworth, 2001).

20. Leonas L. Burlingame, *Heredity and Social Problems* (New York: McGraw-Hill, 1940), 256–57.

21. Leonard Lee Rue III, *Sportsman's Guide to Game Animals* (New York: Harper & Row, 1968), 5, 10, 15.

22. Ecofeminists have been among the first to recognize the deep entanglements of oppression, especially between women and other animals. These scholars tend to point to patriarchal thinking as the primary support of oppressive society. On one level, patriarchy serves male "interests" (interests ranging from the financial to the sexual to the psychological). However, the costs to males alone for such "privileges" are deep and pervasive, with disastrous consequences for their personal identities, relationships with others, and overall quality of their lives. While the role played by patriarchy in oppression is powerful, it is most likely that transcendence of the capitalist system is a necessary precondition for the eradication of patriarchal systems.

23. On the social construction of gender, see, for example, Linda L. Lindsey, *Gender Roles: A Sociological Perspective* (Englewood Cliffs, N.J.: Prentice Hall, 1990).

24. Janis Birkeland, "Ecofeminism: Linking Theory and Practice," in *Ecofeminism: Women, Animals, Nature,* ed. Greta Gaard (Philadelphia: Temple University Press, 1993), 18–19.

25. Antonio Gramsci, *Selections from the Prison Notebooks* (London: Lawrence & Wishart, 1971 [1937]).

26. Michael Parenti, *Make-believe Media: The Politics of Entertainment* (New York: St. Martin's, 1992).

27. Parenti, *Make-believe Media.*

28. Robert W. McChesney, *Rich Media, Poor Democracy: Communication Politics in Dubious Times* (New York: New Press, 1999), 229.

29. McChesney, *Rich Media, Poor Democracy.*

30. David A. Nibert, "The Political Economy of Disability," *Critical Sociology* 21, no. 1 (1995): 71.

31. Nibert, "The Political Economy of Disability," 71–72.

32. Rick McAllister, "They're Here, They're Queer, So What Are They Like? Gay, Lesbian, and Bisexual Characters on Primetime Television," senior thesis, Department of Sociology, Wittenberg University, Springfield, Ohio, 1998.

33. Arnold Arluke and Jack Levin, "Second Childhood: Old Age in Popular Culture," in *Growing Old in America: New Perspectives on Aging,* 3d ed., ed. Beth B. Hess and Elizabeth W. Markson (New Brunswick, N.J.: Transaction, 1987), 151–58.

34. See, for example, Lucinda Joy Peach, ed., *Women in Culture: A Women's Studies Anthology* (Malden, Mass.: Blackwell, 1998).

35. A plethora of films of this type (usually low-budget) have been thrust upon the public—films ranging from a portrayal of a herd of giant rabbits attacking humans to a yarn about a colony of homicidal cats.

36. *The UCLA Television Violence Report 1997* (Los Angeles: UCLA Center for Communication Policy, 1998), 75–76.

37. Jill Howard Church, "In Focus: How the Media Portray Animals," *The Animals' Agenda* 16 no. 1 (1996): 24–28.

38. Quoted in Church, "In Focus," 28.

39. Stephen Jay Gould, "Keynote Address," given at the conference "In the Company of Animals" in New York City on 6 April 1995; reprinted in *Humans and Other Animals,* ed. Arien Mack (Columbus: Ohio State University Press, 1999), 195.

40. For a discussion of the transformation of public into mass, see C. Wright Mills, *The Power Elite* (New York: Oxford University Press, 1956), 302–24.

41. McChesney, *Rich Media, Poor Democracy,* 19.

42. McChesney, *Rich Media, Poor Democracy,* 20.

43. The term "crushing advantage" was used in this regard by Ralph Miliband in his seminal work *The State in Capitalist Society* (New York: Basic Books, 1869), 182.

44. A thoughtful argument for using the term *genocide* to include the mass killing of other animals is given by Steven Wise in his book *Rattling the Cage: Toward Legal Rights for Animals* (Cambridge, Mass.: Perseus, 2000).

45. Dottie Enrico, "The Fifty Greatest TV Commercials of All Time," *TV Guide* 47, no. 7 (3–9 July 1999): 2–34.

46. Enrico, "The Fifty Greatest," 28.

47. Arluke and Levin, *Growing Old in America,* 155.

48. McChesney, *Rich Media, Poor Democracy,* 45.

49. McChesney, *Rich Media, Poor Democracy,* 94, 108.

50. Dave Larson, "Atlantis' Search Made in Vain," *Dayton Daily News,* GO! section 12, no. 14 (15 June 2001): 9.

51. Slavoljub Milekic, "Disneyfication," in *Encyclopedia of Animal Welfare and Animal Rights,* ed. Marc Bekoff and Carron A. Meaney (Westport, Conn.: Greenwood, 1998), 133.

52. Phrase borrowed from C. David Coats, *Old MacDonald's Factory Farm: The Myth of the Traditional Farm and the Shocking Truth about Animal Suffering in Today's Agribusiness* (New York: Continuum, 1989), 61.

53. Edward S. Herman and Noam Chomsky, *Manufacturing Consent: The Political Economy of the Mass Media* (New York: Pantheon, 1988), 1.

54. Samuel Bowles and Herbert Gintis, *Schooling in Capitalist America: Educational Reform and the Contradictions of Economic Life* (New York: Basic Books, 1976).

55. Associated Press, "Students Witness Slaughter of Steer," *Columbus Dispatch,* 19 May 2001, A1, A2.

56. Lawrene Trump, "After Auction Is Over, the Bond Is Broken," *Springfield News Sun,* 28 July 2000, 1.

57. Mark Crispin Miller, www.fair.org/extra/9705/ch1-miller.html.

58. Dayton Daily News, "Ads in Math Textbooks Adding Up to Controversy," 21 March 1999, 9A.

59. Lynda Birke, *Feminism, Animals and Science: The Naming of the Shrew* (Philadelphia: Open University Press, 1994), 7.

60. Harrington, *The Other America*, 4.

61. Cleveland Amory, *Man Kind? Our Incredible War on Wildlife* (New York: Dell, 1974), 9–11.

62. Carol J. Adams, *The Sexual Politics of Meat: A Feminist-Vegetarian Critical Theory* (New York: Continuum, 1990), 40.

63. *Dayton Daily News,* "Veal Cuts on the Bone Have a Fuller Flavor," 10 March 1999, 1C.

64. See Coats, *Old MacDonald's Factory Farm,* 61–68.

65. *Dayton Daily News,* "Tiny Cornish Game Hens Rock Palates," 3 March 1999, 1C.

66. *Dayton Daily News,* "A Fresh Start: Rabbit is Comparable to Chicken—But with Fewer Calories, It's a Lean Option," 28 April 1999, 1C, 4C.

67. Robert L. Kidder, *Connecting Law and Society* (Englewood Cliffs, N.J.: Prentice Hall, 1983), 29.

68. David Nibert, *Hitting the Lottery Jackpot: State Governments and the Taxing of Dreams* (New York: Monthly Review Press, 2000), 3.

69. Helen M. Muller, *Lotteries,* Vol. X, no. 2 of the Reference Shelf Series (New York: Wilson, 1935), 108.

70. See Nibert, *Hitting the Lottery Jackpot.*

71. For a discussion of the prejudicial nature of the term *wildlife,* see Adams, *The Sexual Politics of Meat.*

72. Mike Markarian, "Targeting Teens: Government-Sponsored Youth Hunts," *Threshold: The Movement Magazine of the Student Environmental Action Coalition* (February/March 1996): 20–21.

73. "Youth Movement," *Petersen's Hunting Magazine* (January 1999): 70–73.

74. "Should Kids Hunt?" *Time* 162, no. 22 (30 November 1998): 105.

75. Everett K. Wilson, *Sociology: Rules, Roles and Relationships* (Homewood, Ill.: Dorsey, 1966), 92; cited in D. Stanley Eitzen and Maxine Baca Zinn, *In Conflict and Order: Understanding Society,* 9th ed. (Boston: Allyn & Bacon, 2001).

76. See, for example, Randall Lockwood, "Animal Cruelty and Violence against Humans: Making the Connection," *Animal Law* 5 (1999): 81–87; Randall Lockwood and Frank R. Ascione, eds., *Cruelty to Animals and Interpersonal Violence: Readings in Research and Application* (West Lafayette, Ind.: Purdue University Press, 1998).

77. "Gap in Wealth in U.S. Called Widest in West," *New York Times,* 17 April 1995, A1.

78. Abraham H. Maslow, *Motivation and Personality* (New York: Harper, 1954).

79. Maslow, *Motivation and Personality,* 149, 148.

80. Michael Harrington, *The Next Left: The History of a Future* (London: Tauris, 1987), 21.

81. Michael Harrington, *Socialism: Past and Future* (New York: Arcade, 1989), 127.

82. Joe R. Feagin and Clarece Booher Feagin, *Racial and Ethnic Relations,* 4th ed. (Englewood Cliffs, N.J.: Prentice Hall, 1993), 94.

83. Susan Previant Lee and Peter Passell, *A New Economic View of American History* (New York: Norton, 1979), 214.

84. James Serpell and Elizabeth Paul, "Pets and the Development of Positive Attitudes to

Animals," in *Animals and Human Society: Changing Perspectives,* ed. Aubrey Manning and James Serpell (New York: Routledge, 1994), 134.

85. For a discussion of this expansion, see Eric Hobsbawm, *The Age of Capital: 1848–1875* (London: Abacus, 1995 [1975]).

86. Joyce E. Salisbury, "Changing Attitudes throughout History," in *Encyclopedia of Animals Rights and Animal Welfare,* ed. Bekoff and Meaney, 80.

87. Serpell and Paul, "Pets and the Development of Positive Attitudes," 135.

88. Linda Pifer, Kinya Shimizu, and Ralph Pifer, "Public Attitudes toward Animal Research: Some International Comparisons," *Society and Animals* 2, no. 2 (1994): 108–9.

89. Patricia Greanville and Doug Moss, "The Emerging Face of the Movement," *Animals' Agenda* 5, no. 2 (1985): 10.

90. *Animals' Agenda,* "What Sort of Person Reads *Agenda?*" (May/June 1983): 26.

91. Associated Press, "Porkers Go on Lam Six Days, No Baloney," *Dayton Daily News,* 17 January 1998, 4A.

92. While this observation should not be construed as supporting the purposeful taking of many other animals—such as those referred to as "wildlife"—as "pets," it recognizes that there are situations in which contact occurs and relationships develop.

93. Margaret A. Stanger, *That Quail, Robert* (New York: HarperCollins, 1966), 88–89.

7

Toward a United Struggle against Oppression

[T]he end to class exploitation is not a panacea but merely an essential precondition for our true liberation and self-determination.

—Tomás Almaguér[1]

The emancipation of . . . [humans] from cruelty and injustice will bring with it in due course the emancipation of animals also. The two reforms are inseparably connected, and neither can be fully realized alone.

—Henry Salt[2]

In myriad ways, over centuries and millennia, the oppression of humans and of other animals have been connected and intertwined. And, as Henry Salt notes, the social changes that will lead to the liberation of both humans and other animals will and must be inseparable. The question is, how is true liberation to be achieved, particularly in a society in which stratification and oppression are inherent elements of the social structure?

We have used the theory of oppression as an etiological compass to chart the roots of speciesism, racism, sexism, classism, and other malignant belief systems. Based on Donald Noel's 1968 theory on the origins of ethnic conflict, this model helps bring into focus the inadequacies of previous efforts to explain oppression by psychologisms—that is, explaining oppression largely as the result of deficiencies or pathology in those who are prejudiced and who discriminate. Individual-level analysis also has characterized much of the work of advocates for other animals, who largely locate the problem in prejudices grounded in moral positions. Although activists sometimes recognize these objectionable moral positions as the result of cultural values, their strategies for change focus on promoting increased individual awareness that, it is hoped, will eventually lead to a change in societal morals. Those who take this position suggest that this course and consequent political reforms within the existing social structure will bring other animals liberation, ostensibly already won by oppressed human groups. Some powerful advocates for other animals—such as Regan, Stallwood, and Spiegel (discussed in chapter 1)—suggest either overtly or implicitly that economic systems, capitalism in particular, are not primary in the causation of oppression. To the contrary, however, the general position offered here is that exploitation of "others" is motivated primarily by economic self-interest— that, in the words of sociologist Ted Benton, they are "indissolubly intertwined"[3]— and that exploitation largely serves the interests of elites.

As we have seen, the economic factors that primarily cause the oppression of humans and other animals go back thousands of years to the latter stages of hunting and gathering society, when systematic hunting of other animals and the devaluation of women developed hand in hand. The advent of early agricultural society brought with it opportunities for individual privilege and power—primarily for elite males—by intensifying and broadening systematic oppression of both humans and other animals. Countless humans were assigned to hegemonically created social positions, including those of "slave" and "serf," that devalued them individually and collectively. And so it was with other animals, whose use and placement in such social positions as "livestock" and "game" greatly facilitated the development of highly stratified and oppressive agricultural societies. Untold numbers of "others" were yoked to pestles, plows, wagons, and chariots for their entire lives, while countless more were used as currency or devoured as victuals, largely by the privileged. Humans and other animals were forced to fight each other to the death to amuse the elites and to distract the masses from their experiences and the sources of their deprivations. Similar entertainment and diversionary uses of devalued others occurred during the Middle Ages, when mass exploitation was continued by manorial lords and high-placed church officials. Under conditions such as these, women and cats, for example, were scapegoated for system-produced "misfortunes" and executed as witches and their conspirators.

Capitalism continued the ten-thousand-year-old tradition of exploiting humans and other animals for the production of wealth and privilege, an exploitation that continued to bind the fate of devalued humans and other animals. For instance, the enclosure movements in Europe saw exploited humans forced from the countryside only to have the land used for raising captive sheep. The sheep were robbed of their body hair, which was sent to developing urban areas where the former country residents, transformed into an urban proletariat, worked and suffered in nascent textile mills. The Irish, subjugated by the British military, were forced from their homeland to have much of it used to raise cows, whose bodies were sent back to feed the elite in Britain. In the Western Hemisphere, Astor killed tens of thousands of other animals—whose skin and hair were worn largely by the elite to advertise their elevated social status—while exploiting indigenous humans. Meanwhile, countless other animals were massacred and "cleared" from the land so that humans of color who were enslaved could be used to produce profitable cash crops. "Cattle kings" accrued great wealth raising cows destined for the horrors of the slaughterhouse where the "meat producers" exploited countless workers who had the task of killing and dismembering other animals. Contaminated and tainted "meat" was sold to the public and the U.S. military at inflated prices.

The unfolding of the twentieth century brought the onset of corporate dominance of the economy, and millions of farmers were forced from the countryside as the chemical-driven Green Revolution and large-scale factory farming escalated the level of suffering experienced by "farm" animals and accelerated destruction of the environment. Today, "meat" production is based on almost unimaginable suffering for billions of other animals every year. Third World elites (empowered by the International Monetary Fund and the World Bank) create poverty and destitution in their nations by taking over the land to send inexpensive feed and the bodies of other animals to countries like the United States, where giant corporations and their legions of advertisers exhort everyone to consume "burgers" and "fried chicken." The critical health problems associated with eating the bodies, secretions, and eggs of other animals bring growing profits for the pharmaceutical industry. Drug companies staunchly defend their use of countless other animals in horrific experiments every year as necessary for the good of the public, a clear misrepresentation by an industry that has demonstrated callous and deadly disregard for consumers and that strongly resists sharing its products with those who cannot afford them.

Meanwhile, financial exigencies created by virtually total corporate control over the global economy lead many desperate humans to turn to poaching, to murdering and selling gorillas and chimpanzees, elephants bearing ivory, and any other being whose exploitation and death can help them to survive, or gain an edge, in the "new economic order."

The examples of the interdependent nature of oppression of humans and other animals mentioned in this book scarcely begin to cover the actual extent of the economic entanglements. However, these illustrate that today the mistreatment of devalued humans and other animals is deeply embedded in the capitalist system and the social positions generated by the system; their oppression is profoundly intertwined and mutually reinforcing. We have seen that the economic arrangements largely created by, and certainly facilitating the interests of, the most privileged have been sanctioned and protected by the various powers of the state. Military and police power and rigged legal systems have created and protected oppression for thousands of years. From Hammurabi's laws to the defeat of Spartacus, from the sanctification of slavery to the creation of "humane" slaughter policies, the beneficiaries of oppression have firmly controlled and used the power of the state. This control has become increasingly ideological in nature with the advent of political capitalism. Reforms under capitalism have been relatively modest, underenforced, and prone to reductions, reversals, and eliminations.

Capitalist influence over ideology also has helped "naturalize" oppressive arrangements, making them seem to be normal and innate elements of worldly existence. The metaphysical and theological belief systems that taught the "natural" place of the enslaved, women, children, other animals, and other devalued and oppressed groups for thousands of years have been supplanted to a considerable degree with more recent "scientific" and social scientific ideologies that defend and naturalize the contemporary socioeconomic order. Still more powerful is the lifetime propaganda from such diverse but powerful sources as the mass media, schools, museums, the state, families, and organized religion, all of which shape a day-to-day reality that fosters widespread and deep acceptance—indeed, internalization—of this hegemonically constructed reality. Both the conscious and subconscious minds of human members of society are imbued with ideas about the largely "inferior" qualities and the "otherness" of women, humans of color, those with disabilities, those of advanced age, other animals, and other oppressed groups.

THE LEFT AND THE LIBERATION
OF OTHER ANIMALS

Many on the political Left, broadly defined, are largely accepting of anticruelty laws but unfriendly to the movement for the *liberation* of other animals, a condition both documented and lamented by John Sanbonmatsu, who writes, "Within the mainstream progressive community, activists continue to eat their Big Macs, buy their rabbit-tested floor polish, and show little interest in finding out more about the animal suffering they materially support."[4]

To activists in other liberation movements, assertions of commonality between the oppression of humans and of other animals are frequently viewed with hostility or disdain.[5] Indeed, some on the Left have seen any public effort to link human oppression with the oppression of other animals as a trivialization of human suffering. For example, in a 1978 article Leslie Pickering Francis and Richard Norman write:

> [E]quating the cause of animal welfare with genuine liberation movements such as black liberation, women's liberation or gay liberation . . . presents an implausible guise in the quite valid concern to prevent cruelty to animals. At the same time the equation has the effect of trivializing those real liberation movements, putting them on a level with what cannot but appear as a bizarre exaggeration. Liberation movements have a character and a degree of moral importance which cannot be possessed by a movement to prevent cruelty to animals.[6]

More recently, even after years of activism and efforts by advocates for other animals, many other activists still view the use of energy and resources for other animals as examples of misplaced priorities. For instance, speaking before a class at Harvard Law School in the Academy Award–winning documentary *Defending Our Lives,* the nationally recognized campaigner against domestic violence, Sarah Buel, states:

> Well, we've come a little ways in fifteen years. There are now twelve hundred battered women's shelters across this country. But you need to keep that in perspective. There are about thirty-eight hundred animal protection shelters. No matter how much you love animals, it seems to me our priorities are a little skewed when we have three times

the number of shelters for homeless animals than we have for battered women and their children.[7]

Similarly, in her important and powerful book *Chaos or Community? Seeking Solutions, Not Scapegoats for Bad Economics,* Holly Sklar rightfully laments the inadequate wages of child care teaching staff; she punctuates her point, however, with the following observation: "People who take care of animals in zoos make an average of $2,500 more a year than child care teachers."[8] Buel's and Sklar's statements are characteristic of many such observations from the Left, being based on hierarchical paradigms and reflexive responses to the relationships of humans and other animals. In Buel's case, the "animal shelters" she refers to are mainly death houses for most of the "sheltered" other animals, who are killed by government "animal control" agencies. Sklar mistakenly views other animals confined in zoos as coddled fortunates, instead of the awful prisoners of tourism that most are. They are kept by "experts" in quarters that are usually small, sterile, and profoundly unnatural— mainly because of their entertainment value for humans and their contributions to the local economy, not because they are valued or respected as individuals.

The resistance of many distinguished liberation activists and others on the political Left to acknowledging oppression of other animals is grounded, in part, in the fact that they, too, have been raised not in a vacuum but in a society that uses powerful propaganda to naturalize that oppression. While many may have developed an awareness of human oppression through academic study, most classrooms and teachers are silent on the issue of the oppression of other animals. As a consequence, as John Sanbonmatsu points out, many on the Left exhibit the same views on other animals as their conservative capitalist adversaries.[9] Many civil rights and liberation activists and others on the Left perceive the movement for the liberation of other animals as disconnected from their own struggles, and they are unaware of the profound economic entanglements of these various forms of oppression and their relationship to the capitalist system.

It is important that members of other contemporary liberation movements come to realize that the current oppression of other animals, especially as "food," is ethically atrocious and causes unimaginable pain and suffering. What is more, it simply is not possible to feed the more than six billion humans on the earth—a number that is growing rapidly—with "meat." As long as the flesh of other animals is defined as food, it will always be consumed disproportionately by the elite and privileged. The consumption of "meat"—particularly the more expensive forms—will remain a symbol of elevated social rank, a desirable status to which everyone is expected to aspire. Unaltered, we will continue to see the terrible consequences of "meat" production and consumption: the barbaric and grotesque treatment of billions of other animals, the expropriation of land by elites, the violent repression of resistance movements, the waste of precious arable land and grain, the pollution of dwindling supplies of freshwater and further intensification of global warming, the serious health problems that afflict those who produce "meat" and consume it, the plague of hunger and starvation—and ever-increasingly concentrated and centralized agribusiness that profits from all these nefarious practices.

Many on the Left, who otherwise will challenge authority and question the status quo, nonetheless accept the social positioning and treatment of other animals determined by agribusiness; the pharmaceutical, biomedical, and chemical industries; state departments of "wildlife"; and the like and their view that it is natural and necessary to treat other animals as they do. As long as social critics and activists accept this state of affairs, odds are great that, among the numerous other disastrous consequences, the dispossessed of the Earth will continue to experience malnutrition and oppression while the masses in more affluent countries are pacified in part by making themselves obese and sick eating "meat," "dairy" products, and eggs.

When issues of food and hunger surface, some on the Left criticize advocates for other animals as elitist for condemning hunting. The criticism takes the form of an assertion that those who can purchase all the food they need at a supermarket should not moralize over those who cannot and who must hunt in order to eat. This defense of hunting puts many on the Left in the awkward position of defending the "right" to hunt—an ethically bankrupt custom that is, in fact, disproportionately practiced by the privileged. Inherent in this violent custom are patriarchal ideas and practices that have been criticized by a number of ecofeminist scholars.[10] What is more, the defense of hunting by some on the Left also puts them in the position of supporting the National Rifle Association and the powerful lobby of manufacturers and sellers of guns and other armaments. If the production of food were done ethically and its consumption regarded as a basic right ("food for people, not for profit"), hunting other animals for food as a means of survival, where it does exist, would become unnecessary.

Leftists, activists, and scholars also must become more aware of the ideological entanglements among the forms of oppression. Most largely accept the pseudoscientific arguments for the oppression of other animals rather than seeing and challenging its hierarchical basis. What most do not realize is that efforts to distance the constituents of social movements from other animals actually *strengthen* the ideological rationalization for oppression. Barbara Noske observes, "Time and time again new versions of Darwinism have cropped up providing genetic justifications for class oppression and sexual and racial discrimination, all of which have been labelled 'natural.' . . . In order to safeguard humans from another onslaught of biological determinism social scientists tend to be quite defensive about the non-animalness of humans."[11]

Acceptance of the notion of a hierarchy of worth of living beings helped create and sustain caste and class systems throughout the ages. In more recent times, male workers challenged their devalued status as labor but believed themselves superior to women. Women struggled for suffrage, but some distanced themselves from the "lower class" and humans of color. Members of some ethnic groups differentiated themselves from other groups that were perceived to be inferior, and a hierarchy of value and worth surfaced even within ethnic groups. The poorest of the poor could take refuge in the assertion that "I may be poor, but I'm not stupid," an obvious distancing from those with disabilities, and many proclaimed their dignity in the face of oppression by asserting, "I am not an animal."

This tendency for some members of oppressed human groups to challenge their own subjugation while accepting the concept of hierarchy is noted by Paulo Freire in *Pedagogy of the Oppressed.*

> [T]he oppressed . . . tend themselves to become oppressors, or "sub-oppressors." The very structure of their thought has been conditioned by the contradictions of the concrete, existential situation by which they were shaped. . . . This phenomenon derives from the fact that the oppressed, at a certain moment of their existential experience, adopt an attitude of "adhesion" to the oppressor. . . . Every revolution, which transforms a concrete situation of oppression by establishing the process of liberation, must confront this phenomenon. Many of the oppressed who directly or indirectly participate in revolution intend—conditioned by the myths of the old order—to make it their private revolution. The shadow of their former oppressor is still cast over them.[12]

Many on the Left are largely unaware of the activists, reformers, and revolutionaries throughout history who have observed and criticized the oppression of other animals.[13] For example, workers who saw their fate as similar to that of other animals led the Old Brown Dog Riots in early twentieth-century England[14]—a powerful lesson to the capitalist class in the need to promote a profoundly speciesist reality. The lack of awareness of just how deeply human oppression is rooted in the oppression of other animals, and the resultant diminished potential for progressive unity, help the elite to remain comfortably in control.

The Left's reluctance to accept the movement for the liberation of other animals is also grounded in strategic concerns. Many feel that it is already an enormous challenge to educate and rally the public around issues pertaining to human oppression without also trying to generate sympathy and action for those at the "bottom" of the social order. However, such a strategy will produce only limited and illusory gains if it does not challenge the dominant belief in a hierarchy of life. Such well-motivated but ultimately self-interested views contribute to the fragmentation of liberation movements in which activists for a specific devalued group strive to obtain more resources or better treatment for their group—variations on previous, self-interested "revolutions from above."

The powerful forces that both drive and are driven by contemporary capitalist economic arrangements, and the dreadful consequences we have seen, are unlikely to be altered in any meaningful way by welfarist reforms or by factionalized liberation movements. Overcoming the formidable system of economic arrangements, the rigged state apparatus, and the effects of profound ideological indoctrination—all of which give the elite a "crushing advantage"—will require a much more unified and focused effort.

ADVOCATES FOR OTHER ANIMALS AND CAPITALISM

Increased awareness of the common roots and contemporary entanglements of the oppression of humans and other animals would empower and further the progress of the Left in the struggle against injustice and exploitation. Likewise, those active in the movement for the liberation of other animals must examine their tendency to view capitalism as a largely benign social force. They rightly decry many examples of speciesist economic practices and denounce entire industries, such as agribusiness and the fur industry. In general, though, they call for social transformation largely through changed perceptions and priorities on the part of individuals and through welfarist reforms.

This is not to say that the numerous books, articles, pamphlets, lectures, conferences, and protests challenging the oppression of other animals in the last quarter century are unimportant. Certainly, activists for other animals have had some notable successes in the United States in recent years, such as increasing public awareness of the testing of commercial products on other animals and reducing the social acceptability of wearing "fur." But an approach that is largely silent about the role of capitalism is very unlikely to stem the growing level of oppression of other animals in the era of the new global economic order.

Many activists for other animals continue to agree with the position taken by Kim Stallwood, cited in chapter 1: "in every human society, whether communist, capitalist, or developing world, the labor of nonhuman animals is used without any moral consideration to provide services and to produce commodities for human consumption."[15] This assertion of the universality of the oppression of other animals, past and present, discounts the impact of social structural arrangements and overlooks two important points. First, human history does not consist of an uninterrupted trail of blithe and unconcerned use of other animals. To the contrary, as we have seen, for most of our history humans lived fairly harmoniously with other animals, and there was little economic motivation to mistreat them. When systematic oppression of other animals began, evidence suggests many humans experienced a great deal of guilt and uneasiness. In the later stages of foraging society, humans created religious beliefs and rituals that rationalized the killing of other animals, indicating that the practice disturbed members of the society and thus required legitimation. Throughout the centuries, moral challenges to the treatment of animals have been plentiful. However, in societies developing agricultural modes of economic production, speciesist ideologies were created and promulgated to legitimate killing and exploitation of other animals. Such ideologies subverted views that might give moral consideration to the treatment of other animals and controlled efforts of those who expressed concern about oppressive practices.

Second, and very importantly, a view that ignores the possibilities that socialism may offer for liberation of other animals unduly limits visions and strategies for political alliances and social change. It is not surprising that today many activists distance themselves from socialism. Liberation activists and their liberal supporters and potential allies are aware that efforts to establish socialist systems in the twentieth century were fraught with conflict and deprivation and that the regimes they built were bureaucratic and frequently oppressive. Even many on the Left, often joining the defenders of capitalism, are far too anxious to throw out the socialist baby with the totalitarian bathwater.

Many feel it is better to live under a system that affords the right to vote, free speech, and the promise of liberty, equality, and fraternity—even though such rights are precarious and social progress largely illusory. Some highly visible advocates for other animals, like Alex Pacheco of People for the Ethical Treatment of Animals (PETA), actually embrace the capitalist system as a tool for the advancement of the liberation of other animals. After interviewing Pacheco, philosopher Susan Finsen summarized his approach as follows:

> [H]e stated that he was marketing compassion. The idea is that compassion, just as soap or toothpaste, can be effectively sold to the public. If enough people learn about the issues, they will demand change (for example, cruelty-free products). On this view, there is seemingly no incompatibility between status quo corporate capitalism and the ends of animal rights. The familiar fact that large corporate interests, profiting from animal exploitation, generally crush any attempts to legislate protection for animals is not necessarily decisive in rebuffing this view. It could be that the fight for animal rights is analogous to the little family-owned company that eventually triumphs against all odds and becomes a big corporate giant, buying out the competition. The correct approach is to continue to educate the public, and create a demand for products which do not exploit animals. If properly educated, people will only buy fake fur, vegetarian food, and non-leather shoes.[16]

Finsen, however, is skeptical. "[T]here are reasons to think that this approach won't work," she writes. "Most fundamentally, corporate capitalism focuses on the bottom line. The profit motive ignores other values, such as family, community, and environmental integrity. The results for family farms, family owned businesses, ecosystems, and endangered species have been dismal."[17]

Still, the capacity for a better life for all has developed under capitalism. Even Marx recognized how social, political, economic, and technological developments under capitalism could be used to build a rational and just social system. Under capitalism, in the past several hundred years the rule of monarchical dictators collapsed, economic opportunities were created for many, powerful technology was developed, and a large middle class emerged in industrialized nations. Growing numbers of humans have shown their capacity for empathy and have both made and heeded calls for justice. But the growth of the capitalist system, past and present, has exacted enormous costs (disproportionately exacted from those perceived as "others"), and the oppressive practices and ensuing social problems have reached critical levels. The possibilities that capitalism once may have held—the promise of an enhanced quality of life for all and the widespread and sustained development of empathy and respect for "others"—are not at all likely to emerge now, with the economic exigencies of contemporary global capitalism.

The technological innovations developed under capitalism, while having the potential to serve everyone and improve the quality of life for all, have been largely used selfishly to create more personal wealth, to intensify centralized control and to neutralize or eliminate dissenters. Reflecting on the misappropriation of modern technology, Michael Harrington writes, "Our technology has produced unprecedented wealth, rotted great cities, threatened the very air and water, and embittered races, generations, and social classes."[18]

Apologists for capitalism point to the current plethora of electronic gadgets available to those who can afford them as an indicator of social progress. Of course, one could debate whether cell phones that allow one to check stock quotes over the Internet, mobile computers that make every place the workplace, and children's toys that require more battery power than imagination truly improve our quality of life. At best, however, such items largely constitute a superficial indicator of the state of only a particularly affluent segment of the modern world.

Reflecting on the condition of U.S. cities, Holly Sklar observes that we now live in a "violent world of crumbling cities sprinkled with high-tech gadgets. A world of voice-mail mazes and fewer interactions with real people. A world where children are free to explore their computers, if they have one, but not their neighborhoods."[19]

Renowned Harvard professor of economics John Kenneth Galbraith observes:

[C]apitalism performs excellently in providing those things—automobiles, disposable packaging, drugs, alcohol—that cause problems for the city. But it is inherently incompetent in providing the things that city dwellers most urgently need. Capitalism has never anywhere provided good houses at moderate cost. . . . Nor does capitalism provide good health services. . . . Nor does capitalism provide efficient transportation for people. . . .

In the United States there remains the conviction that, however contrary the experience, private enterprise will eventually serve.[20]

Many in the United States hold to the view that capitalism is both good and synonymous with freedom—as Galbraith says, often despite their own harsh experiences with it—because of the force of such ideology in so many basic institutions and the unending efforts of corporate capitalists to support these beliefs. Nonetheless, as we have seen earlier, in every generation activists and scholars, from W. E. B. DuBois to Oliver Cox to Michael Harrington to Holly Sklar have dissented. In his seminal work *How Capitalism Underdeveloped Black America,* Manning Marable assesses the quality of life and experiences of African Americans in the twentieth century, concluding, in agreement with other scholars, that "Black economic, political and social development is possible 'only on the basis of a radical break with the capitalist system.' "[21] Sounding the same note, acclaimed feminist theorist bell hooks observes, "[c]apitalism [is] a system that exploits female labor and [is interconnected] with sexist oppression."[22]

Observing the incongruity between hopefulness for liberation and justice with the actual nature of corporate capitalism, sociologist Immanuel Wallerstein writes, "Liberals have always claimed that the liberal state—reformist, legalistic, and somewhat libertarian—was the only state that could guarantee freedom. And for the relatively small group whose freedom it safeguarded, this was perhaps true. But unfortunately that group always remained a minority perpetually en route to becoming everyone."[23]

Some of the most notable activists, scholars, and leaders of the modern era (including former U.S. presidents, as we have seen) have denounced the new dictatorial rule of the corporate capitalists and the havoc it has brought to the world and its reliance on oppression.

One does not have to be a president, scholar, or liberation activist to be aware of the profusion of serious and critical problems confronting the world in the twenty-first century. Every local newspaper—even though usually corporate owned and hegemonically controlled—chronicles incidents of injustice and disparity, fraud and corporate wrongdoing, and aggression and violence. Unlike a huge segment of the world's population, most in the United States do not face basic survival problems. However, growing numbers here experience rising debt, joblessness, underemployment, serious health and health care problems, high levels of violence and racial conflict, and increased personal isolation. Outside the realm of academia or progressive critiques, which appear mainly in little-seen alternative publications, such problems are almost never connected to the nature of the modern capitalist system. The economically marginal or insecure often seek salvation in the hope, or the fantasy, of joining the ranks of millionaires—a small segment of the population that is nonetheless growing as the middle class shrinks and the amount and level of poverty increase. Some hope to secure a spot on a television quiz show or "survival" program, while others hang on to the hope of transcendence through unending purchases of lottery tickets. Such substitutes for the development of a just and rational society are encouraged by the most socially powerful technological development of the last century, the broadcast media. The media both distract the majority and buttress support for the status quo. The state remains firmly under the control of powerful capitalists. Corporate interests have recently become more directly involved in U.S. domestic and foreign policy in ways that are so extreme and obviously self-serving that the United States is being soundly criticized by activists and leaders from around world, and even by leaders of other capitalist-dominated nations.

Still, many decent, concerned, and politically active citizens in the United States—including many advocates for other animals—can envision no alternative to the capitalist system. While they may fight against factory sweatshops, child labor, hunger, forced prostitution, weapons sales, and other manifestations of the new global order, many are vehemently against "socialism" and what they view as "failed" efforts at creating alternatives to the capitalist system. From this perspective, moderation and centrism are the keys in the development of a "kinder, gentler" capitalism. The elusive and illusory goal of securing social justice and an end to oppression under capitalism, particularly in the form of the liberation of other animals, is highlighted in Susan Finsen's question, "Is it likely that this massive system, which has so far ignored the most basic interests of human beings around the globe, can be bent to consider the interests of animals?"[24]

THE ABSENCE OF SOCIALIST SYSTEMS

Modern capitalism is characterized by private ownership or control of most of the Earth's life-sustaining resources, private ownership of the technology and facilities needed to meet basic societal needs, and an emphasis on personal profit and glorification of wealth. The result has been a world that would cause Adam Smith to recoil in horror. But, hasn't socialism been proven to be just as bad, or perhaps worse? The honest answer is that the benefits of a true socialist system have not been demonstrated because one has yet to be created. Before explaining this statement, it is useful to note the basic characteristics of a socialist system. A socialist system is one in which the important resources and key production technology and facilities are owned by the members of the society and used for their collective benefit. A socialist system would be characterized by democratic decision making and the development of strong and much more egalitarian communities. It is in the context of such a social system that liberty, equality, and fraternity, a reversal of environmental destruction and the reduction of oppression of humans and other animals (especially in a world of nine billion humans by 2050) could be realized.

Efforts by revolutionaries and reformers to move social systems in some parts of the world toward this ideal have been difficult and at times disastrous. Of course, few worthwhile developments in human history were successful after the first try. It is understandably difficult, especially within a few years or decades, to develop a more democratic, egalitarian, and empathetic society in a world generally steeped in ten thousand years of violence and oppression. While an extended discussion of the problems and issues that have foiled efforts to establish socialist systems in the twentieth century will not be attempted here, it is worth noting several particular impediments such attempts have faced.

In the nineteenth and twentieth centuries, many humans around the world were challenging the capitalist system and the widespread misery, suffering, and oppression it brought. However, capitalists in Western, industrialized nations were able to forestall social transformation with "reforms" that actually bolstered the system, victim-blaming ideologies, hegemonic control of the media, and the substantial use of covert and overt police and military power, as we have seen.

At the same time, the depth of exploitation and suffering in countries like early twentieth-century czarist Russia, which combined agriculture-based, nascent capitalist economies with the plague of colonial rule or monarchical control, spurred revolutions that relied on various interpretations of Marxist philosophy. The largely agricultural nature of these countries, the high levels of exploitation and privation, and the long-standing traditions of exploitation of other animals precluded almost any thought of embracing other animals within the early socialist vision. As one can construe from Maslow's work, social stability and economic security are important if the majority of the human members of society are to develop substantial and sustained empathy and respect for "others." Unfortunately, however, the Soviet Union, Cuba, and other countries that began as alternatives to both monarchical and capitalist systems were permitted to experience neither stability nor security.

In the Soviet Union, for example, the potential for a democratic and equitable society was undermined in part by significant counterrevolutionary forces, from both within and outside its borders. Seeking to keep the world safe for continued capitalist growth, the elite in Western nations, including the United States, saw the Soviet system as a serious threat to the status quo and attempted to oust the revolutionary government using military force. A Western international army, calling itself the "white" army, fought to crush the revolutionary state and its "red" army. Failing that, the Western capitalists launched a cold war.

In the face of such exigencies, and without a model or blueprint for the creation and maintenance of a socialist system, Soviet leaders thrust their society on a course of rapid industrialization. Instant industrialization was viewed as necessary, in part to develop the military capacity necessary to resist powerful counterrevolutionary threats. A centralized, command economy was adopted to implement the economic priorities dictated by issues of national security, diverting vast resources that could have enhanced the quality of life of the citizenry. Under constant siege by counter-revolutionary forces for well over half a century, the government took on a profoundly repressive character.

The tragedies and atrocities of the Soviet experiment should not be forgotten or excused any more than those that have occurred under the capitalist system. However, we will never know whether the highly centralized and repressive practices of the Soviet system would have occurred if it had not been attacked and constantly undermined by nations controlled primarily by powerful capitalists.

Indeed, most progressive parties and governments that have attempted alternatives to capitalism have been subverted by practices and policies of the United States and other large capitalist nations, including economic sanctions and boycotts, CIA infiltrations, sabotage, and assassinations of political leaders. It is extremely difficult to go where no modern social system has gone before without a map or blueprint, and nearly impossible when powerful global elites use any means necessary to build obstacles in the road and launch frequent ambushes along the way.

Due consideration should also be given to Paulo Freire's caution about the propensity for human members of society to be led by "the myths of the old order" and to turn efforts at structural change into "their private revolution." The "long shadows" cast by former oppressors no doubt influenced those who had power in previous experiments with socialism and undermined attempts to establish systems free of oppression and truly characterized by liberty, equality, and fraternity. Strategists and activists for a rational and just economic and social system should heed lessons to be learned from Marjorie Spiegel's work—that the "battle against oppression . . . [should also] . . . be waged within each of us."[25]

Workers, consumers, students, environmentalists, liberation activists, scholars, and others striving for a just, sustainable, and oppression-free world must seriously reevaluate their own ideas about the nature and promise of a socialist system, ideas largely shaped by a self-serving capitalist elite that has distorted and demonized socialism. The movement for the liberation of other animals must recognize the improbability of substantial or lasting success within the capitalist system, convince others why this transition is imperative, and unite with other liberation activists in a renewed and thoughtful struggle for real socialism.

There is evidence that Western nations with prominent socialist and labor parties have managed to avoid, or at least to minimize, some of the most serious and critical problems that characterize the United States. The existence and influence of these parties, such as the Greens in Germany or the Social Democratic Party in Sweden, have been enhanced by political systems that provide for proportionate representation. Under this form of government structure, each political party receives parliamentary seats in proportion to its share of the total vote. Countries such as the Netherlands, Switzerland, Germany, and France have such systems. If Germany, for example, used the same system as the United States, direct representation in which citizens cast a vote for individual candidates, the hundreds of thousands of Green Party supporters there likely would have little or no political power. A switch to a proportionate system of representation in the United States would constitute a substantial challenge to corporate control of the state.

While the presence of progressive political parties within capitalist systems certainly has not led to the elimination of oppression, the levels of deprivation, violence, environmental destruction, and other social ills are less intense in those countries than in the United States—and many entitlements, such as health care, frequently are guaranteed to all.[26] The United States is unlike virtually every other Western nation in that it has no viable political party that represents what generally can be called the public interest.

While most other animals suffer horribly in capitalist systems even with socialist and labor party presences, those societies do show signs of increased empathy and respect for other animals. (We can posit that such developments are due, in part, to a higher level of material security generally experienced by the citizenry.) In Western European countries, where socialist and labor voices have some influence, there is a greater tendency to "strike a . . . balance between human desires and the animals' interests"[27] than in the United States. European nations seem more inclined to take a respectful and compassionate view toward other animals, and to treat them accordingly, at least to the extent that their principles do not unduly interfere with profit taking. For instance, as Elaine L. Hughes and Christiane Meyer observe, the members of the European Union have created treaties to establish protocols for the treatment of other animals. They note that the preamble to the treaty established for the Protection of Pet Animals states:

> "[M]an has a moral obligation to respect all living creatures," looking at the value of pets to society as a consequence of their contribution to human quality of life. It is also noted that wide variations in attitudes toward pets are sometimes due to "limited knowledge and awareness"; thus, the treaty looks at "a basic common standard of attitude and practice which results in responsible pet ownership" as being a realistic (as well as desirable) goal. The provisions of the treaty are then directed toward the "keepers" of pets or the "persons responsible" for them, not the animal "owners." Activities such as the use of animals in entertainment, exhibitions and competitions are prohibited unless the pets' health and welfare are not put at risk.
>
> The convention also provides that human preferences and convenience are not to be placed ahead of animal welfare. For example, docking of tails, cropping of ears, devocalizing, declawing, and defanging are all prohibited by the treaty in Europe.[28]

While the convention's statement of the rights of "pets" certainly does not equal the liberation of other animals, its acknowledgment of human moral obligations, recognition of the interests of other animals, and rejection of the concept that "companion animals" are not "property" move much farther in that direction than any broad declarations of public policy in the United States.

Another example of the link between economics and social and material security on one hand, and empathy and justice on the other, comes from New Zealand, a nation with a strong Labour Party, a rich socialist tradition, and a relatively secure and unusually progressive citizenry. In 1999, its Parliament adopted the Animal Welfare Act, which substantially restricts using any "non-human hominid"—that is, primates such as chimpanzees—for research, testing, or teaching.[29] Like the nations of the European Union, New Zealand still is profoundly capitalist, notwithstanding the moderating influences of its socialists. Indeed, it has established a niche in the global capitalist system as a supplier of "beef" and is responsible for a great deal of the "beef" imported into the United States. However, as Hughes and Meyer note, New Zealand does not have a large biomedical industry, and little research was performed there on "nonhuman hominids" before the law was enacted. In a society in which there is little economic incentive to oppress a particular group of other animals and no corporate vested interest in the abusive practices, efforts to protect other animals can be pressed more strongly and are more likely to succeed than in the United States.

These concrete examples suggest that steps toward the liberation of other animals are more possible and probable under social systems in which the power and control of corporate capitalism are not entirely unfettered. A substantial movement to socialism—particularly important in the United States because of its global economic, cultural, and military dominance—would likely increase citizens' material security and heighten public attention to preventive health care, creation of safe and sustainable sources of food, and environmental restoration. Concern for these issues, combined with the increased possibility for empathetic response and action of citizens in a more secure and equitable society, would no doubt reduce greatly the oppression of other animals in this country, in all its forms. Such changes in the United States would improve the lot of other animals around the world for practical reasons beyond just the cultural influence of the United States. Reduced demand here for "beef" and other products would take away much of the economic basis for the awful treatment of cows in New Zealand and the Americas for "beef" imports to the United States and for related forms of oppression around the world.

This is not to say that socialism is a panacea for all earthly conflicts and problems or that development of a viable socialist system will automatically reduce speciesism, racism, sexism, classism, and other forms of oppression in that society. Such forms of oppression predated the emergence of capitalism and certainly have accompanied nearly all economic systems with substantial unequal distribution of resources. However, socialism holds out the possibility of constructing human social systems in which economic, political, and ideological power are controlled much more democratically. It presents the best, perhaps the only, hope for eliminating oppression of both humans and other animals.

The powerful observation of scholar Tomás Almaguér, reflecting on the material basis of Chicano oppression, can be generalized to all liberation movements. He notes that Chicano oppression is not only a manifestation of racist ideology but also has strong material roots that must be dug out and removed before prejudice and discrimination can be significantly reduced. He writes:

> [I]t becomes clear that Chicano oppression in the United States has not been simply the outgrowth of a 'cultural conflict' between Anglos and Chicanos, not merely the result of a vicious racist ideology. Rather, the many forms of social, political and cultural oppression Chicanos have faced have ultimately been shaped by the material conditions of our labor. The racial oppression of the Chicano, and of other racial minorities, has largely stemmed from the place we occupy in the working class and from the fact that class exploitation in the United States has taken on a racial form. To do away with the class basis of this racial oppression, however, will not automatically ensure that racism will altogether disappear. For racial minorities, the end to class exploitation is not a panacea but merely an essential precondition for our true liberation and self-determination.[30]

So, the answer to the question by philosopher and activist Susan Finsen posed in chapter 1—"Is corporate capitalism compatible with animal rights?"—is no. Nor, for that matter, is corporate capitalism compatible with an end to racism, sexism, classism, and other injustices. The social system that is most conducive to the liberation of both devalued humans and other animals is socialism—a *true* socialism that reconfigures contemporary technological and productive capacity to meet the material needs of the world's inhabitants without oppression. It must be a socialist system that is guided through democracy and that can grow, mature, and correct the inevitable mistakes without being hindered and sabotaged by powerful procapitalist forces.

How should a movement toward socialism take place? Great minds have pondered this question for well over a century, and that topic is not the focus of this book. Briefly, though, it is unlikely that a spontaneous or rapid social revolution will occur, particularly in an era in which control of the mass media and popular culture is concentrated primarily in the hands of corporate capitalists. However, if widespread unrest and rapid social change do begin, advocates for other animals and all those desiring a more just and sustainable world should be aware of the necessity of using that opportunity to transcend, not merely repair and restore, the capitalist system. Liberal illusions should be set aside, and advocates for other animals should foster and join efforts to replace corporate control of the economic and political system with democratic control.

It is more likely that the social structural transformation necessary to bring an end to the oppression of humans and other animals will occur—if it comes at all—more gradually. Efforts for the end of oppression of other animals therefore should be what Gary Francione calls "incremental abolitionist"—which he defines as measures of "change achievable through prohibitions that recognize that animals have nontradable interests and where those prohibitions do not substitute alternative forms of exploitation."[31] Francione's strategy for liberation is very similar to that of French sociologist André Gorz, who called for the necessity of "nonreformist reforms" in order to bring about significant structural changes in capitalist society. An example of a nonreformist reform is "the right to organize labor unions, embodied in the Wagner Act of 1935, but won by the sit-down strikes and mass organizing efforts of the CIO," which provided workers with a new and fundamentally important right to organize and take collective action.[32] (Another example would be actions that compel McDonald's to stop selling fried body parts of chickens altogether, compared to a reformist effort to require it to use only chickens from slaughterhouses that use "humane" methods of killing.) The socialist Michael Harrington calls this type of struggle for a true socialist order "visionary gradualism."[33] Manning Marable puts it this way:

> The achievement of "nonreformist reforms" . . . can be won within the present capitalist state. These would include, for instance, the passage of: the Equal Rights Amendment; abortion rights; antidiscriminatory legislation; massive job training programs; universal health care; the abandonment of nuclear power plant construction, and so forth. The successful achievement of these legislative socioeconomic reforms does *not* create a socialist society or state. But combined with legislation which restricts the legal prerogatives of private capital, and a mass mobilization of popular forces in the streets as well as in the legislatures, it will create the social and material foundations for a logical "alternative" to the bourgeois authority and hegemony.[34]

Marable is convinced that the Democratic Party in the United States is not the vehicle that will usher in a socially just and oppression-free system.

> Critical support for progressive and anticapitalist politicians . . . who run for office within the Democratic Party, at the present time, may be necessary and constructive activity in building an anticorporate consensus within the working class. Yet to view either major capitalist party as the primary or fundamental terrain for building socialism would be a disaster. The Democratic Party will never be transformed into an appropriate vehicle for achieving the political hegemony of Blacks, Latinos, feminists and the working class. This requires the creation of an antiracist and antisexist political formation which is distinctly anticapitalist, and represents the interests of working and poor people.[35]

After the 2000 presidential election, Ralph Nader was chided by many on the Left for running as the Green Party candidate, taking votes away from Al Gore and facilitating the highly conservative, corporate-directed presidency of George W. Bush. Such a perspective, however, is shortsighted. The creation of a viable progressive third party in the United States would be an important means of transcending the existing economic and political system. If the Left continues to support the somewhat more liberal party that is merely the lesser of two evils, corporate capitalists will always remain firmly in control of the social system. The current system neutralizes progressive voters with its system of direct representation, which severely limits the potential involvement of any alternative party. These same voters are also held hostage to the Democrats, who are financed by corporations and their constituents just as much as the Republicans, because of the continual threats that important social programs will be eliminated or that judicial gains for one devalued group or another will be reversed under the Republicans. Many progressives feel compelled to vote for the less-than-satisfactory Democratic candidates.

The increasing concentration of economic control in record mergers, the rising disparities in wealth and income, and the draconian reforms that brought about "the end of welfare as we know it" during the Clinton administration prove that voting for the lesser of two evils results in just that. Furthermore, even if the less objectionable party or candidate is elected one year, the "greater evil" may come to power in the next round of elections and eliminate or reverse what the former government did. An electoral strategy that works solely within a corporate-controlled, two-party political system will never bring about the conditions necessary to change the social system in any meaningful way.

The opportunities and possibilities available within the capitalist system must be used to *transcend* it. To abolish oppression we must be able to use television, radio, and other forms of mass media to develop the human mind instead of to increase human appetites and expand markets. Technology must be transformed to create tools that further freedom and quality of life instead of instruments for profit accumulation and social control. We must use and democratize the existing media, while also continuing to develop ways to produce and more widely disseminate alternative news and information—information not molded and packaged by corporate interests. The goal is to create a social system in which the social positions that humans occupy neither compel violence nor encourage passive complicity in oppressive practices and arrangements. We must create a system in which oppression is not naturalized and rationalized but is *visible* and thus can be seen and remedied. Today, most forms of oppression are *invisible*, at least to relatively affluent Western citizens (read: consumers). Abused workers toil in sweatshops in Third World countries, the working poor and homeless are hidden in neighborhoods bypassed by interstates, the reality of pain and death that other animals suffer to become "meat" is glossed over and sanitized by supermarket packaging and enticing restaurant menus, and humans with diseased hearts and plaque-laden arteries after countless other-animal-based meals are sequestered in cardiac wards and nursing homes.

Hope for change is provided today by the millions around the world who are committed to the struggle for justice, the end of corporate dominance, and the abolition of oppression. At the beginning of the twenty-first century, tens of thousands began organizing and participating in increasingly strong protests in Washington, D.C., Seattle, Quebec, and other cities around the globe at meetings of such institutions as the World Trade Organization, the International Monetary Fund, and the World Bank. In the summer of 2001, thousands of demonstrators protested the summit of the Group of Eight, or G-8, consisting of the world's seven wealthiest nations plus Russia. (The elite of the nations formerly known as the G-7 deigned to include Russia in acknowledgment of its attempt to enter the capitalist system, a venture that, predictably, has increased wealth for the few, gross disparities among the population, and privations and oppression for many.) The power and passion of the demonstrations at the G-8 summit motivated conservative President Jacques Chirac of France to remark, "One hundred thousand people don't get upset unless there is a problem in their hearts and spirits."[36]

The demonstrations against the policies, practices, and very existence of these organizations—nominally international but actually controlled by the wealthy capitalist nations—are often referred to as "antiglobalization" protests. However, they are really directed against corporate control of the global economy and the environmental degradation, material inequities, reduction of democratic influence, and increased oppression it has brought. One of the most striking and important aspects of these demonstrations is the way they have brought together labor, liberation, and social justice groups from around the world. Among these diverse groups, who increasingly are seeing common interests and goals, are many strong advocates for other animals who have begun to recognize the structural basis of the oppression they oppose.

The beginnings of concerted political action by those on the Left and those working for the liberation of other animals, and the growing ability of hundreds of thousands around the world to see through the hegemonic legitimations for oppression, should give hope to all those determined to make plain the often invisible oppression of other animals and devalued humans and to reduce, if not eliminate, that oppression in the twenty-first century. We need to dedicate ourselves to stopping twenty-first-century versions of the Hinckley and Panzos massacres and the countless day-to-day attacks and routine killing of those most vulnerable. This requires an understanding of the ways in which the oppression of so many groups and other animals are intertwined and interdependent, of the fundamental economic basis of oppression—and of the ultimate necessity of building a true political and economic democracy.

NOTES

1. Tomás Almaguér, "The Historical Roots of Chicano Oppression," *Socialist Revolution* (July/September 1975), in Richard C. Edwards, Michael Reich, and Thomas E. Weisskopf, eds., *The Capitalist System,* 3d ed. (Englewood Cliffs, N.J.: Prentice Hall), 304.

2. Henry Salt, *Seventy Years among Savages* (London: Allen and Unwin, 1921), quoted in *The Extended Circle: A Commonplace Book of Animal Rights,* ed., Jon Wynne-Tyson (New York: Paragon House, 1985), 229.

3. Ted Benton, "Animal Rights: An Eco-Socialist View," in *Animal Rights: The Changing Debate,* ed. Robert Garner (New York: New York University Press, 1996), 19.

4. John Sanbonmatsu, "Animal Liberation: Should the Left Care?" *Zeta Magazine* (October 1989): 108.

5. For other thoughts on the Left's view of the movement to liberate other animals, see Anna E. Charlton, Sue Coe, and Gary Francione, "The American Left Should Support Animal Rights: A Manifesto," *Animals' Agenda* (January/February 1993): 28; and Gary Francione, "Animal Rights and the Left," at www.animal-law.org/commentaries/mr14.htm (visited 24 July 2001).

6. Leslie P. Francis and R. Norman, "Some Animals Are More Equal Than Others,"

Philosophy 53 (1978): 527; cited in Ted Benton, *Natural Relations: Ecology, Animal Rights and Social Justice* (New York: Verso, 1993), 10.

7. This quote from Sarah Buel was taken from the documentary film *Defending Our Lives* (1993), Cambridge Documentary Films, Inc., P.O. Box 385, Cambridge, Mass. 02139.

8. Holly Sklar, *Chaos or Community? Seeking Solutions, Not Scapegoats for Bad Economics* (Boston: South End, 1995), 93.

9. Sanbonmatsu, "Animal Liberation," 108.

10. Marti Kheel, "License to Kill: An Ecofeminist Critique of Hunters' Discourse," and Maria Comninou, "Speech, Pornography, and Hunting," in *Animals and Women: Feminist Theoretical Explorations,* ed. Carol J. Adams and Josephine Donovan (Durham, N.C.: Duke University Press, 1995), 85–146.

11. Barbara Noske, *Beyond Boundaries: Humans and Animals* (New York: Black Rose, 1997), 88.

12. Paulo Freire, *Pedagogy of the Oppressed* (New York: Seabury, 1970), 29–31.

13. See, for example, Jon Wynne-Tyson, ed., *The Extended Circle: A Commonplace Book of Animal Rights* (New York: Paragon House, 1989).

14. Coral Lansbury, *The Old Brown Dog: Women, Workers and Vivisection in Edwardian England* (Madison: University of Wisconsin Press, 1985).

15. Kim Stallwood, "Utopian Visions and Pragmatic Politics: Challenging the Foundations of Speciesism and Misothery," in *Animal Rights,* 195.

16. Susan Finsen, "Obstacles to Legal Rights for Animals: Can We Get There from Here?" *Animal Law* 3 (1997): ii.

17. Finsen, "Obstacles to Legal Rights for Animals," ii.

18. Michael Harrington, *Why We Need Socialism in America* (New York: Institute for Democratic Socialism, 1974), 1.

19. Sklar, *Chaos or Community?* 177.

20. John Kenneth Galbraith, *The Age of Uncertainty: A History of Economic Ideas and Their Consequences* (Boston: Houghton Mifflin, 1977), 319.

21. Manning Marable, *How Capitalism Underdeveloped Black America* (Boston: South End, 1983), 256.

22. bell hooks, *Feminist Theory: From Margin to Center* (Boston: South End, 1984), 159.

23. Immanuel Wallerstein, *After Liberalism* (New York: New Press, 1995), 2.

24. Finsen, "Obstacles to Legal Rights for Animals," ii.

25. Marjorie Spiegel, *The Dreaded Comparison* (New York: Mirror, 1996), 106.

26. "Study Rates U.S. Low on Helping Poor," *St. Louis Post Dispatch,* 9 September 1991, 1; Harold Kerbo, *Social Stratification and Inequality: Class Conflict in Historical and Comparative Perspective* (New York: McGraw-Hill, 1991).

27. Elaine L. Hughes and Christiane Meyer, "Animal Welfare Law in Canada and Europe," *Animal Law* 6 (2000): 46.

28. Hughes and Meyer, "Animal Welfare Law in Canada and Europe," 45.

29. Paula Brosnahan, "New Zealand's Animal Welfare Act: What Is Its Value Regarding Non-Human Hominids?" *Animal Law* 6 (2000): 189.

30. Almaguér, "The Historical Roots of Chicano Oppression," in Edwards, Reich, and Weisskopf, eds., *The Capitalist System,* 304.

31. Gary Francione, "Animal Rights: An Incremental Approach," in *Animal Rights,* 59.

32. Martin Carnoy and Derek Shearer, *Economic Democracy: The Challenge of the 1980s* (White Plains, N.Y.: Sharpe, 1980), 18.

33. Michael Harrington, *Socialism: Past and Future* (New York: Little, Brown, 1989), 248.

34. Marable, *How Capitalism Underdeveloped Black America,* 258–59.

35. Marable, *How Capitalism Underdeveloped Black America,* 257.

36. Alessandra Stanley and David E. Sanger, "Italian Protester Is Killed by Police at Genoa Meeting," *New York Times,* 21 July 2001, A1.

Index

About the Author

David Nibert is a former tenant organizer and community activist who is now associate professor of sociology at Wittenberg University in Springfield, Ohio. He is the author of *Hitting the Lottery Jackpot: State Government and the Taxing of Dreams* (2000) and articles in such journals as *Critical Sociology, Society and Animals,* and *Race, Gender and Class.* He lives in Yellow Springs, Ohio, with his spouse, Julie Ford, and their son, Taylor, in a home shared with numerous other animals who make up their extended family.